"Mel Goodman shines a critical whistleblower light into the dark recesses of the CIA as a former insider. His book serves in the public interest as a warning and wake-up call for what's at stake and why we cannot trust the CIA or the intelligence establishment to do the right thing."

—Thomas Drake, former NSA senior executive and whistleblower

"Mel Goodman's *Whistleblower at the CIA* is not just an insider's look at politics at the highest levels of government. It's also a personal account of the political odyssey Goodman had to negotiate for telling the truth. The CIA likes for its employees to believe that everything is a shade of grey. But some things are black or white, right or wrong. Mel Goodman did what was right. He may have paid with his career, but he's on the right side of history."

—John Kiriakou, former CIA counterterrorism officer and former senior investigator, Senate Foreign Relations Committee

"Mel Goodman's *Whistleblower at the CIA* confirmed for me what my own experience had revealed during six hectic days and seven sleepless nights at CIA headquarters, getting Colin Powell ready for his presentation to the UN Security Council on Iraq's 'Failure to Disarm' on February 5, 2003. Mr. Goodman provided exhaustive detail on why the agency has failed, again and again, and will continue to fail if some future president and congress do not step in and dramatically change the way CIA functions."

—Lawrence Wilkerson, former Chief of Staff to Secretary of State Colin Powell

D1125020

"A refreshingly honest, well-sourced expose of the CIA that not only furnishes the author's compelling personal story of standing up to inflated estimates sprinkled with little-known but historically significant details of the jewels and the warts, the successes and failures of decades of U.S. intelligence analysis. Especially instructive to our current era plagued by faulty group-think and the 'war on whistleblowers,' the book chronicles how 'contrarian' analysts are often 'the best source for premonitory intelligence.' This book is a must-read not only for political historians and American citizens wanting to know the unvarnished and often surprising truth about the intelligence side of the CIA but for all students contemplating a career with the CIA or other intelligence agency."

—Coleen Rowley, retired FBI agent

"In this fascinating and candid account of his years as a senior CIA analyst, Mel Goodman shows how the worst enemies of high quality intelligence can come from our own midst, and how the politicization of intelligence estimates can cause more damage to American security than its professed enemies. *Whistleblower at the CIA* is a must-read for anyone interested in the intricate web of intelligence-policymaking relations."

—Uri Bar-Joseph, author of *The Angel: The Egyptian Spy Who Saved Israel*

WHISTLEBLOWER AT THE CIA
A PATH OF DISSENT

Melvin A. Goodman

City Lights Books | San Francisco

Cover design: Herb Thornby

Library of Congress Cataloging-in-Publication Data

Names: Goodman, Melvin A. (Melvin Allan), 1938- author.
Title: Whistleblower at the CIA : an insider's account of the politics of
  intelligence / Melvin A. Goodman.
Other titles: Whistleblower at the Central Intelligence Agency
Description: San Francisco : City Lights Publishers, 2017.
Identifiers: LCCN 2016047282 (print) | LCCN 2017000887 (ebook) | ISBN
  9780872867307 (paperback) | ISBN 9780872867314 (ebook)
Subjects: LCSH: Goodman, Melvin A. (Melvin Allan), 1938- | United States.
  Central Intelligence Agency—Officials and employees—Biography. | United
  States. Central Intelligence Agency—Management. | United States. Central
  Intelligence Agency—History. | Intelligence service—Political
  aspects—United States. | Whistle blowing—United States. | BISAC:
  POLITICAL SCIENCE / Political Freedom & Security / Intelligence. |
  BIOGRAPHY & AUTOBIOGRAPHY / Political. | POLITICAL
  SCIENCE / Political
  Freedom & Security / International Security. | POLITICAL SCIENCE /
  Government / General.
Classification: LCC JK468.I6 G6633 2017 (print) | LCC JK468.I6 (ebook) |
  DDC
  327.12730092 [B] —dc23
LC record available at https://lccn.loc.gov/2016047282

City Lights Books are published at the City Lights Bookstore
261 Columbus Avenue, San Francisco, CA 94133
www.citylights.com

CONTENTS

Introduction: The Path to Dissent *1*

ONE Joining the CIA *29*

TWO The Joy of Intelligence *69*

THREE Leaving the CIA *99*

FOUR Landing in the Briar Patch *139*

FIVE Jousting with the Senate Intelligence Committee *169*

SIX The CIA's Double Standards and Double Dealing *211*

SEVEN CIA Directors and Dissent *239*

EIGHT Goodman v. Gates *277*

NINE The Press and the Whistleblower *313*

TEN Conclusions: Maintaining the Path of Dissent *345*

Acknowledgments 380
Glossary 381
Notes 389
Index 407
About the Author 422

To my mentors who were models of courage and integrity: the late Professor Amin Banani, professor emeritus at UCLA; the late professors Owen Lattimore and Robert Slusser of Johns Hopkins University; the late ambassador Robert White, who heroically exposed the crimes of the Reagan administration in Central America; the late Professor Alvin Z. Rubinstein of the University of Pennsylvania; Professor Robert Ferrell of Indiana University; and once again my wife, Carolyn McGiffert Ekedahl, who made sure that the crimes of the George W. Bush administration and the CIA could not be forgotten.

THE PATH TO DISSENT: A WHISTLEBLOWER AT THE CENTRAL INTELLIGENCE AGENCY

"The reasonable man adapts himself to the world. The unreasonable one persists in trying to adapt the world to himself. Therefore all progress depends on the unreasonable man."

—George Bernard Shaw

This is the story of an unreasonable man at the Central Intelligence Agency. There will be insights about the CIA and the forces of top-down corruption within the intelligence process, some settling of old scores within the Agency, and introspection about a 42-year career spent serving my country in the military and intelligence communities during the height of the Cold War. I joined the agency in the 1960s, a decade of radical change and upheaval in American culture. My closest friends questioned the decision of a self-confessed progressive to join one of the most secretive agencies in the government when the U.S. war against Vietnam was becoming increasingly ugly and divisive. Ironically, I found a more spirited and intelligent debate over the war in CIA corridors than I experienced in graduate school at Indiana University where I participated in the teach-in movement against the war.

There has been a great decline in the stature and influence

1

of the CIA over the past two decades. The CIA's failure to anticipate the fall of the Berlin Wall in 1989, the collapse of the Warsaw Pact in 1990, and the dissolution of the Soviet Union in 1991, which ended the Cold War that fostered the CIA, deeply damaged the credibility of the entire intelligence community. The manipulation of intelligence for political ends—politicization—was responsible for these failures, and two decades later this process of corruption helped the Bush administration make the catastrophic decision to invade and occupy Iraq without any evidence of a threat or provocation. The insistence of Vice President Dick Cheney to conjure phony intelligence in order to go to war against Iraq in 2003 was particularly criminal. With the end of the CIA's anti-communism mission, the Agency had to come up with other missions; the ethical and operational failures in these missions further damaged its reputation. The CIA's role in the Terror Wars has included extrajudicial killings, assassinations, secret prisons, torture and abuse, and extraordinary renditions that have violated the U.S. Constitution and international law.

The CIA's decline over several decades was marked by mediocre leadership, particularly by directors such as William Casey, Robert Gates, Porter Goss, and George Tenet, who tailored intelligence to satisfy the neoconservative biases of Presidents Ronald Reagan and George W. Bush. Tenet and Goss as well as Michael Hayden and John Brennan endorsed barbaric interrogation methods, and Brennan tried to block the Senate Intelligence Committee's investigation of torture in secret prisons. CIA directors who tried to prevent manipulation of the intelligence process, such as Richard Helms and William Colby, were either exiled to Iran as ambassador or simply fired, respectively. Meanwhile, the CIA refuses to recognize the harm of politicization and hasn't introduced bureaucratic barriers that protect intelligence analysts from coercion.

There have been too few people of conscience willing to risk their careers in order to call attention to the turpitude that occurs in the CIA headquarters building in the tranquil suburbs of Virginia. I am proud of the fact that I was one of the dissidents, having testified before the Senate Select Committee on Intelligence in 1991 in an unsuccessful effort to stop the confirmation of Robert Gates as director of central intelligence and having written profusely on the dangers of politicization—the systematic manipulation, distortion, and falsification of intelligence to serve ulterior motives outside the Agency's mission.[1]

Why would someone who spent more than four decades in the United States of America's national security system become a dissident or a contrarian? I entered the United States Army as a teenager with the reluctant permission of my parents, and served as a cryptographer at the Joint United States Military Mission in Greece in the 1950s. If any single experience kindled my passion for a career in international relations and led me to the CIA, it was serving in the U.S. Army in Athens. It was an eventful two-year period from 1956 to 1958, marked by the Hungarian Revolution and the Soviet invasion; the British-French-Israeli invasion of Egypt; the launching of Sputnik; and the U.S. invasion of Lebanon, which threatened an unwanted extension of my tour of duty. I was enthralled by my work coding and decoding sensitive messages about these historic flash points while they were situations in progress; my father, a telegrapher with the Pennsylvania Railroad for 50 years, was proud and bemused.

I was fortunate to hold intelligence positions that provided unusual access to the U.S. foreign policy process. The CIA and the National War College provided an excellent vantage point for observing the national security system in the nation's capital. I witnessed one of the great turning points for U.S. national security with the collapse of the Soviet Union, and observed events that members of my generation never expected to witness. I was an intelligence advisor to the U.S. delegation to the Strategic Arms Limitation Talks (SALT) in Vienna, where intense negotiations led to the conclusion of SALT I and the Anti-Ballistic

Missile (ABM) Treaty in 1972. I was in the audience at the National War College in 2001 when President George W. Bush announced that the United States would abrogate the ABM Treaty, destroying the keystone of strategic deterrence.

For 24 years, I served as an intelligence analyst at the CIA and the Department of State's Bureau of Intelligence and Research. When I left the intelligence community in 1990, I crossed the river to join the Department of Defense as a professor of international security at the National War College. For several decades, I held sensitive security clearances that gave me access to clandestine reports from the CIA; cables from foreign service officers; military attaché reports from the Department of Defense; satellite photography from the National Reconnaissance Office; and signals and communications intelligence from the National Security Agency (NSA). I was privy to the most sensitive political and intelligence issues of the Cold War, and served on task forces on virtually every crisis with the Soviet Union for nearly a quarter of a century. It was incredibly challenging and exciting.

I was polygraphed four times by the CIA, and always encountered difficulty in passing these tests because of the amateurism of polygraph operators and the bizarre and unreliable nature of the technology. The most notorious CIA mole, Aldrich Ames, had no difficulty passing the polygraph. At some point during these tests, an operator would leave the room, demonstrating some impatience, and then return as much as an hour later to report that there was one area of concern that blocked passage of the examination. He would invariably ask if I "would take a stab in determining what area that may have been." This is probably one of the hoariest devices of the polygraph process, and, having been warned by senior colleagues, I never rose to their bait. I may have seemed fishy to the security troglodytes, but I had nothing to hide and no intention of getting snagged on their hook.

Although I served more than four decades in the secret shadows of the national security system, this was hardly an exclusive domain. The bloated U.S. intelligence infrastructure produces millions of classified documents every year and certifies several million civilians, service members, and contractors to receive confidential, secret, and top-secret documents. The Department of State even adds such categories as Limdis, Exdis, and Nodis to their sensitive cables, which translates to limited distribution, exclusive distribution, and no distribution, respectively. The CIA uses red and blue borders to create the same level of caution for its clandestine reports.

In many cases, the added layers of classification aren't designed to protect sensitive matters that would jeopardize national security. More often, security caveats are designed to avoid embarrassment, making sure that no one learns, for example, that the CIA once proposed creating a pornographic film starring Bing Crosby as part of a scheme intended to embarrass an Indonesian head of state. Nevertheless, if I had used personal email during my tenure at CIA, as Hillary Clinton did as secretary of state, I would currently be out on bail . . . or worse.

Unfortunately, the American people seem to have become fully inured to the government's aggressive and self-aggrandizing pursuit of power, privilege, and prerogatives. The U.S. national security establishment has established layers of secrecy and a grid of constant surveillance, while the citizenry has become increasingly obedient and compliant. There is little protest or public outcry when the United States massacres civilians abroad or when it inadvertently bombs a wedding procession or a hospital in Afghanistan. There was little public outrage following the disclosures that reasons for going to war in Iraq were cooked up, that U.S. soldiers committed perverse and sadistic crimes at Abu Ghraib; that CIA officials used torture and abuse; that tapes providing evidence of CIA torture were intentionally destroyed; and that secret U.S. prisons and extraordinary renditions violated international norms and regulations. Not even the disclosures of Edward Snowden and Chelsea Manning, which fully documented the excesses and improprieties of the U.S. government and military, shocked the American people into demanding that their government comply with the law.

As Andrew Bacevich warns, the revelations of Manning and Snowden have "confronted Washington with something far more worrisome" than "al-Qaeda, Iran's nuclear program, and the rise of China."[2] Bacevich argues that their leaks undermine the authority that the White House has amassed during the Terror Wars. Unless Americans insist that diplomacy, dialogue, and substantive debate precede acts of military aggression, it will remain easy for the United States to deploy military coercion and violence in response to crises.

If the wars in Iraq, Afghanistan, Syria, Somalia, Libya, and Yemen could not serve as a catalyst for a massive American protest movement, then it is unreasonable to expect that the disclosures from Snowden and Manning could do so. On the one hand, Americans are quick to ignore or forget the criminality and false premises of the U.S. wars waged against Iraq and Vietnam; on the other hand, the conventional wisdom of the mainstream media is typically supportive of the government's position on national security. Meanwhile, the authors of the Justice Department's torture memoranda, John Yoo and Jay Bybee, hold significant positions at the University of California's law school in Berkeley and the federal appeals court in California, respectively.

The CIA has now long pursued a double standard in order to protect its reputation. It allows its employees to defend policies such as human torture while trying to censor those authors who are critical of such policies. The agency endorsed the publication of a memoir by a clandestine operative who destroyed the torture tapes and denied that torture and abuse took place.[3] It subverts democracy when those who have access to official secrets are allowed to violate laws with impunity and without accountability, and to publish "official history" that obfuscates illegalities without facing scrutiny or criticism.

Several years ago, a major documentary film, *The Gatekeepers*, arrived from Israel. The film, starring former Israeli spymasters as whistleblowers, challenged Israel's ruthless tactics against Palestinians. *The Gatekeepers* had far-ranging impact because it featured whistleblowers from the intelligence establishment—the keepers of the secrets—who were willing to speak out against Israel.

Imagine a comparable film in the United States that featured former directors of the CIA who exposed CIA involvement in a military coup in Chile in the 1970s; support for the Contras in Nicaragua in the 1980s; manipulation of intelligence that exaggerated the Soviet threat prior to the breakup of the Soviet Union; willingness to provide phony intelligence to the White House to justify a catastrophic invasion of Iraq in 2003; and the details of secret prisons, torture and abuse, and extraordinary renditions to Vice President Dick Cheney's "Dark Side."

WHISTLEBLOWERS. DISSIDENTS. CONTRARIANS.

The terms are used synonymously by pundits and the public, and I've been all three at one time or another in order to expose improprieties and illegalities in the secret government, and to inform the American public of policies that compromise the freedom and security of U.S. citizens and weaken U.S. standing in the global community.

I have never liked the terms contrarian or dissident. I've always believed that my criticism should be conventional wisdom. The term whistleblower is more complex because it often raises questions of patriotism or sedition. Chelsea Manning received commutation from her 35-year prison sentence for revealing so-called secrets that documented the terror and violence of the baseless U.S. war in Iraq. Members of the Bush administration who launched the invasion of Iraq in 2003 are considered honorable members of our society, although their acts involved the corruption of intelligence; caused the death of thousands of U.S.

soldiers and foreign civilians; terrorized civilian populations; perpetrated the criminal use of torture and abuse; sanctioned use of secret prisons and extraordinary rendition; and caused the destabilization of the region that has set the stage for strategic advances by Al Qaeda and ISIS.

Edward Snowden, if he had remained in the United States, would have faced an even longer prison sentence because he revealed the massive NSA surveillance program that was illegal and immoral, and that violated the Fourth Amendment protection against illegal seizures and searches. Manning and Snowden admit to breaking U.S. laws, but their actions were never as serious as the law-breaking, including massive violations of privacy, that they exposed.

The debate over whether Snowden was a traitor is fatuous. As a result of Snowden's revelations, we learned that the National Security Agency logged domestic phone calls and emails for years, recorded the metadata of correspondence between Americans, and, in some cases, exploited the content of emails. The case against Private Manning was similarly fatuous. Manning provided evidence of the U.S. cover-up of torture by our Iraqi allies; a U.S. Army helicopter opening fire on a group of civilians, including two Reuters journalists; and the use of an air strike to cover up the execution of civilians. Some of these acts were war crimes.

There is no more compelling evidence of the unconscionable behavior of U.S. personnel in Iraq than the callous dialogue between the crew members of the helicopter regarding the civilian deaths and particularly the firing on those Iraqis who came to recover the dead bodies of Iraqi civilians. Manning's documents exposed this behavior, but her efforts were ridiculed by former secretary of defense Robert Gates, who described it as examining war by "looking through a straw."

To make matters worse, American journalists have criticized their colleagues (Julian Assange of WikiLeaks and Glenn Greenwald of *The Guardian*) who brought the Snowden-Manning revelations to the attention of the public. David Gregory, then host of the venerable *Meet the Press* on NBC, asked Greenwald "to the extent that you have aided and abetted Snowden . . . why shouldn't you . . . be charged with a crime?"[4] Jeffrey Toobin, a lawyer who labors for CNN and *The New Yorker*, called Snowden a "grandiose narcissist who belongs in prison" and referred to Greenwald's partner, David Miranda, who was detained by British authorities for nine hours under anti-terror laws, the equivalent of a "drug mule."[5]

The king of calumny is Michael Grunwald, a senior correspondent for *Time*, who wrote on Twitter that he couldn't "wait to write a defense of the drone strike that takes out Julian Assange." The *New York Times* also targeted Assange, although the paper cooperated with WikiLeaks in 2010 in publishing reams of information from Private Manning's revelations. Of course, if *Time* or the *New York Times* had broken these stories, they would have built new shelves to hold their Pulitzer Prizes. Their hypocrisy was exposed by David Carr of the *New York Times*, who expressed shock at finding Assange and Greenwald "under attack, not just from a government bent on keeping its secrets, but from friendly fire by fellow journalists."[6]

I didn't reveal abuses as great as those revealed by Manning and Snowden or Daniel Ellsberg, but I do claim status as a whistleblower because of my revelations before the Senate Select Committee on Intelligence during confirmation hearings for Bob Gates, who was nominated by President George H.W. Bush in 1991 to be director of central intelligence. According to U.S. law, the term "whistleblower" applies to anyone who "reasonably believes" he or she is disclosing a violation of law or gross mismanagement, gross waste, or abuse of authority. My testimony documented for the first time the intentional distortion of intelligence by CIA director William Casey and Deputy Director Gates in order to serve the agenda of Ronald Reagan and his administration.

Bob Gates was an old friend, but the friendship ended when

he routinely distorted intelligence throughout the 1980s as deputy director for intelligence and deputy director of the CIA. In destroying the political culture of the CIA, he created a toxic and corrupt environment at the Agency, and the Senate Intelligence Committee's report on CIA detention and torture reminds us that the Agency hasn't recovered.

Being a contrarian was easy and natural for me. In fact, no one should think about entering the intelligence profession without good contrarian instincts. Such instincts would include an innate skepticism, the doubting of conventional wisdom and a willingness to challenge authority, which translates to an ability to tell truth to power. These contrarian instincts are essential to the success of any intelligence organization. As Rogers and Hammerstein would have it, it was "doing what comes naturally!"

My book *The Failure of Intelligence: The Decline and Fall of the CIA* was the first insider account from an intelligence analyst regarding the skewed and politicized assessments of the CIA's Directorate of Intelligence—the Agency's analytic arm. I also exposed the strategic failure of covert actions that were never intended to be a part of President Harry Truman's CIA. I wrote the book for many reasons, including the need to describe the inability of journalists to take into account, let alone understand, the dangers of politicization and the actions of CIA directors such as Casey, Gates, and more recently Goss and Tenet. The political pliancy of these directors fully compromised the intelligence mission of the CIA, and it was political pliancy that made directors such as Gates and Tenet so attractive to Presidents Reagan, Bush I, and Bush II.

For the past quarter century, my testimony and writings have exposed the failure to honor President Truman's purpose in creating a CIA to provide policymakers with accurate, unbiased accounts of international developments, and have highlighted the CIA's readiness to cater to the White House. This view is not original with me; in fact, it was President Truman who first acknowledged that the CIA he created in 1947 had gotten off the tracks under Presidents Dwight D. Eisenhower and John F. Kennedy in the 1950s and early 1960s.

In December 1963, less than a month after the assassination of President Kennedy, Truman wrote an op-ed for the *Washington Post* to document the wrongs of the CIA. He concluded that his efforts to "create the quiet intelligence arm of the Presidency" had been subverted by a "sinister" and "mysterious" agency that was conducting far too many clandestine activities in peacetime. I lectured at the Truman Library in the summer of 2014, and found a note in Truman's hand that stated the CIA was not designed to "initiate policy or to act as a spy organization. That was never the intention when it was organized."

In *The Failure of Intelligence*, I documented the CIA's resistance to reform and the corruption in both the analytical and operational directorates. I made a case for starting over at the CIA, not dissimilar from the case made by Senator Daniel Patrick Moynihan 25 years ago as a member of the Senate Select Committee on Intelligence. Not every agency or department of government can be reformed, and it is possible that the intricate web of habits, procedures, and culture places the CIA in the nonreformable category. Once the political culture of an institution such as the CIA has been broken, it is extremely difficult—if not impossible—to rebuild or repair it.

Serious organizations, including both houses of Congress, the Council on Foreign Relations, and the 20th Century Fund, have made realistic and substantive proposals for changing the agency. But here we are in the 21st century with a CIA that develops phony intelligence arguments for launching wars, employing torture and abuse, operating secret prisons, making erroneous renditions, and censoring details of its operations. Federal courts are permitting the CIA to block the public from seeing intelligence documents dealing with the invasion of Cuba more than 50 years ago, and the former chairman of the Senate Select Committee on Intelligence, Dianne Feinstein, has produced a seminal document on CIA abuses that the White House and the CIA will not declassify, and the Department of Justice won't read. The fact that the report is a partisan document representing only Democratic members of the committee is troublesome.

Reviewers of *The Failure of Intelligence* acknowledged that the book exposed the militarization and manipulation of intelligence that has taken place in the U.S. intelligence community since the Cold War ended in 1991.[7] Seymour Hersh credited me with trying to "right a dangerous wrong," which is the definition of whistleblowing. Burton Hersh, the author of *The Old Boys: The American Elite and the Origins of the CIA*, noted that my "corridor battles" with Casey and Gates were taking place long before I testified to the Senate Select Committee on Intelligence about the soft-pedaling of evidence that the Soviet Union was falling apart in order to promote the Reagan administration's bloated defense spending. Gates can be forgiven by some, but not by me, for exaggerating the Soviet threat when in reality the system was heading toward collapse; Gates should never be forgiven for insisting that his subordinates in the analytic cadre of the CIA be similarly wrong.

The negative connotations of the word "whistleblower" are worrisome. Until consumer advocate Ralph Nader popularized it in the 1970s, the term had a negative meaning. According to the *Wall Street Journal*, the idiomatic "blowing the whistle" emerged in the American vernacular in the early 20th century to describe a boxing referee ending a bout or a football official stopping play to announce a penalty.[8] In a 1909 story by Sewell Ford, the earthy protagonist Shorty McCabe cuts off the garrulous Sadie Sullivan by saying, "Blow the whistle on that, can't you?" By the 1930s, "blowing the whistle" on someone could imply the dramatic revelation of something illicit, and in certain walks of life that meant getting painted as a "rat" or a "snitch." In 1936, a New York sportswriter referred to someone who had exposed the fakery of professional wrestling as a "whistleblower, which is unforgivable."[9]

Nader rescued the term in the 1970s, acknowledging that the term whistleblower was not appreciated, but asserting that it was not a synonym for "fink or stool pigeon, a squealer or an informer, who rats on his employer." Ironically, when Nader raised the issue he was speaking to the annual convention of the Association of Computing Machinery, warning that the collection of huge "data banks" might prevent people from "speaking out and blowing the whistle against the system." By exposing the National Security Agency's large-scale surveillance of the American people, that's what Edward Snowden has done, and continues to do.

Whistleblowing begs the question of loyalty to government and country. Whistleblowers must decide whether they owe loyalty to the government agency or military service they represent or to the U.S. Constitution they are sworn to honor. Leaks of classified information in the field of national security are particularly complicated, because laws protect such information. Whistleblowers may be naïve about the consequences of their actions, particularly the risk of lifting the veil on secrecy. Nevertheless, they deserve recognition as dissenters or contrarians who want to bring some semblance of truth to the American people.

Legitimate whistleblowing within the government typically follows a breakdown in the moral compass of some department or agency. In my case, it was the intentional and systematic manipulation of intelligence within the CIA; in the case of Daniel Ellsberg, it was an unnecessary war; in the case of Thomas Drake, it was a constitutional breakdown at the National Security Agency; and in the case of Chelsea Manning, it involved war crimes being committed by the United States. A decade after my exposure of chronic corruption at the CIA, the deliberate and systematic falsification of intelligence to coerce the nation to launch an unprovoked war demonstrated that the problem had metastasized. A decade after that, we learned about the CIA's role in the Terror Wars, which involved secret prisons, torture, and the targeted killing of people only suspected of crimes.

In 2014, the Senate Select Committee on Intelligence under the chairmanship of Senator Feinstein produced the 6,300-page report on CIA torture that revealed that even innocent individuals had been held in secret prisons and tortured. The Senate report was validated by a review ordered by then CIA director Leon Panetta. The Senate report and the Panetta Review recorded the sadistic interrogation of more than 100 al Qaeda members and suspects under the euphemism "enhanced interrogation techniques." The report and review confirmed that no significant intelligence was produced by torture, and that the CIA lied to the White House and the Congress about the true nature of the interrogations and the intelligence that was (or, in this case, was not) obtained. Former CIA officials (including Directors Tenet, Goss, and Hayden) and CIA apologists, including journalists, maintained that torture gets results and that the interrogations were valuable. The immorality of the CIA's use of violence, humiliation, and coercion was never a factor for these individuals.

CIA director John Brennan was critical of torture and abuse in 2009, when he was serving on President Obama's staff, but he referred to interrogators as "patriots" when he became director. As director, he went to unusual lengths to block the release of the report, lying to the committee chair and even threatening a constitutional crisis over the separation of powers by sanctioning the hacking of Senate computers and the emails of Senate staffers.

When former CIA director William Colby was faced with evidence of CIA crimes during the Vietnam War, he released the dispositive documents to the Senate. Brennan was neither courageous enough nor independent enough to do this. Instead, Brennan permitted the CIA to conduct electronic searches of Senate computer programs in order to learn what documents the Senate staffers had obtained, even hacking into the emails of key committee staffers. The CIA ran this program like any covert operation aimed at an adversary, but the target was the Senate Intelligence Committee of the United States of America and there could be no "plausible denial."

In an unusual attack, Senator Feinstein charged the CIA with secretly withdrawing hundreds of documents from the Senate staff's archives, including the authoritative Panetta Review that corroborated the charges in the Senate report. The CIA falsely claimed that the White House had ordered the withdrawal of the documents, which led to a CIA apology. Senator Feinstein called for additional CIA apologies, but what was needed was the release of the full report and the Panetta Review. The most tantalizing aspect of Feinstein's remarks was her view that the Panetta Review may have been placed in the Senate's documents by a CIA whistleblower.

As soon as the Republicans took over control of the Senate Select Committee on Intelligence as a result of their election victory in November 2014, they reclassified the Panetta Review and ordered it returned to the CIA. The chairman of the Senate Select Committee on Intelligence, Richard Burr (R-NC), even blocked the confirmation of a former staffer of the Senate Select Committee on Intelligence, Alissa Starzak, as general counsel for the United States Army. Burr's reason for blocking the confirmation? Starzak was the lead investigator in the writing of the torture report. The deceit never stops.

At least 200 CIA officers who took part in illegal activities relating to the Terror Wars continue to work at the Counterterrorism Center, which probably explains why the Obama administration refused to seek accountability. Any serious accountability would discover that a small group of CIA officials, including lawyers, were acting as both judge and jury in deciding who was guilty of terrorism and who would be detained and tortured. The CIA is deeply damaged, but no one appears to want to fix it or even knows how, including the congressional intelligence committees charged with oversight.

* * *

In view of the catastrophic losses in terms of death and destruction, it is appalling that so few whistleblowers have emerged during the Terror Wars. It takes an unusual personality to challenge the government, in part due to the lack of protection and the likelihood of retribution. One of the reasons why so few are "doing what comes naturally" is the lack of trust in the system. People of conscience contemplating whistleblowing fear retaliation and punishment for reporting even illegalities. The fear is real and documented; it was particularly obvious during the scandal at the Department of Veterans Affairs in 2014 over the cover-up of terrible abuses. The series of abuses at the Secret Service from 2011 to 2014 revealed that there were agents who would not step forward to report security concerns because they didn't trust the system or their supervisors. At the CIA, I was aware of numerous individuals who wouldn't go to the Office of the Inspector General, let alone the Congress, and believed that it would be a career-ending move to do so.

There is no protection for whistleblowers in the intelligence community, and intelligence officers face the possible loss of a security clearance for going public regarding abuses. Any individual with a security clearance who goes to the media is subject to loss of security clearance, which is the same as being fired. The system for oversight, moreover, is broken in the Congress and at the CIA.

Federal employees fear that they can not disclose violations of law without reprisal.[10] There has been a lack of accountability at the Department of Veteran's Affairs, the Federal Emergency Management Agency, the Internal Revenue Service, and the Department of Health and Human Services. The Obama administration used the Espionage Act of 1917 to pursue whistleblowers and prevented legitimate oversight by not naming inspectors general to national security agencies. The State Department lacked an inspector general during Clinton's stewardship; the CIA was without an inspector general for nearly two years in President Barack Obama's first term until an extremely weak appointment was made; the Pentagon wouldn't permit the inspector general to act independently. The CIA lacked a statutory inspector general (one appointed by the president) during most of Obama's second term as well.

The worst abuses took place during times of warfare, and since September 11, 2001, the U.S. has been in a constant state of war. Countless civilians have been killed by U.S. operations and drone attacks in Afghanistan, Pakistan, Iraq, Syria, Yemen, and beyond. In April 2015, a disconsolate President Obama had to tell the American people that a U.S. strike in the Afghan-Pakistan border region killed a U.S. aid worker held hostage. In October 2015 the U.S. bombed a Doctors Without Borders hospital in the city of Kunduz, Afghanistan, killing 22 people, mostly doctors and staff.

Meanwhile, America's vast national security apparatus continues to grow like Topsy. The USA PATRIOT Act permits wholesale use of national security letters from the FBI to compel financial officers, librarians, and physicians to turn over vast amounts of data about American citizens without a court order. The Foreign Intelligence Surveillance Act (FISA) allows intelligence agencies to eavesdrop on communications between Americans and people overseas without a probable-cause warrant. FISA investigations require an order from the Foreign Intelligence Surveillance Court, which meets in secret, but from 1979 to 2013 it rejected only 11 applications out of more than 30,000 requests from federal agencies. They are subject to no review.

The efforts of Thomas Drake to expose corruption and deceit at the National Security Agency, where he was a senior exeutive, marked the most outrageous pursuit of a whistleblower. Drake took his story of government waste to the *Baltimore Sun* only after failing to interest the inspectors general at the NSA and the Pentagon as well as the Senate and House Intelligence Committees. Drake exhausted most of his retirement savings and had to take a second mortgage on his house to fight the federal government in court. As a result, he faced 10 felony charges involving mishandling classified information and obstruction of justice, which a judge wisely dismissed.

Drake has been a guest lecturer at my classes at Johns Hopkins University, where he has mesmerized audiences with his experiences with an out-of-control federal government. During the search of Drake's house, one embarrassed FBI agent even whispered to Drake, "Who in the world did you piss off?" The government's treatment of Drake was disgraceful; it may explain why Snowden left the country before telling the world about the NSA's vast grid of surveillance operations.

Like Drake, Thomas Tamm, an attorney with the Justice Department, went to James Risen and Eric Lichtblau of the *New York Times* only after striking out with the Pentagon's inspector general and the U.S. Congressional Intelligence Committees. Tamm returned home one day to find 12 cars parked all along his street and 18 federal agents (some in body armor) banging on the door and yelling at his wife, who was in her bathrobe.

My own efforts in the early 1990s to expose corruption of intelligence reporting by William J. Casey and Robert M. Gates were far more modest. In testifying before the Senate Select Committee on Intelligence in the fall of 1991, and then mounting a random but persistent public campaign in books and editorials, I called attention to the misuse of power and secrecy at our most elite intelligence organization. I didn't face prosecution and ruin, but, like Daniel Ellsberg and others, I experienced the isolation of whistleblowing and the frustration of being ridiculed and marginalized in the political arena and the mainstream media. Like Drake, I encountered no serious efforts to understand my motivations for becoming a whistleblower, and instead faced efforts to dismiss my expertise and experience as a senior CIA veteran.

Whistleblowers go through an exhausting period of self-examination before taking on a path of dissent that involves secret and sensitive materials, but they underestimate the impact of taking on the national security state. Again, I cannot really compare my actions to those of Ellsberg, Drake, Manning, or Snowden, but taking on a presidential nomination in front of a Senate Intelligence Committee, whose chairman had unwisely "guaranteed" confirmation to the White House, could have been construed as a fool's errand.

Snowden argued that he wanted to start a debate on privacy; he certainly has achieved that goal. Snowden's documents raised the central issue of whether the National Security Agency undermines our democracy and violates our right to privacy. The debate over whether Snowden is a hero or a traitor continues to be a distraction from this discussion. Manning's documents should have led to a major debate on the Iraq War in terms of how we went to war and how we fought the war, but the American public was insufficiently responsive.

The fact that I was a professor at the National War College and therefore an employee of the Department of Defense added to my problems. My boss at the college, Major General Walter Stadler, summoned me to his office to suggest that I not testify before the intelligence committee, and added that there were lawyers at the Pentagon who could get me "out of this." When I reminded him that such a proposal to someone who had received a subpoena from the Congress was a violation of federal law, he backed off. Nevertheless, he hoped that I would not use my notoriety to "jump on a white horse" to lead a campaign against the Bush White House.

Senator Warren Rudman (R-NH) told his colleagues on the intelligence committee that he would "take care of Goodman because he's a government official." Rudman's threats never panned out to more than petty whining. After the confirmation hearings were over, he wrote a personal letter to the commandant of the National War College to bark about my failure to provide an honorarium to a speaker, a desperate, empty gesture from a senator who wrongly presumed my duties at the college included cutting checks.

Despite widespread abuse of both government and corporate power, commercial media often ignore the civic motives of people who expose high-level wrongdoing. Instead, media often marginalize people who dare to challenge authority. For Snowden, the media carried titillating stories about a high school dropout and his girlfriend, a pole dancer. Manning was disparaged as a cross-dresser, which had nothing to do with her reasons for revealing state secrets. The White House circulated malicious rumors about me in 1991, but I was alerted by reporters from *Time* magazine and the *Washington Post*. The deputy director for intelligence at the time, John Helgerson, who later became an inspector general, refused to corroborate these tales. There is no better way to dilute the debate about our national security state than to lie about whistleblowers.

There are rational motivations for whistleblowing, but it is easier for journalists to use accusations from official sources than to dig for greater meaning. The media has been particularly derelict in examining the worst side of politics, particularly the conduct of public affairs for private or personal advantage. After all, the main task of the press should be to hold those in power accountable for their actions, and to expose those who violate the public trust. Investigative journalism is central to democracy for precisely this reason, but corporate media are too often a compliant extension of power, not its independent auditor. The rise and fall of Gary Webb's career and personal life following his investigation of the CIA connections with narcotics trafficking is a good example. Years after his "Dark Alliance" story rocked the CIA, Webb was found killed by two gunshot wounds to his head. Despite this, his death was officially declared to be a suicide.

People and organizations face similar attacks and destabilization when they blow the whistle in the corporate sector. General Motors (GM) spied on Ralph Nader and hired women to lure him into compromising situations after Nader revealed lethal safety flaws in GM cars. Nader's organization, Essential Information, produced a report on how this criminal activity against whistleblowers continues to this day as corporations continue to target individuals and public interest organizations, including groups devoted to food safety, consumer rights, pesticide reform, nursing home reform, gun control, social justice, the environment, anti-war efforts, animal rights, and arms control."[11] According to the report, corporations regularly infiltrate and violate the privacy of individuals and nonprofits that dare to step up and investigate possible corporate crime.

There is a lesson from these examples of whistleblowing. If you are unwilling to accept the possible consequences, then you should keep your head down and do as you are told. There is a cost to revealing corruption at the NSA or the CIA, just as there is a cost to exposing high-level corporate crime. Officials within the United States government will claim that the release of so-called sensitive information will harm national security, even when the unveiling of such information points to serious improprieties. In actual fact, whistleblowing could help the government. My own experience regarding the exposure of high-level corruption should have led the CIA to recognize the problem and to make sure that there was no more tailoring of intelligence to satisfy the wishes of those in power. Nevertheless, a decade after my testimony, a corrupt National Intelligence Estimate and an unclassified white paper on non-existent Iraqi weapons of mass destruction were prepared in order to justify the U.S. invasion of Iraq that resulted in thousands of American soldiers and countless Iraqi people being killed, and the regional destabilization that has been an invaluable gift to the territorial advances of Al Qaeda and ISIS.

Several documentaries on whistleblowing have helped us to understand the importance of the Manning-Snowden revelations.

Robert Greenwald's *The War on Whistleblowers* and Alex Gibney's *We Steal Secrets: The Story of WikiLeaks* provided an excellent framework for debating the legality and morality of our national security state and the culture of secrecy created in the wake of 9/11. *Citizenfour* won an Oscar in 2015 for its compelling examination of Snowden's motivations, which the press overlooked. I took part in Greenwald's earlier documentary, *Uncovered*, which exposed the Bush administration's lies about weapons of mass destruction and the failures of the media.

President Obama has contributed to the need for whistleblowers by weakening the traditional institution for oversight in the national security process, the CIA's Office of Inspector General. Inspectors general are not popular within the federal government, but they are essential for keeping government corruption in check. The Obama administration focused from the outset on weakening the Office of Inspector General at the CIA by taking more than a year and a half to replace an outstanding inspector general, John Helgerson, whose staff had exposed a host of illicit activities, including torture, abuse, and improprieties linked to extraordinary renditions. When the White House eventually appointed an inspector general, it was a weak one, and in 2015, the Office of Inspector General was moved outside of the headquarters building, making it difficult for the office to conduct genuine oversight. This documents the nation's drift away from an open and accountable democracy and toward the kind of authoritarian society that George Orwell warned about.

Since the Vietnam War, we have witnessed a system of congressional acquiescence and judicial tolerance. Congress has acquiesced in the questionable actions of both the Bush and Obama administrations since 2001, permitting foreign policy to be the sole preserve of the executive branch and not the shared responsibility of the president and the Congress. Instead of serving as rigorous watchdogs, congressional intelligence committees have become advocates for the CIA. The Supreme Court only intervenes on foreign policy matters to endorse the policies and powers of the president. This deferential attitude has led to an absence of judicial scrutiny of illegalities, including warrantless eavesdropping and the destruction of the CIA's torture tapes. The destroyer of the 92 videotapes, Jose Rodriguez, ignored a White House order not to destroy the tapes and published a book sanctioned by the CIA that maligns the Office of Inspector General for its supposed "holier-than-thou attitude and the prosecutorial ways they routinely treated fellow CIA employees."

In addition to the failure of Congress and the courts to provide necessary oversight of national security, the media have been complacent about their investigative watchdog role in a democracy. The media are an essential partner in the whistleblowing process, but they typically ignore the reprisals taken against the people who risk all to challenge the authority of state and corporate power. Often, media disdain the information provided by whistleblowers that is critical of the establishment—preferring, instead, to side with official versions of events for the perks that doing so affords them.

There has been a great deal of vindication for the whistleblowers, however. Pulitzer Prizes were given to journalists (Barton Gellman, Glenn Greenwald, and Laura Poitras) from the newspapers (*Washington Post* and *The Guardian US*) that published Snowden's revelations. Forty years ago, Daniel Ellsberg's efforts led the Pulitzer's board to give its public service award to the *New York Times*. Like Ellsberg, Snowden has been portrayed as a traitor; the *New York Times*, the *Washington Post*, and the *Guardian US* have been vilified by congress members and even some journalists as enabling espionage and harming U.S. national security.

Representative Peter T. King (R-NY), chairman of the House Homeland Security Committee's subcommittee on counterterrorism and intelligence, termed the Pulitzer Prize "disgraceful" and charged that "enabling a traitor like Snowden is unjustifiable."[12] King stated that news organizations should be prosecuted for violations under the Espionage Act of 1917, which makes it illegal to disclose classified material that aids a foreign enemy. It took the nation several years to realize that the Pentagon Papers represented no threat to national security and that it was important to expose the official chicanery that led to the horrors of the Vietnam War. We are a long way from realizing that an intrusive national surveillance grid does far more harm to U.S. national security than Snowden's leaks do.

As a result of the imbalance in the process of foreign policy decision-making, we have come full circle from President Woodrow Wilson, who wanted to make the "world safe for democracy," to Presidents George W. Bush and Obama, who find the world too dangerous to permit honoring constitutional democracy. The excesses of the Vietnam War, Watergate, Iran-Contra, and the Terror Wars have contributed to the creation of a national security state and a culture of secrecy. Whistleblowers can help all of us decide whether the ends justify the means regarding these excesses.

Meanwhile, secrecy itself has fostered ignorance in the United States. The overuse of secrecy limits necessary debate on foreign policy and deprives citizens of information on which to make policy and political judgments. Only a counter-culture of openness and a respect for the balance of power can reverse the damage. As long as Congress defers to the president in the conduct of foreign policy; the courts intervene to prevent any challenge to the power of the president in making foreign policy; and the media defer to authorized sources, we will need courageous whistleblowers.

The Senate's response to disclosures regarding the culture of secrecy in the United States has been to resort to greater secrecy. In 2012, the Senate Intelligence Committee approved misguided legislation that would further limit news coverage of national security issues. The provisions, part of the intelligence authorization bill for fiscal 2013, were drafted in secret without public hearings; they were designed to deny Americans access to information essential to national debate on critical issues such as the extent of government spying activities and the use of torture. Under the measure, only the director, deputy directors, and designated public affairs officials of intelligence agencies would be permitted to provide background information on intelligence activities to the media. Briefings on sensitive topics by lower-level or career officials would be prohibited, shutting off routine news gathering that provides insight into policy. These measures weaken democracy and strengthen the trend toward authoritarianism in the United States.

* * *

At no point in my congressional testimony in 1991, or in my publications and speeches since then, have I believed that I was anything but patriotic in revealing political corruption at the CIA. Only time will tell if the American people conclude that the actions of such whistleblowers as Drake, Snowden, and Manning were patriotic efforts to awaken a sleeping nation to the extent of the criminal misuse of state power at home and abroad. National security whistleblowers are typically vindicated, but it often takes public opinion many years to catch up.

Far too often the secrecy of the national security state has been used to conceal miscalculations and malfeasance. The CIA tailored intelligence in the 1980s to justify enormous U.S. weapons spending in peacetime. Two decades later, the CIA falsified intelligence to justify the Iraq invasion, which cost more than 4,500 American lives, trillions of dollars, and the radical destabilization of the entire region. The CIA violated constitutional and international law when it engaged in torture and abuse and operated secret prisons. Excessive secrecy within the CIA and the absence of oversight permitted these crimes.

Dissidence in the intelligence community should not be

considered controversial, let alone subversive. It is not criticism that is cynical, but the absence of criticism among public servants that undermines the integrity of any organization, particularly a secrecy-bound community like that of U.S. intelligence workers and officials. In looking back, I am thankful for my mentors at Johns Hopkins University and Indiana University, who encouraged critical inquiry in pursuit of truth. The CIA itself (as well as Johns Hopkins) prides itself on the biblical wisdom that "You shall know the truth and the truth shall make you free," inscribed in the lobby of the CIA's headquarters and on my college ring.

The intelligence failures regarding the Soviet Union and Iraq were marked by the absence of sufficient critical inquiry, which the academic community might have provided, as is its traditional role. Indeed, there should be no fundamental contradictions in the worlds of liberal education and intelligence, even though education depends on openness and universal access and intelligence requires secrecy and the "need to know." But strong critical skills and integrity are required in both worlds. I tried to break down the insular culture that dominates the CIA, taking advantage of every opportunity to bring educators into the intelligence process.

Ultimately, however, it is the American people, not the academic elite, who must demand that the systemic failures of the U.S. intelligence community be addressed by public officials, politicians, and presidents. The intelligence community, particularly the CIA, has accumulated far more power than the Founding Fathers would have permitted or President Harry Truman ever intended. The statutes creating intelligence agencies, particularly Truman's CIA and the National Security Act, were far too vague, and the oversight process of the U.S. Congress is dysfunctional. The steady expansion of domestic and foreign intelligence in an era of permanent war demands that whistleblowers expose the criminal excesses and abuses that too often take place in the name of national security. The first obligation of any American, particularly a member of the intelligence community, is to defend and protect the Constitution of the United States. The lies and distortions that have become commonplace in the first several months of the Trump administration indicate that intelligence analysts must speak truth to themselves in order to deliver truth to power. There has never been a greater need for contrarian thinking and even dissent in the departments and agencies of government.

ONE

JOINING THE CIA

"In order to know what is going to happen, one must know what has happened."
—Niccolò Machiavelli

I never planned to join the Central Intelligence Agency. In looking back, there were signposts on my path to CIA headquarters in Langley, Virginia, in the summer of 1966. My three-year tour in the U.S. Army as a cryptographer exposed me to the intelligence world, and my two years in Athens, at the Joint United States Military Mission to Greece led to a love of travel and global politics. The training for my assignment at Fort Gordon in Augusta, Georgia, was secretive. My first tour of duty at the Pentagon involved encoding and decoding sensitive messages involving U.S. national security. My duties in Athens introduced me to behind-the-scenes developments during the Suez War in 1956, the Soviet invasion of Hungary in 1956, the launching of Sputnik in 1957, and the U.S. invasion of Lebanon in 1958. The latter invasion posed such a threat that my commanding general considered extending my tour as an "essential soldier" due to the possibility of warfare in the region. For the first and perhaps only time, at the age of 20, I was termed essential.

The assignment in Athens was important in another way. It gave me the opportunity to take college courses at a University of Maryland classroom on a U.S. air base. My professor, the late

Dr. Amin Banani, a brilliant scholar from Iran, sparked my interest in Russian history and opened many academic and cultural doors. As a result of Dr. Banani's encouragement, I applied to Johns Hopkins University, which I did to please him but without any expectation of being admitted. Following Hopkins, I went to Indiana University for graduate school where another professor, Dr. Robert Ferrell, took an interest in me and my work. He directed my Ph.D. dissertation on Soviet-American relations, which I completed largely because I didn't want to disappoint this generous man. Without Professors Banani and Ferrell, my life would have been far different and much less interesting.

My initial interviews with the CIA and the State Department were in 1964 and 1965, when both agencies conducted interviews on the Bloomington campus of Indiana University. I was also approached by the National Security Agency (NSA) because of my background in cryptography and Russian studies. I pursued all three agencies because I was unhappy with the academic openings for Indiana University graduates at that time; I had no interest in going to Stevens Point, Wisconsin, or to Denton, Texas, to teach. I decided to look elsewhere as long as I could make use of my background in Russian studies.

The selection process was easy. The security environment at the NSA was oppressive, which is ironic in view of the extensive leaks regarding NSA surveillance of American citizens. There were security mobiles hanging from the ceilings at Fort Meade, Maryland, and political posters ("Loose lips sink ships!") facing visitors in every corridor. There were badge checks within the building even after you got through security at the entrance. The foreign-service examination of the State Department was rigorous, but the personnel board of senior United States Foreign Service officers was off-putting. These officers had no interest in the work I was doing in graduate school and didn't indicate that I could specialize in the Soviet and East European areas. The personnel board was unwilling to give me an entry waiver of 12 months so I could complete my dissertation research. I didn't get the impression that the Foreign Service was interested in Russian area specialists with a serious academic background.

The introduction to the CIA didn't have the pervasive security atmosphere of the NSA and, unlike the State Department, it was willing to accommodate my academic pursuits. I had no interest in working in clandestine operations, so I met no one from the Directorate of Operations, which coordinates covert actions worldwide. I emphasized my interest in the Soviet area and was directed to the CIA's Office of Current Intelligence, where I met with the chiefs of the Soviet and East European regions. We discussed my dissertation topic on Soviet-American relations and held a lively exchange on national security and the role of intelligence in policymaking. Most importantly, they offered a one-year waiver to enable me to complete my research at the National Archives, the Library of Congress, and the Roosevelt Library in Hyde Park, New York.

I was interviewed by the *crème de la crème* of the CIA's Directorate of Intelligence—the analytical division of the CIA that produces reports and briefings for the White House and policymakers. Senior managers in those days had joined the CIA in the late 1940s and early 1950s when the Cold War was heating up, and the Soviet Union had become the "evil empire." This was probably the golden age for the CIA as an intelligence organization because of its sense of mission. Large numbers of liberal Ivy League graduates had been attracted to the CIA along with veterans of the military and the Office of Strategic Services, who were proud to serve a national security team's international mission. This was a political generation that had been willing to take risks on behalf of U.S. interests, and had encountered no serious political criticism of the CIA or U.S. foreign interventions when they were recruited. When I arrived in the 1960s, however, there was widespread criticism because of Vietnam.

I arrived at the CIA in 1966 as the war was becoming costly

and unpopular. Several supervisors were curious as to why someone who opposed the Vietnam War would join a CIA that was becoming infamous due to the war's horrors, particularly the violent Phoenix program, which was responsible for the deaths of innocent Vietnamese people. I'm embarrassed to say that I didn't give much thought to the role of the CIA in Vietnam or in places such as Iran, Guatemala, the Congo, or Cuba, where the CIA had conducted some of its most destructive operations. The CIA's involvement in the overthrow of the government in Iran in 1953 and Guatemala in 1954 as well as the targeting of Patrice Lumumba in the Congo in 1959 and Fidel Castro in 1961 at the Bay of Pigs were far from my mind.

I was naïve, leaving the first round of CIA interviews believing that it was a large research institution specializing in international relations. I gave little thought to the security investigation that would take up most of that year, which included an oppressive lie detection test. The CIA had an excellent library in my fields of interest, a helpful and professional staff to assist in research, opportunities for additional language training, and access to the most sensitive secrets of the U.S. government on the Soviet Union and East Europe. I was impressed with the people I met in the interviews, and I was excited by the possibility of overseas travel.

There is no excuse for not focusing on the clandestine operations of the CIA, and not weighing the pros and cons of the agency's violent role in undermining the governments of other nations, many of which were democracies. While the CIA had a legitimate role to play in the collection and analysis of intelligence, its role in the field of clandestine operations and covert action was questionable at best. CIA training courses were quite boastful of the covert actions behind the overthrow of governments in Iran and Guatemala, but I eventually concluded these events were strategic failures. We are still dealing with strategic setbacks caused by the pursuit of regime changes in nations lacking political stability outside the authoritarian strongman model. It took me too long to realize that CIA covert actions, as well as military intervention, had registered no strategic successes, but had been responsible for a series of strategic failures for the United States, and catastrophe for families and communities in foreign lands. It was particularly shocking to learn that the father of containment, George F. Kennan, whose books I had devoured as a graduate student, was a leading proponent of a covert action role for the CIA in the late 1940s—over the objections of the first CIA directors and their general counsels.

I learned early on, however, that the CIA was no "rogue elephant out of control," but a secret agency that simply carried out the orders of the White House. CIA director Gates ordered the destruction of nearly all of the operational documents on the overthrow of Iran's government (Operation Ajax) in 1953, presumably because one of the coup's planners prepared a secret history that described the Eisenhower administration's direct involvement. The coup may have been a tactical success, but it was a strategic nightmare that still burdens U.S.-Iranian ties. The same could be said for most covert actions.

The bureaucratic wall between the CIA's Directorate of Intelligence and Directorate of Operations contributed to my belief that I was doing legitimate work as an intelligence analyst and had nothing to do with the covert activities of the CIA's "case officers." The CIA headquarters building contributed to this feeling, because it was divided physically and ideologically between the two major directorates, or the "two sides of the house." Analysts resided in the northern half of the building, and operations officers in the southern half. We ate in different cafeterias to make sure that visitors to the CIA would never stumble into covert operatives who worked under cover. The physical layout was cumbersome, and it inhibited contact and communication between analysts and collectors. The latter wanted this system because analysts were viewed as progressive eggheads who didn't understand the harsh international environment. Few analysts objected, because we viewed many of the operatives as knuckle-draggers with little substantive expertise.

There was a double standard in the training of new hires. The CIA's Directorate of Operations—in charge of clandestine activities in foreign countries—recruited operations types who were given rigorous training for nearly a year at a training facility in Virginia. They received training in paramilitary activities as well as operational tradecraft. The career trainee program was devoted to preparing incoming officers for a career in clandestine activities. There was no comparable training for new analysts. A few analysts received mentors when they got to their regional offices, but most were on their own.

A useful preparation for life as an intelligence analyst was reading studies from the senior research staff. I learned that the research in the academic community was not as up-to-date as the work being done by the senior research staff. The work of this small, elite group suggested that the best way to get good assessments is to recruit good students and give them enough time and independence in their areas of expertise to pursue their work. Since papers by the senior research staff were considered "working papers" and not final intelligence, they did not require formal coordination within the CIA or the intelligence community, which is the best way to encourage out-of-the-box thinking. National Security Advisor Henry Kissinger knew that the best intelligence in Washington came from informal papers and not the formal estimates and assessments that carried the endorsement logos of myriad intelligence organizations. Coordinated intelligence is typically intelligence that forswears the most radical or experimental thinking.

Before facing the cultural challenges of the Intelligence and Operations Directorates, however, I encountered a personal challenge. Returning to my graduate studies at Indiana University's Russian and East European Research Institute, I encountered strong hostility to the CIA among faculty members and fellow students. They were aghast at my career choice. One member of my dissertation committee, Professor Bernard Morris of the Department of Government, immediately resigned from my committee without any explanation either to me or to the Department of History. He refused to speak to me for years, let alone help with my research.

Morris had had a bad experience while serving in the State Department's Bureau of Intelligence and Research, which was the intelligence arm of the State Department. He told a mutual friend that the "Goodman thing" really bothered him because he did not want to be perceived as a former government official from the intelligence community whose students were seeking job counseling and, in my case, a job with the dreaded CIA. The episode with Morris left me angry and frustrated.

I learned later that Morris had faced a rigorous and unfair security investigation at the Bureau of Intelligence and Research and wanted nothing to do with anyone considering a career in intelligence, let alone at the CIA. Professor Morris, an engaging and exciting professor, was victimized by the wave of McCarthyism that swept over the State Department in the 1950s.

Morris was extremely important to me because he had arrived at Indiana University in 1963, a year after my enrollment, as a vigorous and articulate critic of the U.S war in Vietnam. I was opposed to the war too, but Morris had a deeper understanding of the relevant history and politics, and their implications for international stability. He soon developed a close circle of followers within the graduate student community, and a few of us became active in the teach-in movement against the war, which was later investigated during my polygraph examination for the CIA.

I was also sympathetic toward Owen Lattimore, another professor who was victimized by McCarthyism in the 1950s and, as a result, was treated shabbily by our university, Johns Hopkins, where he was a professor. Neither Morris nor Lattimore received the protection they should have had from their institutions, and their experience should have made me more critical about bureaucratic politics in Washington, craven bureaucrats who occupy important positions, and the cowardice of academic and governmental institutions.

The reaction from some of my closest friends at the university was equally passionate and outraged. There were several individuals who cut off all contact with me, although this group did not include such fellow students as James Collins, who became ambassador to the Soviet Union in the late 1980s; Richard Miles, who became ambassador to Azerbaijan in 1992; and another close friend—who must remain unnamed—who headed the CIA's operational desk on the Soviet bloc. There were ugly letters from some graduate students, but they didn't cause me to rethink my career choice.

Losing friends at Indiana University was good preparation for my experiences with another former student there, Robert M. Gates, a close friend before he became an adversary at the CIA. When Gates was nominated to be CIA director and I became his leading opponent at his confirmation hearings in 1991, more friendships were lost. I had great respect for my Indiana University friends who were expressing strong opposition to the CIA. I had little respect for my CIA critics, who seemed to be careerists or opportunists. At the same time, I had my supporters at the agency—including some in management positions—who took risks in providing examples of politicized intelligence to support my congressional testimony. And there were analysts who also took great risks in submitting sworn testimony against the confirmation of Gates. One of them, Carolyn McGiffert Ekedahl, became my wife two years after the hearings.

I entered the CIA with great enthusiasm in the summer of 1966. The agency's headquarters are in McLean, Virginia, less than 10 miles from the White House. The 258-acre compound has a campus setting, which helped me ignore the heavily guarded main gate and the various barricades, which were fortified in 1993 after a young Pakistani national, Aimal Khan Kansi, killed two CIA employees and wounded several others, firing an AK-47 into cars headed into the CIA grounds. Shortly after the shootings, I got a call from the Virginia police, telling me that they had found an old copy of *Newsweek* in Kansi's apartment from the time of the 1991 hearings. The police wanted me to know that the pictures of Gates and me were circled. I asked if Gates had also been called, and they assured me that he was getting 24-hour police protection. I asked what I was "getting," and they replied that I was getting "this call."

The CIA's headquarters was designed in the 1950s by the same New York architects who designed the United Nations complex in Manhattan. The facade was impressive; the entrance offered an airy and open feeling. The compound itself was known as "Langley," the name of the McLean neighborhood where the CIA is located. There is a statue of Nathan Hale, who was captured and executed by the British for spying for the United States, to the right of the entrance, and an egg-shaped auditorium nearby, where the jazz legend Lionel Hampton gave a concert for his neighbor from Connecticut, the CIA director George H.W. Bush.

The two major cultures of the CIA, the analytical and the operational, were quite distinct. The operatives believed the primary mission of the CIA was the collection of foreign intelligence. The recruitment of case officers involved a search for extroverts who would be trained at a facility in Virginia, to recruit foreign sources of secret information for policymakers, and not necessarily for intelligence analysts. Analysts had access to the raw information of the intelligence community, including the sensitive intercepts of the NSA, and used facts and inference for policy-relevant estimates and assessments. "Open source" materials, such as newspapers, official statements, and published statistics, were often more valuable than secret information from clandestine sources. Both directorates were good at dealing with the capabilities of adversaries; neither did a good job of dealing with intentions.

Clandestine operatives or case officers are deeply involved in policy; they rely on secrecy and hierarchy and share information on a strict need-to-know basis. They are typically generalists who serve overseas and rarely have regional or country-specific expertise. They typically move from one country to another every few years. The best of them gather important information by serving in key countries, but very few are good at incorporating that information into a global picture to serve the needs of policymakers. There were always exceptions, however. Most are hard working because they must do both the job that their cover status demands as well as their clandestine mission. Their political views tend to be on the right.

There was rarely agreement between clandestine operatives and intelligence analysts. Operatives were quick to support administration positions, giving upbeat assessments of the Vietnam War that were contradicted by the intelligence assessments coming from the Directorate of Intelligence. The differences between the two directorates on the war couldn't have been more stark, moving Director Helms to remark "I felt like a circus rider standing astride two horses."[1] CIA analysts and operatives differed on the impact of Mikhail Gorbachev on Soviet domestic politics and Soviet-American relations.

Intelligence analysts are tethered to their desks at Langley and get insufficient opportunities to travel overseas. It was particularly frustrating to learn that the Directorate of Operations did not permit Soviet analysts to travel to the Soviet Union, although this policy was altered in the 1970s. Intelligence analysts should have no policy axes to grind; their credibility rests on that fact. Unlike operatives, analysts tended to be progressive in their political thinking, which led President Richard Nixon to refer to them as "clowns." They received short orientation trips to their areas of expertise, but got insufficient support from overseas case officers, who viewed analysts traveling with marginal and ineffective cover as a threat to their clandestine missions. I traveled to countries where the CIA station would not allow me to come into the U.S. embassy (for example, the USSR, India, Costa Rica) and I was denied travel to important countries (for example, Iraq, Pakistan) for no good reason. If the CIA had a genuine "one Agency" culture, intelligence analysts would have gone overseas regularly for temporary duty, and served tours in CIA stations. This would allow regular discussion of sources with case officers and assessments of the information that sources provide. When I was on the faculty of the National War College, the overseas trips were particularly rewarding, because we had support from defense attachés assigned to the embassies in countries we visited. The CIA needs a similar culture.

Unlike the Operations Directorate and the military, which offers extensive training to its recruits, the CIA in the 1960s was extremely casual in preparing intelligence analysts. I received no training and only informal mentoring upon entering the CIA, and no exposure to the problem of intelligence manipulation. The testimony I provided to the Senate Select Committee on Intelligence about corruption at the CIA was fully transcribed in official congressional publications, but there was no effort to incorporate these accounts into training manuals or actual case studies. An ombudsman post was finally created in the wake of the hearings, but there were no junkyard dogs among those who filled the post.

The CIA culture was challenging due to the differences between the Directorates of Intelligence and Operations. These two distinct cultures were formed during World War II in the Office of Strategic Services (OSS). The OSS had an operational element that served in Europe and Asia with some members becoming CIA directors: Allen Dulles, Helms, Colby, and Casey. The analytical element of the Office of Strategic Services served primarily in Washington, D.C., and their members were influential in forming the CIA's Office of National Estimates, particularly Yale University's Sherman Kent and Harvard University's William Langer.

The culture of the clandestine service remains dominated by the secrecy of the mission; its hierarchical nature has its roots in the quasi-military origins of the Office of Strategic Services. The Directorate of Operations is a closed fraternity; even CIA analysts are considered outsiders who can't be trusted. The risks confronting operatives are similar to those of Foreign Service Officers and military officers, but clandestine agents believe they are part of an exclusive club. The Directorate of Operations has become a paramilitary organization in many ways.

Operatives are extroverts by nature, getting their energy from other people, useful in recruiting foreign agents to do the bidding of the United States. The culture of the Directorate of Operations is inherently contradictory; it represents a closed, secret society inside an open democracy. It claims to have the highest morality, but represents a lawless organization overseas. The willingness to break laws leads to a resentment of congressional oversight. As former director of central intelligence General Walter Bedell Smith has conceded, "The CIA has committed every crime there is except rape." The need to manipulate others and to obfuscate their own identities leads many to drop out of the directorate. For the overwhelming majority that remain, their own families, particularly their children, have no idea that they are clandestine operatives of the CIA. There is typically great anger when they become aware.

Unlike operatives, analysts are classic introverts. Many analysts are recruited from graduate school, where they were preparing for life in the ivory tower. The dominant culture of the Directorate of Intelligence in the mid-1960s was shaped by Sherman Kent, who believed that analysts must keep a distance from policymakers and must shield themselves from the prejudices and motivations of the consumers of intelligence. Unlike operatives, analysts are often critical of the excesses of U.S. national security policy, such as the Vietnam War and U.S.-sponsored coups in Iran, Guatemala, Vietnam, and Chile.

Intelligence analysts have registered serious failures, such as the lack of warning about the decline of the Soviet Union or the phony assessments of Iraqi weapons of mass destruction. These failures occur when intense policy pressure distorts the flow of intelligence information. CIA directors and deputy directors (Casey and Gates) were involved in the failure to accurately assess the Soviet decline; Tenet and John McLaughlin played key roles, providing tailored intelligence to allow the Bush administration to invade Iraq.

When I left the CIA in the mid-1980s, the dominant culture was shaped by Robert M. Gates, who could not have been more different from Kent, lacking both his stature and his intellect. Gates believed it was the duty of the analyst to study and serve the agenda of policymakers. The ethos of Robert Gates created the conditions that led to the corruption of intelligence.

President Truman designed the CIA so that the intelligence analyst would be at the center of the organization; it soon became obvious that clandestine operatives were the real center. Analysts typically resent their association with clandestine operatives, who are perceived as "spooks." Operatives see analysts as naïve, idealistic, and unrealistic. Those senior officers of the CIA, such as Harvard University's Robert Bowie of the National Foreign Assessment Center in the late 1970s, who thought they could merge the two cultures, did not succeed. Director John O. Brennan has created an unprecedented merger of the Directorates of Intelligence and Operations without consulting the Congressional Intelligence Committees and without debate within CIA itself.

I was wrong not to learn more about the CIA's clandestine foreign interventions that were so abhorrent to many friends and academic colleagues, including my faculty advisors. I believed that my work in the Directorate of Intelligence, which was openly acknowledged, was far different from the work of the Directorate of Operations, which was covert and unacknowledged. I had little contact with officers of the Directorate of Operations, even in my own field of Soviet affairs. I developed an academic interest in the CIA's clandestine operations, but I felt no responsibility for covert actions that involved destabilizing foreign governments, let alone assassinations and support for brutal regimes.

The CIA's secret operations, particularly regime changes and political killings, were not the rogue actions of an out-of-control agency, however. These acts were authorized and conceptualized at the White House with the approval of the president. The National Security Act of 1947 that created the CIA did not refer to covert actions, but it did assign to the CIA "duties related to intelligence affecting the national security." There is no evidence that President Truman wanted to use the CIA in such covert deeds, but his immediate successors, Eisenhower and Kennedy, gave the CIA a major clandestine role in foreign policy. Their successors endorsed covert actions that violated international law, and were not in accordance with U.S. law.

President Truman wanted a firewall between the Directorate of Operations and the Directorate of Intelligence because he didn't want the policy role of clandestine operations to compromise the analytic role of the Directorate of Intelligence. In 2015 Brennan destroyed the bureaucratic wall between intelligence and operations to create regional and functional "fusion centers," which now situate analysts and operatives side by side. This creates greater centralized control and more opportunities for manipulating intelligence, and harms the production of strategic intelligence and authoritative National Intelligence Estimates.

The intelligence from CIA's fusion centers concentrates on tactical warning, but does a poor job of explaining the "why" and "wherefore" of geopolitical events. The CIA was wrong, for example, in failing to anticipate the emergence of the Islamic State in Iraq and Syria, and never warned the White House in 2002–2003 about the domestic consequence of using force in Iraq. The CIA clearly underestimated the military capabilities of the Islamic State, and the intelligence failure led to a policy failure in responding to a new challenge in both Iraq and Syria.

There were immediate rewards in joining the CIA's Office of Current Intelligence, which provided timely intelligence to the president and key policymakers, particularly the friendship of a group of Soviet foreign policy analysts, about a half dozen or so, in their late twenties, most newly married, and one or two with young children. All had advanced degrees from good universities; all were progressive; all were committed to becoming good intelligence analysts. We held potluck parties at a time when Washington had few decent restaurants and salaries in the range of $6,000–$8,000 didn't allow for dining out. When we moved from apartments to houses, we banded together with rented trucks and got the job done.

There was great esprit de corps in the first years. I pitched for the CIA's Office of Current Intelligence softball team and played point guard for its basketball team. When CIA director Helms was asked by *LIFE* magazine to do a photo essay on the softball league, he agreed, if a healthy honorarium was paid. Helms was interested in padding the CIA's budget; *LIFE* wasn't that interested in our softball league. My contribution to the *esprit* was organizing small groups of analysts to go to Baltimore for baseball games, since Washington was deprived of the sport. On one occasion, I got management of the Orioles to welcome the CIA contingent on the electronic scoreboard, which was a great delight for all of us. In 1984, I chartered a bus to conduct a one-day tour of Charm City for 45 colleagues, another great source of merriment. I have a wonderful picture of a half dozen of us standing in front of the CIA's Family Inn, a down-to-earth Italian restaurant in Fells Point.

We were an interesting mix, and became rather formidable within the Office of Current Intelligence. We gave no thought to the fact that there were no female analysts in our group. We worked long hours without any provision for overtime. We were feisty for the most part, and some of us manifested a contrarian streak. I developed a reputation for being particularly prickly, but there were few shrinking violets in the group. Some of us were simply quicker than others to go to the mat. I wrestled in junior high school, so I loved to go to the mat. We had no mentors inside the office so we nudged and badgered each other; some dealt with that better than others.

The group included, at one extreme, Bob Gates, who went on to become CIA director under President George H. W. Bush and secretary of defense under Presidents George W. Bush and Barack Obama. I took Gates to the cafeteria for his first lunch in the building in 1968, and told my colleagues that we would be working for this guy one of these days. It simply happened much sooner than I expected. Bob started out as a very good, hard-working analyst, but his ambition and ego eventually prevailed over his ethics and professionalism.

At the other extreme was Raymond McGovern, who currently heads a small group of former intelligence analysts who lobby the White House on sensitive issues and contribute regularly to various websites. Like Gates, McGovern came to the CIA as part of his tour as an Air Force officer; they locked horns immediately and they haven't disengaged 50 years later. When the young McGovern became our branch chief, it was the even younger Gates who went to our bosses and succeeded in getting McGovern replaced.

I'm not a member of Ray's group of activists because I prefer to pick my own causes and make my own cases. Ray's civic activity has led to a great deal of notoriety, including an arrest in 2014 in New York City simply for trying to attend a talk by General David Petraeus at the 92nd Street Y. So much for the 92nd Street Y's commitment to free speech, tolerance, and openness. Federal agents have also escorted Ray from public meetings where he merely tried to question former secretary of defense Donald Rumsfeld or former secretary of state Hillary Clinton.

If anyone doubts the massive nature of surveillance of the American population, then just ponder the fact that McGovern had a ticket to the Petraeus event that was purchased online, and that the 92nd Street Y and New York City's finest were waiting for McGovern at the door to bar his legitimate and lawful entry. The head of counterintelligence for the New York City police department may have had something to do with this. The counterintelligence chief is the former head of operations at the CIA, David Cohen.

My best friend in the CIA was the late Barry L. Stevenson. Barry and I traveled together in China; taught a course in Soviet politics and policy at the National War College; attended anti-war rallies in the Vietnam era; and forged a close personal relationship that lasted until shortly after the confirmation hearings for Gates in 1991. Barry, Bob, and I had been close in the 1960s and 1970s, and Barry did his best to bridge the gap when Bob and I became antagonists. Barry was one of the analysts who provided me with important documents that revealed how Gates was tampering with intelligence to satisfy those above him, but eventually Barry felt he had to choose between the two of us. He chose Gates, so I felt an ironic satisfaction when Barry was named the CIA's ombudsman to prevent corruption in the mid-1990s. The position didn't exist until several of us made the issue of politicization the thrust of our opposition to Gates's confirmation as CIA director.

Another close friend was Eugene Wicklund, whose wedding reception was held at my apartment in Washington because it was within walking distance of the ceremony at the National Cathedral, and the cost was right. A favorite delicatessen in McLean, Virginia, for CIA analysts and operatives did the catering. Wicklund was a new and inexperienced analyst in 1968 when he accurately forecast the Soviet invasion of Czechoslovakia, but he was silenced and even ridiculed by senior managers at the CIA and the Department of State's Bureau of Intelligence and Research, who argued the Kremlin didn't do that kind of thing anymore.[2] Fast forward to Russian aggression in Ukraine and Crimea in 2014–2015 for a similar CIA failure.

Many, if not most, of my colleagues in the Soviet Division of the CIA's Office of Current Intelligence were opposed to the war in Vietnam and took part in anti-war rallies in Washington. More importantly, the CIA's political intelligence on the war was implicitly critical of the U.S. effort and extremely pessimistic on the chances of U.S. success. The most memorable march occurred in 1967 and was memorialized in Norman Mailer's *Armies of the Night*. Stevenson and I proudly marched behind veterans of the Abraham Lincoln Brigade that had fought in Spain 30 years earlier. We went as far as the Pentagon, but when it turned ugly we took the advice of Kenny Rogers: "You gotta know when to hold 'em, know when to fold 'em, know when to walk away, and know when to run." We imagined the absurd political imagery of J. Edgar Hoover's FBI agents taking pictures of the two of us as CIA anti-war protesters.

The environment and work in the Office of Current Intelligence suited my temperament and disposition. Our task was to provide timely political intelligence to U.S. decision makers. Pride of place was given to the President's Daily Brief, which went to the president, the national security advisor, the secretaries of state and defense, and very few others. President Richard Nixon demanded that a copy go to the attorney general as well, which pointed to the close relationship between Nixon and John Mitchell. The fact that a very junior analyst could contribute to an intelligence document for the president of the United States was a major part of the excitement of our work.

The President's Daily Brief was an all-source document that incorporated sensitive materials from the CIA's Directorate of Operations; intercepts from the National Security Agency; cables from U.S. embassies; defense attaché reporting; and the excellent and under-appreciated media coverage from the CIA's Foreign Bureau of Information. The National Security Agency is defined as a collection agency rather than an analytic one, but in the 1960s and 1970s they boasted some of the best analysts in Washington, and I soon learned to use the scrambler telephone to call my counterpart at the National Security Agency, Eugene Rowe, an outstanding intelligence analyst.

One of the peculiarities of the CIA during my tenure from 1966 to 1990 was the fact that so few people were delegated and so little attention was paid to the President's Daily Brief, which was read at the highest levels of government, compared to the time and attention given to National Intelligence Estimates, which were rarely read by senior policymakers. The CIA tailored the Brief to the interests of the president, some of whom were readers (Kennedy, Clinton, and Obama) and some of whom were not (Johnson and Reagan). With the changes in the intelligence community, the Brief is now directed by the Director of National Intelligence—a retired military officer—and not the director of CIA—an intelligence professional.

In order to prepare items for the President's Daily Brief or to contribute to National Intelligence Estimates, I had an in-box with the best of U.S. intelligence from an outstanding collection system is unmatched. We had the most challenging intelligence requirement in the community, judging the capabilities and intentions of the major adversary facing the United States—the Soviet Union. We were not fully appreciative of the great responsibility we had at the time, particularly in view of our inexperience and modest professional backgrounds. We had academic degrees, typically master's degrees, but none of us had ever worked in foreign policy or intelligence communities. We had successes and failures. Our failures had nothing to do with collection; they were due primarily to the lack of rigor and imagination among analysts and, in the 1980s, to chronic political interference from Casey and Gates.

In addition to writing short intelligence items for the President's Daily Brief and the National Daily Bulletin that went worldwide, we conducted briefings before congressional committees, traveled overseas for orientation and briefings of foreign liaisons, participated in the preparation of National Intelligence Estimates, and coordinated intelligence throughout the multi-agency intelligence community. I served on task forces at all hours of the day and night during crises such as the Six-Day War in the Middle East, the Soviet invasion of Czechoslovakia, the October War of 1973, and even the Iranian hostage crisis and the Chinese invasion of Vietnam in the late 1970s, because there was always a Soviet angle to be investigated.

No one has ever studied the intelligence products of these task forces, although they produced the best assessments of fast-breaking situations around the world. These products were superior to the work of other intelligence agencies, and far more valuable than what appeared in the mainstream media. When I served on the task force on Vietnam in 1979, I fielded a call from former CIA director George H.W. Bush, who was traveling in Texas and wanted to be brought up to speed on the Chinese invasion.

I soon learned that the CIA's intelligence support is invaluable in any negotiating arena, whether arms control negotiations such as SALT or negotiations on the Middle East. Harold Saunders, one of the leading Arabists in the State Department, who accompanied Kissinger in negotiations between Israel, Egypt, and Syria, affirmed to me the importance of CIA support. "When you are a mediator . . . you quickly realize you're particularly naked because the Syrians had lived on, and the Israelis were sitting on, the Golan Heights, and the Egyptians had pumped oil from the Gulf of Suez and the Israelis were sitting on that territory," Saunders said.[3] "We weren't, so our ability to keep people in the mediation honest and not trying to pull wool over each other's eyes was entirely dependent on our having knowledge from in-dependent sources." He considered CIA support "superb." If I sound overly enthusiastic, then it is because I was. I found all of this exhilarating.

It was impossible to hold a conversation in Washington in the mid-1960s without debating Vietnam. It didn't take many social occasions for me to realize that the CIA wasn't a popular institution, but a good way to disarm critics was to protest the war with chapter and verse evidence of U.S. perfidy and poor judgment in deploying a huge force to Southeast Asia. Twenty years later, the various annexes to the Pentagon Papers carried several National Intelligence Estimates that recorded CIA assessments from the early 1960s indicating that U.S. bombing of Vietnam would not hinder Hanoi's ability to carry on the war against the South, and that the North Vietnamese would match every U.S. act of escalation, no matter how great the physical suffering.[4] U.S. bombers dropped more ordnance on Vietnam than on Germany in World War II, with no impact on the outcome of the war in Southeast Asia. CIA director Richard McGarrah Helms soon wore out his welcome at both the Johnson and Nixon White House because of the pessimistic messages he carried to policy meetings.

The CIA prepared a series of studies for President Lyndon B. Johnson, National Security Advisor Walt Rostow, and Secretary of Defense Robert McNamara that concluded that bombing operations such as Rolling Thunder, designed to complicate the enemy's war effort, had not reduced enemy operations in the South or the amount of enemy supplies moving into the area. A good friend of mine at the State Department's Bureau of Intelligence and Research, Louis Sarris, was reaching identical conclusions, but McNamara ordered that Sarris be taken off the Vietnam account. Secretary of State Dean Rusk meekly carried out McNamara's outrageous order, which may have been the first personnel reprisal of the war. Sarris was treated as a pariah by most of his colleagues because of his opposition to the war. Some of my colleagues, including my wife, encountered similar experiences in the wake of their testimony to the Congress to counter the confirmation of Robert Gates as CIA director.

Secretary of Defense McNamara responded to Sarris's trenchant analysis with an angry and chilling warning to Secretary of State Rusk, saying, "If you were to tell me that it is not the policy of the State Department to issue military appraisals without seeking the views of the Defense Department, the matter will die."[5] Rusk assured McNamara that future memoranda that contained "military appraisals (would) be coordinated with your Department."[6] At a pivotal time in October 1963, only several weeks before the assassination of President John F. Kennedy, when the groundwork was being laid for the tragic escalation of the war, key decision makers were denied ground truth about the situation in Vietnam from the CIA and the State Department's Bureau of Intelligence and Research.

Policymakers looked at CIA operatives and intelligence analysts with the same suspicion that operatives and analysts had toward each other. It is the rare memoir from a policymaker that extols the virtues of the CIA; for the most part the CIA became a whipping post for failed policy. Secretary of Defense McNamara lied about the intelligence he received on Vietnam and denied having access to good intelligence that provided sufficient warning of the fool's errand that he supported. He used his memoir and a documentary film to argue that a lack of reliable information about Vietnam led to incorrect decisions in the early 1960s.[7] "Our government lacked experts for us to consult," he wrote. This was not true. Four decades later, the key members of the Bush administration used their memoirs to blame the invasion of Iraq on bad and inadequate intelligence.

A CIA colleague, Samuel Adams, fourth cousin seven times removed of the second president of the United States, became another outcast. He wore out his welcome with the CIA establishment by fighting the deliberate undercount of Viet Cong by military intelligence, particularly the Defense Intelligence Agency. Adams was taken off the Vietnam account, but was not moved far enough away, because after his lateral arabesque to the Cambodian desk, he found that the Khmer Rouge in Southeast Asia were also being deliberately undercounted. Policymakers had a difficult time dealing with the larger estimates of enemy fighting forces because such estimates exposed the exaggerated body counts of the military and begged serious questions about the need for a greater U.S. troop presence. Presently, military intelligence is being investigated for politicizing and exaggerating the results of U.S. actions against ISIS in Iraq and Syria.

Adams was the *enfant terrible* of the CIA and indeed the entire intelligence community. He wrote one of the best books ever written on the politics of intelligence analysis, but, like most "best books," it has been read by very few and understood by even fewer.[8] Sam was the model of the crusading intelligence analyst. He had conclusively established that the intelligence community, led by the military, had severely and deliberately undercounted the numbers of Viet Cong with the prodding of military commanders who wanted to make the war effort appear successful. The bureaucratic infighting took place at the highest levels of the policy and intelligence communities, and the eventual release of thousands of documents supported Adams.

Many of these documents were available because Adams simply decided to take them home, which is far removed from standard security procedures at the CIA. The end-of-the-day security drill was a simple one that included taking paper bags of classified trash to the appropriate burn chutes; tugging at safe and file drawers to make sure they were locked; and combing the area for stray pieces of classified trash. But in 1969, when the CIA's deputy director, Admiral Rufus Taylor, delivered a letter that suggested Adams should "submit his resignation" if he could not be a "helpful member of the intelligence team at CIA," Adams tried a new drill.

Adams had no intention of quitting, so he began to remove documents in a daily paper, usually the *Wall Street Journal*, and bury them on a neighbor's heavily wooded property in a wooden box that once held cheap Spanish wine. Like other whistleblowers, Adams walked the halls of Congress to interest our representatives in the intelligence failure that had destroyed so many lives in Vietnam, but he encountered a deafening silence, the same silence that would confront whistleblowers such as Daniel Ellsberg, Thomas Drake, and William Binney years later. When Adams and other contrarians were accused of exaggerating the numbers of Viet Cong, National Security Advisor Walt Rostow would typically add, "I'm sorry you won't support your president." Too many Republican senators on the intelligence committee dismissed my testimony because they thought it was nothing more than a reflection of a personal rivalry between two former friends at the CIA.

A good contrarian, Adams took his protests to the highest levels, circulating blistering criticism on various National Intelligence Estimates and accusing drafters of "self delusion."[9] The head of the Board of National Estimates was no longer a fellow contrarian such as Sherman Kent, but a more academic leader, Abbot Smith, who was not a bureaucratic infighter with sharp elbows, but someone who believed that National Intelligence Estimates should present agreed judgments and not sharp alternative views. This is exactly why so many policymakers choose to ignore the substance of these estimates. Helms knew that any estimate dealing with enemy strength could become a sensitive political document and told President Johnson that he considered not publishing some of them.[10] There was one estimate on Vietnam that Helms simply didn't carry to the White House. The dereliction of duty had reached every level of the policy and intelligence communities.

Like Ellsberg and Drake, Adams eventually chose to go public. First, there was an article in *Harper's* magazine that I used in my courses on the CIA at American University, and then a CBS documentary, *The Uncounted Enemy: A Vietnam Deception*. The article hit the stands only a few days before the fall of Saigon, but it had no impact. The CBS documentary had the lowest ratings of any national program for the week. The Adams saga is a reminder that the job of the intelligence analyst is not to ease the job of policymakers, but often to complicate it and to provide information they don't want to hear. That is why whistleblowers are needed, and why messengers (i.e., whistleblowers) are shot.

Adams gained notoriety because General William C. Westmoreland, who was charged with a "conspiracy" to hold down the numbers of Viet Cong, sued the network for $120 million, with Adams named as a defendant because he was a consultant to the show. So a middle-level intelligence analyst found himself guiding the evidentiary search at a trial that turned into the only major investigation of the Vietnam War. It is difficult to prove conspiracy but, thanks to Adams and his purloined documents, Westmoreland withdrew his suit before the case was scheduled to go to the jury.

The Institute of Defense Analysis, a think tank for the Pentagon, corroborated Adams's work and added its own pessimistic assessment of the bombing program, which was the "most categorical rejection of bombing as a tool of our policy in Southeast Asia to be made by an official or semiofficial group."[11] CIA publications led to President Johnson's decision after the Tet Offensive to curtail U.S. bombings in the North. Unlike Louis Sarris, who became a non-person at the Department of State with a windowless office that lacked a phone, Adams was treated as a hero by some of us at the CIA, because not only did he stick his finger in the eye of the policymaker, he was right to do so. The Adams affair sent a positive message to me about the importance of an independent intelligence service, an analytic corps prepared to tell truth to power, and the importance of tenacity in the process. It requires taking evidence where it leads and then standing up for it.

Just as Gene Wicklund got it right on the Soviet invasion of Czechoslovakia in 1968 and Sam Adams got it right about the numbers of Viet Cong in Vietnam in the 1960s, another young colleague whom I admired—Bob Layton—got it right on the Tet Offensive of December 1968 that destroyed the Pentagon's phony estimates of enemy strength. Layton was an intelligence analyst detailed to Saigon in mid-1967, and he prepared three major assessments in November and December 1967 that warned of a powerful, nationwide enemy offensive. One of the assessments uncannily predicted that the offensive "would in all likelihood determine the future direction of the war."[12] These three assessments marked the finest predictive performance of any intelligence agency prior to Tet, but they had no impact on senior White House and CIA officials.

Layton was the best kind of contrarian, because he strived to get the attention of Walt Rostow, the war's chief cheerleader in the White House. Just as George W. Bush got a completely distorted picture of the Iraq War from Dick Cheney, Lyndon Johnson got an incorrect assessment of Vietnam from Rostow. This is exactly why analysts need to be tenacious in getting the attention of obtuse decision makers, and this is exactly what Gates worked to prevent. He constantly warned against "sticking your finger in the eye of the policymaker."

Layton was prophetic. In his third and final assessment, he predicted an all-out Viet Cong–North Vietnamese push and a willingness to accept "staggering losses" to accelerate a sharp decline in the American will to continue the war. In other words, the war was nearing a "turning point" that would determine the future direction of the country.[13] The CIA's special assistant for Vietnam, George Carver, gave this assessment to Rostow, and distanced himself and the CIA from the conclusions, which paved the way for the surprise in Washington when Tet hit. Carver was helped by the Intelligence Directorate's North Vietnam analysts, who continued to believe Hanoi would follow a careful policy of attrition and resented a radical new assessment from outside their ranks.

The official histories of President Johnson and Walter Rostow want you to believe they read Layton's assessments, and agreed with them. President Johnson claimed that he "agreed heartily with one prophetic report from our Embassy in Saigon [that the war was probably nearly a turning point]. I was increasingly concerned by reports that the Communists were preparing a maximum military effort and were going to try for a significant tactical victory."[14] Rostow even quoted Layton's assessments at length and disingenuously claimed they indicated the extent to which the White House "appreciated" the structure of the Tet Offensive and the "data available to Johnson" as early as December 1968.[15]

This is why the U.S. intelligence community must protect the contrarian, often the best source for premonitory intelligence. During the worst days of Cold War McCarthyism, when the leading diplomatic voices such as those of Ambassadors George Kennan, Tommy Thompson, and Charles E. (Chip) Bohlen were muffled because of their conciliatory slant, it was the CIA and the Board of National Estimates that ignored McCarthyism and pursued "new thinking." The ambassadors believed that the Soviets were more concerned with maintaining their own power than with expanding communism. CIA assessments supported this view, but McCarthyism ensured that hard-line neoconservatives would carry the day in the policy community. This was the feisty culture existing at CIA when I arrived, and the culture that dominated CIA debates until Casey and Gates introduced their brand of "McCarthyism" in the 1980s—a brand that dished out more than enough to turn a contrarian into a dissident.

My first 15 years at the CIA were a time of great excitement and fulfillment on a personal and professional level. My daughter was born in 1970, and my son was born in 1972. I took on a great professional challenge in going to Vienna in 1971 as part of the

SALT delegation, which led me to miss my daughter's first steps and first words. That was a mistake that I still regret as I watch my 11 grandchildren go through such developmental landmarks. My son was born during a teaching sabbatical at the University of Connecticut in Storrs. Soon after returning from Storrs, I went to the State Department's Bureau of Intelligence and Research for a two-year rotation, where I worked with a talented group of Soviet analysts with strong academic backgrounds.

I spent a summer in Moscow at the U.S. embassy in 1976, working in the political section on Soviet relations with Asia. I traveled to most of the Soviet republics, and celebrated the 200th anniversary of U.S. independence with an interesting group of expatriots at a rooftop restaurant in Uzbekistan. The trips to Ukraine, Georgia, Estonia, and Lithuania, my ancestral homeland, were particularly rewarding. For the first time, I could actually study first-hand the places that I had read about in graduate school or examined from satellite photography at the CIA. I realized as never before that intelligence and academic reporting had greatly exaggerated the power and prospects of the Soviet Union. I conversed with Soviet officials and citizens at every level. If only I had taken my Russian language studies more seriously.

In Moscow, I shared an apartment with Lynn Jones, a former graduate school classmate from Indiana University, who was the bureau chief for ABC. As a result, I met many Soviet media personalities, and traveled with Jones on weekends to various places outside of Moscow to cover stories. We prepared interesting pieces on racetracks, wedding receptions, and dog shows. The chief of the political section, Jack Matlock, an excellent Soviet scholar and linguist, probably would not have approved. Twenty years later the *New York Review of Books* published Matlock's favorable review of the book that my wife and I co-authored on Eduard Shevardnadze.[16] The review made a big impact on my academic mentors.

There were many intelligence successes during this period that were a source of great professional and personal pride. The

CIA's analysis of the Sino-Soviet split in the 1960s opened the door to U.S. triangular diplomacy between Washington, Moscow, and Beijing that established better U.S. relations with Moscow and Beijing than the Soviet Union and China had with each other. The improved relations with China opened the door with the Soviets to the SALT Agreement on limiting offensive strategic ballistic missiles; the Anti-Ballistic Missile Treaty, which was the cornerstone of strategic deterrence; and the Treaty of Berlin kept the divided city of Berlin from becoming a possible flashpoint between the United States and the Soviet Union in Europe. The arms control treaties of 1972 would not have received congressional ratification without the CIA guarantee of verification of the terms of the treaties.

These events took place despite the vulnerability the U.S. created for itself by waging an unwinnable war in Vietnam. The CIA's intelligence throughout the 1960s and 1970s described the weakness of the U.S. military and political position in Southeast Asia, and, if that intelligence had been accepted, the United States might have been spared the Vietnamese setback, including the loss of more than 56,000 servicemen and women in an egregious war. There is no utility in good intelligence if it is not read and absorbed.

In my first 15 years, until Casey's arrival as director, the CIA performed its analytical role as President Truman intended. In the late 1960s and early 1970s, the CIA produced excellent intelligence that demonstrated that U.S. air power was meaningless against the guerrilla struggle in Vietnam and that the absence of an ally in South Vietnam meant no possibility of success against North Vietnam. CIA verification of the SALT and ABM treaties created the conditions for congressional ratification of the treaties as the agency stood up to the Pentagon's opposition to disarmament. The CIA had a good understanding of the Soviet reasons for invading Afghanistan in 1979, which conflicted with the view of the White House and the National Security Council.

Intelligence analysts have a great deal of regional expertise and are often in a position to inform policy options, but only if policymakers are willing to engage. A typical example of conflict between policy and intelligence took place in the mid-1970s when Secretary of State Kissinger refused to recognize the qualifications of the leftist Movimento Popular de Libertação de Angola (MPLA) because he wanted to pursue a wrong-headed policy on behalf of South Africa against the Soviet Union and Cuba.

Several of us were contrarians in trying to prevent the unnecessary dust-up over the Soviet combat brigade in Cuba in 1979, but we were unsuccessful. This wasn't a case of intelligence corruption, but it demonstrated the ability of a national security advisor, Zbigniew Brzezinski, to have untoward influence over the CIA's national intelligence officer, Arnold Horelick, which spoke to the dangers of intelligence officials getting too close to policymakers. Several of us, however, managed to convince CIA director Casey and President Reagan that the "war scare" in Moscow was genuine and that U.S. actions had something to do with it. These events depicted the different worlds of intelligence and policy that are discussed in the following chapter.

FAILURE AS WELL AS SUCCESS

There were major intelligence failures during this period as well, particularly the failure to anticipate the Egyptian-Syrian attack on Israel in 1973, the October War. There is no doubt that Egyptian president Anwar Sadat surprised Israel's Mossad as well as the CIA in organizing the attack on Israel. Less than 24 hours before the attack, the CIA told President Nixon that "both sides are becoming increasingly concerned about the activities of the other. Rumors and agent reports may be feeding the uneasiness that appears to be developing. *The military preparations that have occurred do not indicate that any party intends to initiate hostilities.*"[17] Israeli intelligence also failed, despite the availability of an Egyptian spy who happened to be the son-in-law of former Egyptian

President Gamel Abdel Nasser and who provided advance intelligence of the Egyptian military operation.

Not only was the CIA terribly wrong about the possibility of hostilities, it told the president two days after the war began that "after several days of heavy fighting" the Israelis would complete the destruction of the Syrian army and "destroy as much as possible of Egypt's army."[18] This was a much greater intelligence failure, involving group think and flawed intelligence that had dire consequences for Israel, because Kissinger dragged his heels on resupply of military equipment for the Israelis. Secretary of Defense Schlesinger finally convinced Kissinger that Israel was suffering huge losses and needed U.S. resupply as soon as possible.

The CIA's track record on military intervention, the outbreak of war, and revolution is particularly weak. In addition to the October War, the stunning list of failures includes Korea in 1950, Hungary in 1956, the Cuban missile crisis in 1962, Czechoslovakia in 1968, the Iranian Revolution in 1979, martial law in Poland in 1980, the Tiananmen Square nightmare in 1989, and Iraq's invasion of Kuwait in 1990. More recently, the Arab Spring in 2010–2011, the rise and consolidation of Islamic militants in Iraq in 2014, the Russian seizure of Crimea in 2014, and the introduction of Russian military forces in Syria in 2015 were not anticipated by the CIA. War is an irrational process in many respects, and intelligence analysts pride themselves on being rational, which may explain some of these failures. But in the cases of the October War, martial law in Poland and particularly September 11, 2001, there was ample early warning and strategic intelligence. Overall, the intelligence collection was good; the analysis was poor.

The value of intelligence in wartime should not be written off, however, as intelligence analysis during any war or crisis pays huge dividends in terms of up-to-date situation reports for military planners and policymakers. Decision-making during the Cuban missile crisis benefited from timely CIA intelligence that allowed President Kennedy to know how much time he had to respond in view of the time the Soviets needed to deploy medium-range and short-range missile systems. One of the CIA's most important Soviet agents, Colonel Oleg Penkovsky, had provided sensitive Soviet manuals on medium-range and short-range ballistic missiles, which were invaluable during the missile crisis.

Similarly, National Security Advisor Kissinger had access to important intelligence when he was in Moscow to arrange a ceasefire in the Middle East during the October War. The CIA kept Kissinger apprised of Israeli ceasefire violations, which allowed him to press Israeli Defense Minister Moshe Dayan to honor the ceasefire. Kissinger used a provocative nuclear alert to intimidate the Soviets during the war, which intelligence couldn't support; he threatened the Israelis with unilateral intervention if the ceasefire was not honored, which intelligence did support.

In addition to having intelligence collection that was good enough to anticipate the Egyptian-Syrian attack in October 1973 and to track early Arab successes, the CIA knew that Egyptian President Sadat had decided to expel Soviet military advisors. In July 1972, the Egyptian analyst Gordon Sund and I were the first analysts in the intelligence community to report President Sadat's decision to expel Soviet military technicians. In the wake of the summit meeting between Presidents Brezhnev and Nixon in May 1972, Sadat became convinced the Soviets would never lean on the United States to arrange an Israeli return of the occupied Sinai Peninsula.

Following our article on the likely ouster of the Soviets, Sund and I received phone calls from the deputy director for Intelligence, Sayre Stevens, saying that Kissinger had called CIA director Helms to say that it was "gratifying to learn about an important development from a CIA publication and not from the *New York Times*." Sadat hoped the ouster of the Soviets would attract U.S. support for resuming the peace process, believing that Moscow was no longer a factor in the Middle East. Kissinger ignored the signal and, in his memoirs, falsely claims that Sadat's "decision came as a complete surprise to Washington."[19] Kissinger conceded that he was "handicapped by my underestimating of the Egyptian president," but he offered no explanation for failing to respond to Sadat's "bombshell," which could have prevented the war that began 15 months later. The CIA had provided premonitory intelligence, but Kissinger chose not to pay attention.

More importantly, Kissinger misused the intelligence that was available during the October War to declare an unjustified nuclear alert, a provocation that could have had terrible consequences. Kissinger declared Defense Condition III (DefCon-III) at a meeting of the National Security Council that he chaired late in the evening of October 24, 1973, arguing that the Soviets had sent nuclear materials through the Dardanelles and that General Secretary Brezhnev was prepared to intervene unilaterally due to Israeli violations of the ceasefire.

Neither assumption was valid. The intelligence system that tracked nuclear materials in the Dardanelles was a famously inaccurate system with numerous false positives, and the actual intelligence reading that Kissinger cited took place two weeks earlier. The note from Brezhnev to President Nixon was in fact a plea to the United States to rein in Israeli forces and return to the ceasefire that the United States and the Soviet Union had endorsed several days earlier.

Kissinger was the only principal at the National Security Council meeting who believed there was any likelihood of a Soviet intervention in the Middle East, and that a military alert involving nuclear systems was necessary. I spoke to other participants at the meeting, Secretary of Defense Schlesinger, CIA Director Colby, and Chairman of the Joint Chiefs of Staff Thomas Moorer, who considered DefCon-III risky and unnecessary. I served on the CIA task force at the time, and there was no intelligence that pointed to Soviet preparedness to intervene; there was no preparation of the air transport fleet; no resumption of an airlift of military equipment; no introduction of airborne forces. I argued at the time that the Soviets were not able to introduce forces at crucial points during previous Arab-Israeli confrontations in 1956 and 1967 because the Israeli Air Force had destroyed Egyptian air bases. The Soviets, moreover, had never used their airborne forces in a combat situation, and intelligence indicators showed they weren't preparing to do so this time. By late October 1973, the Israelis had once again destroyed Egyptian air bases.

At an academic conference 25 years later, chaired by Ambassador Richard Parker, I repeated these charges against Kissinger and received support from former secretary of defense Schlesinger, who participated in the roundtable discussion. Interestingly, one of Kissinger's most active acolytes, Peter Rodman, challenged my arguments and added that the United States "would have and should have been willing to go to war to prevent" Soviet military intervention. Rodman was still unwilling to concede that there was no intelligence evidence of such intervention.[20]

Although the CIA's Middle East analysts missed the October War of 1973, they understood the threat of Palestinian terrorism, particularly the threat to Jordan's King Hussein; the foolhardiness of the Israeli invasion of Lebanon in 1982; and the callous disregard for the safety of U.S. Marines who were dispatched to Lebanon in 1983 without proper rules of engagement. These are examples of the CIA being more alert than the community of policymakers, who were insufficiently responsive to intelligence alerts.

The combination of the policy failure in not exploiting President Sadat's ouster of the Soviets in 1972 and the intelligence failure in not anticipating the surprise invasion led to an unnecessary setback for the policy of détente with the Soviet Union. The combination of a threat to Israel and Kissinger's trumped-up notion of a Soviet threat to intervene unilaterally in the Middle East, possibly with nuclear weapons, led the right wing to renew its attacks on arms control and détente with Moscow and caused the liberal supporters of détente to reverse their position due to concern over a Soviet threat to Israel. The current Russian-American confrontation over Syria is having similar consequences, with a renewed call for more active opposition to Moscow's maneuvers.

Neoconservatives and the right-wing community in the United States have been traditionally hostile to CIA intelligence, often charging that CIA analysts are apologists for Russian or Chinese behavior. They totally dismissed the CIA's success in refuting the so-called "gaps" in Soviet-American weaponry and exposing the myth of Soviet military superiority. Starting with the non-existent bomber gap of the 1950s, the CIA convinced President Eisenhower that the true gap was Moscow's significant inferiority in air power. The missile gap was a fiction of the 1960 presidential contest between Kennedy and Nixon, with the Democratic candidate fabricating the notion of a U.S. lag in missile capability. Again, the true situation was Soviet inferiority, but Kennedy was having too much success in the campaign with the charge of a missile gap and refused to correct his accusations.

There were other gaps that the CIA challenged, particularly the so-called intentions gap that was floated by Harvard Professor Richard Pipes in the early 1980s, when he argued speciously and even risibly that the Soviets believed they could fight and win a nuclear war. Charges of a gap between the anti-ballistic missile stocks of the two sides were pure fiction. Nevertheless, Deputy Director Gates gave public speeches that distorted the message of his own Intelligence Directorate and even supported the phony charge of a civil defense gap.

Another phony gap that the CIA contributed to was the charge of a "relentless Soviet buildup" in strategic forces, even though military intelligence was more exaggerated than CIA assessments. The CIA overestimated the growth of Soviet defense spending throughout the late 1970s and early 1980s, and it took several years for the CIA's military analysts to convince Gates that the Congress had to be informed of the errors in earlier briefings. There were no increases in Soviet military procurement or investment, which were the most important indexes. It was not until 1983 that we were able to inform Congress that the "Soviets did not field weapons as rapidly after 1976 as before. Practically all major categories of Soviet weapons were affected—missiles, aircraft, and ships."[21]

In addition to the neoconservative critics of Nixon's policy of détente, there were liberals such as Senators Moynihan and Henry Jackson (D-WA) who joined with labor leaders such as George Meany and Lane Kirkland to malign the policy of détente. As a result, key players in the Ford administration, Dick Cheney and Donald Rumsfeld, successfully maneuvered against Kissinger and his policy of détente and made a special effort to toughen the CIA's assessments on the Soviet Union.

In order to sabotage arms control, particularly the SALT agreement of 1972, Cheney and Rumsfeld convinced President Ford to weaken Kissinger's influence by ending his dual role as secretary of state and national security advisor, thus allowing General Brent Scowcroft to direct the National Security Council. Cheney and Rumsfeld then pressed the new CIA director, George H.W. Bush, to agree to the creation of a competitive threat assessment that would be prepared by an outside group of experts. The idea seemed harmless on the face of it, but those of us who had worked on SALT knew that a parallel estimative team of neoconservatives would manipulate the estimate process to satisfy the needs of their political agenda.

Our concerns were validated when we learned that members of the competitive team, know as Team B, included certified hard-liners or neoconservatives such as Harvard Professor Pipes, a Polish immigrant with extremely hard-line views of the Soviet threat; William Van Cleave, who served on the SALT team in Vienna and was an obstreperous foe of disarmament; Paul Wolfowitz; General Danny Graham; and Seymour Weiss. This would be tantamount to selecting Dracula to run a blood bank. If

Cheney and Rumsfeld had set out to recruit a predictable team of troglodytes on the Soviet Union, they could not have selected a more reliable squad to heighten anxiety about Moscow.

I weighed in with my former boss on the SALT team, Howard Stoertz, who was now the national intelligence officer responsible for intelligence estimates on Soviet strategic forces. Stoertz knew that the Team A/B exercise was an "ideological and political foray" and not a substantive or intellectual exercise, but he was unwilling to block it. The deputy director of the CIA, E. Henry Knoche, not one of the sharpest tools in the CIA shed, was in favor of the idea and totally unsympathetic to the possibility of a manipulated National Intelligence Estimate. The Team A/B exercise was an excellent example of the pressure on the CIA from neoconservatives trying to tailor intelligence. The neoconservatives triumphed in 1980, when the United States elected a president who wanted to confront the Soviet Union, and installed an ideologue as CIA director to ensure that intelligence documented the charge of the "evil empire."

The deputy director for intelligence in the mid-1970s, Sayre Stevens, aggressively fought the idea of a right-wing team entering the CIA, but couldn't persuade CIA director Bush to block the efforts of the Ford administration. Stevens was one of the finest analysts that the CIA ever produced, and I knew him well from my experience with the SALT talks. On a key technical issue involving the Anti-Ballistic Missile Treaty in 1972, Stevens stood up to the Pentagon to argue that the Soviet surface-to-air missile system could not be considered an anti-ballistic missile system. This debate was overtaken by events several years later when both sides accepted a total ban on anti-ballistic missiles, which became the cornerstone of strategic deterrence until another President Bush recklessly repudiated the ABM Treaty in 2001 in order to deploy an ineffective national missile defense system.

Stevens also fought the Pentagon on a key issue involving the SALT treaty in 1972. The Department of Defense and the

Pentagon didn't want a ban on MIRVs—weapons of mass destruction that launch as a single missile but separate into multiple bombs directed at multiple targets—and believed that a demand for on-site inspection of MIRV sites would ensure there would be no agreement. Stevens and our verification team, along with the Department of State and the Arms Control and Disarmament Agency, convinced President Nixon and Kissinger that satellite reconnaissance could monitor a ban on MIRV deployment. The military representatives didn't want to give up deployment of MIRVs, and they chortled privately over confronting the Soviets with on-site inspection. Ironically, the Department of Defense eventually found on-site inspection a bitter pill to swallow when it was introduced into treaty provisions.

Sayre liked a good fight and knew we had to "deal with contentions that we are wrong." I took the same approach to the challenges from the White House on our position regarding Moscow and international terrorism, and again it was Professor Pipes leading the charge against the CIA's intelligence. Twenty years later, CIA analysts rolled over for Vice President Cheney and offered intelligence assessments that were tailored for a post-9/11 White House obsessed with conjuring reasons to invade Iraq, instead of marshaling its full attention to defeating the enemies that had attacked the Pentagon and World Trade Towers.

The results of the Team A/Team B exercise were predictable. Just as the Soviet Union was beginning to reduce the growth in defense spending and Brezhnev was signaling interest in détente and arms control, Pipes's team persuaded the CIA to adopt more threatening estimates of the Soviet strategic threat. Pipes's worldview was stamped on the Team B assessments, which labeled the Soviets an aggressive imperialistic power bent on world domination. According to Team B, the Soviet Union rejected nuclear parity, was bent on executing and surviving a nuclear war, and was radically increasing its military spending. Team B predicted a series of Soviet weapons developments that never took place, including directed-energy weapons, mobile anti-missile systems, and anti-satellite capabilities.

CIA deputy director Gates used Team B assessments in speeches and articles in the *Washington Times* to ingratiate himself with the Reagan administration and to garner increased defense spending. By pitching policy, Gates violated the CIA's charter, which stipulated that there should be no policy advocacy from the agency. As CIA director in 1992, Gates exaggerated the threat from Iran and the threat of nuclear proliferation to stave off cuts in the intelligence budget.

The sad lesson in the political use of right-wing ideologues to craft hard-line assessments is the susceptibility of intelligence to political interference and corruption. Just as Vice President Dick Cheney's relentless pressure on the CIA led to false reports on Iraq in 2002–2003, Team B's pressure led to exaggerated estimates of Soviet military spending and the capabilities of Soviet military technology. It was nearly a decade before the CIA began to correct and lower its estimates of Soviet defense spending and the Soviet strategic threat. In the case of Team B, the next administration—President Carter's—ignored its bogus findings just as President Eisenhower had ignored the trumped-up conclusions of the Gaither Report on Soviet air power in the 1950s. The Reagan administration in the early 1980s, however, used the estimates to double defense spending, garnering $1.5 trillion in additional spending against a Soviet Union in decline and a Soviet military threat that was exaggerated.

The U.S. intelligence community should neither indulge in worst-case analysis, which distorts the international picture for policymakers, nor play the role of devil's advocate, which panders to decision makers. Casey and Gates played devil's advocate in the 1980s to link the Soviets to the Papal assassination plot in order to derail Secretary of State George P. Shultz's resumption of détente. Tenet and McLaughlin did the same in the run-up to the Iraq War in an attempt to link Iraq to al Qaeda in order to strengthen Bush Junior's campaign for war. In his self-serving memoir, Michael Morell acknowledged that the deputy director for intelligence, Jami Miscik, directed the Counterterrorism Center to prepare a classified memorandum "to see how far the analysts could push the evidence" to link Saddam Hussein to al Qaeda. The paper generated the impression of a connection, and Morell blithely noted that "well-placed staffers in the Pentagon and the Office of the Vice President liked it."[22] Is there any wonder?

Inflated threat assessments have become an inherent part of the U.S. national security system, which is why the CIA was created in the first place—to prevent or at least counter such exaggerations. President Truman wanted the CIA to be the "quiet intelligence arm" of the White House, and the analytical successes of the Directorate of Intelligence from 1966 to 1981 were quiet ones. In the absence of effective oversight to assess the influence and impact of manipulated threat assessments on operations and diplomacy, we need whistleblowers to call attention to the misuse of an intelligence community shrouded in secrecy.

TWO

THE JOY OF INTELLIGENCE

"There were so many things that I did not know when I became president."

—Harry S. Truman

"The truth that makes men free is for the most part the truth which men prefer not to hear."

—Herbert Agar

The term "speaking truth to power" originated with the Quakers in an effort to expand the idea of anti-war pacifism. The term has special meaning in the field of intelligence, which requires giving information to policymakers who prefer not to listen. A key aspect of being an intelligence analyst was the opportunity to tell truth to power.

For most, the CIA's greatest challenge is the recruitment of spies and the stealing of secrets. For me, the challenge revolved around providing intelligence to policymakers. It meant telling the administrations of Kennedy, Johnson, and Nixon that the Vietnam War was essentially unwinnable. It meant telling the Pentagon that its views on Soviet weapons systems were wrong, which opened the door to arms control agreements in the 1970s. It meant telling the Carter administration that the Soviet invasion of Afghanistan had nothing to do with the "urge to the sea," and telling the Reagan administration that Gorbachev was a different Soviet leader.

This challenge was enhanced by having access to the intelligence community's vast collection of information: communications intercepts from the National Security Agency (NSA); satellite photography from the National Reconnaissance Office; sensitive cables from the Department of State; field reports from military attachés as well as clandestine reports from CIA operatives. There is a great deal of information in the public arena, but it cannot compare to the collection of the intelligence agencies.

Intelligence work is exhilarating and exhausting, particularly when intelligence analysts accept the importance of informing policymakers of the historical and social factors that should be considered in decision-making regarding U.S. actions in foreign lands. Decisions regarding Vietnam in the 1960s and 1970s ignored these factors, and U.S. policy suffered as a result. U.S. decisions on Iraq, Afghanistan, and Syria also ignored these factors, and too often U.S. intelligence failed to provide relevant information.

SPOT-ON ABOUT THE SIX-DAY WAR

My baptism as a CIA intelligence analyst took place less than one year after I came onboard. As a member of the task force preparing situation reports for the White House on the increased tensions in the Middle East, I helped to draft the report that described Israel's preemptive attack against Egypt on the morning of June 5, 1967. We had sensitive NSA intercepts that documented Israeli preparations for an attack and no evidence of an Egyptian battle plan.

The Israelis had been clamoring to Washington that they had indications of Egyptian preparations for an invasion, but the U.S. intelligence community saw no Egyptian readiness in terms of its air or armored power. We assumed that the Israelis were engaging in disinformation in order to gain U.S. support. My own view was that Egypt would be unlikely to start a war with Israel while half of its army was tied down fighting in a civil war in Yemen. My Egyptian colleagues believed that Egyptian president Gamel Abdel Nasser was bluffing, and all of us emphasized the low quality of Cairo's military equipment.

We were therefore shocked when President Lyndon Johnson's national security advisor, Walt Rostow, wouldn't accept our intelligence assessment of the Israeli preemptive attack. Rostow cited "assurances" from the Israeli ambassador in Washington that under no circumstances would the Israelis attack first. Over the protests of Israeli defense minister Moshe Dayan, the Israeli government lied to the White House about how the war started. President Johnson was told that the Egyptians had initiated firing on Israeli settlements and that an Egyptian squadron had been observed heading toward Israel. Neither statement was true.

Rostow had convinced the president that Israel would never consider a preemptive attack, and as a result, three days before the war President Johnson's letter to Israeli prime minister Levi Eshkol noted that Israel would be alone if it preempted, but he couldn't "imagine that [Israel] would make this decision."[1] As a result, our report the morning of June 5, 1967, that described a series of surprise attacks on Egyptian, Jordanian, and Syrian airfields, met with a hostile response from the National Security Council. Rostow returned the report with some angry remarks, but CIA director Richard Helms supported our decision to return the report with modest and meaningless editorial changes. When the National Military Command Center corroborated our assessment, Rostow summoned Clark Clifford, chairman of the President's Foreign Advisory Board, to examine the intelligence along with Harold (Hal) Saunders, the leading Arabist on the National Security Council staff. Clifford and Saunders corroborated our assessments.

President Johnson admitted in his memoirs that he strongly disagreed with the CIA estimates regarding a quick Israeli victory and asked Helms to recalculate the intelligence because it seemed so unbelievable. Rostow never conceded his errors of judgment, although he did order the U.S. ambassador, Walworth Barbour, to see Israeli Prime Minister Eshkol and to demand a military briefing on the war. When the ambassador asked if the Egyptians had attacked, the Israelis responded with vague references to movements of Egyptian troops and tanks. The CIA, with the benefit of satellite intelligence, could inform the White House that Egyptian planes were parked on their airfields wingtip-to-wingtip, which pointed to no plan to attack.

Twenty years later, I learned that Harry McPherson, a confidant of the president, was in Israel at the start of the war and accompanied the ambassador to the prime minister's office. During this meeting, Israeli air raid sirens began to wail, but when the ambassador suggested moving the meeting to the Foreign Ministry's underground bunker, Israeli intelligence chief General Aharon Yariv assured him it wasn't necessary. As a result, McPherson concluded that the "Egyptian air force had been destroyed . . . on the ground," which he immediately cabled to Washington.[2] It would have been useful to have this information on a timely basis, but our intelligence indicated that the Israelis had destroyed more than 200 Egyptian planes on the ground.

In any event, Helms stood by our analysis, even when we predicted an Israeli victory in a matter of days. Once again, our analysis differed from that of Rostow's National Security Council, which believed that Soviet arms shipments to Egypt, Syria, and Iraq would bring a different result than the Israeli success in the Suez crisis of 1956. Some staffers from the National Security Council argued that Israel might even be "driven into the sea." We predicted an Israeli victory in seven to ten days, which was close enough.

In addition to lying about the start of the war, the Israelis were deceitful in attributing the attack on the USS *Liberty* in 1967 to a random accident. If so, it was a well-planned accident.

The ship was a U.S. intelligence vessel in international waters, both slow-moving and lightly armed. It brandished a five-foot-by-eight-foot Stars and Stripes in the midday sun, and certainly didn't resemble a ship in any other navy, let alone a ship in the arsenal of one of Israel's enemies. The Israeli attack took place after six hours of intense, low-level reconnaissance. The attack was conducted over a two-hour period by unmarked Mirage jets using cannons and rockets. Then more jets with napalm and more rockets. Israeli boats fired machine guns at close range at those helping the wounded, then machine-gunned the life rafts that survivors dropped in hope of abandoning ship. The NSA investigation of the disaster remains classified.

As a result of the CIA's spot-on intelligence, President Johnson invited Helms to attend the White House's important Tuesday Lunch Group, which until then had only included the president, Secretary of State Dean Rusk, Secretary of Defense Robert McNamara, and the national security advisor. Helms was generous with his praise for our analytic efforts, but within several years the CIA's pessimistic and accurate assessments on Vietnam made him an unwelcome member of the group.

CIA SUPPORT FOR ARMS CONTROL AND DISARMAMENT

My headiest experience as an intelligence analyst was an assignment to Vienna in 1971 as intelligence advisor to the U.S. delegation at the Strategic Arms Limitation Talks (SALT). In my 42 years of government service, it was the only time that I was involved in intense diplomatic negotiations, the implementation of strategic policy, and the bureaucratic infighting that complicates formation and implementation of policy. Negotiations between the U.S. agencies were no less difficult and protracted than negotiations between the U.S. and Soviet delegations.

The CIA's assessments on strategic arms were the best within the U.S. intelligence community, so the SALT experience played an important role in my career as an analyst. The CIA's ability to verify and monitor all aspects of a disarmament treaty, particularly the development and deployment of Soviet strategic forces, enabled the U.S. Senate to ratify the SALT and Anti-Ballistic Missile treaties with confidence.

The CIA plays an important role in allaying the concerns of U.S. congress members, both liberal and conservative, regarding the verification and monitoring of international treaties. This was particularly true in 1972, when there was a great deal of opposition to the SALT and Anti-Ballistic Missile Treaties. Informal CIA briefings to influential senators such as John Glenn (D-OH), and formal briefings to key committees such as Foreign Relations and Armed Services, contributed to congressional approval of the treaties. Tensions between the White House and Congress over the nuclear deal with Iran in 2015 were alleviated by expert CIA briefings to recalcitrant members of Congress.

In order to prepare for a role in the world of strategic arms control, I had to leave the Office of Current Intelligence, which concentrated on political intelligence, and spend two years in the Office of Strategic Research, which studied the Soviet strategic arsenal. It was a world of obscure acronyms—MIRVs, SLBMs, SSBN, ABMs, and ICBMs—and special terms—throw weight, counterforce, countervalue—that had little currency outside the national security community. Fortunately, the chief of the Office of Strategic Research, Bruce Clarke, was one of the genuine stars in the Intelligence Directorate and offered a great deal of assistance in my first months on the job. When I couldn't get a handle on Soviet strategic submarines that were nuclear-capable, Clarke said it should be easy for me: the J-class, E-class, W-class, and S-class. Clarke assumed that a Jew could grasp this.

The disarmament process was an interagency one, requiring every aspect of the negotiations to be vetted by five major U.S. policy departments before being broached with the Soviets. The CIA typically lined up with the Department of State and the Arms Control and Disarmament Agency on the disarmament process; the Department of Defense and the Joint Chiefs of Staff were dedicated to blocking arms control. The CIA played the key role in enabling civilian agencies to overcome opposition from the Pentagon and the Joint Chiefs of Staff, which falsely argued that a Soviet ground-to-air missile defense could be upgraded to an anti-ballistic missile system and that the Soviet SS-9 had multiple warheads. The military's arguments were designed to block the Anti-Ballistic Missile and SALT agreements, respectively.

One of the major blunders in the SALT I treaty was the failure to ban multiple warheads on intercontinental ballistic missiles. Even Secretary of State Kissinger acknowledged this failure as a serious policy blunder. The Department of State, the Arms Control and Disarmament Agency, and the CIA favored a ban and strongly believed prohibition of multiple-warhead missile testing could be verified with satellite photography. The Department of Defense and the Joint Chiefs of Staff wanted to pursue production of multiple-warhead missiles, which they had not yet developed, so an opportunity was lost to put a ban on multiple-warhead missiles in the treaty. The militarization of the CIA and the dissolution of the Arms Control and Disarmament Agency complicate the bureaucratic task of reaching a new consensus on any disarmament treaty.

One of the key reasons for the opposition of presidential Chief of Staff Dick Cheney and Secretary of Defense Donald Rumsfeld to the CIA (and the Arms Control and Disarmament Agency) in the 1970s was these agencies' support for arms control. The conflict was renewed during the administration of President George W. Bush, when the CIA pushed back against some of their arguments for invading Iraq. Overall, however, the CIA caved in to Cheney's importuning.

My major job as intelligence advisor to the SALT delegation in Vienna was preparing a daily briefing for the delegates, providing the opportunity to discuss political and military issues with the chief of the U.S. delegation, Ambassador Gerald Smith; the

Joint Chiefs of Staff representative, General Royal Allison; the Department of Defense representative, Paul Nitze; the Department of State representative, Ambassador Raymond L. Garthoff; and the representative from the Arms Control and Disarmament Agency, Harold Brown. The Nitze briefing was the toughest one because he followed all military and political issues and had definite ideas about the intelligence problems associated with geopolitical issues, not merely strategic weapons issues. He was initially unfriendly to negotiating with the Soviets, although he reversed course and led the efforts to eliminate all intermediate nuclear forces 15 years later. I assisted Nitze in other ways, because he had a drinking problem and I had to help him make his goodbyes from several social occasions.

The Brown briefing was easy, because he wasn't interested in getting intelligence briefings; in fact, he was often not in attendance at the talks in Vienna. When the bilateral discussions became intense, Brown was around; when they grew desultory, Brown wasn't even in Austria. General Allison was an interesting figure, because his riding boots were always on his desk, either returning from being shined or placed to be picked up for shining, which was a daily ritual for the general's enlisted aide. Only the general, of course, had an aide. Briefing Ray Garthoff was a pure pleasure; he was one of the savviest people I dealt with in my 24 years at the CIA and the State Department.

The assignment in Vienna offered discussions on arms control and geopolitical issues with Soviet counterparts, including representatives of Soviet intelligence, the KGB. Whereas U.S. representatives had a rich social life that included trips to the Vienna opera and wonderful banquets, the Soviets did not permit their representatives to mix with the Austrian populace, let alone other diplomatic representatives. When I discussed this fact with my Soviet counterparts, they replied that they were simply "birds in a gilded cage." The Soviet delegation didn't even have access to secure communications back to Moscow, and had to travel to Czechoslovakia to report sensitive negotiating matters to the Kremlin.

The CIA's role in the arms control process was a central one, because no treaty would garner Senate ratification unless the U.S. intelligence community could verify all aspects of the terms. Director Helms didn't like having the CIA identified with verification of the treaties; he told us at a meeting in his office that "verification was a political process, and only policy agencies could verify" a treaty. He preferred to call the interagency process the Monitoring Panel, but Kissinger preferred the title "Verification Panel," and verification it became.

Kissinger understood that throughout the Cold War the CIA had the best record in tracking Soviet weapons developments, which ensured that Moscow never developed or procured, let alone deployed, a strategic weapon without the CIA analysts providing advance warning to the National Security Council and the Pentagon. Sadly, several decades later, the CIA's mishandling of Iraqi weapons assessments in 2002–2003 compromised the Agency's credibility, leading to the creation of the Office of the Director of National Intelligence in 2004 and diminishing the role of the director of CIA in producing the President's Daily Brief and National Intelligence Estimates.

Disarmament negotiations made little progress from 1969 to 1971, until the Vienna round that coincided with the beginning of the U.S.-China rapprochement. Soviet representatives at SALT understood that the U.S.-inspired initiative was aimed at Moscow. As a result, the Kremlin knew it must improve relations with the United States by coming to terms with the SALT agreement to limit offensive strategic ballistic missiles; the Anti-Ballistic Missile Treaty to protect strategic deterrence; and the Treaty of Berlin to quell tensions between the United States and the Soviet Union around the divided city of Berlin. My background cables from Vienna emphasized that Soviet anxiety over the new Washington-Beijing diplomatic channel provided opportunities for the United States. I was not crossing the line into policy advocacy; I was merely calling attention to an opportunity for the United States, a key aspect of intelligence reporting.

The Soviets feared rapprochement between the United States and China would be at their expense, diminishing the importance of the Kremlin's ties with Washington. Prior to the news of an improvement in Sino-American relations, the Soviets pursued an unorthodox device to bring the United States into a bilateral treaty against Beijing. In Vienna in March 1971, in the best spy-novel tradition, the Soviet ambassador to SALT, Vladimir Semenov, passed a note to his U.S. counterpart, Ambassador Smith, proposing a bilateral agreement to prevent or retaliate against a provocative attack by third parties (i.e., China). Kissinger believed the proposal was a Soviet attempt to get a free hand against China in a crisis situation without concern for the U.S. response. Semenov's initiative demonstrated the Kremlin's concern with a Sino-American rapprochement, and thus pointed to an opportunity for U.S. diplomatic dividends.

The unsigned note called for Moscow and Washington to take retaliatory action if one or the other were attacked by a third party. Both Moscow and Washington were using the SALT dialogue to prevent accidental or unauthorized use of nuclear weapons, which led to the Agreement on Measures to Reduce the Risk of Outbreak of Nuclear War in September 1971, but Semenov's initiative was a bizarre effort to draw the Soviet Union closer to the United States and to make sure that China remained an outsider looking in. I was one of the few members of the U.S. delegation aware of the Soviet proposal, because sensitive State Department cables went through CIA communications, which were more secure.

What none of us knew in Vienna was that Kissinger immediately used the back channel to Soviet Ambassador Anatoly Dobrynin to reject Semenov's proposal. It was typical for Kissinger to take matters into his own hands in this fashion and not inform

U.S. diplomats who were discussing sensitive matters with Soviet counterparts. We were caught off guard by Moscow's use of the SALT dialogue to collude against China, which would have been a major success for the Soviet Union if it had worked, but the Nixon White House would never accept a Soviet initiative that would have given Moscow a free hand against Beijing.

It was no accident that within several months after the announcement of ping-pong matches between the U.S. and China, an understanding was reached in May 1971 to conclude an Anti-Ballistic Missile Treaty and a treaty to limit offensive missiles. A U.S.-Soviet summit meeting for 1972 was agreed upon in addition to the Berlin agreement that prevented the kind of confrontations that had occurred in 1948–1949, 1958–1959, and 1961, which led to the building of the Berlin Wall. It was exciting to be an eyewitness—even from the back bench—to events that led to an U.S.-Soviet summit and détente; North Atlantic Treaty Organization's readiness to accept a Conference on European Security and Cooperation; and the Warsaw Pact's willingness to join the Mutual and Balanced Force Reduction talks. Nearly a decade after the Cuban missile crisis, the Cold War ice was breaking up.

The SALT and ABM agreements were a great achievement in U.S. national security policy, but key members of the SALT delegation lost their careers in arms control as a result. Senator Henry "Scoop" Jackson (D-WA), who gets far more praise for his congressional career than he deserves, demanded that the leaders at the State Department and the Arms Control and Disarmament Agency who worked on the SALT and Anti-Ballistic Missile treaties never again work in the disarmament field. In January 1973, President Nixon, who was honored by many for his achievements in the fields of détente and disarmament, bowed before Senator Jackson's insistence that his vote for ratification of the treaties (as well as the Trident submarine program) depended on a purge of the SALT delegation, even a hard-liner such as General Allison.

Garthoff, the most important member of the U.S. delegation, was made ambassador to Bulgaria. In addition to purging delegates to the SALT talks, President Nixon purged 14 of the top 17 Arms Control and Disarmament Agency officials. The agency's budget and personnel were cut and a conservative leadership was introduced. Two decades later, President Clinton bowed to pressure from Senator Jesse Helms (R-NC) and Representative Newt Gingrich (R-GE) and finished the job by abolishing the Arms Control and Disarmament Agency altogether. Neither Nixon nor Clinton referred in their memoirs to their pusillanimous behavior in confronting a form of McCarthyism.

THE CIA'S ROLE IN THE ARTIFICIAL "COMBAT BRIGADE" CRISIS IN CUBA

Debates over intelligence are hard fought and often tendentious, and the public rarely learns about the political differences between intelligence agencies. One such debate took place in the fall of 1979, when the NSA intercepted a Soviet message that referred to a "combat brigade" in Cuba. A combat brigade of less than 3,000 men that had no airlift capability or sea transport did not represent a threat comparable to a possible Soviet submarine base as in 1970 or the deployment of Soviet MiG-23s as in 1978, let alone the Cuban missile crisis of 1962. But the fate of SALT II between Washington and Moscow hung in the balance, and national security advisor Brzezinski, no friend of Moscow or of détente, feared any effort by the Kremlin to steal a march on the United States. As a result, he put a great deal of pressure on the CIA and its national intelligence officer on the Soviet Union, Arnold Horelick, to find evidence of any Soviet chicanery.

Brzezinski and his military assistant, Colonel William Odom, both anti-Soviet and anti-disarmament, were fearful that Moscow would exploit the period during the run-up to the scheduled summit between President Carter and General Secretary Brezhnev in Vienna, where the SALT II agreement would be signed. Brzezinski asked CIA director Turner to take a hard look at all intelligence dealing with Soviet activities in Cuba and to increase intelligence collection over the island with a Lockheed SR-71 Blackbird. Brzezinski and Horelick spoke often on a secure line during this period, and the subject of possible Soviet violations of agreements regarding Cuba was a hot topic.

The "threat" turned out to be the possibility of a Soviet combat brigade in Cuba. In 1962, Moscow had deployed ground combat units to Cuba at four major locations as part of its deployment of medium- and intermediate-range missiles. General Secretary Khrushchev withdrew all ground forces that were protecting missile installations or bombers as part of the diplomatic agreement that ended the crisis. The so-called combat brigade was located at one of these four locations, which contributed to the confusion over the unit.

The combat brigade, however, was a praetorian guard for Castro that pre-dated the Cuban missile crisis, and Moscow had reason to assume that U.S. intelligence would confirm this. Therefore, they believed Carter was creating an "artificial issue" to avoid fighting for the ratification of a SALT treaty in a recalcitrant Senate. When a powerful opponent of détente with the Soviet Union and arms control, Senator Henry Jackson, leaked intelligence on the "brigade" and used the information to attack the treaty and the Soviet Union, there was grist for the Soviet mill.

Ignoring our concerns, Horelick immediately proposed "warning notices" regarding the combat brigade to the policy community, which created the impression of an impending crisis. Several of us took the position that there was nothing new about references to a combat brigade, and attempted to convince Horelick not to push an intelligence panic button that was nothing more than an exercise we referred to as CYA—"cover your ass." We were the contrarians within the analytical community, challenging the conventional wisdom in order to defuse the crisis atmosphere that Brzezinksi and Horelick were creating. Our arguments to Horelick were both sane and sound, and—more importantly—correct. Unfortunately, the CYA exercise prevailed, which often happens in the intelligence community, particularly with military intelligence.

The State Department contributed to the crisis atmosphere by leaking news of the intelligence to two liberal senators, the chairman of the Senate Foreign Relations Committee, Frank Church (D-ID), and Richard Stone (D-FL), who favored ratification of the SALT II agreement. The Department believed that Church and Stone, both influential within their party, would tamp down speculation of a possible Soviet violation of agreements that ended the Cuban missile crisis. Church and Stone were facing election challenges in their states from neoconservatives, however, and they exploited the intelligence they were given.

Provocative rhetoric from two dovish senators put the Carter administration on the defensive, and Secretary of State Cyrus Vance made it worse when he proclaimed on September 5, 1979, that this was a "very serious matter affecting our relations with the Soviet Union." Church put the ratification of SALT II on the back burner, and presented himself as a tough foe of the Soviet Union. No one anticipated that he would take a hawkish stance and put an important arms control agreement at risk, because he was an experienced political figure and a strong supporter of SALT. He demanded the withdrawal of the Soviet force, a gratuitous demand. Seventeen years earlier, however, the Kennedy administration had falsely assured Senator Church that the Soviets hadn't introduced missiles into Cuba, which led the right wing in Idaho to vilify him.

Stone, moreover, decided to pander to his anti-Castro constituency. He cited leaks from NSA staffers regarding a recent buildup of Soviet forces in Cuba, "perhaps as much as a brigade," which proved to be wrong. Stone joined the Republican opponents of arms control, led by Senator Robert Dole (R-KS), who would not begin ratification hearings for SALT II until Soviet troops were withdrawn from Cuba. Ironically, as mentioned, the so-called combat brigade had been placed in Cuba prior to the Cuban missile crisis and was permitted to remain there to prevent a U.S. invasion similar to the Bay of Pigs, the CIA's "perfect failure" in 1961.

The combat brigade "crisis" and the misuse of intelligence led to election defeats of both Church and Stone as well as the failure to gain ratification of SALT II, intended as a major keystone of the Carter administration. This led to a fundamental weakening of Soviet-American détente that wasn't corrected until President Reagan's second term, when Washington returned to arms control with Moscow. This was a classic example of intelligence being mishandled by the National Security Agency, poorly analyzed by the CIA, and misused by the Carter administration and the State Department. We have no idea what the Soviet leaders concluded from this amateurism, but they had reason to believe that Carter had lost interest in détente and arms control or that there was a right-wing conspiracy to block SALT II. In view of Moscow's predilection for conspiracy, it probably assumed conspiracy.

The intelligence community had dropped the ball, and the CIA contributed to an unnecessary flap. The National Security Agency failed to have good archival records that would have established that the brigade had been in Cuba prior to the missile crisis, had no connection with Cuban combat units, and never should have been labeled a "combat" unit. The CIA, led by National Intelligence Officer Horelick, was too quick to accommodate the importuning of Brzezinski by issuing warning notices that added fuel to an unnecessary fire regarding Soviet intentions prior to a summit meeting and the signing of a strategic arms agreement.

The brigade did not compromise, let alone violate, the Soviet-American understandings about Soviet activities in Cuba. As with the unnecessary missile alert six years earlier during the October War, when Kissinger misused sensitive intelligence, the Soviets were left to scratch their heads and try to determine U.S.

reasons and motivations for an unnecessary flap that brought détente to a halt. The CIA was created to provide the institutional memory on these occasions when new and inexperienced administrations lack a political background.

The media contributed to the crisis atmosphere, which is typical in these situations. *Time* magazine carried an article on "The Storm over Cuba" with a photograph captioned "Soviet-Built Intelligence Station in Cuba." The station was described as an "advanced electronic monitoring complex east of Havana," but it was a complex that had been built by an American company, ITT, before Castro took power in 1959. Flawed CIA intelligence on Cuba and Iran in 1979 undermined confidence in President Carter, which contributed to his election defeat in 1980. Presently, the mainstream media are playing up the notion of a renewed Cold War, which is becoming a self-fulfilling prophecy

Even though the Carter administration and the CIA were wrong about the combat brigade, Brzezinski remained stubbornly critical of "backing down" to Moscow, and it was the one time in his stewardship as national security advisor that he considered resigning. He angered the president by arguing that the Kremlin would find weakness in U.S. reaction and therefore would miscalculate in the future, citing the relationship between Khrushchev and Kennedy that contributed to the Cuban missile crisis. Brzezinski took no responsibility for the mishandling of the issue, and blamed the State Department for "inexcusably precipitating the crisis with premature briefings" to the senators. His stewardship for U.S. national security policy did more harm than good during the Carter era.

THE CIA'S DISPUTE WITH THE WHITE HOUSE ON AFGHANISTAN

Policy and intelligence communities can have different explanations for crucial events. I was in the middle of such a dispute in the winter of 1979–1980, when the Soviets invaded Afghanistan and the Carter administration wanted to justify a strong response to Moscow's use of force. The debate began in the intelligence community in the first months of 1979, when I was the first analyst to draft an assessment that argued the Soviets would use force to prevent the Afghan civil war from spilling over to their Muslim republics. I wrote a warning memorandum to that effect that was circulated throughout the policy community in March and April, receiving special attention in the Pentagon, where Doug MacEachin—a former colleague—was serving a rotational tour as a warnings officer.

When the Soviet invasion did take place in December, there were factions, led by Secretary of State Vance and National Security Advisor Brzezinski, that found Soviet actions morally and politically unacceptable. President Carter led the U.S. reaction to Moscow's actions, which he repeatedly characterized as the "greatest threat to peace since the Second World War." Brzezinski, who typically took a conspiratorial view of Soviet decision-making, was out in front of the December invasion, having put in place covert support against Soviet interests in Afghanistan months before the actual invasion. The CIA's clandestine operatives were aware of this at the time; intelligence analysts weren't.

As author of the first piece of premonitory intelligence, in March 1979, that anticipated the Soviet use of force, and as branch chief for Soviet–Third World policy, I was selected to go to Brussels in January 1980 to brief the NATO delegations on the reasons for the Soviet invasion and the likely short- and long-term outcomes. The U.S. delegation was unhappy with my presentation, because it didn't argue the Brzezinski line that the Soviet move was a harbinger of more aggressive actions throughout the region, the first step in the Soviet desire to move to the Indian Ocean. This was the position of Secretary Vance, and the U.S. delegation to NATO wanted confirmation of his position in order to get the European delegations to support forceful actions. The recent U.S. overreaction to Russian policy toward Ukraine suggests that history may be repeating itself.

I had no prior guidance from either an intelligence or policy perspective prior to my briefing trip to NATO. I was accompanied by a military analyst who provided a nuts-and-bolts assessment of Soviet military operations in Afghanistan, while I was given carte blanche to discuss all political aspects of Soviet decision-making, particularly their reasons for resorting to military force. I was rather relaxed about the briefing trip, but my military counterpart was extremely nervous about protecting the sensitive intelligence information he carried in a CIA-supplied aluminum suitcase that never left his side. I had been given a similar aluminum suitcase for my assignment in Vienna in 1971, but I refused to use it because of its obvious, practically ostentatious appearance.

My intelligence presentation was radically different from the views of Vance and Brzezinski. As a result, I was not invited back to Brussels for additional briefings to NATO, although I led background briefings to members of the Washington press corps, who traveled to CIA headquarters on a regular basis. I was told by Karen House of the *Wall Street Journal* and many others that the CIA briefings were the best of any policy or intelligence agency. Intelligence analysts have a decided advantage in these briefing sessions, because, unlike policy analysts, they can simply tell it like it is without a policy axe to grind. It was difficult to be a contrarian in the intelligence community; it was virtually impossible in the policy community.

Intelligence analysts had an easier assignment than policy-makers because they did not have to exaggerate the Soviet invasion's impact on Soviet-American relations, which in my analysis was a separate, albeit related, issue. Vance and Brzezinski considered the Soviet invasion a threat to the balance of power, which in my analysis was not a primary motive of Moscow's actions. The key difference between Vance and Brzezinski was over whether the Soviets could be made to withdraw. Vance was stubbornly optimistic that Moscow would withdraw; Brzezinski didn't agree and, as an anti-Soviet ideologue, was far more interested in providing enticement for the Soviets to increase their presence in Afghanistan in order to bring détente to a halt.

Unlike Kissinger and earlier Vance, Brzezinski was never deferential to the idea of keeping détente alive. Brzezinski considered this an important opportunity for the United States to draw the Soviet Union into greater conflict on its borders. I didn't know about Brzezinski's views at the time, and, because of the bureaucratic wall at the CIA between intelligence analysis and operations, I didn't know about the aggressive covert steps that had been taken by CIA operatives in Afghanistan. I eventually learned that Brzezinski believed that the Soviet invasion of Afghanistan was the "most direct case of Soviet military aggression since 1945," requiring a "broad strategic response."[3] He was appalled when Secretary of State Vance and his Soviet advisor, Marshall Shulman, favored taking the initiative to improve relations with the Kremlin. Brzezinski and Shulman were academic rivals at Columbia University and policy rivals in the Carter administration. When I was on the faculty of the National War College, I made sure that Shulman delivered an annual lecture to the class on Soviet-American relations. The fact that he wheeled in annually on his Harley-Davidson was a huge hit with his military audience.

My analysis of the situation had nothing to do with détente or covert action. In early 1979 I drafted my paper on possible Soviet force when, in the wake of the abduction and assassination of the U.S. ambassador to Afghanistan, Adolph "Spike" Dubs, I concluded that Moscow was playing a heavy role in Afghan affairs and would use force to maintain this role in Kabul as well as to prevent the emergence of a radical Islamist regime in Afghanistan, a battle that is still being waged. I argued that Moscow would not let the Afghan situation worsen; that they had great concerns about the leadership of Prime Minister Hafizullah Amin, who was an unpredictable hard-liner; and that there was no evidence that Moscow had plans beyond Afghanistan itself. I believed the Soviets were convinced that the United States would find a way to return to Iran after its ouster in 1979 and that they wanted to be in Afghanistan to counter that eventuality.

I was satisfied with my two days of briefing in Brussels in January 1980, but there were policymakers who wanted the NATO delegations to echo the so-called threat to the balance of power and to prepare for harsh measures, including sanctions, against the Soviet Union. The comparison with the current situation in Ukraine is revealing, with the Obama administration divided over the proper response and some European nations opposed to additional harsh sanctions. Once again, the issue of the threat assessment is important to both policymakers and intelligence analysts, but the former typically exaggerate the threat in order to ramp up policy, maintain support from the American public, and arrange for Allied unanimity. Presently, the Obama administration is exaggerating the Russian threat in East Europe for similar reasons.

Intelligence analysts are often caught between intelligence information and policy considerations, the problem of being caught between the fire hydrant and the pissing dog. If the past is any guide, policy demands will trump the intelligence evidence and lead to greater exaggeration of the threat, which will be reflected in media accounts of the crisis based on official and anonymous sources. The exaggerations that accompany the Terror Wars are another example of the mishandling of the threat.

I was never told that there was unhappiness with my briefings in Brussels, and never suffered personally or professionally from going off the policy reservation with my analysis. I went back to work analyzing Soviet actions in the Third World, and remained initially oblivious to the actions of the CIA Directorate of Operations on behalf of the Mujahideen. I was certainly aware of the covert aid by 1986, when I was leaving the building on the way to an assignment as a faculty member at the National War College. Prior to my departure, I encountered the CIA's chief of operations in Afghanistan, Milton Bearden, and offered my criticism of military assistance for fundamentalist groups that had taken up residence in Pakistan's disputed territories. Bearden merely replied, "We simply send the arms over there and will let God sort it out." God is still sorting, and probably won't be finished until the United States completes its withdrawal, a distant objective three decades later.

Bob Gates wrote in his CIA memoir that covert action in Afghanistan marked the greatest clandestine adventure of all. My own view is radically different. I believe that the most vehemently anti-American Islamists currently operating in Afghanistan are part of the very organizations, such as the Haqqani network and the forces of Gulbiddin Hekmatyar, that the CIA assisted, which tags military support as a glaring CIA failure. Afghan militants such as Haqqani and Hekmatyar have long been considered "global terrorists" by the intelligence community. There were individuals linked to al Qaeda that received support from the CIA. The United States took steps against the perceived ideology of the Soviet Union, only to create a more virulent ideological enemy, militant Islamic jihadism. We have been at war with this new historical enemy for three decades.

With the president, the secretary of state, and the national security advisor in complete agreement that Moscow's invasion would be followed by additional Soviet force to "improve its strategic position in Southwest Asia," the role of intelligence was severely circumscribed. Even Secretary Vance anticipated that the Soviets would try to exploit events in Iran, exert "strong influence and pressure" on Pakistan and India, and counter U.S. moves into the Indian Ocean and the Persian Gulf. Brzezinski believed that the Soviet move into Afghanistan would lead to the "domination of Afghanistan," the promotion of a "separate Baluchistan," access to the Indian Ocean, and the dismemberment of Pakistan and Iran. The intelligence evidence suggested the Soviet move into Afghanistan was a defensive one, but the political record was dominated by those who believed it was an offensive one that had to be countered.

Vance's memoirs show him to be a prime example of a headstrong policymaker who had little interest in the intelligence evidence on Afghanistan. He had many false notions about the USSR and Afghanistan that intelligence could have corrected, and no understanding of the domestic political situation in Afghanistan or Moscow's concerns with spillover of the violence into the Muslim republics in the Soviet Union. He underestimated Moscow's concerns with political instability in Kabul, and even confused the two key Afghan leaders fighting for supremacy, Nur Mohammad Taraki and Hafizullah Amin.

Vance ignored Moscow's security concerns in the region, and both Vance and Brezhnev wanted to use the Afghan situation to return to the policy of containment that President Nixon and Kissinger had abandoned. President Obama's conservative critics used the crisis over Crimea and Ukraine to return to the case for containment as well.

CONVINCING THE PRESIDENT OF THE SOVIET "WAR SCARE"

Unlike the CIA's handling of the Soviet combat brigade, an analytical failure with negative consequences for U.S. policy, the handling of the Soviet "war scare" in 1983 was an analytical success, convincing President Reagan that Moscow genuinely feared the United States was planning a surprise attack against the Soviet Union. Many politicians and pundits in the United States believe to this day that the war scare in Moscow was no more than Soviet disinformation. My reading of the intelligence materials and my understanding of U.S. military exercises as well as my debriefing in 1985 of the former deputy KGB chief in London, Oleg Gordievsky, convinced me that the war scare was real. I was part of a small group of analysts who convinced Director Casey that the scare was genuine, which led Casey to carry the message personally to President Reagan. This was a rare occasion when

Casey sided with his Soviet analysts over the objections of his deputy director for intelligence, Bob Gates.

Once the British had exhausted Gordievsky's knowledge of the war scare and Soviet operational activities, they delivered him to the U.S. intelligence community for debriefings. According to Gordievsky, who was recruited by British intelligence in 1970 after the Soviet invasion of Czechoslovakia, the KGB had demanded information from all KGB stations regarding the possibility of U.S. preparations for an imminent nuclear strike against the Soviet Union. This order from the KGB "Center" in Moscow took place during the week-long Able Archer exercise, and, although not all KGB officials overseas shared the view of such a possible attack, the "Center" was convinced. Soviet military doctrine, according to Ray Garthoff, had long held that a possible U.S. *modus operandi* for launching an attack would be to convert an exercise into the real thing.

For the first time, the exercise was going to include President Reagan, Vice President Bush, and Secretary of Defense Weinberger, but when the White House understood the extent of Soviet anxiety regarding U.S. intentions, the major principals dropped out. In his memoirs, Reagan did not mention Gordievsky, but he noted that he was surprised to learn that Soviet leaders were afraid of an American first strike. More importantly, one of the reasons why Secretary of State Shultz was able to convince President Reagan of the need for summit meetings with his Soviet counterpart in 1985 was the president's belief that it was necessary to convince Moscow that the United States had no plans for an attack.

Although it was not known to the American public at the time, 1983 was the most dangerous year in Soviet-U.S. relations since the Cuban missile crisis. Moscow and Washington were going in different directions, with Reagan declaring a political and military campaign against the "Evil Empire" while Soviet leaders, in the wake of the death of Brezhnev, were looking to end the confrontation that was hurting the Kremlin. The intelligence in that year made it clear that the Soviet Union was in a downward spiral internationally, marked by the quagmire in Afghanistan; the drain of funds in developing countries, particularly Cuba; political and military setbacks in Angola and Nicaragua where covert actions were limiting pro-Soviet regimes; and the growing cost of competing with the largest peacetime increases in the U.S. defense budget since the end of World War II. Soviet leaders believed that the "correlation of world forces," Soviet terminology in weighing the international balance, was working against the interests of Moscow and that the U.S. government was in the hands of a dangerous anti-Soviet crowd. The Kremlin seemed to have good intelligence on its American problem.

The events of 1983 pointed to a renewal of the Cold War, which made the role of intelligence analysis at the Agency more immediate and controversial. President Reagan began to refer to the Soviet Union as the "focus of evil in the world" and an "evil empire." The new Soviet general secretary, Yuri Andropov, the former chief of the KGB, suggested that President Reagan was insane and a liar. U.S. media paid close attention to Reagan's sensational charges, and Soviet media launched a verbal offensive that matched Reagan's rhetoric. Reagan was compared to Hitler and accused of "fanning the flames of war." Andropov was portrayed in the U.S. press as a Red Darth Vadar. Reagan's demonization of several Soviet leaders was counter-productive; the same could be said for Obama's demonization of Vladimir Putin, president of the Russian Federation at the time of this writing.

European media were declaring the resumption of the Cold War, comparing the crisis in the early 1980s to the Berlin blockade in 1948 and the Cuban missile crisis in 1962. These were exaggerations, but any level of tension in relations between Moscow and Washington created reminders of previous confrontations. Soviet-American détente and arms control were pushed to the background, and the possibilities of superpower conflict to the foreground.

The public's reaction in 1983 would have been more tense if it had shared Soviet knowledge of aggressive U.S. military exercises and intelligence activities. The Reagan administration authorized unusually aggressive military exercises near the Soviet border that, in some cases, violated Soviet territorial sovereignty. American, European, and Soviet publics had no knowledge of the "war scare" in the Kremlin, particularly Operation RYAN, a sensitive KGB collection operation launched to determine whether the United States was planning a surprise nuclear attack.

One of the great mutual misunderstandings between the Soviet Union and the United States was that both sides feared surprise attack. The United States suffered psychologically from the Japanese surprise attack at Pearl Harbor, and it has still not recovered from 9/11. At the same time, the United States has never appreciated that Moscow has similar fears due to Operation Barbarossa, the German invasion in the same year as Pearl Harbor, a far more devastating assault.

One of the great ironies of WWII is that the United States and the Soviet Union both suffered from surprise attack, although both had the intelligence capacity to limit, if not prevent, the attacks. The intelligence failures contributed to the national traumas caused by these attacks, which marked the worst military disasters in their history. U.S. leaders should be more aware of the impact of this trauma on their Russian counterparts. This was not the case for President Reagan, who issued a radio warning into an open mic in August 1984 that "I've signed legislation that will outlaw Russia forever. We begin bombing in five minutes." Those of us in the intelligence community who understood the importance of de-escalating the possibility of war with the Russians weren't amused.

Russia's fear of surprise attack was accentuated in 1983, when the Reagan administration deployed the Army's Pershing-II missile and land-based cruise missiles in Europe as a counter to the Soviet Union's SS-20 missiles. The SS-20 was not considered a "strategic" weapon because of its limited range—3,000 miles, well short of the United States. The P-II, however, could not only reach the Soviet Union, but could destroy Moscow's command and control systems. Since the Soviets would have limited warning time—less than five minutes—the P-II was viewed as a first-strike weapon that could destroy the Soviet early warning system. I asked Undersecretary of Defense Lynn Davis whether anyone in the Pentagon thought of the P-II as a first-strike weapon, and she appeared nonplussed. Currently, U.S. policymakers fail to understand Moscow's legitimate concerns with the deployment of a regional missile defense in Poland and Romania.

In addition to the huge strategic advantage from the P-II and numerous cruise missiles, the U.S. deployment of the MX missile and the D-5 Trident submarine placed the Soviets in an inferior position with regard to strategic modernization. Overall, the United States held an advantage in political, economic, and military resources. The United States and NATO presently have significant advantages over Russia, which makes the current exaggeration of the threat particularly odious.

President Reagan authorized a high-risk psychological warfare program to intimidate the Kremlin, including dangerous probes of Soviet borders by the U.S. Navy and Air Force. These activities were unknown to intelligence analysts at the CIA. In fact, very few U.S. officials at the White House or the Pentagon were fully briefed on these measures. These risky operations included sending strategic bombers over the North Pole to test Soviet radar, as well as conducting exercises in maritime approaches to the Soviet Union where U.S. warships had never previously ventured. There were secret operations that simulated surprise naval air attacks on Soviet targets. Operation RYAN was a response to the detected aspects of the U.S. psychological warfare campaign, which began several months after President Reagan was inaugurated.

The CIA was at a disadvantage in trying to analyze the war

scare, because a major flaw in the intelligence process is the un-willingness of the Pentagon to share U.S. military maneuvers and weapons deployments with the CIA. The CIA was slow to anticipate Soviet military maneuvers in the Mediterranean Sea and the Indian Ocean because there was no awareness of U.S. deployments of strategic submarines in those waters, which led to a Soviet response. In 1983, the CIA had no idea that the Pentagon's annual Able Archer military exercise would be conducted in a provocative fashion with high-level participation. The exercise was a test of U.S. command and communications procedures, including procedures for the release and use of nuclear weapons in case of war.

The intelligence community was unwitting of these provocative exercises, and the CIA regularly turned out National Intelligence Estimates that assessed indications of an "abnormal Soviet fear of conflict with the United States." The national intelligence officer for Soviet strategic weapons, Larry Gershwin, believed that any notion of a Soviet fear of an American attack was risible, but six years later the President's Foreign Intelligence Advisory Board concluded that there had been a "serious concern" in the Kremlin over a possible U.S. attack. I believed that Soviet fears were genuine at the time, and President Reagan's national security advisor, Robert McFarlane, remarked, "We got their attention" but "maybe we overdid it." At the time of this writing in 2016, Gershwin, who manipulated intelligence on strategic matters throughout the 1980s, is still at the CIA as a national intelligence officer. *Plus ça change, plus c'est la même chose.*

INTELLIGENCE LESSONS LEARNED

It would be wonderful if intelligence could predict the future, but it can't. Good intelligence should at least be able to create the possibility of better, more effective national defense, but that is similarly uncertain. In 1972, with the benefit of excellent clandestine sources, I learned that Egyptian president Anwar Sadat had decided to expel the Soviet military presence from his country, because he had concluded (correctly) that Moscow would never take military risks to challenge the Israeli occupation of Egyptian territory. But it was also likely that the ouster of the Soviet advisors was designed to attract the attention of the United States and provide an opening for pressure from Washington on Israel to get serious about direct talks with Cairo over the Israeli occupation. Kissinger called Director Helms to thank him for premonitory intelligence that he did not acquire from the media. I received a call from Helms's office thanking me for the assessment and noting that it was well received in the White House. But it did not lead to any policy considerations of a new diplomatic opening in the Middle East that could have advanced the cause of peace and stability.

In a rare passage in his memoir, Kissinger conceded that the national security advisor first turns to the CIA for the "facts in a crisis and for analysis of events." He was particularly complimentary toward Helms for "never misusing his intelligence or his power." Helms knew that his integrity guaranteed his effectiveness, that his best weapon with presidents was a reputation for reliability.

The sad fact is that accurate intelligence is no assurance of effective national security policy, but intelligence failure will surely compromise the possibility for effective policy. If the Kennedy and Johnson administrations had been reading the CIA's estimates on Vietnam in the 1960s, there would have been good reasons for not escalating forces in Southeast Asia. But Kennedy was convinced of the need to check what he believed to be the actions of a Soviet proxy, which North Vietnam wasn't, and Johnson was insufficiently confident to follow his intuition against the policy arguments of the so-called "best and brightest," the key players of the Kennedy administration, particularly the Rostow brothers (Walt and Eugene) and the Bundy brothers (McGeorge and Bill) as well as Secretaries Rusk and McNamara.

Two decades later, if the Reagan administration had been

paying attention to CIA intelligence on the Middle East, perhaps President Reagan would have thought twice about accepting the advice of National Security Advisor Colonel Robert McFarlane, who pressed the president to send U.S. Marines into Beirut in 1983 to pull Israeli chestnuts out of the fire in Lebanon. Thus began the downward spiral in Lebanon that continues to this day. If the Bush administration had not been committed to the use of force in Iraq 20 years later, then perhaps the initial intelligence assessments of the Arabists at the CIA would have indicated that Vice President Cheney and Secretary of Defense Rumsfeld were wrong about a "cakewalk" for the U.S. military.

The policy process will always overrule the intelligence process when there are differences between the two. Policymakers look for intelligence to further their own agenda; they typically reject and even resent a contrary viewpoint. National Security Advisor Rostow displayed typical stubbornness when he believed that "assurance" about preemptive war from the Israeli ambassador would trump authoritative signals intelligence from the National Security Agency and the assessments of the CIA. When intelligence assessments differed from policy assessments, President Nixon dismissed the analysts as "the clowns" at Langley.

A major problem is that senior intelligence analysts are largely anonymous to senior policymakers. Unlike clandestine operatives who serve abroad with senior foreign service officers and therefore build professional connections to their State Department counterparts, intelligence analysts rarely have professional or personal experiences with policymakers. Thus, when policymakers receive intelligence, they find it to be random assessments of unknown provenance from intelligence analysts whose names ring no bells. The separation of intelligence and policy contributes to the objectivity of intelligence, but it also creates serious gaps and communications breakdowns between the seasoned analyst with ground truth and the policymaker who knows more about the domestic situation in the United States than domestic situations overseas. Unfortunately, the intelligence analyst is often bringing the worst news possible, and the delivery of negative messages on a regular basis over a period of time will lead to "shooting the messenger." The fact that Dick Helms regularly carried negative messages to the White House on Vietnam led to his posting as an ambassador to Iran.

There were great personal and professional rewards for me from the day I entered the CIA in 1966 until Casey arrived at the CIA in 1981. There were times when I thought that what we did in its Office of Current Intelligence really mattered. And there were times, such as during the Vietnam War, when what we did could have mattered if we had been taken seriously. Unfortunately, there were times when we were flat-out wrong. Nevertheless, the work is important and the culture of telling truth to power must be restored. It was this culture that Casey and Gates, then Tenet and McLaughlin, destroyed.

THREE

LEAVING THE CIA

"Don't worry, it's a slam dunk."
—CIA Director George Tenet's response when
President Bush wanted more intelligence on Saddam
Hussein's weapons of mass destruction. He got the
intelligence even though no such weapons existed.
December 21, 2002

In the summer of 2014, I was invited to lecture at the Truman Library in Independence, Missouri. The library was running a special exhibit on "Lies, Spies, and Paranoia" to honor President Truman's establishment of the CIA in 1947, and the chief archivist wanted a speaker with CIA experience. I jumped at the chance to give a talk on "The CIA and the Presidency: From Truman to Obama." I've always been a fan of the Truman presidency. Little did I know that I would get to see important documents at the library that bolstered my reasons for leaving the CIA in 1990. I was introduced to the audience as a CIA dissenter and contrarian, although I continue to believe that my views aren't contrary. It's simply a matter of my insistence on forming views irrespective of whatever the day's dominating political agenda may be.

Fifty years ago, former president Truman wrote a rarely cited op-ed for the *Washington Post* that criticized the CIA's covert operations during the Eisenhower-Kennedy era and called for restoring the agency to its "original assignment as the intelligence arm of the President."[1] President Truman was leery of the intelligence provided to the White House by policy departments that had an axe to grind, and wanted an independent agency outside of the policy process to provide intelligence in its "natural raw" state. He was supportive of the need for occasional clandestine operations, but thoroughly opposed "peacetime cloak-and-dagger operations" that would make the CIA a "symbol of sinister and mysterious foreign intrigue—and a subject for cold war enemy propaganda." Truman didn't want the CIA to be "seized upon as something akin to a subverting influence in the affairs of other people." The fact that the CIA was used as such a "subverting influence" against Americans during the Cold War and the Vietnam War would have saddened Truman.

My decision to leave the CIA was unwittingly framed by Truman's retrospective, particularly the need to return the agency to its original assignment as the intelligence arm of the president. Truman understood that an intelligence agency that conducted massive subversive activities abroad, particularly regime change and political assassination, could no longer be the "quiet arm of intelligence." My decision to leave the CIA was formed over a five-year period due to chronic abuse at the agency, particularly the falsification of intelligence, which became commonplace under Casey and Gates. My decision to become an open dissident was driven by a remarkable event: the nomination of Gates—who had corrupted intelligence in the 1980s to please his bosses—to become director in 1991. The arrival of William J. Casey in 1981 and the nomination of Bob Gates in 1991 were shocking bookend events that framed the deepening corruption of the CIA over a 10-year period. A decade later, similar malfeasance occurred with the conjured intelligence that marked the disastrous post-9/11 campaign to invade Iraq. The full cost of such corruption may never be fully accounted for in terms of the death and misery that the United States invasion delivered to the people of the region, or in terms of the radical deterioration of regional security, which continues to be exploited by our greatest enemies: al Qaeda and the Islamic State.

Although I didn't decide to leave the CIA until the Casey-Gates era of the 1980s, there was an event in the 1970s—the Church Committee hearings—that had forced me to question my view of the agency. Senator Frank Church (D-ID) understood the Vietnam War to be a "monstrous immorality" and promised that he would do whatever he could "as one senator, to bring about a full-scale congressional investigation of the CIA." One of the ironies of the various investigations of the mid-1970s was that there were two politicians who hoped to use the investigations to support a run for the White House. Senator Church was one of these individuals; Governor Ronald Reagan, a surprise appointment to the Rockefeller Commission, was the other. When Reagan was named, he ran true to form and warned President Ford that his "speaking engagements might conflict with the meetings."[2]

The hearings caused panic at the highest levels. The *New York Times* knew about the assassination schemes long before they surfaced at the hearings, but withheld publication following pressure from the Ford administration. President Ford warned that there could be revelations of CIA involvement in attempted assassinations of foreign leaders. Director William Colby acknowledged that his agency had kept files on members of congress who had attended anti–Vietnam War rallies and were considered dissidents.

One after another, the Church Committee in the Senate, the Pike Committee in the House, and the president's Rockefeller Commission revealed the details of the CIA's campaign against freedoms of speech and assembly. The campaign, appropriately code-named Operation Chaos, involved surveillance of more than 300,000 American citizens and organizations, including Martin Luther King. There were tests on unsuspecting individuals, primarily prisoners in a federal penitentiary, but one—Frank Olson—was an army civilian employee who died in mysterious circumstances after being drugged with the powerful hallucinogen LSD. The Ford administration paid a settlement to Olson's family after he either jumped or was pushed out of a hotel window in New York City; this is more than the Bush and Obama administrations have been willing to do for the innocent people killed or victimized as a result of U.S. drone attacks, indefinite detentions, torture, and abuse.

The chairman of the House intelligence investigation, Representative Lucien Nedzi (R-MI) had been briefed by the CIA on its domestic spying and possible involvement in assassination attempts. On his weekly radio show, Governor Reagan blamed all three investigations, including the one on which he nominally served, for engaging in "anti-intelligence hysteria" at a time when we need "more intelligence gathering." Once again, fast forward to the National Security Agency's Orwellian violation of the nation's privacy, and American indifference to the increasingly authoritarian concentration of government power and violations of the U.S. Constitution.

The Ford administration did its best to squelch the Church Committee's report on "Alleged Assassination Plots Involving Foreign Leaders," which documented the CIA's involvement in attempts to kill Fidel Castro, Rafael Trujillo, Ngo Dinh Diem, and—as I eventually learned—Patrice Lumumba. Just as President Obama claimed that the CIA's use of torture and abuse is "not who we are," Senator Church added a three-paragraph epilogue to his committee's report stating that the committee "didn't believe that the acts which it has examined represent the real American character."[3] Nor did the acts "reflect the ideals which have given the people of this country and of the world hope for a better, fuller, fairer life." Church referred to the assassination plots as "aberrations"; if so, they were aberrations that involved four presidents over a 20-year period. And just as the apologists of the *Washington Post* refused to confront the CIA's torture and abuse over a 10-year period, the paper strongly endorsed Church's epilogue and added that "to believe otherwise is to assault the basic process of consensus and correction by which a democratic society must proceed."[4]

The reports of the three investigative bodies were hugely uncomfortable for me, but it took the arrival of a right-wing ideologue, Bill Casey, to make me confront the corruption of the CIA and ask, "Who are we?" Casey had worked hard to make Reagan president, and he wanted to be rewarded with a top position in the new administration. Casey had worked almost as hard to elect Richard Nixon 12 years earlier, but then had waited two years before being named to an unexciting position as assistant secretary of state for economic affairs. In 1980, Casey garnered a top position in the transition process, heading the committee on foreign policy. He took no interest in the committee on intelligence because he hoped to become secretary of state. Unfortunately for Casey (and the Reagan administration and ultimately the United States), the appointment at Foggy Bottom went to General Alexander Haig. Vice President George H.W. Bush considered Casey an "inappropriate choice" for the CIA, and prophetically warned "if you pick Al Haig, I predict you'll have problems."[5]

Vice President Bush had few original ideas about national security policy, but he was spot on regarding his impressions of Casey and Haig. Neither one should have been considered for a key policy or intelligence position. A CIA analyst, Ruth Worthen, briefed Haig during the 1981 war between Argentina and the UK over the Falkland Islands, when the secretary of state wanted to know what the Pentagon and the CIA were going to do about the strategic Soviet submarines headed for the Falklands. When Ms. Worthen told him there was no such activity, he was dismissive. The following year, the Israelis gave Haig a heads-up about their invasion of Lebanon, which became a strategic nightmare for the Israelis. Unlike his various predecessors at Foggy Bottom, Haig found no problems with Israel's attack, an operation that went all the way to Beirut and eventually cost Israeli Prime Minister Menachem Begin his job and his health. Fortunately, the Reagan White House finally had had enough of Haig, and accepted one of his routine threats to resign. Haig's mishandling of Israel's aggression against the Lebanese wore out his welcome at the White House.

Haig's greatest sin was the firing of my good friend, Ambassador Robert E. White. White was posted to El Salvador when members of the Salvadoran National Guard murdered four American Maryknoll churchwomen whom he knew well. Ambassador White was at the scene when the bodies were dug up, and he angrily vowed, "This time the bastards won't get away with it." He and his wife Maryanne ignored death threats in El Salvador and professional threats from Haig that eventually cost him his job. Bob became my mentor 10 years later, a role model as well for his integrity and courage.

Not long after President Reagan was inaugurated, Ambassador White was kicked out of the Foreign Service and devoted himself to testifying at trials that determined the guilt of high-ranking Salvadoran generals. He also testified about the Reagan administration's attempt at a high-level cover-up. Many of these trials took place in Florida, where the United States was involved in resettling high-level Salvadoran defense and military officials who were complicit in war crime atrocities, including the murder of the American nuns. Presciently, when Ambassador White was assigned to El Salvador, neoconservative senator Jesse Helms (R-NC) remarked that a "torch had been tossed into a pot of oil." Like Bush, Helms was rarely right, but he knew White and spiked this observation.

Soon after being removed from the Foreign Service, Bob White told the *Fletcher Forum*, a publication of the Fletcher School of Law and Diplomacy, that "U.S. policy toward Latin America can be summed up in three words: fear of revolution. Because we feared revolution, we consistently opposed the forces of change and uncritically supported dictatorships and small economic elites. We blinked at repression and participated in the perversion of democracy throughout the hemisphere."[6] No one has provided a better description of the U.S. failure in this hemisphere and the misuse of the CIA over the past 60 years.

Casey, who had a fear of revolution, reluctantly accepted the post of director of central intelligence, and President-elect Reagan sweetened the offer by making Casey the first CIA director to be a member of the Cabinet. The Cabinet is a policymaking instrument, and the CIA was not designed to be part of policymaking. Casey's egregious interventions in policy toward the Soviet Union and Central America over the next five years were a harsh reminder that no CIA director should ever serve in a president's cabinet. President Truman's ideas about the danger of placing the CIA director in a policy role were validated.

Meanwhile, intelligence analysts at the CIA, who keep their ears close to the political fences, began to get rumors of the Casey appointment and that his deputy would be Admiral Bobby Ray Inman, the director of the National Security Agency. Bureaucrats are a nervous lot, and CIA intelligence analysts are no exception. Every leadership change brings concerns over the changes and appointments of a new director, particularly a concern about whom the new director would bring along. We knew that Casey and Inman would be a difficult team, and feared that their hardline views would create problems for intelligence analysts. What we didn't expect was that Inman would challenge Casey's imperious and tendentious approach, and that he would resign.

Casey sailed through the confirmation process in record time, spending less than three hours before the Senate Select Committee on Intelligence; he received approval from 14 senators. I listened to excerpts from Casey's testimony and realized that his muddled syntax and muffled delivery would lead to headaches, if not problems, and not just for intelligence analysts. As several journalists observed at the time, Casey would be the first

CIA director who would not require a scrambler telephone; his speech was naturally scrambled.

Casey was a challenge not only for the directorates of intelligence and operations. The CIA's Division of Science and Technology even devised a meter for Casey to take to briefings on the Hill that would alert him when his voice was inaudible. Casey tried it for two weeks without success, so the Senate Intelligence Committee provided him with a particularly sensitive microphone. Nothing worked; he was incomprehensible.

The arrival of Casey as director of central intelligence in January 1981 turned the CIA upside-down and turned me into a dissident. Casey was an ideologue and the worst possible fit for a CIA director. He held three bedrock convictions: the world is a hostile place; the Russians are the root of all evil; and the United States must be "strong, resolute, and purposeful."[7] He had no interest in objective intelligence analysis.

Casey loathed communism; he was a strong supporter of Senator McCarthy in the late 1940s and early 1950s. He was on the board of directors of the right-wing publishing house of Henry Regnery and a strong supporter of William Buckley, one of Regnery's prime authors and the publisher of the right-wing magazine *National Review*. In 1951, Casey organized the American Friends for Russian Freedom in order to lure Red Army personnel in Berlin and Vienna to desert to the West. When the Czechs stood up to the Soviet invasion in 1968, Casey and a conservative friend, Leo Cherne, drove into Czechoslovakia and almost reached Bratislava before they were turned back by the Red Army.

When Casey arrived at CIA headquarters, his first order of business was making sure that the Directorate of Operations had covert actions designed to weaken every government that the Soviets favored. It was strictly zero sum for Casey; any net gain for Washington and the Reagan administration was a net loss for Moscow and Leonid Brezhnev. Casey pressed the clandestine divisions concerned with Cuba, Vietnam, Cambodia, Angola, Ethiopia, South Yemen, Mozambique, and particularly Nicaragua, as the latest Soviet "conquest," to step up their efforts to weaken the regimes and expose Soviet machinations.

Casey was quite emphatic regarding the selection of those who would serve on his staff, preferring those who "lie, cheat, and steal" for the United States. Among his first appointments was one of my closest friends at the Agency, Bob Gates, who became Casey's executive assistant and not long after, his deputy director for intelligence. The two of them were joined at the hip for the next six years. Casey's behavior during this period was increasingly erratic, but Gates was too ambitious to care. As secretary of state, George P. Shultz concluded, "The CIA's intelligence was in many cases simply Bill Casey's ideology."[8]

In 1982, Casey named Gates to replace John McMahon as the deputy director for intelligence, which sent shock waves through the Agency. We knew McMahon had stood up to Casey and that Gates, then 43 years of age and extremely ambitious, would become the cat's-paw of the director. As Bernie McMahon, the staff chief of the Senate Intelligence Committee, said, "Bob wasn't going to talk to the boss the way John did. He's not the kind of guy who's going to say to Casey, 'That's a stupid idea, and if you go through with it, I'm walking out the door.'"[9]

Quite the contrary. Gates became the filter for Casey's views on intelligence matters dealing with the Soviet Union, Central America, and Southwest Asia. Gates and I were still on ostensibly good terms, so I occasionally found myself in his office, watching him cutting articles from *National Review* and other right-wing journals to reify Casey's hard-line views on Soviet foreign policy. I made a jocular reference to the "Gates's Clipping Service"; he didn't seem embarrassed by it.

Casey and Gates were an odd couple. The director was slovenly and unkempt; his eventual deputy was buttoned-down and precise. Casey was fleshy and frizzled, and was described as an "unconscious dresser." Gates was diminutive and compulsively neat. However, both were obsessed with security. Casey up-graded security around the "campus," ordering huge boulders to be placed on the lawns to keep threatening vehicles away from the building and bringing new security personnel to guard the building itself. Gates, for his part, was the only deputy director and acting director of the CIA in my 24 years in the building who patrolled the halls with security personnel.

Gates campaigned for the post as deputy director for intelligence by providing Casey numerous memoranda denigrating the directorate's intelligence analysts and even the deputy director for intelligence himself, John McMahon. He convinced Casey that McMahon was turning the place into the Department of Agriculture with an "advanced case of bureaucratic arteriosclerosis."[10] Upon becoming deputy director for intelligence, Gates immediately earned our contempt with memoranda and private comments that described us as "close-minded, smug, arrogant" people whose work was "irrelevant, uninteresting, too late to be of value, too narrow, too unimaginative, and too often just flat out wrong."[11] These notes earned him the sobriquet "The Little Shit," which is what we called him whenever one of his *billets-doux* arrived.

Casey took on the CIA's Directorate of Operations as a special project, and allowed Gates autonomy in running the Intelligence Directorate. For the Directorate of Operations, Casey brought in an old friend, Max Hugel, a profane business mogul who knew nothing about the CIA or international relations with the exception of the things he learned as a used-car salesman in Japan after World War II. Hugel didn't realize that top-flight operatives had direct links to the mainstream media, and their leaks to the *Washington Post* about the "tiny man with the toupee" who favored lavender jumpsuits soon forced Casey to get rid of him. Casey settled on a bold covert operative, Clair George, who fit Casey's model—the type to lie, cheat, and steal for his country. Indeed, several years later these very traits got George indicted for his role in Iran-Contra and convicted of lying to Congress, but a presidential pardon from Bush Senior saved him.

Casey and Haig, called "brilliant" by various political pundits, were terribly wrong in their perception of threats faced by the CIA and the United States, particularly those posed by a Soviet Union in decline. Let me be blunt and immodest about this: I was right and so were many of my colleagues, including Douglas Garthoff, the late James Noren, and my wife, Lyn Ekedahl. We understood that the Soviet Union was rotting from inside out, although none of us predicted the collapse of the empire. But we were naïve, not understanding that Casey, Gates, and their operational allies at the CIA needed an all-powerful geopolitical nemesis to allow increased defense spending and to support a policy dependent on the military. Gates and his apparatchiks prospered professionally by feeding Casey and the Reagan administration the intelligence that was needed to increase defense spending and covert operations. The fix was in, and we weren't prepared for the accompanying chicanery.

In addition to manipulating the intelligence inside the building, Casey and Gates strategically manipulated the media and the Congress, two institutions that prefer to acquiesce when confronted with authoritarian and official viewpoints and feel far less comfortable with contrarian, let alone dissident, views. And don't think that similar manipulation is not taking place in the current international arena, particularly in regard to Ukraine, where we are plied with the details of Russia's links to pro-Russian activists but we learn nothing about the CIA's assets among their pro-Western counterparts. The CIA has a history of manipulating anti-Russian forces in East and Central Europe; it began doing so in the late 1940s with Operation Gladio and continued this activism in the early 1980s in Poland on behalf of *Solidarnost*. Russian President Vladimir Putin has reason to believe that there is a CIA role in Ukraine today.

Greater covert activity expanded the opportunity for clandestine collection in support of official policy, making it more difficult to challenge the policies of Casey and other neoconservatives in the Reagan administration. The increased opportunity for manipulating intelligence required a bureaucratic wall between operations and analysis, because analysts cannot rely on the credibility and integrity of clandestine collection. Clandestine officers rarely share background information on their sources, and analysts often have no way of deciphering the access or credibility of a clandestine source. This problem will worsen with former CIA director Brennan's creation of fusion centers that will place clandestine operators and intelligence analysts in the same office, and thus increase opportunities for the politicization of intelligence. The Congressional Intelligence Committees did nothing to stop the creation of these centers.

It was politicization that led me to leave the CIA. The key documents were the National Intelligence Estimate of 1981 that falsely linked the Soviets to international terrorism and a spurious assessment prepared *in camera* in 1985 linking the shooting of Pope John Paul II to the Kremlin. The assassination attempt against the Pope took place on May 14, 1981, in the middle of the CIA's debate over the role of the Soviet Union in the conduct of international terrorism. The two documents were bookend developments that marked the decline of integrity in the CIA and my glide path to leave. In today's parlance, they would be considered "fake news."

Prior to 1981 and the inauguration of President Reagan, the CIA had never prepared a National Intelligence Estimate on international terrorism. Reagan, however, had appointed General Alexander Haig to be secretary of state, and Haig arrived at Foggy Bottom with an anti-Soviet agenda that was based in part on his belief that the Soviets were the source of all acts of international terrorism, including an attempt to assassinate him in June 1979, only several days before he stepped down as Supreme Allied Commander of Europe. Haig made the accusation about the links between Moscow and international terrorism for the first time at his confirmation hearing on January 14, 1981, the same day that the Senate confirmed Casey as director of central intelligence by a vote of 95-0, a decision that many key senators soon came to regret, even before Iran-Contra.

One senator, Joe Biden (D-DE), was wise enough to abstain. Ten years later, Biden voted against the confirmation of Gates as CIA director. The two events led to Gates's caustic treatment of Biden in his memoir, which covered his stewardship of the Defense Department.

Shortly before becoming secretary of state, Haig was given the galley proofs of Claire Sterling's sensationalized description of international terrorism, *The Terror Network*.[12] Haig accepted Sterling's thesis that the Soviets were behind international terrorism, including the attack on his life. In January 1981, he identified terrorism as the "new enemy," a "Wurlitzer being played by people in the basement of the Kremlin."[13] This was an ironic use of the term "Wurlitzer" to explain covert actions; it was the term that early operatives of the CIA and their journalistic supporters, such as Frank Wisner and Joseph Alsop, respectively, used to describe CIA shenanigans, including manipulation of the media.

From the very beginning, Haig, the retired Army general, indicated that he was going to poison relations with the Soviet Union. At his confirmation hearings, he charged Moscow with "training, funding, and equipping" international terrorists and, in an aside that dismissed the foreign policy of the Carter adminis-tration, added that "international counter-terrorism will take the place of human rights" as the main policy priority. He promised to put a stop to Moscow's "conscious policies that foster, support, and expand" rampant international terrorism. With the exception of Assistant Secretary of State Paul Wolfowitz, another anti-Soviet ideologue and hard-liner, who played a key role in the march to war against Iraq in 2003, I knew of no State Department officials who agreed with Haig's views on the Kremlin and terrorism.

A colleague of mine, Richard Kerr, was Haig's intelligence briefer for a spell, and was treated to frequent earfuls about Soviet perfidy, particularly with regard to terrorism. Haig saw the Soviet hand in every event that challenged U.S. global interests. When Kerr would push back, Haig would respond, "You don't know what you're talking about."

A State Department official who pushed back was Ronald J. Spiers, the director of the State Department's Bureau of Intelligence and Research, where I worked from 1974 to 1976. He was a wonderful gentleman but somewhat naïve, believing that he could defuse the issue of the Soviet Union and terrorism by commissioning a National Intelligence Estimate to evaluate the role of the Kremlin that would disabuse Haig of his geopolitical biases, if not his personal paranoia. Spiers told Haig privately that the intelligence record would not support his hard-line views of the Soviet Union and international terrorism. (A good friend of mine at the State Department, Phillip Stoddard, an outstanding Arabist, facetiously confirmed Haig's notion, remarking, "Yes, the Soviet Union orchestrated terrorism like a giant Wurlitzer organ.") Spiers, according to Stoddard, gave Haig an earlier study by the Department of State's Bureau of Intelligence and Research that examined Soviet attitudes toward terrorism, which concluded that Moscow saw terrorism as an unpredictable two-edged sword at best.

The Bureau of Intelligence and Research study concluded there was no good evidence of Soviet involvement, let alone leadership or direction. Haig rejected this study out of hand, scribbling several undiplomatic comments in the margins.[14] The marginalia scatology of Haig, Casey, and Gates would make an interesting study. In any event, the Bureau of Intelligence and Research and my colleagues agreed that the Soviets provided arms and training to groups such as the Palestine Liberation Organization, but did not encourage, let alone direct, these groups or their activities. There was no credible evidence of Soviet support to such nihilistic terrorist groups as the Italian Red Brigades or the West German Baader-Meinhof Gang in the files of any of the various intelligence organizations. These conclusions were unacceptable to the neoconservatives: Casey and Gates at CIA; Haig and Michael Ledeen at State; and National Security Council Advisor Richard Allen and National Security Council staffer Pipes.

Haig was so frustrated by the failure of the Bureau of Intelligence and Research to reify his strongly held views that he allowed Ledeen, a former colleague of Claire Sterling's, to press the Haig line on Soviet involvement in international terrorism. Haig returned the Bureau of Intelligence and Research study and accused Spiers and his staff of "naïveté." (Twenty years later, Vice President Cheney and Secretary of Defense Rumsfeld employed a similar technique by relying on neocons such as Douglas Feith and David Wurmser at the Defense Department to provide the intelligence needed to justify the invasion of Iraq when the CIA dragged its heels on corroborating some of the more outlandish ideas from the vice president.)

Failing to make an impression on Haig with their moderate views, Spiers and Stoddard decided that a National Intelligence Estimate on the subject would be a safe and non-confrontational way to disabuse Haig of his hard-line views. The two State Department bureaucrats, both high-minded and sophisticated, simply had no idea of the games that Casey and Gates were playing with intelligence at the CIA. I warned my former colleagues at Foggy Bottom, but the State Department had always played an effective role in leavening the more provocative assessments within the intelligence community and believed they could do so again on the issue of the Kremlin and international terrorism. They didn't realize that a new cast of characters had changed the game at the CIA.

Spiers had not considered the anti-Soviet paranoia of the new CIA director, and the director's interest in making a personal mark on his first National Intelligence Estimate. Casey was bent on emulating the efforts of Secretary of Defense Rumsfeld and Chief of Staff Cheney in the administration of President Ford to push the CIA's intelligence analysis in a hard-line direction. Rumsfeld and Cheney were dissatisfied with the CIA's independent analysis, particularly its ability to monitor and verify strategic arms agreements with the Soviet Union that they opposed. As a result, they introduced the Team A/Team B concept to the CIA. When Director William Colby refused to accept such a group of ideologues, he was removed as director and replaced by a political appointee, George H.W. Bush, who did. No one needed to push Casey to the far right; he had already taken up residence.

After meeting with his Soviet analysts, who agreed there was no evidence for the Haig thesis, Spiers requested that the acting national intelligence officer for the Soviet Union, Jeremy Azrael, prepare a special National Intelligence Estimate on the Soviet Union and international terrorism. Spiers believed that a special estimate would reinforce the views of the Bureau of Intelligence and Research, but in the guise of a more authoritative community judgment. Azrael was a well-meaning but ineffective intelligence bureaucrat, and he was unable to stand up to the pressure exerted by Casey and Gates.

Haig agreed with the idea of a National Intelligence Estimate, knowing that, regardless of the estimate's conclusions, he had a high-level supporter for his views, President Reagan. Reagan's campaign oratory against Moscow regularly referred to "Soviet-trained terrorists who are bringing civil war to Central America," requiring a "stand against terrorism in the world."[15] Haig and Casey knew they were in a battle that they could not lose. CIA intelligence analysts, and I was among them, simply failed to take this into account. We naïvely believed that the evidence was on our side, and that we would therefore prevail.

The timing of the estimate could not have been worse. Spiers and his colleagues didn't know that Haig had found a close friend and confidant in Director Casey.[16] Haig's reference to the Sterling book at a White House meeting piqued Casey's interest in the book. Casey's biographer, Joseph Persico, as well as Bob Woodward, noted that former president Nixon wrote to Casey in early March 1981 to recommend Sterling's article in the *New York Times*, which summarized the thesis of her book.[17] There was a special relationship between Sterling and the editors of the *Times* because it was unusual for stringers to get front-page bylines on stories on a regular basis. Obviously someone at the *Times*, probably her close friend William Safire, also wanted to link Moscow to international terrorism. Safire was the *Times*'s neoconservative op-ed writer, who was hired by the paper's publishers over the objections of every member of the editorial staff.

Unlike so many of the bland and corporate characters who surrounded Reagan in the White House, Haig and Casey were testy, mercurial, and prickly, and they shared strong views about the necessity of opposing the Soviet Union everywhere around the globe. Haig was suave and debonair in blue serge suits and crisp monogrammed shirts; Casey was rumpled and sloppy, and spoke in a rancorous mumble. But they both agreed—and indeed were obsessed—with fighting the influence of communism, particularly in Central America. I should have known that, when Secretary Haig fired Ambassador White for investigating the murders of the churchwomen in El Salvador, there would be a price to pay for opposing the ideas of our "masters."

Spiers's well-intentioned efforts to produce a National Intelligence Estimate on international terrorism to disabuse Haig of his ideological and paranoid views on Moscow played into Casey's hands. For the new director, a National Intelligence Estimate on terrorism would offer him an excellent opportunity to demonstrate that a new era had begun at the agency. It was unfortunate that Casey cut his bureaucratic teeth on this particular estimate, because it convinced him that CIA analysts were not only naïve, but apologists for the Soviet Union. At the same time, the exercise convinced the analysts that Casey was an ideologue, a polemicist, and a bully.

As national intelligence officer for the Soviet Union, Bob Gates influenced the new director's views about the CIA's Soviet analysts, telling him they were ignorant and wrongheaded. In all of our meetings with Casey about the estimate, Gates sat directly behind the director, snickering at Casey's put-downs of the analysts and passing him notes of support. Gates's supportive snickering earned him a promotion from national intelligence officer to a position as Casey's special assistant, on the way to becoming the deputy director for intelligence and eventually deputy director of the CIA. After Casey's sudden death from a brain tumor during the Iran-Contra investigations, Gates became acting director of CIA and President Reagan nominated Gates to be Casey's successor. Key members of the Senate Intelligence Committee, including the chairman, believed that Gates was withholding information about Iran-Contra, if not lying, which kept him from becoming CIA chief in 1987.

As the deputy division chief for Soviet relations in the Third World, I was tasked with directing the first draft of the estimate on the Soviet Union and international terrorism. I appointed the senior analyst in the branch, Lyn Ekedahl, who had a well-earned reputation for tough-minded and balanced analysis, to write the draft. This was a dozen years before she became my wife, which is another story for another time.

The draft was coordinated at a working-level meeting of analysts from the CIA, Defense Intelligence Agency, Department of State's Bureau of Intelligence and Research, and various military agencies, but it ran into a blistering attack from Casey—another proponent, along with Haig, of the "giant Wurlitzer in the Kremlin" theory. In a meeting with the author of the draft, the senior leadership of the CIA's Directorate of Intelligence, agents from the Directorate of Operations, and a representative from the Bureau of Intelligence and Research, Casey denounced the draft as an "exculpatory brief" and ridiculed everyone around the table who didn't share his polemical views. Casey, although often a less than coherent mumbler in the best of circumstances, was forceful and even brutal in dealing with senior CIA analysts and the top leaders of the Intelligence Directorate.

In trying to defend his department's views on terrorism and his analysts, the deputy director for intelligence, Bruce Clarke, encountered Casey's rancor. At one point, Casey glowered at Clarke and said, "Half of what you say makes sense and the other half makes no sense, but the problem is, I can't tell which is which." Clarke soon retired, and he and his wife moved to Vienna, far away from his beloved agency and its erratic leader. I was too young to retire, but due to these events I began to think that my days at the CIA might be coming to an end as well.

One of the truly interesting aspects of the exercise on international terrorism was the unanimity between members of the CIA's Directorates of Operations and Intelligence in working to counter the misuse of intelligence. In my 24 years at the CIA, I cannot recall another time (with the exception of the Papal plot assessment, which will be discussed later) when there was such collegiality between the hard-nosed collectors of intelligence and the less flamboyant analysts of intelligence. In addition to the parochial rivalry between the two groups and all the very different personalities, there was a tendency for clandestine operators to look for conspiratorial Soviet behavior in the international arena and for intelligence analysts to try to explain the Soviets in terms of national interest. In this case, operatives and analysts cooperated to try to prevent misuse of clandestine intelligence.

In denouncing our draft as an "exculpatory brief," Casey ridiculed everyone who had anything to do with it. He cited the writings of Claire Sterling and noted that he had stopped at a bookstore to pick up her latest work, *The Terror Network*, for $13.95, and "it told me more than you bastards whom I pay $50,000 a year." All of us knew that Sterling was a polemicist and that her writings were replete with disinformation and misinformation that CIA agents had planted in European newspapers and magazines. Sterling was a very willing user of CIA propaganda on virtually any subject.

Casey, unfortunately, was not the only high-level reader of Sterling's *Terror Network*. Several days before his comments linking Moscow to international terrorism, Haig read the book. Haig had brought Sterling's collaborator, Michael Ledeen, into the Department of State as a special assistant. Ledeen, who played a major role in bolstering Haig's view that the Soviets were behind international terrorism, had close ties to the chief of the Italian Military Intelligence and Security Service, General Giuseppe Santovito, and SISMI operative Francesco Pazienza, who were convinced that the Soviets were behind the plot to kill the Pope. The gullible victims of Ledeen's disinformation included Kissinger, Brzezinski, and former ambassador to the Soviet Union Malcolm Toon, who accepted the notion of a Bulgarian-Soviet link to the Papal Plot. Brzezinski went so far as to say that it was "utterly scandalous" that State and CIA officials were "unwitting . . . or witting tools" in a campaign "pooh-poohing what turns out to be a very serious plot."

Italian intelligence officers were also behind the fraudulent view two decades later that Iraq was purchasing uranium from Africa. In a speech to the U.S. Congress in January 2003, President George W. Bush cited a report alleging that Saddam Hussein purchased uranium from the African government of Niger. Many knew the report was a fraud, but Bush used it as part of his battle cry for launching a preemptive attack against Iraq. In his January 29, 2002, State of the Union address, Bush attributed the Niger intelligence to the British, but it was the Italian Military Intelligence and Security Service report, which was delivered to the British and French intelligence agencies, that the president used to go to war. The European intelligence agencies believed the report to be rubbish, indeed a forgery, but the White House and the CIA had uses for it. The CIA published a National Intelligence Estimate in October 2002 that falsely claimed that Iraq "began vigorously trying to procure uranium ore and yellowcake," a charge that was lifted out of a Defense Intelligence Agency report from February 2002.[18]

Using a forgery to make a case for war against Iraq was far more serious than Casey and Gates taking black propaganda that the CIA embedded in the European press to draft a National Intelligence Estimate on the Soviets and international terrorism. Nevertheless, Casey and Gates had violated the sacred credo of the intelligence world, which is to provide objective and honest intelligence to the policy community. In his memoir, Gates took his usual dog in the manger approach, claiming falsely that he was "on the sidelines in this fight."[19] In fact, he took advantage of every opportunity to provide misinformation to the CIA director in order to enhance his own standing and to move the estimate to a hard-line position, concluding that "Casey had been more right than the others."[20]

Nevertheless, the key analytical and operations officers at the CIA and their counterparts at the State Department stuck by their principles. They knew Casey and Haig were wrong about their assessment of the Soviet Union and terrorism and had to be disabused. A senior intelligence official in the Intelligence Directorate, Richard Lehman, who facetiously referred to policymakers as "our masters," told a group of us, "Casey and Haig will have to be let down, but you must let them down easily." We were aware of the difficult bureaucratic task that we faced, but we naïvely believed that senior leaders such as Lehman would support us.

There was no credible empirical evidence of Soviet support for international terrorism in Western Europe and the Middle East. To the contrary, there was excellent evidence of Soviet efforts to persuade insurgent and radical groups, particularly the Palestine Liberation Organization, to forswear terrorism. As the security archives of various East European government have opened, we have seen additional evidence of the limits of Soviet Bloc support for groups that engaged in the use of terrorism.

During the battle over the estimate on terrorism, a meeting was called at the National Security Council to discuss Moscow's role. The meeting was to be chaired by Professor Pipes, who had taken a leave of absence to become an advisor on Soviet affairs in the Reagan administration. Pipes had been the key driver of the Team A/Team B exercise in the 1970s and an important ideological driver for branding the Kremlin responsible for all major acts of international terrorism. My boss at the time, Helene Boatner, a recipient of a CIA trailblazer award, would not allow me to attend the meeting at the National Security Council because she knew that my views would have clashed with Pipes's polemic. I'm not sure if Boatner was trying to protect me from a serious challenge at the National Security Council or simply trying to protect herself and her agency from having one of her analysts ridiculed in such an august setting.

Boatner was a typically cautious bureaucrat, so I assume it was the latter. A few months later, Lyn Ekedahl and I wrote a hard-hitting memorandum to Casey, challenging his views on Moscow and terrorism, and warning that his position would undermine the CIA's credibility. Boatner allowed us to forward the memorandum, but insisted that it come from us as analysts and not from her Office of Soviet Affairs. Interestingly, I had known Boatner since 1955, when we met in Athens. She was the daughter of Major General Hayden Boatner, my commanding general in Athens. I was General Boatner's cryptographer.

Ekedahl and I weren't the only ones to challenge Casey. Key members of the CIA's Directorate of Operations tried to tell Casey that much of Sterling's "evidence" was black propaganda they placed in the European press, but he was dismissive. He was comfortable bullying the operatives as well as the analysts. To paraphrase UN inspector Hans Blix, who was critical of CIA intelligence on Iraqi weapons of mass destruction two decades later, it was another case of "100 percent certainty and 0 percent knowledge." Meanwhile, Gates held onto his back-bench role, remaining inscrutable but doing great damage behind our backs in meetings with the director.

Casey's solution for the problem of our initial draft on Moscow and terrorism was to take it out of our hands and give the job to the more "reliable" Defense Intelligence Agency, which had no problem politicizing intelligence. Military intelligence is typically subject to pressure from the chain of command, which was one of President Truman's reasons for creating the CIA in the first place. The chief of the Defense Intelligence Agency, General Eugene Tighe (known to CIA analysts as "General Tighraid"), had written Casey a letter outlining his differences with the CIA draft and arguing that the Soviets were involved in international terrorism, even if there was no evidence to say so. Like Vice President Cheney two decades later, Casey and Tighe considered the absence of evidence as evidence.

The draft estimate from the Defense Intelligence Agency had no support from CIA analysts and operatives, but it was just what Casey and Gates desired. It concluded that any violent action against constituted authority was a form of terrorism, which opened the gates to a frivolous debate over activities that had nothing to do with terrorism. Even Gates finally conceded in his memoir that the Defense Intelligence Agency draft led to "something of a donnybrook" inside the intelligence community. Following our memorandum to Casey, Ekedahl and I went to the deputy director for intelligence, John McMahon, and made it clear that the draft was unacceptable, and he agreed to take the matter to Casey. McMahon cooperated in our efforts to organize both the Agency directorates in opposition to Casey and his ultra hard-line views.

As a result of the opposition, Casey finally agreed to permit a third draft with significantly altered and more vague terms of reference, and a new title ("The Soviet Role in Revolutionary Violence") that permitted the CIA to dodge the more provocative question of international terrorism and to incorporate virtually every report of Soviet activity in the Third World, including a great deal of unconfirmed reporting. The estimate concluded that Moscow supported wars of liberation against entrenched autocratic regimes, and provided arms and training to encourage liberation, which no one disputed. The estimate was initially ordered to examine whether Moscow supported such armed organizations as the Baader-Meinhof Gang in West Germany, the Red Brigade in Italy, and the Red Army faction in Japan, for which there was no evidence.

Gates stated in his memoir that this draft was prepared by "an old hand in the estimates business" and that both sides accepted it "grudgingly," which was a lie. The final draft was written by an academic-in-residence, Professor Richard Mansbach from Rutgers University, who had arrived at the CIA only several months earlier with no background in intelligence or international terrorism. To make matters worse, he made no attempt to exploit the CIA's extensive files, particularly those of the directorates of intelligence and operations on terrorism and Soviet activities in the Third World. Lyn Ekedahl was permitted to attend coordination meetings on the Mansbach draft, but instructed not to speak unless spoken to.

Although the estimate on Moscow and terrorism went further than the intelligence allowed, Casey and Gates were never satisfied with a product that argued non-state actors could conduct terrorism on their own without superpower backing, and that there was no evidence that the Soviets directly fomented international terrorism. The estimate was so tendentious and polemical that it was quickly ignored and quietly shelved by the policy community that it was intended for. We may have lost the internal battle over Moscow and international terrorism, but the policy community understood the CIA product was phony. Several years later, we fought a similar campaign, with similar results, over another issue related to terrorism.[21]

The next campaign was initiated by Casey, who remained dissatisfied with the inability of the CIA to link the Soviet Union with the 1981 shooting of the Pope. The intelligence record clearly exonerated both the Soviet Union and Bulgaria, and, as late as the winter of 1983–1983, even Gates's briefings to Congress emphasized the non-involvement of Moscow and Sofia. Just as Vice President Cheney pressed to prove a non-existent link between Saddam Hussein's secular regime and al Qaeda in 2002–2003, Casey would not stop linking Moscow to the plot to assassinate the pope. He was getting a great deal of pressure from right-wingers on Capitol Hill, such as Senator Alphonse D'Amato (R-NY), to produce evidence of Moscow's role. Sterling was needling CIA officers in Rome about their unwillingness to point an accusing finger at Moscow. At one cocktail party, where Sterling was elaborating her perspective on CIA complicity, a CIA operative dismissed her views as conspiracy theory, which—according to one witness—"pissed her off. She climbed all over the guy."[22]

The 1985 assessment "Agca's Attempt to Kill the Pope: The Case for Soviet Involvement," became a classic example of the political corruption of intelligence. Two Agency post-mortems took the assessment and its co-authors (Kay Oliver, Beth Seeger, and Mary Desjeans) to task for their flawed work. Their careers did not suffer as a result, however. All three continued to be promoted in the CIA's bureaucracy, with Desjeans becoming chief for intelligence on the former Soviet Union and even an assistant to the deputy director for intelligence, and Oliver becoming the chief of the Agency's historical staff. All three also received generous cash awards for their efforts in support of Casey and Gates.

The papal plot assessment provided another example of Gates's lack of candor. The flawed character of the secret report was indicated by its tendentious reasoning, which framed a document created out of whole cloth. "The Soviets were reluctant to invade Poland" in 1981, the report said, "so they decided to demoralize [the Polish] opposition" by killing the Polish Pope. The conclusion of the report was nothing short of menacing: "Since the Soviets haven't been blamed by world opinion thus far, they are then more inclined than before 1981 to undertake adventurous actions."[23] In other words, about the same time that Mikhail Gorbachev was taking the reins of the Soviet Union and pointing toward improved relations with the United States and an invigoration of the disarmament dialogue, the CIA was predicting a new round of Kremlin adventurism, a fixed notion with Casey and Gates. Fortunately, Casey's efforts to worsen Soviet-American relations failed, because Secretary of State Shultz was one of many important policymakers who ignored the estimate.

Soon after Gates removed me from my position as chief of the division on Soviet–Third World relations, I learned of yet another effort to distort intelligence on behalf of White House policy. This involved an effort by the National Security Council and the CIA to produce a document that would provide intelligence justification for the scandal known as Iran-Contra. Iran-Contra was a scheme to use the profits from secret arms sales to Iran to supply the Nicaraguan rebels known as the Contras. Iran ultimately paid more than $30 million for U.S. weaponry, and part of these funds were channeled into a Swiss bank account where money from arms sales was commingled with money for the Contras. In order to conduct arms sales to Iran, however, the Reagan administration had to demonstrate that Iran was no longer involved in the conduct of state terrorism, which of course was not true. Gates was intimately involved in the effort to change the CIA's analytical line on Iran in order to demonstrate that Tehran had ended support for international terrorism.

In May 1985, the national intelligence officer for the Middle East, former Directorate of Operations officer Graham Fuller, orchestrated a flawed estimate on Iran to justify arms sales. Fuller worked closely with the deputy director for intelligence, Bob Gates, and the National Security Council officer charged with monitoring the arms sales, Howard Teicher, to make sure the conclusions of the estimate matched the operational needs of the covert program to initiate arms sales. As a result, the estimate falsely concluded that Iran was reducing its support for international terrorism, that the Soviet Union was gaining a foothold in Iran, and that there were moderates in Iran who wanted to open a dialogue with the United States. This was the worst example of falsifying a National Intelligence Estimate in order to support operational policy until 17 years later when CIA senior analysts Robert Walpole and Paul Pillar produced a phony National Intelligence Estimate and an unclassified "white paper," respectively, to convince the policy community and the U.S. Congress that Saddam Hussein had extensive stocks of weapons of mass destruction.

There was no evidence for any of these conclusions on Iran, and many analysts in the Directorate of Intelligence opposed the draft estimate. These efforts were unsuccessful because Gates used his positions as director of the National Intelligence Council and deputy director for intelligence to make sure there would be no opportunity to counter the final product. Just as Gates had picked the drafters of the Papal Plot assessment that was done *in camera*, he picked the major players in the estimate on Iran. When I testified against Gates in his 1991 confirmation hearings, I referred to this process as "judge-shopping in the courthouse," for there is no better way to assure the outcome of a tendentious intelligence product. You can get the sentence that you desire with the right judges; you can do the same with the appointment of the right analysts to draft an intelligence product. (We will never know the full extent of the CIA's involvement in Iran-Contra, because President George H.W. Bush pardoned key CIA officials who played a major role in the crimes.)

In selecting Graham Fuller to draft the estimate on Iran, Gates selected one of the strangest characters I encountered in the directorate of operations. Fuller was a major supporter of the Mujahideens' campaign against Soviet forces in Afghanistan in the 1980s, believing that an Islamic insurgency would be the best path to creating instability in the Soviet Union. Fuller drove the outcome of the Iran estimate in 1985 in order to create a revived U.S. relationship with Iran that would be anti-Soviet. More recently, we learned that Fuller had family connections to Ruslan Tsarnaev, the uncle of the brothers responsible for the Boston Marathon bombings, and that Fuller wrote a letter of recommendation for the Green Card application of Turkish Islamic leader Fethullah Gulen, whom Turkish president Recep Erdogan blames for the coup attempt in Turkey in July 2016.

In any event, short of resignation, there was nothing that an analyst, even a contrarian one, could do about three politicized CIA intelligence assessments, let alone the CIA's operational nightmares orchestrated with the approval of the White House. The worst nightmare took place in March 1985, in Lebanon, about the time that I was learning about the phony assessment to link the Kremlin to the Papal Plot. In a situation reminiscent of the current debacle in Syria, the CIA found itself in the middle of the Lebanese civil war, struggling against such opponents as Hezbollah as well as such putative allies as the Phalangists, whose brutality against the Palestinians on behalf of Israel exceeded what CIA operatives were willing to sanction.

Casey even sanctioned a car bombing in March 1985 against Shia cleric Muhammad Hussein Fadlallah, who played a key role in the attacks against U.S. personnel in Lebanon. The bomb detonated over 400 pounds of explosives outside Fadlallah's house in the Beirut suburbs. It killed more than 80 innocent people and injured 200 more, but Fadlallah escaped without injury. *Washing-*

ton Post journalist Bob Woodward reported that Casey had by-passed the CIA's traditional channels to funnel money to the hit squad that planted the bomb.[24]

The production of corrupt intelligence tailored specifically for U.S. political maneuvering against the Russians drove me out of the CIA, but it was the decision of President George H.W. Bush in May 1991 to nominate Gates for the position of CIA director that led me to blow the whistle. The fact that Gates, who had been instrumental in the distortion of findings at the CIA and in the crimes and cover-up of the Iran-Contra scandal, could then become a CIA director for the Bush administration (and eventually a secretary of defense for the administrations of Presidents Bush and Obama) remains mind-boggling. It proves that there are not only second acts in the world of politics, but even third acts as well.

When Casey was struck down by a brain tumor in December 1986, leading to his death the following year, Gates was considered his heir apparent by the White House. President Reagan was in no rush to appoint a successor to Casey, but Nancy Reagan began hounding her husband's chief of staff, Donald Regan, to "get rid" of Casey, even though he had been instrumental in Reagan's election in 1980.[25] President Reagan's popularity was sinking like a stone because of Iran-Contra, and Regan was convinced that Nancy was "looking for somebody to throw off the sled to save the administration."[26]

Finally, on January 29, 1987, Donald Regan and one of Casey's closest friends in the administration, Ed Meese, the attorney general, carried a letter to Casey from the president, offering Casey the job of counselor to the president when he was well. Later that day, Gates brought Casey a two-sentence letter of resignation that he showed to Casey's wife Sophia, before handing it to his boss. No one who visited Casey understood a word that Casey was saying in the hospital, but Gates seemed to think that Casey, after the letter of resignation was signed, said, "That's the end of a career."[27] The following day, President Reagan nominated Gates to be the CIA's new director, the youngest appointee ever at the age of 43.

Gates's confirmation problems in 1987 began immediately. Gates's view of his failure to gain confirmation is very different from the actual reasons for his decision to withdraw his nomination. The one certainty is that the Iran-Contra scandal was the reason for his failure. Gates claimed that he had "virtually nothing to do with the operational side of CIA's activities in Central America" and was "surprised and a little dismayed" by the Senate Intelligence Committee's demand that he testify on the subject.[28] The Casey-Gates relationship was a tight one, and Gates's claim that he had no knowledge of the CIA director's close working relationship with the National Security Council on Central America or his aggressive involvement in the arms-for-hostages deal was not believable. The seamless relationship between Casey and Gates undermined Gates's claim that he was out of the chain of command on the operational decisions. (CIA director Brennan used a similar defense in 2009 and 2013 to claim his innocence about CIA decisions on torture and abuse. Like Gates, Brennan had to withdraw his name from consideration as CIA director in 2009, and, like Gates, Brennan laundered his credentials to gain confirmation four years later in a vote even more divisive than the one for Gates.)

The fact that I didn't believe Gates in 1987 was of no importance. The fact that the independent counsel of the Iran-Contra investigation, the chairman of the Senate Intelligence Committee, and most members of the committee didn't believe Gates was dispositive. Gates used his memoirs to portray himself as being on the "side of the angels."[29] And like Brennan in 2014 regarding torture and abuse, Gates relied on the "reassurance from Agency lawyers that there was nothing illegal about the Iran operation." What I knew and what the intelligence committee didn't know was that Gates had been instrumental in forging the intelligence case for Iran-Contra that was based on disinformation and outright lies about Iran and terrorism, Iran and the Soviet Union, and Iran's domestic politics.

Gates also used his memoir to blame his predecessor as deputy director, John McMahon, one of the finest gentlemen I worked for in my 24 years at CIA. Gates correctly noted that McMahon "had been a real stickler for the rules," an odd choice of words to describe an individual with a genuine sense of ethics.[30] As a result, Gates contends that McMahon "would have blown the whistle, or at least warned me," if he had been aware of any impropriety or continuing questionable actions with respect to Iran or Central America." In fact, it was common knowledge throughout the agency that McMahon was encountering problems with Casey over operational and analytical matters and was disgusted with the director's performance. McMahon was no fan of Bob Gates.

The Iran-Contra operations were run by Ronald Reagan's National Security Council, but several high-ranking CIA officials, not only Gates, were witting. My source for this information is another former colleague at the CIA, James McCullough, then head of the CIA's executive staff and therefore responsible for supporting both Casey and Gates in preparing congressional testimony. The key events took place in the latter part of 1986, when the operational security of Iran-Contra began to break down. This was a particularly eventful year for the CIA, including the U.S. air raid on Libya; a series of counterintelligence issues in what become known as the "Year of the Spy"; intelligence leaks from Moscow; and a number of Soviet-American arms control issues culminating with the summit in Reykjavik. It was also the year that I left the CIA to go to the National War College.

Ironically, I had very close relations with both McCullough and Stanley Moskowitz, who served two reckless masters, Casey and Gates, respectively. The three of us were devoted basketball fans and shared season tickets for years to the Washington Bullets.

We discussed McCullough's knowledge of the role Gates played in making sure that the Directorate of Operations prepared Casey's testimony on Iran-Contra to the Congress. It should have been McCullough's job as director of the Executive Staff to prepare the testimony, but Gates put it in the hands of Clair George, the deputy director for operations, a sure sign that the CIA deputy director wanted the cover-up to continue.

I was in my first year as a faculty member of the National War College when Gates was nominated in 1987 and still employed by the CIA. I considered reaching out to the Senate Intelligence Committee to present my case against his confirmation. But before I could decide one way or the other about testifying, Gates had to drop his nomination because the committee did not believe his denials about knowledge of Iran-Contra. There was no hesitation in 1991, however. I was no longer an intelligence analyst at the CIA and had been appointed to the war college faculty as a professor of international security. I lost the battle against the nomination, but nevertheless won some major campaigns in getting acknowledgement inside and outside the government on the CIA's politicization of intelligence on terrorism in 1981and on the plot to assassinate the pope.

These issues pointed to the corruption of the intelligence process, and revealed Gates's direct involvement. They also illustrated my personal battles with Gates and his acolytes, leading to my decision to leave the CIA and become a dissident. The candor of Gates was a prime issue in both of his confirmation battles with the Senate Intelligence Committee, in 1987, when he had to withdraw his name from the nomination, and in 1991, when he attracted more opposition than all previous and subsequent nominations to the post of CIA director, except for John Brennan in 2014.

Casey and Gates demonstrated that it was relatively easy to destroy the political culture of the CIA by ignoring the rules of analytic tradecraft. Moreover, the legacy of the politicization of intelligence in the 1980s and the Team A/B exercise in the 1970s was revived two decades later at the CIA in a classic exercise of "*déjà vu* all over again," to quote Yogi Berra. Just as Team B contributed to exaggeration of the Soviet strategic threat in the 1970s and 1980s, the CIA produced a National Intelligence Estimate in 1998 that exaggerated the overall threat of ballistic missiles. The 1998 estimate is a classic case of the way hyperbole works its way into intelligence on threat perception. I was involved in this issue, co-authoring a book that made the case against national missile defense and revealed how intelligence was manipulated to bolster the threat.[31]

In 1998, the Commission to Assess the Ballistic Missile Threat to the United States, chaired by Donald Rumsfeld, made headlines with a dire warning that Iraq, Iran, and North Korea could deploy an operational intercontinental ballistic missile (ICBM) with "little or no warning." It is no accident of history that several years later Iran, Iraq, and North Korea became President George W. Bush's "axis of evil," which led to the invasion of Iraq in 2003 and the exaggeration of Iran's nuclear program. Two decades later, none of these countries has intercontinental missiles, and only North Korea has medium-range missiles.

The CIA was created to challenge incomplete and distorted assessments of strategic threats, but in this case the political pressure from Rumsfeld's commission led to a National Intelligence Estimate in 1999 that concluded the United States, over the next 15 years, would most likely "face ICBM threats from . . . North Korea, probably from Iran, and possibly from Iraq." In 2016, the United States faced no ICBM threats other than the decades-old ones from Russia and China.

The CIA reached its bogus conclusion in 1999 with one of the standard tools of politicization, lowering previously established standards for judging threats. This technique is exactly how the CIA prepared its estimate on international terrorism in 1981 and its estimate in October 2002 that conjured a threat of weapons of mass destruction in Iraq without evidence. In the case of the 1999 estimate, which concentrated almost exclusively on the non-existent threat from Iraq, Iran, and North Korea, the CIA emphasized that these three nations "could" test a long-range missile instead of the previous standard of "would" they deploy one.

The 1999 estimate gauged the threat against the United States to include the westernmost parts of Hawaii and Alaska instead of the continental United States, which shortened the distance required for a long-range missile to strike. It's highly unlikely that ICBMs would be deployed against the sparsely inhabited areas of those two states. Finally, the CIA abandoned the idea of "deployment" of an ICBM and substituted a "test" of a weapon. It is noteworthy that, in the case of the Indian program involving medium-range weapons, the Agni missile program began in the mid-1980s and was not flight tested until the late 1990s. Nowhere did the estimate mention that a shorter test program would produce a less reliable missile.

These examples of skewed intelligence represent the worst-case analysis that the CIA was designed to prevent. To please those in authority and satisfy their agenda, the agency tweaked its assessments without any new corresponding developments on the ground. CIA officials simply changed the standards for assessing situations. There had been no technological breakthroughs producing missile systems in developing nations, but the CIA's tweaked estimate was used to justify the abrogation of the Anti-Ballistic Missile Treaty in 2001, the deployment of a national missile defense system in 2002, and even the unprovoked invasion of a foreign nation in 2003.[32] There are few stronger examples of the dangerous consequences of corrupting intelligence to meet political ends.

In addition to the conjuring of threats, there were cover-ups of U.S. and CIA violations of human rights, particularly in Central and South America. The CIA's Directorate of Operations abetted the cover-up of human rights violations throughout the hemisphere to satisfy the Reagan administration in the 1980s. My good friend, Ambassador Bob White, protested this cover-up in El Salvador and was fired by Secretary of State Haig in 1981. The mass slaughter of Guatemalan Maya peasants between 1978 and 1983 is rarely cited in any discussion of genocide. In South Asia, the Directorate of Operations censored or ignored reports on strategic weapons programs and human rights abuses in Pakistan to satisfy the Nixon and Reagan administrations. The few reports that did get to the analysts were difficult to circulate, because Gates, as the deputy director of intelligence, blocked their distribution. Casey and Gates knew that, if intelligence on Pakistan's nuclear weapons reached the Congress, all aid to Pakistan would have to stop.

Ten years earlier, President Nixon had protected Pakistan because it served as an intermediary for secret diplomacy with China; therefore, intelligence analysis and collection was politicized. President Reagan protected Pakistan as a conduit for arms shipments to the Mujahideen fighting the Soviets in Afghanistan. The politicization of clandestine collection of intelligence has always been a problem for the intelligence analyst, but the years under the stewardship of Casey and Gates were the worst.

Director Brennan's creation of fusion centers with operatives and analysts working cheek by jowl will make it easier to return to the politicization of the 1980s. In addition to the misuse of clandestine collection to please the day's dominant political agenda, there will be restricted circulation of information to protect so-called sensitive sources. It will continue to be difficult for intelligence analysts to get background information on clandestine sources, which is needed to judge access and credibility. Operatives are trained to manipulate, and the manipulation of intelligence analysts would not be difficult.

The vulnerability of the intelligence process to political manipulation involves the conscious decision *not* to share relevant information that fails to support policy preferences of the White House. For example, an informant told the CIA in the spring of

2001—a full two years before the invasion of Iraq, that Iraq had abandoned its uranium enrichment program, a major element of the nuclear weapons program, and that centrifuge components from the scuttled program were available for examination and even purchase.[33] But in October 2002, without any additional new evidence, the CIA reversed direction and charged Iraq with taking energetic steps to reconstitute its nuclear weapons program.

In the wake of 9/11, Vice President Cheney and Secretary of Defense Rumsfeld, who created the Team A/B exercise to compromise the integrity of intelligence analysis, further reduced the role of the CIA. Their support of the Intelligence Reform Act of December 2004; the creation of a director of national intelligence; and the appointment of military officers to the positions of both director of the CIA and director of national intelligence in 2006 weakened the role of the CIA. President Obama continued this trend, appointing General James Clapper to serve as director of national intelligence and General David Petraeus, briefly, as director of the CIA.

In addition to protesting politicization, I called attention to the mythology regarding the Intelligence Reform Act of 2004. One myth was that the act's creation of a director of national intelligence, the so-called intelligence "tsar," would make the intelligence community more accountable. In fact, the Reform Act made a bad situation worse by creating a new bureaucracy beholden to the White House and unable to challenge, let alone prevent, militarization of the community. With the exception of the first tsar, a retired Foreign Service Officer, John Negroponte, every director of national intelligence has been a general or admiral with little understanding of strategic and long-term intelligence. Negroponte was a deplorable choice because of his connection to the cover-up of human rights atrocities in Central America in the 1980s. Negroponte wasn't the Bush administration's first choice to be the tsar; the honor in that category went to Gates, who declined the offer.

A greater myth was that the intelligence tsar exercises control over the intelligence community. In fact, the Pentagon has veto power over the director of national intelligence with respect to personnel and budgetary authority. Meanwhile, the director of national intelligence has built a bloated bureaucracy with no fewer than 19 assistant deputy directors with a management staff coming largely from the CIA and the State Department, thus weakening two key institutions. Important positions and functions are in the hands of contractors with extravagant salaries and insufficient accountability.

President George W. Bush designed the position of director of national intelligence to enhance the power of the Pentagon and weaken the civilian leadership at CIA. He was cynical, however, with regard to those he selected to be the intelligence tsar. In 2007, when Bush replaced his secretary of defense and the top three military commanders—the military chain of command that opposed the surge of forces in Iraq—he offered General John Abizaid the face-saving offer of becoming the intelligence tsar. Abizaid chose to retire. The current director of national intelligence, former senator Dan Coats, has no background in intelligence.

History does repeat itself. When the White House encountered some resistance from the CIA in 2002 against providing the worst of the false intelligence in the run-up to the invasion of Iraq, Cheney and Rumsfeld created a "super-secret intelligence analysis operation at the Pentagon, totally separate and unknown to the members of the Intelligence Community."[34] They even called the office Team B, which—like the earlier Team B in 1976—reported directly to Cheney and Rumsfeld. The new Team B opened initially with just two analysts, both neoconservatives, David Wurmser and Michael Maloof, who reported to Undersecretary of Defense Douglas Feith, a well-known critic of the CIA's analysis. By late summer 2002, with the Bush administration moving toward a drop-dead decision to go to war, Team B was renamed the Office of Special Plans, absorbed the staff of the

Pentagon's Iraq desk, and grew to 18 staffers. Its sole purpose was to provide intelligence to the White House that made the case for war, using whatever information it could, including intelligence that the CIA did not consider credible.

Team B in 1976 and Team B in 2002 shared another aspect: both were wrong. In 1976, at the very time when Soviet leaders were signaling an interest in détente with the United States and more arms control, Professor Pipes's team falsely concluded that the Soviet Union rejected nuclear parity, was bent on fighting and winning a nuclear war, and was radically increasing its military spending. Team B also applied worst-case thinking to predict a series of Soviet weapons developments that never took place, including directed-energy weapons, mobile anti-missile systems, and anti-satellite capabilities. In 2002–2003, the Pentagon's Team B information was wrong on every aspect of Iraq's (non-existent) weapons of mass destruction; Saddam Hussein's (non-existent) relationship with al Qaeda and Osama bin Laden; and Iraq's (non--existent) connection to 9/11.

The false intelligence created by the White House, the Pentagon, and the CIA in 2002 regarding Iraq harmed the credibility of the United States and the CIA, and led to the incorrect challenge of intelligence on Syria's use of chemical weapons 10 years later against civilians. Thousands of American soldiers have met their death, and tens of thousands have been maimed, dismembered, and seriously wounded as a direct result of the deliberate falsification of intelligence about Saddam Hussein's regime in Iraq. The U.S. invasion of Iraq was a devastating distraction from military operations against al Qaeda, and created the conditions for regional destabilization that fueled the territorial advances of both al Qaeda and its much larger, better-funded, and more heavily armed rival, the Islamic State—ISIS.

Like Cheney and Rumsfeld in 1976 and 2003, Casey and Gates in the 1980s were dedicated to pushing the CIA's analysis far to the right to support Reagan's efforts to increase defense

spending and the use of covert action against an exaggerated Soviet threat. Casey and Gates used a National Intelligence Estimate
on international terrorism in 1981 and an intelligence assessment
on the so-called Papal Plot in 1985 to pursue their own political agendas. Like Cheney and Rumsfeld, Casey and Gates were
a perfect bureaucratic pair: Casey a mean-spirited and bullying
commander; Gates a perfect bureaucratic filter for Casey's views.

Over the past seven decades, the CIA has registered one covert
nightmare after another with disastrous consequences for U.S. interests. And to make matters worse, too much of the clandestine
collection of intelligence is designed to support covert action and
other U.S. policies, which contributes to analytical failures.

The CIA has encouraged the myth of successfully recruiting
foreign assets. In fact, the CIA's Directorate of Operations relies
on walk-ins and rarely recruits major espionage assets. The most
successful walk-ins, such as Colonel Oleg Penkovsky, often have
great difficulty in getting CIA operatives to accept them. Vasili
Mitrokhin, a KGB archivist who brought thousands of pages of
valuable notes to the West, volunteered twice to the CIA, was
turned away, and then went to the British, who recognized the
gold mine that he carried with him. During my years at the CIA,
most of the agents recruited from Cuba and East Germany were
double agents reporting to their host governments.

I left the CIA in 1986 to protest political corruption, and
joined the National War College as a professor of international
security. My first four years were part of a rotational assignment,
but in 1990 I became a part of the college faculty as a member of
the Department of Defense. My colleagues from the Agency who
predicted in 1986 that I was being thrown into the briar patch
were right. I had no desire to return to the CIA and no desire to
leave the National War College. The students were professional
military officers and senior foreign officers, providing an excellent teaching opportunity. Some of them were curious as to why I
would leave the Senior Intelligence Service to take on a position

at lower pay and prestige. It was an easy decision. The National War College is one of the best-kept secrets in Washington, and the seminar experience is challenging and dynamic. I remained there for 18 years and enjoyed virtually every aspect of it. Leaving the CIA was easy because it had abandoned the intelligence role that President Truman envisaged in 1947. The CIA had violated my political and social contract, becoming a political extension of whatever president was in power and a powerful instrument used to implement his agenda. President Truman would have been aghast.

FOUR

LANDING IN THE BRIAR PATCH

"The winner of the Cold War would inevitably face the imperial problem of using power in global terms but from one particular center of authority, so preponderant and unchallenged that its world rule would almost certainly violate basic standards of justice."

—Reinhold Niebuhr

"America is no mere international citizen. It is the dominant power in the world, more dominant than any since Rome. Accordingly, America is in a position to re-shape norms, alter expectations and create new realities. How? By unapologetic and implacable demonstrations of will."

—Charles Krauthammer

Leaving the CIA was the right thing to do. I had temporarily left the Agency before, to recharge my batteries and examine the possibility of a career elsewhere, and the experiences were always gratifying. From 1972 to 1973, I was visiting professor of government at the University of Connecticut in Storrs. This was a period of heavy student dissent against U.S. military violence in Vietnam, and student protesters were interrupting classes in history and political science. Many faculty members in the department were strongly opposed to the idea of a CIA analyst holding a teaching position, even on a one-year basis. Fortunately, the chairman of the department, Professor Louis Gerson, was a genuine advocate of academic freedom and believed that a different perspective for one year would not be a threat to the academy. Professor Gerson also happened to be a good friend of my dissertation advisor, Professor Robert Ferrell. I had just completed my PhD dissertation at Indiana University, and Ferrell's recommendation went a long way.

At the end of the academic year, however, it was time to leave. The teaching was thoroughly enjoyable at an institution with many students who were the first members of their families to attend college. But I missed the immediacy of intelligence work, which was ample incentive to return. Moreover, toward the end of the academic year, the CIA connection to Watergate in the form of an operative, Howard Hunt, was making big headlines, and the so-called progressives on the faculty renewed their objections to my place at the college. Decades later, in 2000, I was invited back to Storrs to give the tenth annual Louis Gerson Foreign Policy Lecture, which is designed to promote careers in Washington that span both policymaking and scholarly pursuits in the field of international relations. I felt vindicated.

I was back at the CIA for only a year when the new director of the Department of State's Bureau of Intelligence and Research, William Hyland, invited me to join the Bureau. Hyland had been a senior member of the CIA's Office of National Estimates before joining Henry Kissinger's staff at the National Security Council. When Kissinger became secretary of state in addition to being national security advisor, he took Hyland with him to run the intelligence bureau. Hyland knew me as a fast pen, at a time when the Bureau suffered because its extremely bright and experienced individuals were slow to put pen to paper. I was grateful for the invitation. Although I knew it sent the wrong signal to the CIA to follow one sabbatical with another, that kind of thinking was never a part of my professional DNA.

The State Department afforded opportunities that the CIA could not provide. During the Cold War, the CIA had several hundred political, military, and economic analysts working on the Soviet Union; the Bureau had less than half that number working on all global issues and only a dozen or so working the Soviet problem. As a result, CIA analysts worked on narrow problems and rarely got an opportunity to look at the bigger strategic picture. The State Department's Bureau of Intelligence and Research specialists had a much bigger piece of the Soviet mosaic to analyze, and typically had a more sophisticated view of most intelligence issues. The Bureau also had the advantage of trying to explain issues for key policymakers and foreign service officers. The CIA, on the other hand, had no constituency in its own building and tried to serve too many clients throughout the policy community and even on Capitol Hill. This often led to research projects and analysis that were unfocused and not particularly relevant.

The immediate audience at the Bureau of Intelligence and Research consisted of high-level policymakers and, unlike at the CIA, there was immediate feedback from the policymakers and their ambitious staffs. The difficulty of generating feedback at the CIA—or most other intelligence organizations, for that matter—is perennial, and points to one of the serious weaknesses of the intelligence community as a support mechanism for policy. With a little energy and imagination at the State Department, however, it was possible to anticipate the issues that were uppermost in the minds of policymakers, and even gain access to memoranda of conversations between State Department officials and their foreign counterparts that were essential to the craft of intelligence.

The experience at the Bureau of Intelligence and Research forced me to change my view that intelligence analysis needed to come from a department or agency outside the policy process in order to be truly objective. Although the Bureau was embedded in the Department of State, I never doubted the objectivity of its analysis. I received a great deal of pressure from overzealous staffers of high-level State Department officials, but it never got in the way of my analysis and I was always supported by my bosses. I made some of them nervous when I challenged the key aide to Ambassador Malcolm Toon on sensitive Soviet-Israeli matters. The aide and Toon were known for their unpredictable tempers, but their complaints to my front office went nowhere.

I was admonished by my front office in 1974, however, when I was too glib with a reporter from Drew Pearson's syndicated column, "Merry-Go-Round." Unlike at the CIA, reporters merely had to sign up to gain access to virtually all parts of the building, at least in the 1970s. Journalists did have to report those State Department officials that they interviewed, and intelligence professionals had to report their contacts with reporters. In the wake of Secretary of State Kissinger's ominous and exaggerated remarks about a Communist takeover in Portugal, I gratuitously noted that "Henry loves to do a nervous jig about these issues, but in the case of Lisbon a communist threat is greatly overstated." Of course, these remarks found their way into the papers, and I found myself admonished by the high command of the Bureau of Intelligence and Research. I learned to be more careful in future contacts.

At the end of my two-year tour at the Bureau in 1976, I was offered the opportunity of a permanent position as an intelligence analyst on Soviet foreign policy. This was a difficult decision at the time, because the Bureau was an interesting and challenging environment. The access to policymakers, including the seventh floor of the State Department building, was enticing, and the State Department itself was certainly a better corporate address than the CIA. But if you are not a foreign service officer in the State Department, you are a second-class citizen.

Before I returned to the CIA in 1976, I had one more blandishment thrown my way—a summer tour at the U.S. embassy in

Moscow, sort of a "Kelly girl" experience as a temporary replacement for a political officer who was on extended home leave. I was given an account on the foreign policy desk with responsibility for all the countries of Asia, including South Asia and East Asia. With the use of the rolodex that came with the "desk," I could call counterparts at various Soviet ministries, including the Foreign Ministry, and Soviet academies and think tanks such as the Institute for the Study of the USA. I also forged an important collegial relationship with Richard Combs, the chief of the Soviet internal section, who was Senator Sam Nunn's legislative assistant when I testified to the Senate Intelligence Committee 15 years later.

Analysts from the CIA rarely get the opportunity to gain access to Soviet policymakers, so the summer tour was an unusual experience. It allowed me to travel to more than half of the 15 Soviet republics. Soviet authorities knew from my SALT tour in 1971–1972 that I was a CIA officer with official cover, so my KGB counterparts kept a close eye on me. Once they realized that I had not taken full advantage of the excellent language teachers that I had at Indiana University's Russian and East European Institute, I believe they became less suspicious. At the same time, my Indiana University ties were professionally important, because I had encounters with former classmates who were foreign service officers and eventually became ambassadors to Russia, Georgia, Estonia, and Azerbaijan. Back at Langley, another former classmate became the CIA's director of operations for the Soviet Union.

The summer tour was a great opportunity to feel confident about my nonconformist perspective regarding the low level of economic and political development within the Soviet Union. I had served a U.S. Army tour in Athens, in the 1950s, and it was obvious to me that the economy and standard of living in the Soviet Union in the 1970s rivaled the destitute Greek economy I witnessed during my military tour in the 1950s. When you got outside the major cities of the Soviet Union, it became evident that living conditions were even more impoverished than those of the Greeks. I was able to return to the CIA in the fall of 1976 confident that economic analysts had underestimated the burden of backward Soviet and East European economies and misunderstood the military burden of trying to compete with the United States. Of course, with very few exceptions, academic and think-tank economists did no better than their CIA counterparts. I'm still convinced that the Soviet Union collapsed like a house of cards simply because it was a house of cards. President Reagan had nothing to do with it.

By 1986, I had completed 20 years with the CIA: 15 wonderful years that included two years at the Bureau of Intelligence and Research; a one-year teaching sabbatical at the University of Connecticut; and two years on a rotational assignment for the SALT talks that involved an important round of talks in Vienna. But this was followed by five miserable years, marked by the right-wing corruption of intelligence by a grizzled veteran of the Office of Strategic Services, Bill Casey, and his obedient deputy, Bob Gates. Casey was a hard driver, a neoconservative who believed his own hard-line ideology; Gates was a windsock, serving his master in order to maintain his steady climb up the bureaucratic ladder.

Gates wanted me out of the CIA's Directorate of Intelligence, presumably out of the CIA, because I fought every one of his ideological points of view and ultimately had the gall to call him out for his lack of integrity. Of all the charges that I leveled against Gates over the years, the accusation regarding his integrity was the one that knocked him off his pins. There was a verbal confrontation in his office in 1985, which was followed by a call to my home in the evening. No yelling and screaming, but raising the issue of integrity clearly angered Bob. He could never handle confrontation, at least at that stage of his life, and I never minded it. In any event, I wouldn't take back the charge, and we never shared another social occasion. This upset my kids, because Bob made some of the best ice cream they had ever tasted.

Even today, there is no doubt in my mind that Gates lacked a moral core. He may now be the president of the Boy Scouts of America and an honorary chancellor at William and Mary College, but his long history of pandering, lying, and conniving harmed the integrity of the CIA and harmed the nation. Once a friend and confidant of Gates, I became that quarrelsome counselor (think Thomas Becket) who had to be removed by the kingly bureaucrat (think Henry II). As for "Who shall rid me of this troublesome priest?" Gates anointed Doug MacEachin for that task, but fortunately I survived to tell my story.

As my boss, Douglas MacEachin had trouble delivering the message from Gates, and he screwed it up every which way. First of all, he told me that the decision was his, but I saw the email from Gates that ordered my removal along with that of two other solid analysts who challenged the Casey line; they were Douglas Garthoff, who understood Gorbachev's interest in détente and arms control, and James Noren, who understood the weakness of the Soviet economy. Second, MacEachin told me that he was moving me from my post as division chief for Soviet–Third World affairs to that of deputy chief of the Office for Strategic and Tactical Issues. I had no problem with this assignment, but there was no such position.

I found out about MacEachin's deceit the hard way. Since I'm something of an extrovert, which isn't typical of CIA analysts, I immediately went to the Office of Strategic and Tactical Issues to introduce myself. I knew and respected the chief of the office, Ben Rutherford, but he wasn't around that afternoon. It was the next day that Mr. Rutherford called me into his office to tell me that MacEachin "simply didn't have the guts to say" that I would not have any managerial responsibilities. I immediately confronted MacEachin, and he lamely shifted gears and said that he wanted me in his front office as a senior analyst who would write on all Soviet matters, both foreign and domestic. I assumed that MacEachin couldn't be lying about a position once again, and immediately began to think that writing on topics of my choosing at times of my choosing was ideal.

By CIA standards, I had been a prolific analyst over the years, so it wasn't long before I was turning out various think pieces on Gorbachev and the opportunity for improving U.S.-Soviet relations; Gorbachev and his retreat from the Third World; Gorbachev and arms control; indeed, any topic concerning Gorbachev that would annoy Casey and Gates. At the same time, I was in the perfect spot in the front office to observe the continued tampering with intelligence ordered by Gates, including Moscow and the Papal Plot; Moscow and Iran; Moscow and Nicaragua; Moscow and developing nations. MacEachin actually treated me as a soulmate on these issues, and we chatted candidly about Casey and Gates and the manner in which they imposed their biases on intelligence. It was two-faced MacEachin's way of having it both ways.

No one walked both sides of the street at the CIA better than MacEachin, and the issue of manipulating intelligence was no exception. Indeed, the issue had an interesting twist. As head of the Soviet affairs office, MacEachin often traveled to Capitol Hill to brief the Senate Intelligence Committee. MacEachin loved occasions that allowed him to perform in front of the echelons of power—any echelon. The Senate Intelligence Committee offered a genuine prize for MacEachin, a modest but frustrated athlete who worked sports metaphors into all of his briefings, because a genuine athlete, a superstar, served on the committee: Senator Bill Bradley (D-NJ), a star basketball forward at Princeton University and an all-star with the New York Knicks. MacEachin was torn; he could deliver the intelligence briefing the way that Gates would have wanted it, but he risked the ire of Senator Bradley, who had contempt for Gates and was fully apprised of the corruption of intelligence that Casey was commanding.

I had some great memories from my 20 years at the CIA, but the deceit of Bill Casey, Bob Gates, and Doug MacEachin made it easy to move on, even though the National War College may have seemed an odd corporate address for my anti-war views. I arrived at the CIA in 1966 as an anti–Vietnam War protester and left the National War College 38 years later as an anti–Iraq War protester. Perfect symmetry, but the two experiences were very different. The CIA and the war college are gated compounds with heavy security, so the atmospheres were superficially similar. The CIA is located in a bucolic setting in the suburbs of northern Virginia, and the college has a majestic waterfront location in Washington, DC, on the Washington channel and the Potomac River. The college was established in 1946 by General Dwight D. Eisenhower as a joint military college, so that the various services could study and learn together and have an introduction to the need for joint military training. The CIA was established a year later by President Truman, to do a better job with military intelligence and threat analysis than the Pentagon could ever hope to do.

The National War College is located on a military base, Fort Leslie J. McNair, in the District of Columbia. General Leslie Mc-Nair was the highest-ranking fatality due to friendly fire in World War II. The National War College is its crowning architectural jewel. McNair died in Normandy in 1944 while observing troop movements in the breakout from St. Lô. There are those who believe that the death of McNair along with 100 soldiers was due to the lack of joint understanding on the part of the forces involved.[1] World War II also exposed the lack of a functioning relationship between the War Department and the State Department, which the war college was designed to correct.

On the base, there are a row of Georgian houses along the Potomac River, a nine-hole golf course that pundits love to excoriate, and excellent tennis courts that were placed on the very location where the conspirators against President Abraham Lincoln were hanged. The regimen at the college could not have been more relaxed. There were no classes scheduled for a two-hour period around noon to allow time for exercise. I pitched for the softball team, played shooting guard for the basketball team, and returned to a sport that I indulged in high school, running. I did all of these things at the CIA as well, but on my own time.

The run along the waterfront was spectacular. In leaving the isolated CIA headquarters building in the Virginia suburbs and landing at a national landmark building in the District of Columbia, built during the administration of our most fascinating president, Theodore Roosevelt, I thought I had died and gone to heaven. The National War College itself sits on a spit of land southwest of the Capitol in Washington. As you approach National Airport from the air, you can see the war college, a National Landmark building, and I've never returned to National Airport without twisting and turning to glimpse the magnificent building.

The college was staffed initially at a very senior level with a vice admiral as the commandant, Harry W. Hill, who became superintendent of the Naval Academy, and deputy commandants from the Army and Air Force, who were also general officers and eventually became, respectively, the supreme allied commander of NATO force and commander of U.S. air forces in Europe. George F. Kennan arrived at the college in September 1946 as a deputy commander, and it was at the college that he penned his famous "Mr. X" article outlining the U.S. strategy of containment. The civilian faculty in those days was very distinguished, including Professors Hardy Dillard of the University of Virginia and Sherman Kent and Bernard Brodie of Yale University. Kent was an expert in strategic intelligence and became the director of the CIA's Board of National Estimates in the 1960s.

The National War College was the military's senior college for the study of national security policy, both political and military, and it offered guest lecturers from the government and the academic community. The students were mainly from the military at the rank of lieutenant colonel and colonel, and there were 20 or so foreign service officers. There were also a dozen officers from various foreign countries, some at the level of brigadier general; as a rule, the foreign officers were exceptional and more sophisticated than their U.S. counterparts. Any government agency that had anything to do with national security had an opportunity to send one or two students for an academic year that led to a master's degree in national security policy.

Since I was at the college to teach courses in Soviet domestic and foreign policy, it was a wonderful opportunity to lecture on all those ideas that Casey and Gates were censoring from CIA publications. My views about Mikhail Gorbachev, Soviet political reform, and Soviet-American détente were met with a great deal of skepticism initially, but by 1990 there was a general appreciation for my so-called contrarian views. Again, I never considered myself a contrarian in this respect, because I strongly believed that my thoughts would eventually represent conventional wisdom.

My students were clearly the *crème de la crème* of the military, including several colonels who went on to become chairmen and deputy chairmen of the Joint Chiefs of Staff. A recent chairman of the JCS, General Martin Dempsey, was a student, and so was Admiral James Stavridis, who became supreme allied commander of the North Atlantic Treaty Organization and is the dean of the Fletcher School of Law and Diplomacy at Tufts University. Both Dempsey and Stavridis were modest performers in a seminar setting, but those who stick their necks out in the military limit their career paths. I'm reminded of the old Russian saying "It is the tallest shoot of grain that is the first to get cut down by the wind."

One of my best students was Colonel Montgomery Meigs, who eventually became General Meigs, the commander of the U.S. Army in Europe. Meigs was the great-great-grandson of the legendary General Montgomery Meigs, who was President Lincoln's quartermaster general for the Union, built the bridge in Cabin John, Maryland, that I used in commuting between home in the Maryland suburbs and the CIA, and established Arlington National Cemetery. My student Monty referred to himself modestly as an "armor guy," but he had a PhD in history and taught at West Point. The best and brightest of our military do not constitute a large group, but it is a very talented group. I considered it a great opportunity to conduct seminars for them and their colleagues.

General Dempsey's statements as chairman of the Joint Chiefs suggest, however, that he paid little attention to my observations in seminar or simply kept his disagreements to himself. In 2012, he stated, "We are living in the most dangerous time in my lifetime, right now."[2] A year later, he was even more assertive, stating that the "world is more dangerous than it has ever been." Of course, this view is endemic to today's military. A veteran of combat such as Senator John McCain, who should certainly know better, agrees, believing the world is "a more dangerous place than I have seen."

There was an important lesson to be learned from leading seminars for senior military officers, and that is their recognition of the restraints and constraints on the use of military power. When I think of the fool's errands that this country has pursued in the last 50 years, it is obvious that we have encountered nothing but defeat or stalemate with the exception of Desert Storm in 1991. In all of the major setbacks, it was the professional military that had the best case for not resorting to the use of force. This was true for Vietnam in the 1960s and 1970s as well as Iraq and Afghanistan over the past 15 years. These were civilian wars endorsed and orchestrated by David Halberstam's "best and brightest," those senior civilians with Ivy League and New England pedigrees, who led Presidents John F. Kennedy and Lyndon B. Johnson down the path of militarism in Southeast Asia. Unfortunately, the senior members of our military lacked the political courage to express their disagreements over the use of force, and this was the "dereliction of duty" that a former U.S. Army colonel, H.R. McMaster, wrote about in the 1980s.[3] I made his book required reading for my seminars.

As the Soviet specialist on the faculty, I led the annual student trip to the USSR. I made about a dozen of these trips between 1986 and 2004, and this offered an excellent opportunity to gauge the decline of the Soviet Union between 1986 and 1989, the brief burst of optimism between 1989 and 1991, the overthrow of Gorbachev in 1991, and the steady decline under President Boris Yeltsin in the 1990s. I constantly battled with the college bureaucrats who wanted military-to-military contacts to dominate the trip, because I felt the Soviets and the Russians would not allow us to learn anything of a sensitive military nature, and it was the civilian institutions that offered the best opportunity to gain new perspectives. I did make sure, however, that we met with Soviet veterans from World War II, and it was particularly gratifying to see the respect and the admiration between the soldiers of the two countries. Those meetings in the late 1980s and early 1990s fed my optimism about the future state of Russian-American relations, but the current Cold War environment has ended that. President Obama's legacy will including his mishandling of the Russian problem.

The military students knew that the use of military power should always be the last resort, but I also tried to inculcate a lesson from French foreign minister Talleyrand that "nations ought to do one another in peace the most good, in war—the least possible evil."[4] The career military seems to understand that lesson, but the past decade of permanent war in Iraq and Afghanistan, which has brought no strategic advantage to the United States, indicates that the lesson has been lost. It is not possible to understand the current turmoil in the Middle East and the Persian Gulf without recognizing the illegal and immoral invasion of Iraq in 2003 and the expansion of the war in Afghanistan. President Eisenhower understood the limits of military coercion in the pursuit of political objectives, but his civilian successors in the White House have failed to apply this lesson to their strategic planning. As Eisenhower said in 1961, "God help the United States if the people who eventually occupy my chair in the White House do not know how to talk or deal with the military." Very few of his successors have understood this issue.

The National War College offered an unusual degree of academic freedom for a military college. I wrote several books there and dozens of articles and op-eds that were critical of the White House and the Congress; the CIA and NSA; national missile defense and the use of force; and so on. With the exception of one president of National Defense University, General Michael Dunn, who objected to my severe criticism of the Bush administration's misapplication of force in Iraq in 2003, there was no major attempt to censor my writings.

Similarly, from the National War College there was no open criticism or opposition to my testifying to the Senate Intelligence Committee against the nomination of Bob Gates in 1991 except from its commandant in the early 1990s, Major General Gerald Stadler. My contract renewal in the wake of my testimony offered an unusual two-year renewal instead of the customary three-year contract. A small price to pay. I don't believe that there are many governments that would have permitted their employees to throw themselves in front of their national security machine and oppose a nomination made by a head of state without completely squashing them.

The CIA and the National War College were very different bureaucratic entities in the national security arena, but they did share a common origin as a response to the early stirrings of the Cold War and the Soviet strategic challenge to the United States. The CIA was created in 1947 following a two-year bureaucratic battle that found the Pentagon and the FBI fighting the idea of a civilian intelligence agency as a serious rival in the fields of strategic intelligence and counterintelligence. President Truman knew what he wanted; he dissolved the Office of Strategic Services in 1945 after the war and created the Central Intelligence Group as a civilian entity the following year. The new Central Intelligence

Group was not permitted to conduct covert operations; Truman wanted an intelligence agency that would be a "center for keeping the President informed on what was going on in the world."[5] When the CIA was created by the National Security Act in 1947, along with the National Security Council, the Department of Defense, and the U.S. Air Force, Truman emphasized that he didn't want the CIA to "initiate policy or to act as a spy organization. That was never the intention when it was organized." It is easy to fathom why, years later, not long before he died, Truman said, "If I knew then what I know now, then I wouldn't have created the CIA."[6]

The CIA was designed to prevent another surprise attack such as Pearl Harbor in 1941, to deal with the Soviet threat in the wake of World War II, and to challenge the worst-case assessments of the Pentagon. The sinister role of Joseph Stalin and the unpredictability of the Soviet Union played major roles in justifying an intelligence agency that became the key civilian component in a large, and eventually bloated, intelligence community. Pearl Harbor was clearly the catalyst that overwhelmed the opposition to a permanent intelligence organization in peacetime. The 9/11 attacks, however, opened the door to the misuse of intelligence organizations, allowing the National Security Agency to exceed its constitutional mandates in violating the privacy of U.S. citizens.

The National War College was created in 1946 to provide some structure to the study of international relations for senior military and foreign service officers. The war college is the only military institution devoted to the study of strategy, and remains the leading inter-service and interagency institution for professional military education. It has received great support over the years from senior general officers, which was true from the very beginning when Generals Eisenhower, George Marshall, and Henry "Hap" Arnold wanted an institution to promote better relations between military and civilian departments of government and among the military services themselves.

In many ways, the CIA as an intelligence organization and the National War College as an educational organization were two sides of the same coin. In both places, I was obligated to lay out the evidence and point to possible cause-and-effect patterns; structure assumptions about what is known and unknown; and bring my expertise to bear on threats and opportunities for U.S. policy, without any attempt to advocate policy. Evidence was far more important than opinion, although it was important for military students to understand the importance of informed opinion, which they would be called on to provide as they moved through the ranks. Explanation was far more important than prediction, although once again intelligence analysts and teaching professors were often asked to provide premonitory intelligence.

Like any opportunity in the field of regional studies and international relations, the faculty position at the National War College provided me with opportunities to lecture and to publish. Just as the CIA offered opportunities to serve as an intelligence advisor to the strategic arms control delegation, and the State Department offered me the opportunity to go to the U.S. embassy in Moscow as a political officer, the college opened doors to the academic and think-tank communities. In 1990s, I became a senior fellow at both the Center for International Policy in Washington and the Institute for International Affairs in Moscow. A rather unusual joint appointment for a former CIA analyst, who was exploiting one of the new benefits of globalization.

General Eisenhower lobbied for the National War College as a joint service educational institution; he had high-level support from General George Marshall, Secretary of the Navy James Forrestal, and Admirals Ernest King and Harry Hill. They wanted a military college that would promote understanding between the various services of the armed forces as well as between the military and the civilian agencies. The fact that George F. Kennan, a career foreign service officer and the father of containment, was selected as the first deputy commandant for Foreign Affairs pointed to the importance of the institution for the Department of State. Kennan's seminal article, "The Sources of Soviet Conduct," the so-called "Mr. X" article, was actually drafted in his office at the war college. The article focused on policies and actions short of war to deal with the Soviet problem, an approach that was debated throughout the Cold War. Upon arrival in the summer of 1986 the very first thing that I asked to do was to sit at his desk for a few moments. If that sounds odd to some, I can assure you that I was neither the first nor the last to do so.

There has been a military installation on these grounds since the earliest days of the nation, and an authoritative history of the fort and the land notes that Captain John Smith passed by this location in 1608.[7] The building itself was completed in 1907, and formally dedicated by Secretary of War Elihu Root as the Army War College. President Theodore Roosevelt attended the laying of the cornerstone in 1903, using the same tools used by George Washington to lay the cornerstone of the U.S. Capitol on September 18, 1793. The architectural firm of McKim, Mead, and White designed and built the building, and the chief architects were Stanford White and Charles McKim. The rotunda of the building was magnificent, and I felt a certain satisfaction each and every time I arrived to start the day.

On various occasions, I escorted foreign ambassadors, U.S. journalists, and assorted dignitaries through the rotunda on the way to the auditorium for their lectures, and there were few visitors who failed to note the majesty of the place. No one appeared more overwhelmed than the Soviet ambassadors whom I sponsored for talks at the college. The only negative response I ever received in the rotunda was when I had to tell former secretary of state Larry Eagleburger that he couldn't smoke in the building.

Military parochialism is probably one of the reasons why the college never took root as a rigorous and authoritative educational institution. Although the first semester of the college in 1946 began with a distinguished civilian faculty headed by George Kennan, all of the civilians returned to their Ivy League campuses, or in Kennan's case to the State Department, before the second semester. It was not until 1990, when the college used Title-10 legislation to hire civilian faculty, that the Pentagon got serious about creating a quasi-permanent faculty instead of relying on civilians on detail from other government agencies. Without permanent civilian faculty, the National War College was little more than a speaker's bureau that relied on ad hoc lecturers from the academic and government worlds.

I had been one of the faculty members detailed from 1986 to 1990, and I became the first civilian hired under the Title-10 legislation. The transition was not an easy or even friendly one, however, because the commandant, Major General Stadler, who the following year tried to block my testimony at the confirmation hearings for Robert Gates, was not eager to hire me. "Soviet experts are a dime a dozen these days," Stadler told the dean of faculty, Colonel Roy Stafford, "so why should we hire Goodman?" Well, Stadler had a point, because the Soviet Union was collapsing like a house of cards, but he was probably more concerned about my outspoken views on radio and television as well as my many adversarial writings. I'm indebted to Colonel Stafford, who argued my case successfully.

Not only was I outspoken in my views in the seminar room and in public media, but I made a point of inviting similarly outspoken lecturers to the college's study of geopolitical developments, which I directed for several years. I believed that my job was to enhance the critical inquiry skills of these senior officers, and that the best way to do that was to challenge their conventional wisdom as well as the conventional wisdom of their superior officers. I was proud of the fact that I had established outstanding contacts inside the government as well as outside the government in academe and in the Fourth Estate. I invited former CIA directors such as Bill Colby and Stansfield Turner, who had not received rave reviews in the media, in part due to the criticism of senior operatives who had access to key journalists. I even invited Oleg Kalugin, a former KGB official responsible for operations against the United States, and Victor Israelian, a former Soviet deputy foreign minister. The military students had never encountered such personalities; they loved it.

Colby was important to me because he had informed the Senate Congressional Committee about the secret compilation of CIA violations of its charter, including a massive illegal operation against American dissidents masterminded by James Angleton's counterintelligence staff. In addition to forcing Angleton to retire, which earned Colby the life-long enmity of Richard Helms and other veterans of the Directorate of Operations, Colby briefed Seymour Hersh, an investigative reporter for the *New York Times*, for a story that Hersh was already preparing about CIA transgressions. When Colby realized that Hersh knew more about the illegalities than the CIA director, Colby alerted the White House. As a result, the Senate, the House, and even the White House began their own investigations, leading to cuts in the CIA budget, reduced operational activities, and the creation of two congressional oversight committees. Colby did the right thing, but it cost him his job.

Stansfield Turner had great credibility with the students, having served as a rear admiral in the U.S. Navy with tours as the commander of the U.S. Second Fleet and president of the Naval War College. Turner suffered as a CIA director because the leading members of the Operations Directorate opposed him from the start, and their enmity increased when Turner moved against the deputy director of operations, Ted Shackley, who had close ties to Edwin Wilson, a former CIA officer and an arms dealer with ties to Libyan dictator Muammar Qaddafi and some of the notorious players in the Iran-Contra fiasco. The operatives had good connections with the press, and the mainstream media cooperated in finding fault with Turner. Intelligence analysts at the time should have played their own game of leaking to the press, because, by and large, Turner was popular at the Agency for his integrity and his support for analysts.

I wanted the students at the National War College to understand that the moral courage of government officials was just as important as the physical courage of war fighters. So I introduced them to Chester Crocker, an assistant secretary of state for Africa who took on CIA director Casey over using diplomacy to stabilize the geopolitical situation in southern Africa. Don Oberdorfer and Robert Kaiser of the *Washington Post* and David Shipler of the *New York Times* made strong impressions on the class, which was important because the professional military tended to be suspicious and outright hostile to the working press.

It wasn't until July 2016 that the Pentagon revised its manual on international laws of war, which had portrayed journalism as close to spying and authorized the targeting of reporters who relayed information that would be useful in combat.[8] The new Law of War manual no longer compares journalists to spies and no longer encourages censorship of their work. I don't believe the Pentagon ever understood the danger of encouraging the notion that journalists were a potential threat. Too many so-called military warriors had greater fear of American journalists than of their own Russian counterparts.

During my stay at the college, one of the few journalists who was not afraid to criticize the military, Sam Donaldson, annually lectured to the classes and always refused the modest honorarium of $250. I only mention that because such greedy luminaries as Henry Kissinger and Zbigniew Brzezinski wanted tens of thousands of dollars to speak to the military classes. Many military students in the class always looked forward to the Donaldson lecture because they thought they could beat him in a game of wits. They never laid a glove on him.

In order to corroborate my own views on the weakness of the Soviet Union, which career military men and women found difficult to comprehend, I brought in authoritative members of the intelligence and policy communities who were known for their unconventional thinking. Murray Feshbach from the Department of Commerce, who was the first Sovietologist to make me aware of the existential weakness of the Soviet Union, overwhelmed the class with his factual understanding of the demographic problems of the Kremlin. Paul Goble of the Department of State introduced the class to the nationality problems of the Soviet Union. Swedish economist Anders Aslund spoke about the weakness of the Soviet economy, and Soviet theoretician Lilia Shevtsova provided an introduction to Soviet political backwardness. Robert Blackwell, a CIA colleague, gave the students an excellent understanding of the complexity of the Soviet political system. I gave a series of lectures on weaknesses of the Soviet military, which many of the students found perplexing.

Because of the presentations of the Sovietologists, including my own, the students were prepared for the trip to the Soviet Union that I orchestrated. Toward the end of the academic year, the entire class of approximately 170 students divides into groups of about 15 to 20 and travels the world over. I was assigned to lead the Soviet trip most years, which allowed for the opportunity to gauge Moscow's political and economic progress or lack thereof. Occasionally, I would get to lead a different but related trip, and was able to go to Western and Eastern Europe.

Every year the Congress tried to cut the funding for these regional trips, which they considered to be boondoggles. Boondoggles are those trips that congress members take that serve no obvious purpose. But getting career military officers overseas to have face-to-face discussions with their foreign counterparts and gain some ground truth on areas that are heavily politicized in official propaganda and news accounts is essential. The trips afford military officers a close look at the non-military aspects of an adversary such as the Soviets as well as creating military-to-military contacts.

As long as such important alumni as Generals Colin Powell, James Jones, Eric Shinseki, and Tony Zinni defend these trips, however, the Congress will come out on the short end. These trips provide tremendous insight to military officers who rarely get to travel in this fashion, offering new ways to think about old problems. We also had Capitol Hill alumni on our faculty who made important behind-the-scenes efforts to save the war college budget on several occasions.

At the CIA, clandestine operatives had been notably unhelpful in assisting the overseas orientation trips of intelligence analysts, who rarely got the opportunity to travel. But at the National War College, our overseas orientation trip took full advantage of embassy officers and military attachés, who arranged talks and briefings at foreign military and civilian installations. Graduates of the college serving overseas were particularly helpful as loyal alumni.

I arranged for visits to sites important for their military history, such as Stalingrad, Borodino, and Poltava, but the civilian stops offered a close-up view of the backward Soviet economy, which manufactured very little that the world would buy. The class was particularly bemused when I scheduled an annual visit to meet with the Moscow-based vice president of McDonalds, but we probably learned as much about Soviet culture and society on that occasion as on any other.

The Reagan administration and its supporters took a great deal of credit for fostering the collapse of the Soviet Union, but these trips indicated that the United States had very little to do with it. The Soviet Union collapsed under its own dead weight. Various classes objected to my evening visits to an undesignated factory, but their mood changed rapidly when the factory turned out to be a beer plant with a tasting room. Not a big deal in Moscow, but a huge deal in Prague. There was also grumbling over the night of culture in Leningrad to see one of the leading ballet companies of the Soviet Union. I got a change in mood once again when I told them there was a nude scene in the third act, but there was great disgruntlement at the final curtain when the students realized I was merely pulling their legs.

With the Cold War seemingly over, I joined with other civilian members of the faculty to sponsor travel to countries or former Soviet republics that had never been visited previously, such as Belarus, Bulgaria, Croatia, and Slovenia. Our minders at the Pentagon seriously questioned the introduction of a trip that highlighted international organizations, but it's essential for military officers to visit UN organizations in New York and Vienna as well as the International Red Cross and the World Health Organization. Military personnel are increasingly playing an active role with these organizations, and the contacts formed in regional studies travel are invaluable. In the 1990s, we were less successful in getting the college to emphasize study and travel in likely places for an insurgency, but we were soon vindicated as the professional military took on a greater counterinsurgency mission.

On every trip to the Soviet Union, there would be one or two officers who would become extremely depressed at what they saw and learned from a trip to the "other superpower." They had been force fed a great deal of propaganda about the Kremlin in their careers. When they got close to the decrepit Soviet infrastructure and economy in the 1980s, they couldn't believe they were actually seeing the rival superpower.

As a result, some of these officers were actually prepared for the collapse of the Soviet Union in 1991. In fact, the chairman of the Joint Chiefs of Staff at the time, General Powell, who was a big supporter of the National War College, was out in front of his policy and intelligence counterparts in anticipating the Soviet decline. Long before any department in the government started to prepare for such a demise, Powell was working on alternative budgeting and force strategies for a global arena without a Soviet threat. No planner at the CIA had such foresight.

Powell, moreover, was an important ally in my struggle to charge the CIA with a major intelligence failure for its inability to track the Soviet decline. Powell was particularly critical, charging that CIA analysts could not "anticipate events much better than a layman watching television." Former CIA director Turner was another who could not believe the "enormity of the failure to forecast the magnitude of the Soviet crisis."[9] He concluded that the CIA's "corporate view missed by a mile." CIA director Gates had not only been wrong about the Soviet Union, but had made sure that the entire CIA was wrong as well.

The most interesting guest lecturer I was able to arrange turned out to be the Soviet ambassador, who had never before been invited to speak to the war college class. The Pentagon fought me tooth and nail on this, particularly civilian neoconservatives such as Richard Perle, an undersecretary of defense for policy and a Soviet baiter of long standing. Perle finally got the college to agree that the ambassador could come to the college only if his U.S. counterpart, Ambassador Jack Matlock, could speak to a comparable Soviet military institution. Moscow agreed, sort of. The Soviet ambassador spoke to the National War College; my friend Matlock was invited to speak to the Malinovsky Tank Academy. The Kremlin had a keen sense of humor; the Pentagon's Perle didn't.

The war college is rightfully proud of its graduates who have gone on to become chairmen of the Joint Chiefs of Staff, service chiefs, combatant commanders, ambassadors, and sub-cabinet officials. The seminar room allows for discussion of the most contentious policy issues, and often there were students who had participated in one crisis or another. But the college has failed to train national security professionals who understand grand strategy and has not adapted to the demands of a new strategic era. The training of such professionals should be the major objective of the National War College.

Nevertheless, my 18 years at the war college were deeply rewarding. No one could say that I was preaching to the choir this time. I realized that my campaign against the corruption, falsification, and politicization of intelligence, which I touched on at the college, was a small part of a larger campaign against militarism and secrecy. And what could be more relevant than the opportunity to conduct seminars for military officers whose careers could be affected by the discussions at the college? I used my academic background in diplomatic history to cite chapter and verse examples of the importance of negotiated solutions to geopolitical conflict. And I used my intelligence background to document the risks of ignoring the moral component in dealing with authoritarian leaders or, even worse, resorting to political assassination. Finally, I had a group of military and civilian colleagues on the faculty who had their own expertise on important geopolitical and military matters and were extremely willing to share their knowledge.

I wanted my military students to understand the danger of two insidious notions held dear by U.S. decision makers, both military and civilian, that have created serious problems for American interests at home and abroad. The first insidious notion is that of our so-called superpower status, which is belied by our loss of wars in Vietnam, Iraq, and Afghanistan. The second is the belief that the United States "won" the Cold War, thereby sanctifying our supposed good intentions that led us into huge losses of blood and treasure in these fool's errands. The unwise deployment of our massive military power in the Middle East and the Persian Gulf is directly responsible for the tension and turmoil that dominates that region and is spreading violence to Europe. There are many activists and insurgents who claim that U.S. military power, secret prisons, and torture and abuse are directly responsible for the use of terror against civilian targets. The United States contributed heavily to the current confrontation in Ukraine, particularly with the strategically flawed notion of an expanded NATO. I hope that today's National War College students are getting some understanding of U.S. blunders in Central and East Europe.

Retirement was at my own initiative, because I decided to move to a new corporate address, the Center for International Policy in Washington, to pursue my writings against the Iraq War, the CIA, and the national security policies of the Bush administration. It was also an opportunity to join forces with one of my heroes and mentors, Ambassador Robert White, who was fired by Secretary of State Alexander Haig in 1981 for refusing to cover up the killings of four American churchwomen in El Salvador. Ambassador White was kicked out of the Foreign Service as a reward for his ethics and integrity.

My last year of teaching was the first year of the war, thus my anti-war views were conflicting with the emotional reaction of military students who were fearful for their colleagues in the Iraqi war zone and, in a few cases, even mourning the loss of fellow soldiers. There was never any push-back from my numerous media appearances and editorial writings about the strategic stupidity and cupidity of the decision-making for the use of force. I was simply uncomfortable with expressing my anti-war views in seminars where there were soldiers who had just returned from Iraq and carried a great deal of psychological baggage. It was time to go.

I regretted the serious cultural problems in the professional military that needed to be addressed. The all-volunteer military has drifted too far from the norms of American society and is inordinately right-wing politically. The officer corps is essentially "Republican" in its politics, and the military culture includes the fundamental view that its moral code is superior to civilian norms. I encountered many senior officers who were critical of the moral health of civilian society, but had no understanding of the military's stubborn opposition over the years to healthy cultural change. This opposition included the military's resistance over the years to the service of African Americans, women, and homosexuals in their ranks.

In the 1990s, during the Clinton presidency, there was a deep and abiding military animosity toward the president of the

United States. The hostility the military had for President Bill Clinton; his first secretary of defense, Les Aspin; and his national security team, which was considered too soft, was palpable in the comments and locker room banter of many senior officers. Military officers are known for their jocularity, but their humor also reflected their conservative, anti-progressive views, which dominates the officer ranks.

President Clinton was a particular target because he dodged the draft. When I later reminded some that George W. Bush, Dick Cheney, and former secretary of defense William Cohen, my favorite chicken hawks, were draft dodgers, I was met with silence. There was a joke going around the war college following President Clinton's visit in March 1993 to the aircraft carrier USS *Theodore Roosevelt* that had a sailor throwing a beer at the president, but shouting there was no need to worry because it was "draft beer" and the president could dodge it.

The real political firestorm between President Clinton and the Pentagon broke out shortly after his inauguration, when the president suggested in a news conference that he would allow gays to serve openly in the military. When then secretary of defense Aspin tried to explain this view to the Joint Chiefs of Staff, he was treated to an unprecedented 90-minute tirade. The Marine commandant, Carl Mundy, was the most vociferous opponent of allowing gays to serve in the military, terming homosexuality a "moral depravity that could not be tolerated in the ranks."[10]

When the Clinton administration indicated that it would not abandon the struggle to reform the military, several of us went to the commandant of the National War College, Major General John Fryer, to suggest that he address the class on the importance of respecting the political decisions that were being considered. The session in Arnold Auditorium was quite emotional and reached a low point when General Fryer unwisely asked for a show of hands in gauging support for any decision to support the service of homosexuals in the military, and very few hands were raised. The ultimate compromise of "don't ask, don't tell" was a cynical cop-out that was addressed 20 years later when President Obama moved to allow gays to serve openly.

President Clinton simply failed to understand that, by caving in to the Pentagon with "don't ask, don't tell," he was signaling that he could be pushed around by senior general officers. This is exactly what President Eisenhower warned about when he worried that his successors would not know how to deal with the military. In President Clinton's case, his lack of credibility with the Pentagon led the Joint Chiefs of Staff to ignore his call for more aggressive planning to deal with the security challenge in Afghanistan several years before the 9/11 attacks. I was no longer at the National War College in 2009 when President Obama had his own problems with the military. He was clearly rolled by the Pentagon in the decision-making on troop strength in Afghanistan and eventually came to distrust Secretary of Defense Gates and the joint chiefs with the military.

President Obama had to deal with a serious problem of insubordination when the commander of U.S. and NATO forces in Afghanistan, General Stanley McChrystal, and senior staffers made derogatory remarks about senior members of the Obama administration, including Vice President Joe Biden, that found their way into *Rolling Stone* magazine. Fortunately, the president ignored the advice of Secretary of Defense Gates, who made his own derogatory remarks about the vice president in his memoir, and fired the general. If the president had done less, he would have found himself ridiculed by the senior ranks just as President Clinton had been 15 years earlier.

Nevertheless, it is ironic that the Pentagon has become our most important anti-war institution. Our recent wars have been for the most part civilian affairs brought to us by the "best and brightest." The professional military has dragged its heels on virtually all of these conflicts, so I don't hold them responsible when they try to pursue victory on these fool's errands. However, the

Pentagon is responsible for trying to hold onto its huge number of overseas bases and facilities that these confrontations have generated. Former secretary of state Madeleine Albright was wrong to believe that U.S. power was indispensable and therefore sanction U.S. use of force. Our civilian elites are wrong to believe that we must dominate other nations simply because we have the power to do so. And the Pentagon is wrong to look for ways to return to bases that have been abandoned in places such as Greece, the Philippines, Spain, and Taiwan. These institutions only contribute to the perpetual state of war that has existed since the Cold War ended 25 years ago.

Last year's presidential campaign provided another reminder of those members of the military who understand the demands of American democracy far better than some of their critics. A former student of mine, Martin Dempsey, recently chairman of the Joint Chiefs of Staff, lectured his military colleagues who spoke at the Democratic and Republican conventions in their roles as former general officers. In a letter to the editor of the *Washington Post*, Dempsey admonished retired generals John Allen and Mike Flynn, who compromised the apolitical tradition of the military. They were wrong to take part in the conventions, and Hillary Clinton and Donald Trump were wrong to invite them.[11]

FIVE

JOUSTING WITH THE SENATE SELECT COMMITTEE ON INTELLIGENCE

"You can't do vigorous oversight if the leaders of the intelligence community are misleading the American people and Congress in public hearings."
—Senator Ron Wyden (D-OR)

"Suppose you were an idiot, and suppose you were a member of Congress. But I repeat myself."
—Mark Twain

Novels, movies, and television programs have made the world familiar with American spies who confronted the Soviet Union. But in the fall of 1991, I provided the first glimpse of the world of intelligence analysts who joust with each other about the nation's secrets behind closed doors. Internal CIA feuds over the Soviet Union, Iran, Afghanistan, and Latin America were central to the world of intelligence, and I provided a view of the intensity of these struggles as well as the clash of worldviews within the CIA.

I am asked often whether I regret testifying against an old friend, Bob Gates, to the Senate Select Committee on Intelligence. My children have asked if I've changed my opinion of Gates, a close family friend in the 1970s. No, I haven't changed my mind, and any regret would have come from *not* testifying, which would have been an act of political cynicism. By not doing so, I would have conceded that the political corruption at the CIA could not be corrected and that Gates and others responsible for the rot could not be held accountable. I am a different person now than I was in 1991, and I'm sure the same could be said for Robert Gates. But my story covers a 25-year period between 1966 and 1991; it is still accurate.

I regret not doing more and not being more successful. As a former American ambassador, Robert Hunter, said to me after the hearings: "You did good! You didn't do well, but you did good!" When my wife, Lyn Ekedahl, was interviewed for an analytical position at the CIA after the hearings, Gregory Treverton, currently the head of the National Intelligence Council, asked her if she had "changed her mind" about Robert Gates and the corruption of intelligence. Well,we haven't changed our minds.

I remain disappointed and frustrated that the academic communities and national media did a poor job of utilizing dramatic testimony to educate the American public. Twenty-five years later, I sympathize with the congressional staffers who labored for several years to produce the Senate Intelligence Committee's report on CIA torture and abuse, while the American people and their leaders refuse to acknowledge the crimes committed in their names.

Never before had CIA analysts confronted the Senate Select Committee on Intelligence over the fitness of a nominee for the position of CIA chief. In four full days of testimony in the fall of 1991, a secret and then public debate took place over the suitability of Robert M. Gates to serve the United States of America as the director of the Central Intelligence Agency. I'm proud of my role in that debate.

In his memoir, Gates dismissed the confirmation hearings as nothing more than a "bureaucratic food fight" that was "inconclusive in terms of allegations made against me."[1] To Gates, the confirmation hearings were a "donnybrook" and "soap opera," where he had been "sucker-punched by two old friends who had turned against me."[2] To those of us who took great personal and professional risk in throwing themselves in front of a presidential nomination to be director, it was much more important than that.

Although I left the CIA in 1986 because of corruption, I didn't pursue the issue until five years later, when President George H.W. Bush nominated Gates to replace Judge William Webster as CIA director. Bush did so even though Gates had withdrawn his nomination for the job in 1987, when he couldn't convince the Senate Select Committee on Intelligence that his hands were clean with regard to the Iran-Contra scandal. Of course, they weren't, and Bush's hands weren't clean either. Committee Chair David L. Boren (D-OK), Gates's patron on the committee, called Gates at home on February 27, 1987, to report that his colleagues did not believe Gates's disavowals regarding Iran-Contra. The following day, Gates called President Reagan's new chief of staff, Howard Baker, and withdrew his nomination.

In his memoir, Gates states that there were too many un-answered questions at the Senate Intelligence Committee about the "CIA's role and mine" regarding Iran-Contra, and that Boren recommended putting off the hearings several months until the Iran-Contra Committee reported its findings, when the politi-cal atmosphere would be more favorable toward his nomination.[3] There were "unanswered questions" because Gates would not answer the committee's questions about what he knew regard-ing illegal support for the Contras and when he learned about the illegal diversion of funds. At least two senior CIA officials, including his own deputy, told Gates about the criminal transfer of funds to the Contras. I knew both officials, Richard Kerr and Charlie Allen, extremely well.

Gates met with Baker on March 2, 1987, the chief's first day in the office, and told him that he would withdraw "for the good of the country, the president, and the Agency."[4] They were joined by the new national security advisor, Frank Carlucci, and the three of them trooped into the Oval Office to inform President Reagan. Gates never mentioned to the president, the chief of staff, or the national security advisor that Boren had told him confirmation could not be obtained.

Gates used his memoir to attribute his father's death to the contentious confirmation process in 1987. He noted that on the day of Judge Webster's swearing-in ceremony, he learned from his brother that their father had unexpectedly died. According to Gates, the "strain on him of my DCI nomination, hearings, and withdrawal had hastened his death by months, if not more. The shock of his death, on top of all I had been through during the past six months, was too much. I closed the door to my office, sat down at the desk, and wept."[5]

Gates deeply resented the "needling" of critics who noted that he was among the last to recognize the changes that Mikhail Gorbachev introduced to the Soviet Union, particularly its national security policy. Gorbachev opened the door to détente and disarmament with the United States as well as to the liberation of the East European communist states, but Gates's Cold War mentality left him blind to the notion of change. When Senator Bill Bradley (D-NJ) introduced the possibility of change at the confirmation hearings in 1991, Gates totally dismissed the idea and sarcastically responded that he had more important matters to handle. Bradley knew that Gates was wrong about every key intelligence question concerning the Soviet Union as well as other critical intelligence issues, and thanks to Gates, the CIA was equally far afield.

Gates's memoir didn't reveal his deep affection for CIA director Bill Casey or how the two men colluded. The director wanted to intensify the Cold War with the Soviets, and Gates was Casey's man for tailoring intelligence to justify doing so. Both men were part of a crusade to give the CIA a first-tier seat in the councils of the White House. The ideological fervor of Casey and Gates were anathema to most analysts in the Directorate of Intelligence, including me.

Casey made Gates his chief of staff in 1981, promoted him to deputy director for intelligence in January 1982, then deputy director of the Agency in April 1986, replacing Admiral Bobby Ray Inman, who objected to Casey's pandering to the Reagan administration and his lies to the Congress. Whenever Casey was misleading the Senate Intelligence Committee, Inman would squirm in his chair; the more Casey lied, the more Inman fidgeted. Casey sent his criticism of Inman to the director's good friend at the *New York Times*, William Safire, a fellow neoconservative who began to roast the deputy director in his op-eds.

Unlike Inman, Gates had no problem with Casey's deceit, and offered a large clue to his own thinking when he emphasized that it was U.S. military policy, particularly the weapons we procured, that "won" the Cold War. Two decades later, as secretary of defense in the Obama administration, he was telling his closest friends that a "smaller military would go to fewer places and do fewer things," and that he "did not want to be part of such a U.S. policy."[6] At least he was consistent on the role of defense spending and weapons acquisition in national security policy. Ironically, he kept a huge portrait of President Eisenhower behind his desk, although it was Ike who reduced both spending and weapons acquisition.

Robert Gates has offered few additional clues to his thinking or his personality. He was an inscrutable and faceless bureaucrat, even in the public role of secretary of defense from 2006 to 2011. If Gates ever wrestled with his conscience, then I assume that Gates and not his conscience won. Like George Smiley, the well-known fictional spymaster who was played best by Alec Guinness, Gates worked in the shadows; indeed, his CIA memoir was titled *From the Shadows*. His bosses primarily praised him for his "discretion."[7]

Unlike Smiley, Gates found it easy to cook up intelligence assessments that suited the political appetites of his political bosses, whether they were Democrats (Presidents Carter or Obama) or Republicans (Bush I or Bush II). At the 1991 confirmation hearings, Gates worked to convince Democratic and Republican members of the Senate Intelligence Committee that, while he was the deputy to a controversial, law-breaking director, he was merely an onlooker when Casey was at bat.[8] A passage from John Le Carré echoed the Casey-Gates stewardship at the CIA: "Control's gone potty. And if I'm not mistaken he's also dying. It's just a question of which gets him first." For Casey, it was death that paved the way to the unsuccessful nomination of Gates in 1987.

President Bush's nomination of Gates in May 1991 to be CIA director was a shock. I had known Gates since he joined the CIA in 1968, and he was well known to the members of the intelligence committee, who remembered his false start in 1987 after Casey's death. Gates's close relationship with President Bush was also well known to the committee, as was Gates's close relations with Chairman Boren. Gates made a special effort to forge close relations with Boren (the current president of the University of Oklahoma), which still exist.

Gates testified often to the committee throughout the 1980s as the deputy director for intelligence and deputy director of the Agency. Many members of the committee believed that he had been a good witness during this period, always well prepared and forthcoming on intelligence issues. Committee members tended to like him; staff members believed him to be acceptable. Chairman Boren, who had backed Gates in 1987, immediately declared him an "extremely able and non-partisan professional in the intelligence field."[9] Boren "guaranteed" President Bush's senior aide, Boyden Gray, that Gates would have no problem in facing the Intelligence Committee, a guarantee that a Senate chairman of one party doesn't often give to the president of another party.

On the other hand, before the committee and the Senate voted, Boren issued another unusual guarantee to two CIA analysts, Lyn Ekedahl and John Hibbits, who testified against Gates, obviously putting their careers on the line. In one of my private discussions with Boren and the staff director, Tenet, I mentioned that Gates was known for his vindictiveness. As a result, Boren made a personal commitment and "indeed the commitment of our entire committee" that "no action will be taken against [the critics] in a way that will disrupt or penalize their career advancement."[10] Boren said he would hold Gates "accountable and carefully scrutinize his decisions and actions to ensure that needed changes are made." Boren had no ability whatsoever to enforce such a commitment, and his colleagues on both sides of the aisle were nonplussed and chagrined that their chairman had gone out on the limb with a feckless gesture.

Toward the end of the hearings, the chairman added an additional warning that "for my remaining five years in the Senate, long after I have left the committee, I will intervene on their behalf at the slightest hint of retribution."[11] And, if Gates did not live up to the "standards of decency required . . . I will be the first to take action whether I serve on the Intelligence Committee or not." There is no precedent for a congressional guarantee to a witness, let alone a warning to someone about to be confirmed, that there would be intense scrutiny of personnel practices at his or her agency.

Boren's warning to a future CIA director that the intelligence committee would not tolerate any retaliation against Gates's opponents was thus bizarre.[12] He was committed to Gates because he naïvely believed that he could control him and, in the process, become a powerful committee chairman. Boren was wrong about that and wrong about Gates correcting his previous management mistakes. As Boren's congressional colleagues predicted, the chairman could not live up to these guarantees, not even in the period immediately after the hearings had ended.

The retribution started immediately, when Ekedahl and Hibbits had to submit to intrusive polygraph sessions that had nothing to do with security. It took an angry response from both of them to get the Office of Security to back off from its acts of intimidation. It also helped that the head of the Office, Frank Reynolds, was a former colleague in the CIA's intelligence directorate and shared our opposition to Gates.

In addition to their polygraph examinations, Gates made sure that neither Ekedahl nor Hibbits could return to their previous positions as Soviet analysts, where they had excelled for a total of more than 50 years. Gates called Ekedahl, who was on a teaching sabbatical at Georgetown University, and disingenuously asked what she would like to do upon her return to the CIA. Ekedahl asked to remain at Georgetown for another year, which pleased both of them.

When her sabbatical ended in 1992, Ekedahl returned to the CIA, but was denied a position in either the intelligence directorate or the National Intelligence Council. The head of the Directorate of Intelligence, David Cohen, who is currently the chief of intelligence for the New York City Police Department, said there was nothing for her in his directorate. The deputy director of the National Intelligence Council, Gregory Treverton, who is now its director, gave the same message and blocked Ekedahl and Hibbits from analytical positions in the council. Treverton, a company man, had orders from the National Intelligence Council director, Joseph Nye, currently professor of government at Harvard University, who had been told by Doug MacEachin that Ekedahl was a "failed analyst." Ekedahl had received numerous awards as an analyst, and went on to become the director of inspections for the inspector general. She retired from the CIA in 2005 as an SIS-4, then one of the highest-ranking women at the Agency.

Since Gates had had to withdraw his nomination in 1987 due to the Iran-Contra affair, the staff directors of the committee, George Tenet for the Democrats and John Moseman for the Republicans, expected the issue to be revisited and thought that Gates needed to acknowledge he should have handled the issue better. Congress had investigated Iran-Contra, and a key member of the Senate Select Committee on Intelligence, Warren Rudman (R-NH), had been a major player in the investigation, so the historical record was considered complete and there was no anticipation of a September or October surprise. My charge of politicization was the first surprise!

The committee planned to subpoena key operatives from the CIA, such as Alan Fiers, on the issue of Iran-Contra, but expected no damning evidence to turn up. Fiers, however, as well as Tom Polgar, two former clandestine operatives, indicated that Gates had sensitive knowledge of Iran-Contra. Polgar's testimony, a letter to the committee, was credible because he had been a staffer on the Senate committee that investigated Iran-Contra. A former colleague and well-known Agency officer, Charlie Allen, raised serious questions about the level of knowledge Gates possessed regarding Iran-Contra in a memorandum that challenged Gates's truthfulness. Another old friend and former colleague, Dick Kerr, had sensitive material to use against Gates, but he pulled his punches.

Nevertheless, there was no political stirring in the Intelligence Committee when Gate's name came forward, although some Democrats were concerned that Boren had guaranteed a routine confirmation. The committee, which was created in 1977 after the Church Committee hearings, was known for its bipartisan character, with votes determined without political coloration, but the guarantee of a Democratic chairman to the Republican White House seemed excessive. The Senate majority leader, George Mitchell (D-ME), was particularly critical. Gates acknowledged that Boren "spared no effort on my part."[13]

I was at the National War College when the nomination was announced in May 1991. I was angry but had no idea how I would get my views on CIA corruption to the Intelligence Committee. I learned of the nomination in New York City at JFK Airport when I was returning from the Soviet Union, where I had led a National War College delegation to study the decline of Soviet power. The story was the lead item in the *New York Times*, and I was incredulous that someone who had done so much damage to the CIA would be nominated to lead the Agency.

I didn't know at the time that the committee's staff director, George John Tenet, immediately began to get calls, mostly anonymous, that raised Gates's role in the corruption of intelligence. Tenet thought that the issue should be explored, and he asked a staff member, Marvin Ott, who was assigned to a Republican member of the Senate Select Committee on Intelligence, Frank Murkowski of Alaska, to run this issue to ground. Ott, a sober and conscientious type, began to call CIA analysts and receive tales of the tailoring of intelligence. Whenever Ott asked for more names to buttress the accusations, my name was always mentioned.[14] Ott had accepted a teaching position at the National War College, but he delayed his arrival until the hearings were complete.

In June, I got a call from Ott, who invited me to the Hart Office Building to discuss the problem of intelligence corruption and Gates's possible role. Until that moment, I had discussed the issue with family and friends, but not with any journalist or member of Congress. I jumped at the opportunity to speak to staff members of the committee, and made three trips to meet with staff members, including Tenet and Moseman. Until these sessions with the staff, there had been no hint that the nomination of Gates was going to be a big deal, let alone a controversial one.

Some staff members referred to my sessions as "fire and brimstone." Most accepted some of my accusations; only Moseman was hostile. With each visit, there were more staff members in attendance paying close attention to my accusations. They understood that tampering with intelligence was serious and that, if the issue were not treated seriously, the integrity of the confirmation process would be questioned.

To gain support and provide credibility for my views, I supplied names of analysts as well as documents that could be requested and studied for evidence of manipulation. The documents part was easy because of the flagrant violations in preparing a National Intelligence Estimate on Moscow and international terrorism; a special assessment on the plot to assassinate Pope John Paul II; and a National Intelligence Estimate on Iran that was structured to justify the criminal aspects of the Iran-Contra operations. Providing names was a more difficult task, because doing so implicated more people. If they chose to go before the Senate Select Committee on Intelligence, they would encounter CIA liaison officers assigned to the committee, who would report such contacts. Gates knew from the start from a loyal congressional liaison coordinator, Stanley Moskowitz, that I was talking to the staff and recommending names of others who could do so. Moskowitz, an old friend, even warned me to be careful.

Few of the analysts I recommended were willing to cooperate with Ott's investigation. They had their reasons, and can deal with their consciences. But I am proud of those who cooperated and have remained life-long friends with all of them, particularly Lyn Ekedahl. (Our marriage took place two years after these events.) Ekedahl suffered through the corruption of intelligence on the Soviet Union, as did John Hibbits. Jennifer Glaudemans and Brian McCauley had similar experiences with a paper on the Soviet Union and Iran that Gates tampered with to tilt the case for Iran-Contra. All four willingly testified.

My charges received support from additional colleagues. Wayne Limberg, who left the CIA for the State Department because of the manipulation of intelligence, met with the committee and took personal leave to attend the hearings and provide support. His support included sending notes to me in the hearing room telling me to lower the heat on some of my rebuttals to hostile Republican senators, an activity that was reported by the *Washington Times*. Glaudemans, who left the CIA to attend law school, convinced Ott that I was providing credible accusations regarding corruption at the highest levels of the Agency. She was asked to join me in testifying against Gates, and her ability to recall language from key documents became a high point during the hearings. It helped that she addressed Boren in Naabeehó bizaad—Navajo language—at the start of the hearings; we were all impressed, particularly Boren.

Ott faced a quandary. He was a former CIA analyst, and he knew that pursuing analysts would be putting their careers at risk if they testified against the next director. This made Ott very uncomfortable. He also realized that the issue was a hot potato that put the Senate committee in the crosshairs of executive/legislative branch politics. After all, the committee would be placing itself in front of a White House that wanted a CIA director who had close relations with the president.[15] It did not occur to me until later that I was throwing myself in front of President Bush's candidate for the position of director.

My sessions with the committee as well as the interviews that Ott conducted with Ekedahl, Glaudemans, and Limberg convinced him there were problems with the nomination of Gates, and there was sufficient evidence to challenge it. The committee had never been interested in the politicization problem; Ott was the only staffer working on the issue. I was the first person to use the term in front of the committee and its staff. As a result, Ott decided to brief Tenet on his findings and get his efforts endorsed. To his credit, Tenet, who became President Clinton's CIA chief in 1997 and was later infamous for his "slam dunk" assurance regarding weapons of mass destruction in Iraq, gave Ott the go-ahead to proceed "without fear or favor" regarding the nomination.

This was not acceptable to Tenet's counterpart, Moseman, the Republican staff director and Tenet's closest friend on the staff. He was hostile to my views from the outset. I did not know at the time that Moseman had guaranteed to White House staffers that there would be no problems confirming Gates. He knew my testimony could create problems.

Moseman had received a call from the White House that

President Bush considered the vote on Gates to be a test of loyalty to the president, and that there could be no outliers on this issue. He delivered the message to all Republican staffers in forceful terms. Several staffers indicated to me that, if the vote had been simply on Gates's standing, there would have been significant Republican opposition. There were no Republican senators, however, willing to deny the president his preference for CIA director. For Gates, the position of CIA director would go from one that was his to lose to one that would be a battle to win.

Moseman, who was heavy-handed and gruff, had no trouble disciplining the Republican staff on the importance of the nomination, and even tried to short-circuit the investigation. He wanted Ott to "cease and desist" in his investigations, but Ott considered the warning a "drive-by message" unaccompanied by any genuine threat. Tenet had given Ott the go-ahead, and Ott was not only unwilling to back down but willing to resign from the committee if there had been political interference. Thus far, the system was working.

The Moseman warning was neither the last warning nor the most serious threat to Ott's work. Because of the gravity of the situation, the White House assembled a team of three or four officials, including Ron Marks, a CIA officer assigned to the White House, to attend the hearings and report to the White House and Gates's office. This was unnecessary because the CIA congressional liaison, Stanley Moskowitz, was performing this task, a violation of protocol in such matters. Moskowitz and Marks sensed that the confirmation was in trouble. Marks warned Ott to "watch your back," and Moskowitz warned me to "be careful." The White House knew not only what Agency analysts were saying to the committee, but that Ott was too energetic in collecting information.

On a second confrontation with a member of the White House political team, Ott received another warning to lower his visibility in the confirmation process, but again he refused to back down. Gates was under the gun, I held the weapon, and Ott had been identified as having my back. Ott continued to play it straight. He told the White House staffer, "You should want me to succeed," because it would mean that Gates would have survived a genuine political test and would become a more effective CIA director and advisor to the president on intelligence. As far as Ott was concerned, this silenced the issue.

The Senate Intelligence Committee staff began its preparations for the confirmation hearings several weeks before the nomination formally reached the Senate on June 24, 1991. Unlike the current Senate committee, which has a pedestrian membership, the members of the committee in 1991 were luminaries within their party. On the Democratic side, in addition to David Boren, there was Bill Bradley, Sam Nunn, John Glenn, Howard Metzenbaum, Ernest Hollings, Alan Cranston, and Dennis DeConcini. Bradley, DeConcini, Hollings, and Metzenbaum voted against Gates in committee. On the Republican side, in addition to Vice Chairman Frank Murkowski, there was Warren Rudman, Alfonse D'Amato, Slade Gorton, Richard Shelby, John Chafee, and John Warner, all of whom voted for Gates. The ex officio members were Daniel Patrick Moynihan for the Democrats and Bill Cohen for the Republicans.

It was soon apparent that many members of the committee and the staff, and not just the Democrats, took a dislike to Gates's supercilious and patronizing manner. He was known to us at the CIA as an ambitious bureaucrat who knew how to grease the rails of his upward climb. Many senators who supported him acknowledged that he would have to change his ways if confirmed.

Senator Chafee raised concerns that he might break ranks and vote against Gates. He had problems with Gates's personality, particularly his careerist style, not unfamiliar in Washington, that found him "sucking up and kicking down." A gentleman and patrician, Chafee found that unacceptable; he privately compared Gates's management style to that of Genghis Khan. The White

House was also concerned about the possible opposition of key Republicans, particularly Arlen Specter, who had opposed Gates's nomination in 1987, and was scheduled to return to the committee as the ranking Republican in January 1993.

Senator Bill Cohen, a former chairman of the committee, was brought back as a coach for Gorton and other Republicans on the committee, who failed to follow the substance of the hearings and asked inappropriate or irrelevant questions. Cohen played an important role with the news media as well, feeding favorable information about Gates to Roger Mudd from PBS and Mary McGrory, a syndicated columnist with the *Washington Post*, who were glad to oblige. When Cohen started attending the hearings, Senator Moynihan also began to attend, and delivered some compliments to me during breaks.

Gates was given a list of 80 questions to answer, which he handled easily. There were no issues apparent to the committee until staffers began getting stories that dealt with his role corrupting the intelligence process while serving as the deputy director for intelligence and as the deputy to Casey. I was merely one of several former and current analysts who were willing to go on record as a critic of Gates's management style and his hand in tailoring intelligence to satisfy President Reagan's political agenda. I was the most credible critic with the greatest amount of detail on Gates's interference on issues dealing with the Soviet Union, Southwest Asia, and Latin America.

By late July, key staffers were convinced there was sufficient evidence of corruption to summon additional analysts to explore their experiences. I had already supplied evidence of Gates's manipulation of intelligence to serve the policy interests of Casey and the Reagan administration, and was called back on two more occasions. The third session was standing room only. Moseman didn't speak; he merely glowered at me.

Gates's description of the confirmation hearings as a "bureaucratic food fight" do not begin to capture the unprecedented nature of the political exchanges and revelations that took place in the fall of 1991. Several years later, in an op-ed in the *New York Times*, Gates compared the confirmation process to going through a "prolonged root canal without anesthesia."[16] For the first time, there was an open discussion of the manipulation of the intelligence process at the CIA as well as the tension between the Agency's ideological leadership and its analysts. For the first time since the Senate Select Committee on Intelligence had been created as a bipartisan committee, ideological lines were drawn for defending or blocking a president's appointment of a CIA director.

Gates used his memoir to denigrate those of us who stepped forward to oppose his nomination.[17] He claimed to have heard rumors that several former analysts from the CIA's Soviet office "were whispering to the committee staff accusations that I had 'politicized' or slanted intelligence analysis on the Soviet Union to support my 'hard-line' views and the political agenda of Casey and the Reagan administration." Gates didn't hear "rumors" to that effect. Moskowitz, one of his acolytes, was a company man who relished the opportunity to keep his former boss up-to-date on the opposition.

Limberg was prepared to testify, and Ekedahl and Hibbits submitted sworn affidavits against Gates. Limberg was initially hassled by the director of the Department of State's Bureau of Intelligence and Research, Doug Mulholland, for attending the hearings, but when Mulholland learned that Secretary of State James Baker didn't mind the show of opposition against Gates in the hearings, Mulholland quickly backed off. Secretary Baker enjoyed Gates's difficulty, remembering that Gates had tried to block the secretary's efforts to convince President Bush to resume the détente process that President Reagan began in his second term.

I was anxious to testify and didn't need a subpoena, but the committee lawyers believed I needed legal protection since I was an employee of the Department of Defense, serving as a professor of international relations at the National War College. In fact, the commandant of the college, Major General Stadler, called me into his office to make it clear that "throwing yourself in front of a presidential nomination" was not a particularly good idea and that there were Pentagon lawyers who could "get you out" of testifying. I reminded him that such a comment to a subpoenaed witness was illegal, and he retreated.

Tenet and Moseman collaborated closely to select five witnesses: two would oppose the nomination; two would support it; an authoritative and credible fifth witness would carefully weigh pros and cons but conclude that the nominee deserved confirmation. I was the lead opponent, with backing from a former junior analyst, Jennifer Glaudemans, whom I had hired in 1981. She was described by Gates as "an analyst I did not know (or remember)."[18] It was hoped that Glaudemans's testimony and demeanor would corroborate my views, and thus make it difficult to compromise me. Doug MacEachin and Graham Fuller, two of Gates's acolytes, were selected to support the nominee.

The fifth choice was a sterling one for the committee: a longtime Agency officer, Hal Ford had served in both the CIA's Intelligence and Operations Directorates and even on the Senate Intelligence Committee, where he had earned great respect for his judgment and integrity. Ford left the CIA in the 1970s to become program director of the Institute for the Study of Ethics and International Affairs at Georgetown University. He also had been a consultant to the Senate Intelligence Committee and an assistant on foreign and military affairs to Senator Joseph R. Biden (D-DE). Ford had punched all the right tickets as far as credibility and integrity were concerned.

Picked to seal the deal, Ford created the dramatic highlight of the hearings in not doing so. He started his testimony by acknowledging that he was torn by conflicting loyalties to the CIA and to Gates, but concluded that Gates did not deserve to be confirmed as CIA director. In his lapidary style, Ford alluded to Gates's inability to recall his role in the Iran-Contra scandal: "The forgetfulness of this brilliant officer—gifted with a photographic memory—does not, to me, instill confidence."[19]

Ford was known to the committee as someone who was a dogged defender of the CIA's need to resist political pressure, and he charged Gates with the "skewing of intelligence . . . to suit what the consumer wanted to hear. I think there was no question about it."[20] This was key to Ford, who was known within the Agency as a master of the delicate art of interpreting ambiguous and contradictory intelligence reports. He was one of the first analysts to discern hostility between the two great Communist powers—the Soviet Union and China—which paved the way for President Nixon's trip to Beijing in 1972 and President Carter's recognition of China in 1978.

Hal Ford acknowledged there were problems at the CIA, but he argued effectively that they could not be corrected by Gates, who was "part of the problem and not part of the solution." In the single most damaging remark about Gates, Ford noted that "what is needed . . . is a director of national stature, and there are many such people in American life. I wish the president had nominated such a person." The committee was faced with the dilemma of confirming a nominee who was close to the president and pledged a more cooperative relationship with the oversight committee, but who had politicized intelligence and withheld sensitive information regarding Iran-Contra during the Reagan years.

Thus, the Senate Intelligence Committee's carefully selected lineup didn't perform as expected. In preparing for his testimony and even after clearing his testimony with the committee, Hal Ford had a change of heart. At the very last minute, he came to Ott to say he had changed his mind. Ford told Ott that he had been talking to "people with knowledge [of Gates's machinations] who I respected."[21] Lyn Ekedahl, a highly respected analyst and a close friend of Ford's, helped to lead him to acknowledge that he "now understood" that Gates played a heavy hand in tailoring intelligence on key issues. Ford later told me: "It was tough for me, because he'd been my boss and our personal relations were fine." In 2006, when Gates was nominated to be secretary of defense, Ford and I lobbied the Congress and repeated our criticism of Gates.

With the *volte-face* of Hal Ford, the committee lost the heavyweight who had been chosen to seal the deal for confirmation, and was now left with two defenders for Gates who had their own credibility problems. Fuller and MacEachin were fulsome supporters of Gates and were known to have politicized intelligence on his behalf. After the hearings, Fuller acknowledged to me, "There's a lot of blood on the floor. It dismays me." There was no doubt that Agency careerists were appalled at the display of the bitter divisions and frequent infighting that took place at their Marble Palace in Virginia. Many of my former colleagues, including my erstwhile best friend at the CIA, blamed me for that display.

MacEachin privately told several staff members that my testimony was "95 percent accurate, but 5 percent exaggerated," and that "we're going to hang him on that 5 percent."[22] Overall, I was comfortable with my testimony and knew it was truthful. My advice to future witnesses, however, is make sure that you vet your testimony with someone experienced on the Hill, perhaps with a lawyer, who could identify areas that would be considered overreaching.

Boren and the staff chiefs, Tenet and Moseman, were shocked when their efforts to control the outcome of the confirmation process came apart. Ford's about-face was particularly pleasing to Senator Bradley, the most effective interrogator of Gates and the senator most committed to stopping the confirmation. Bradley knew that Gates, like John LeCarré's George Smiley, remembered everything, but, unlike Smiley, Gates on too many occasions could not recall key events, in order to put distance between himself and Casey, who was symbolically in the dock despite having died five years earlier. And unlike Smiley, who never tailored intelligence, Gates falsely claimed that "I never distorted intelligence to support a policy or to please a policymaker." Bradley failed to defeat Gates in 1991, but he was successful a year later when he convinced President-elect Clinton not to retain Gates as CIA director, even for the one additional year that Gates desired.

My biggest obstacle to stopping Gates was the close relationship between him and Senator David Boren. Boren still regretted the failed confirmation of 1987, believing that, with a "friend" like Gates at CIA, he could influence the next director and become a powerful chairman. Boren's goal was to create a confirmation process that would easily confirm Gates, but only after establishing that arguments against him had been scrutinized. In announcing his opposition to Gates, Senate Majority Leader Mitchell said that, if approved, Gates "will owe that confirmation to one person, and one person only, and that is Senator Boren."[23]

Senator Boren privately orchestrated letters of support for Gates from three former CIA directors (Helms, Colby, and Webster) to persuade the Democrats to support Gates. Two former directors (Schlesinger and Turner), who were lobbied by Boren, refused to do so. A year earlier, Turner had written in *Foreign Affairs*, "We should not gloss over the enormity of this failure to forecast the magnitude of the Soviet crisis. . . . I never heard a suggestion from the CIA . . . that numerous Soviets recognized a growing systematic economic problem. Today we hear some revisionist rumblings that the CIA did in fact see the Soviet collapse emerging after all. On this one, the corporate view missed by a mile."[24] The former chairman of the Joint Chiefs of Staff, General Powell, observed that anyone tracking the news about the Soviet decline could have done a better job analyzing the Soviet political scene than the CIA.

Boren portrayed himself to me as a neutral moderator as the committee chairman, but I soon learned that he privately discussed strategy with White House staffers worried about the committee vote scheduled for October 18, 1991. Republican strategist Kenneth Dubberstein, who helped to craft Gates's opening statement to the committee, played a major role in this campaign. It was Dubberstein who advised Gates to go on the offensive in rebutting the serious charges against him, dismissing the evidence of tampering with intelligence, and concentrating on himself as the good guy, the "new broom," who created resentment for trying to "improve quality, productivity and relevance, to make analysis more rigorous and intellectually tougher."[25] Senator Murkowski and many other Republicans bought that line.

The hearings began on September 16, 1991, with no controversy and no concerns about gaining confirmation for Gates. Key Democratic senators such as Metzenbaum told the press that Gates would easily win confirmation and that the committee was satisfied with Gates's "confession" that he should have asked more questions when the details of Iran-Contra became apparent. As far as the committee was concerned, Gates had laundered his credentials and was fit to serve as director of the CIA.

The real battle began on September 25, 1991, in an unusual evening session closed to the public in order to discuss the classified evidence of Gates's manipulation of intelligence. I was selected to go first because I had the most compelling testimony and factual evidence. The witnesses supporting the nomination, Douglas MacEachin and Graham Fuller, had been promoted to their positions by Gates, when he served as deputy director of intelligence from 1982 to 1985.

It was immediately obvious that the Senate Select Committee on Intelligence was hearing views about politicization that they had never heard previously. Democratic staff members feared I would be perceived as someone with an axe to grind and therefore easily challenged by the Republicans. But before I could complete my remarks, Senator Nunn (D-GE) broke in to say that my "material was much too sensitive to be handled in closed session. We needed to go into open session as soon as possible."[26] Nunn interrupted me as I described the phony intelligence that made the case for Soviet involvement in the Papal Plot. His interruptions led other Democrats to weigh in. It ultimately took more time to confirm Gates than it took to defeat Iraq in Desert Storm that year or, as Gates wryly observed, for the Soviet Union to collapse.

The interruptions led to a shouting match between the Democrats and Republicans, with Nunn pressing for a quick resumption in public session, and Senator Rudman casting aspersions on my testimony and demanding a long delay before any resumption. I relished the opportunity to give my views on politicization to a larger audience.

A red-faced Rudman argued with Nunn against any open discussion of these issues, but it was too late. The arguments proceeded on the basis of *when*—and not *if*—the open sessions would be held. Nunn had won a huge political victory in the committee; Rudman had suffered a defeat. And I was able to witness the politics of the process, which is typically opaque to outsiders. Policies and process are often discernible; politics are the best-kept secrets of the Congress.

Boren belatedly realized that there should be no witnesses to the political skirmish between Nunn and Rudman and eventually cleared the room. Staff members and witnesses retired to the foyer of the committee room, where it took nearly an hour for the senators to agree to go into open session with a delay of only one week. Several of us waited outside as Rudman lobbied for more time before going public so that he could prepare his case against Gates's critics, and Nunn argued for no more than a one-week delay. Again, Nunn got his way, and the committee sessions resumed on October 1 with the issue of politicization the centerpiece.

Senator Nunn was the key to defeating Gates in the committee. In addition to being chairman of the prestigious Senate

Armed Forces Committee, Nunn was influential on all national security matters, with as many as 10 or 12 members of the Senate following his lead. Nunn had declared himself undecided, but his administrative assistant and a longtime friend, Richard Combs, told me that Nunn was extremely opposed to confirming Gates, whom he considered unscrupulous and unreliable. The other undecided Democrats included DeConcini, Cranston, and Glenn; their hands were tied because they were facing problems with the Senate ethics committee and thus found themselves subservient to Rudman, co-chairman of the ethics committee. So Boren concentrated his arm-twisting on Nunn, who eventually gave in to the chairman's importuning.

There were others who did not vote but were opposed to Gates, including Bob Kerrey, Tim Wirth, and Harris Wofford. In view of Nunn's powerful role in the Senate, if he had voted against Gates, there would have been greater Democratic opposition, particularly among Southern Democrats.

My testimony offered chapter and verse of the vulnerability of intelligence to top-down corruption, including examples of intelligence that had been manipulated on the Soviet Union and the Papal Plot; Iran-Contra; Central America; the Middle East; and Southwest Asia. I demonstrated that Casey skewed intelligence to support covert actions that he favored as well as to create an inflated portrait of the Soviet threat to support Reagan's defense budgets. Casey, whom analysts lampooned as the "great white case officer," a sobriquet that he favored, acted as Edgar Bergan in orchestrating the main themes of intelligence support; Gates was Charlie McCarthy, the obedient mouthpiece who made sure that Casey's demands were met. Gates was both the deputy director for intelligence and director of the national intelligence officers, making it impossible to publish intelligence outside Casey's lanes. All analysts reported to the deputy director of intelligence and all participants in estimates reported to Gates's national intelligence officers, a particularly servile group.

In addition to my testimony and Ford's confounding of expectations, when he stunningly recommended against confirming Gates, the senators themselves provided fireworks. Senator Metzenbaum broke in to say that it was the first time that he had ever been told of politicization. When Nunn said that this "material was much too sensitive to be discussed in closed session," Senator Rudman immediately began to malign my testimony, even accusing me of McCarthyism.

My problems with Rudman began that initial evening, as he clearly targeted me. Although the Democratic members of the committee had no strategy for dealing with the witnesses supportive of Gates, the Republican members met on several occasions to discuss compromising Gates's opponents. They developed a plan of attack to neutralize the opposition, and assigned Republican senators to go after specific opponents. Republican members of the Congress typically have much sharper elbows than their Democratic colleagues in these congressional battles, and Democrats tend to fold their tents when the going gets tough. This was true in the hearings for Gates; it became more obvious several weeks later in the lack of support for Anita Hill during the hearings for Clarence Thomas.

Senator Rudman was selected to go after me. He did so with the vitriol he was known for in the Senate. Rudman was furious that I had raised Iran-Contra, because he believed it was a closed issue thanks to his investigations. He challenged my testimony, and told his colleague, Senator John Danforth (R-MS), that he would "fix Goodman's wagon. He's with the government so it should be easy to fix his wagon."[27]

Danforth was given the more difficult task of challenging Glaudemans, whom the Republicans privately referred to as "Bambi." She had no axe to grind and her professional demeanor made her untouchable. The sexist sobriquet "Bambi" wasn't meant to demean her; it was a tribute to her credibility and integrity. Danforth's rectitude and easygoing manner made him a natural to try to neutralize Glaudemans. Danforth failed with her; Rudman had some success with me.

I had been warned by a Republican staffer, Art Grant, a former colleague at the National War College, that Rudman would do his best to make my life miserable when the hearings resumed in open session. Rudman, known for his volcanic temper, was true to his word.[28] Several years later, Grant told me that Rudman considered himself the Senate's expert on Iran-Contra and that it was a "hot button" issue if anyone criticized his investigation.

I overplayed my hand in pushing Rudman's buttons on Iran-Contra. My intention was not to insinuate that there were huge gaps in the Iran-Contra investigation, which there were, but to play to Rudman's interest in ethical issues. He was vice chairman of the Senate Iran-Contra investigation and the Senate Select Committee on Ethics, and played a major role in drafting a federal ethics and lobbying bill that applied to members of Congress. (President Reagan vetoed the bill in 1985.) I believed there was an ethical question for the Senate Select Committee on Intelligence in ensuring that the president received unbiased intelligence from the CIA, and wanted to play to Rudman's reputation for defending ethical issues. I mishandled that aspect of the process, and underestimated Rudman's reputation as a tough prosecutor.

Fortunately, there was a Democratic member of the Senate Select Committee on Intelligence, Ernest (Fritz) Hollings (D-SC), whose temper was equal to Rudman's. On every occasion that Rudman confronted me, including the disturbing accusations of "McCarthyism, pure and simple," Hollings reminded his Republican opponent that the confirmation hearings were not a criminal courtroom and that the room was no place for personal attacks. Some of the Republican members realized that Rudman's intemperate rants were not helpful to the cause of confirming Gates and convinced him to lower his voice at the hearings. Rudman eventually became a non-presence in the committee room and passed up future opportunities to attack me.

The charge of "McCarthyism" is a familiar one on the Hill, designed to embarrass any critic of established policy. When the Pike Committee conducted an aggressive investigation of the CIA in the House of Representatives in the mid-1970s, key policymakers and journalists attacked the "McCarthyite inquisition" of the committee. A relatively junior Foreign Service Officer, Lawrence Eagleburger, an acolyte to Secretary of State Kissinger, testified that Pike was running a "McCarthyite inquisition." The *New York Times* referred to the "neo-McCarthyism" of the committees, and ran an editorial titled "Pike's Pique." There was no reason for making this charge against me, and I eventually learned that Rudman was trying to stem the tide of protests from CIA analysts that were delivered to the Senate Select Committee on Intelligence after my public testimony. There were as many as 50 of these letters, according to the committee's legal counsel, Britt Snider.

Stan Moskowitz, a former colleague and old friend, attended the closed session in order to keep Gates, his former boss, briefed on the turn of events that Gates described as the "high drama." At the end of the evening session, Moskowitz was leaving for the White House to brief Gates on my testimony and the controversy. I told Stan that I knew he was providing "strategic warning" to Gates, and, knowing that it was Bob's birthday, which he shared with Paul McCartney, I jocularly asked Stan to deliver a birthday greeting from me.

I had private exchanges over the course of the hearings with many of the senators and their staffers, and it was obvious that Bradley, Hollings, and Metzenbaum were deeply opposed to the nominee because of his dissembling on a variety of issues, particularly Iran-Contra. Gates had attended sensitive meetings at the White House and CIA where illicit activities were discussed. Senator Frank Lautenberg (NJ) based his opposition to Gates on the nominee's inability to remember any details from those meetings or materials. I can testify to the acuity of Gates's memory; his inability to recall details was not credible.[29] Bradley's opposition to Gates also was based on Gates's pathetic track record on the most important intelligence issue of the day—the power, influence, and threat posed by the Soviet Union.[30]

In two days of rancorous debate over his nomination, Gates faced the committee in open sessions on October 3 and 4 as well as a closed session in the afternoon of October 4. Once again, I was the lead witness, followed by Graham Fuller, a bizarre clandestine operative, who testified on behalf of Gates. In the process, Fuller misinformed the committee by describing himself as a foreign service officer. He was a CIA operative, and I warned Fuller that if he continued to lie I would out him. I eventually did, earning his long-term enmity.

The following day, Glaudemans provided strong testimony against Gates; MacEachin, my erstwhile boss in the Office of Soviet Affairs, spoke in favor of him. In each case of Gates's supporters (i.e., Fuller and MacEachin), there was a conflict of interest, because they would benefit from supporting the future director. I cannot recall a confirmation hearing when senior officials placed in their positions by the nominee were then called to support the candidacy of their future leader. This was an unusual and politicized confirmation process.

In addition to getting support from CIA officials, Gates made sure several analysts produced documents to be used in his defense. The White House placed its own political team in the hearing room as part of the high-stakes political game, turning to a well-known political operative, Kenneth Dubberstein, to guide the process. Dubberstein's main job was to keep Gates, who could be awkward in certain situations, from shooting himself in the foot.

If the Democratic members of the Senate Intelligence Committee had been more adroit and manipulative, they would have offered me counsel regarding my testimony. I should have had strategic warning regarding such the obstacles as Senator Rudman; my old friend Moskowitz, a CIA apparatchik serving as the

Agency's chief congressional liaison; and Dubberstein. Moskowitz and Dubberstein roamed the committee room without any limitations and reported their findings to Gates.

In any event, a genuine legislative deliberation was at work that could not be programmed. Senate Intelligence Committee members and staffers heard testimony about politics and politicization at the CIA for the first time that was credible and provocative. Nunn, a longtime veteran in these matters, called the hearings one of the most riveting he had ever encountered in his career. Metzenbaum and others agreed. This issue was new and inflammatory.

According to Nunn's legislative assistant, Dick Combs, I did get corroboration from an unexpected quarter in the form of a letter to the senator from a veteran CIA operative, Tom Polgar. Polgar had met many members of the Senate Intelligence Committee while serving as chief of station in South Vietnam, and was respected as a critic of the war. In letters to Nunn and others, Polgar recited Gates's involvement in Iran-Contra and reminded the committee members that the Senate study of Iran-Contra documented the "slanting of intelligence under the leadership of Casey and Gates."[31] Polgar charged that Gates was associated with the "errors and misjudgments of the past" and that he "advanced his own career by catering to whomever was in charge while being very hard on his subordinates."[32] Polgar wrote that Gates "was like a bicyclist: his nose was up and he pushed down."

In any event, it was the bombshell from Ford that forced a change in the political geometry at the witness table. The committee had arranged for five witnesses: two former analysts (Glaudemans and myself) to make the case against Gates; two senior CIA veterans (MacEachin and Fuller) to make the case for him; and a fifth tie-breaker (Ford) to lean in the direction of support. Moseman had to buttress the case for Gates, so he added another Gates acolyte: the national intelligence officer for strategic programs, Larry Gershwin, who had slanted intelligence on Soviet military capabilities. Twenty-five years later, Gershwin was still a national intelligence officer at the CIA.

According to a committee staffer, Boren angered many members of his own party with his "covert collusion" with White House efforts to get Gates confirmed. Senator DeConcini complained that the seven Republicans on the 15-member committee had "circled their wagons around Gates," which politicized the hearings before they started. Another committee staffer, who worked for Senator Murkowski, added that "it's pretty clear that Boren's wagon has joined the circle."[33]

Rudman's presence on the committee was intimidating to several Democratic members who would have voted against Gates. Rudman was vice chairman of the Ethics Committee, and three Democrats were members of the "Keating Five" and were facing charges before Rudman's committee. Charles Keating, a one-time lawyer and moral crusader, was the central figure in the multibillion-dollar savings-and-loan scandal of the 1980s and 1990s; he served a jail sentence for his crimes.

Keating gave $1.3 million to five senators who lobbied the Federal Home Loan Bank Board to kill its investigation of Keating; three of those senators were Democrats who served on the Intelligence Committee (Cranston, Glenn, and DeConcini) and would be judged by Rudman's ethics committee. The head of the bank board, Edwin Gray, called the work of the Keating Five "an attempt to subvert the regulatory process."[34] Keating himself, when asked if his payments to the senators had worked, told reporters, "I want to say in the most forceful way I can: I certainly hope so."[35]

As a result, the senators were given modest reprimands by Rudman's committee, a *quid pro quo* for not opposing the Gates nomination. Cranston was formally reprimanded by the Senate Ethics Committee; DeConcini was admonished for interfering with the bank board's investigation; and Glenn was merely cited for "poor judgment." Several staffers told me that all three would have voted against confirmation of Gates, but bowed to pressure from Rudman, Gates's most aggressive supporter.

Senator Nunn was the biggest disappointment, because he was personally and politically opposed to Gates but bowed to pressure from Boren. Instead of a vote in the committee that favored Gates by 11-3, the vote easily could have been a much closer 8-6, thus placing greater pressure on the full Senate to examine Gates more closely.

The Gates hearing became a turning point for the committee. A White House source told me that President Bush was surprised and chagrined to learn how much opposition there was to Gates from Agency rank-and-file. Nevertheless, Bush's call for political loyalty was delivered to the senior Republican staffer on the committee, John Moseman, who lectured the Republican staffers.

The committee has never recovered from this turning point, and to this day the Senate Select Committee on Intelligence is no less politicized than any other committee on the Hill. The controversial chairmanship and irascible personality of Arlen Spector (R-PA) in the mid-1990s worsened the bias, but the die was cast during the Gates hearings. The recent skirmish over the committee's authoritative report on CIA torture was the most recent example of politicization. No Republican staffer from the committee was permitted to work on the report; no Republican member supported it.

The key committee staffers, Tenet for the Democrats and Moseman for the Republicans, did their jobs and were well rewarded in the 1990s with key positions at CIA. Tenet became director in 1997; Moseman was his executive assistant. They created hearings to discuss all sides of the nomination, but made sure that Gates got the benefit of the doubt.[36] Moseman told the Republican staffers that "my job is to get Gates confirmed" and "your job is to cooperate."[37] Tenet and Moseman selected the witnesses to make sure that Gates was favored. Ford was crucial to the process, and Tenet and Moseman were shocked when Ford pulled the rug out from their plan.

Tenet initially tried to leverage his success in getting Gates confirmed to support his own appointment as director of the State Department's Bureau of Intelligence and Research. Several senators, including Boren, intervened at State on his behalf, but the efforts failed. There were too many intelligence analysts at the Bureau of Intelligence and Research who found Tenet unacceptable. History repeated itself a decade later when the CIA tried to arrange Mike Morell's appointment to direct the Bureau of Intelligence and Research. Once again there was great opposition within the ranks of the Bureau, which stopped the appointment of a former CIA acting director who has been described as the "Bob Gates of his generation."

The committee process was flawed. The Senate Select Committee on Intelligence was primarily concerned with the operational side of the CIA and was unprepared to deal with analysis and production. Among the two dozen committee staffers, fewer than ten had experience with any intelligence agency, and only one—Marvin Ott—was concerned with politicization. Ott did a remarkable job, but had his own problems because he worked for the Republican minority chief, Senator Murkowski, who was supportive of Gates. On at least two occasions, Murkowski approached me privately in the hearing room to say that I was simply engaged in a personal battle with Gates. I bit my tongue and dismissed Murkowski as too doltish to be serving in the Senate, lacking the intelligence to serve on an intelligence committee.

Very few staffers understood the problem of politicization. Most of them assumed that slanting was simply a standard part of the process, part of the intelligence cycle, and that the notion of the ingrained independence of professional analysts was alien to subservient staffers ruled by senatorial masters. There were exceptions, primarily Ott, as well as a few others who worked for senators such as Bradley and Metzenbaum, who believed the integrity of the system was sacrosanct.

The committee permitted senior CIA officials who would have to report to Gates to testify on his behalf despite the obvious conflict of interest. I have never witnessed a confirmation hearing where so many unabashed cheerleaders for the nominee would strengthen their professional futures by supporting the nominee. The list included National Intelligence Officers Allen, Fuller, and Gershwin, and my former boss at the Office of Soviet Affairs, MacEachin. The committee rigged the system before the confirmation hearings began, although the October surprise from Gates's critics caused last-minute reshuffling.

Meanwhile, Dubberstein coached Gates to go on the offensive because congress members favor political appointees who are tough on the bureaucracy as long as no jobs are lost by constituents. So, Gates read into the record his blistering speech to CIA analysts in January 1982, three days after he became the deputy director of intelligence, which convinced many Democrats on the committee and even some Republicans that Gates was a martinet and probably too immature to head an Agency that failed to anticipate the collapse of the Berlin Wall, the Warsaw Pact, and the Soviet Union. Gates was the "new broom," but he revealed his bristly nature in the process. Senator Bradley noted that Gates was wrong about every key intelligence question of the 1980s.

Gates's speech blasted the CIA's Directorate of Intelligence for producing "irrelevant or untimely or unfocused" material; for "close-minded, smug, arrogant responses to legitimate questions and constructive criticism"; for "flabby, complacent thinking and questionable assumptions combined with an intolerance of others' views"; for "poor, verbose writing" and a "pronounced tendency to confuse objectivity and independence with avoidance of issues germane to the United States and policymakers."[38] Similarly harsh fault-finding was in Gates's memoir, *Duty*, three decades later, although his targets were far larger, including the president and vice president and the Senate and House.

The Senate Select Committee on Intelligence confirmed Gates by a vote of 64–31, the most contentious vote for a CIA director in the Agency's history up to that point. He argued that the CIA was broken and had to be fixed. Certainly, "fixing" intelligence was his specialty. Gates regretted losing the votes of two senators he "had always respected and liked—Bill Bradley and Pat Moynihan."[39] Bradley and Moynihan went out of their way to thank me for my efforts to bring the issue of politicization before the American public, and both believed that Gates was not fit to serve. Moynihan offered me a job on his staff, and Bradley provided my only memento that I've retained from the hearings, an inscribed picture.

Gates's supporters acknowledged his flaws. Senator Rudman, his chief Republican backer on the committee, said he had been too heavy-handed in dealing with junior analysts.[40] Senate Select Committee on Intelligence vice chairman Murkowski acknowledged that the "question is not whether he did everything right in the early 1980s. . . . The question is whether he has grown and learned."[41] Senator Boren defensively reiterated that Gates had "matured," which the chairman felt was sufficient.[42] Former deputy director Bobby Ray Inman, who mentored Gates, conceded that Gates "broke some china" in the 1980s, but he was "older" and "maturity had been added."[43] Those who are curious about Gates's "maturity" should examine his two memoirs for evidence of a lack thereof.

Gates's campaign to develop close relations with Boren paid off. Boren told staffers that Gates would be beholden to the chairman like no other CIA director. Boren naïvely believed that getting confirmation for Gates would give him some control over the new director and thus create a powerful chairman. Boren soon learned that Gates would be no more forthcoming with him than he had been in hearings. Soon after becoming CIA director,

Gates hid details of the Agency's involvement in a scheme to help fund Saddam Hussein's defense spending in Iraq. Meanwhile, the mutual admiration society that Boren, Tenet, Moseman, and Gates formed during the confirmation continues to this day.

The committee clearly bent over backwards to give Gates the benefit of the doubt. In addition to calling witnesses whose careers would be bolstered by the nominee, the Senate Select Committee on Intelligence ignored Gates's orchestration of support from the CIA's Directorate of Intelligence managers suborned to prepare Gates for the hearings. Analysts and supervisors were tasked with providing documents to support Gates's candidacy, aggressively declassifying documents in the process. According to a former Agency analyst, Acting Director Kerr made sure that the National Intelligence Council provided language from selected National Intelligence Estimates to the committee to support Gates.[44] In addition to Moskowitz in the Congressional Affairs office, David Holmes and other lawyers in the general counsel's office rallied to support Gates.

The committee failed to summon senior officials who could have described Gates's efforts to prevent the truth about Iran-Contra from reaching the Senate Intelligence Committee. I urged the committee to take testimony from senior National Security Council officials implicated in the Iran-Contra schemes, such as Admiral John Poindexter and Oliver North, and senior CIA officials such as Clair George and Dewey Clarridge.

There were numerous occasions when the Senate Select Committee on Intelligence failed to counter Gates's rebuttals—not refutations—of the charges against him. At the request of Senator Bradley, I prepared 20 questions that challenged each one of Gates's rebuttals, but few of these questions were brought into play. Gates's one-sided account of his role in preparing the Papal Plot assessment were refuted by two CIA post-mortems, an unofficial one requested by MacEachin to keep Casey and Gates from making a wider distribution of the specious assessment, and another done by three senior members of the Intelligence Directorate, one of whom—John McLaughlin— went on to become deputy director of the CIA.

Of the four analysts involved in these post-mortems, only McLaughlin tried to hide the role of Gates in manipulating the assessment of the Papal Plot. Twenty years later, it was McLaughlin, as the CIA's deputy director, who slanted intelligence in the run-up to the U.S invasion of Iraq, gave the "slam dunk" briefing to President Bush in January 2003, deceived Secretary of State Powell regarding the substance of his address to the UN, and led the effort against the Senate committee's report on torture in 2014.

Gates's role in preparing an intelligence rationalization for Iran-Contra included the false notion that Iran had ended support for terrorism. In order to justify the sales of surface-to-air missiles to an enemy of the United States, Congress would have to believe that Iran was out of the terrorism business. Similar to his denials in 1987 in the *Washington Post* and *Foreign Affairs*, Gates denied there had been any change in the CIA's view of Iran's role in terrorism. This was at odds with his own product evaluation staff, which concluded in a report given to Gates that there was a "marked discontinuity in the analytical line and, even worse, no apparent evidence cited explicitly or implicitly to justify the abrupt departure." The product evaluation staff report was declassified for the 1991 confirmation hearings, but no journalist exploited the opportunity to compare Gates's testimony to the historical record. They didn't match up.

Fuller, the national intelligence officer for the Middle East, boasted in a conversation with Senate Intelligence Committee staffers that he "strong-armed" Soviet analysts on the issue of Soviet relations with to Iran after a conversation with Gates. Gates and Fuller used their bureaucratic clout to stifle any opposition to the 1985 estimate on Iran, which was declassified and available to the press as a result of my testimony. The estimate was designed to justify dealings with Iran by exaggerating the likelihood of a Soviet-Iranian rapprochement.

The intelligence committee also allowed the CIA's Public Affairs Office to lobby aggressively for Gates. Spokesman Peter Earnest, who is currently the director of the Spy Museum in Washington that lionizes the CIA, told the *Washington Post* that Gates was "uniquely qualified." "He'll be an outstanding DCI and we need him," Earnest remarked.[45] Numerous supportive CIA officials spoke to members of the press, which would have been grounds for dismissal if opponents of the confirmation had done so.

Gates not only escaped the scrutiny of the Senate Select Committee on Intelligence, but also survived, though barely, the investigation of the Iran-Contra scandal led by Independent Counsel Lawrence E. Walsh, who spent seven years (vs. the intelligence committee's seven months) trying to find the perpetrators of one of the clumsiest covert actions in CIA's history. Casey was the great whale in this hunt, but there were smaller whales such as Gates who escaped the pursuit of Captain Ahab, played by Walsh. Walsh's report includes 10 pages on Gates, concluding that there was "insufficient evidence to warrant charging Robert Gates with a crime."[46] Without the threat of conviction and prison time Walsh could not hope to win Gates's "cooperation" in his march up the chain of command toward indictment of the other big fish behind Iran-Contra.[47] The report noted that the "statements of Gates often seemed scripted and less than candid."

The strangest call I received during the hearings was from an FBI agent who wanted to interview me. I could not imagine what the FBI had in mind, but it was soon obvious that Gates was the issue at hand. When I remonstrated that I could add nothing to his connection to Iran-Contra, the FBI agent replied that "you would be surprised at the number of people who say they know nothing about Iran-Contra, who actually know a good deal." In this case, however, I could offer the names of two high-ranking officials at the CIA, Charles Allen and Richard Kerr, who kept

Gates informed of the risk of Iran-Contra, particularly the sale of weapons to a terrorist state, Iran—and the funneling of proceeds to right-wing militants, the Contras.

I had five goals in testifying before the Senate Select Committee on Intelligence in order to block the confirmation of Gates as CIA director. First, I wanted to describe the danger of politicization—tampering with intelligence for political ends—which had never been discussed before the intelligence committee and was unknown to the media and the public. I wanted to describe Gates's central role in slanting intelligence to support the Reagan administration and to advance his own career goals at the CIA. Second, I wanted the committee to understand that they weren't getting sufficient access to reports of inspectors general that required follow-up investigation on the Hill. Third, I wanted the closed, classified session of the Senate Select Committee on Intelligence moved to open, public sessions. Senator Nunn played the central role, in this process. Fourth, I wanted to place a cloud over Gates's head, leading to President Clinton's decision to ignore his importuning to remain at CIA, making his stewardship one of the shortest in history.

Finally, I wanted to cite examples of politicization to get the committee to declassify documents and allow the public to make judgments about the spinning of intelligence at the CIA. My testimony in 1991 against the confirmation of Gates led to declassification of many of these documents, and the National Security Archives at George Washington University have posted many of them on its website. I lost the battle over Gates's confirmation in 1991, but I won the war of exposing his role in politicizing intelligence.

Four out of five wasn't bad. Gates was confirmed, but only after a tumultuous confirmation process that sent him to the CIA as a weakened director. It was cynical for the Senate Intelligence Committee to reward the CIA intelligence official most responsible for politicization by confirming him as the Agency's director.

The subject of politicization received some attention from the media, and those who testified against Gates had ample opportunity to discuss his suppression of good intelligence at odds with Ronald Reagan's neoconservative agenda. For the first time, intelligence assessments were declassified that demonstrated the manipulation of intelligence on the Soviet Union, Iran, Nicaragua, nuclear proliferation, and international terrorism in order to support the neocons in the administration, including Secretary of Defense Weinberger, Secretary of State Haig, and National Security Advisors Allen and Poindexter. On balance, I overestimated the ability of the press to do the required work to report and explain the tailoring of intelligence, and underestimated the degree to which the media was embedded with the CIA.

The hearings were watched closely at the National War College and the CIA. The students, mainly colonels and captains, were stunned by the testimony of a faculty member who was throwing himself in front of a White House nomination for a CIA chief. This was the first time for most of them to witness a public display of the bitter division and bureaucratic infighting in the intelligence community. Virtually no student, colonels and naval captains, made any comment to me about my testimony. Several faculty members sent quiet notes of support, but didn't want to be identified openly with my views, although there were exceptions. The only enthusiastic support came from the African Americans serving at the college, primarily in staff positions, who viewed me as not as a whistleblower but as an underdog being mistreated by the Establishment. Meanwhile, at the CIA, there was little work done in the Intelligence Directorate because eyes and ears were fixed on the publicly televised hearings, most of which can still be viewed today on CSPAN's online archive.

The public airing of the political maneuvering on sensitive intelligence reports that dealt with the Soviet Union, Iran-Contra, and Central America was unprecedented, and created great confusion on arcane issues of intelligence and policy. Senator Glenn conceded that the intelligence committee had never heard such "diametrically opposed testimony, under oath, by a lot of people" and that it might take a "lie detector to find out what's going on."[48]

In addition to the support I received from Senators Bradley and Hollings, the Democratic ex officio member of the committee, Senator Moynihan was very supportive of my testimony. We had lunch together on two occasions, and the senator even offered me the position of staff director of his bipartisan Commission on Protecting and Reducing Government Secrecy. I was tempted, but quickly realized that this was a position for a lawyer; I also learned that Moynihan was not an easy individual to work for. Apparently, he had a well-earned reputation for being tyrannical with his staff. I was pleased that someone as influential and formidable as Senator Moynihan even considered that I might be a good fit for a legislative committee open to reducing secrecy in American government. Secrecy was out of control before 9/11; in the wake of the terrorist attacks, secrecy has hurt all three branches of government.

The CIA's Office of Training failed to use the hearings as a teaching opportunity for new recruits to provide warnings of the dangers of politicization, which became a factor in sending the nation into an unprovoked war a decade later. Testimony and declassified documents could have been used to study the manipulation of intelligence and methods to avoid it. Case studies could have been prepared to address the problems raised at the hearings by using declassified documents, Senate testimony, and political memoirs to examine the impact of politicization on the policy process. Instead, the CIA and its Center for the Study of Intelligence used taxpayer money to fund a case study at Harvard University's Kennedy School to deny that there was any tampering with intelligence and, more incredibly, deny that the CIA got it wrong on the decline and fall of the Soviet Union. Princeton

University and Texas A&M even sponsored two CIA symposia to demonstrate the CIA got it right!

Gates defended Casey from charges of politicization during his confirmation in 1991 and his memoirs in 1996, but he eventually admitted that the intelligence process had been corrupted during the Casey era. When Casey had been dead for over a decade and could do Gates no harm, he acknowledged watching Casey "on issue after issue, sit in meetings and present intelligence framed in terms of the policy he wanted pursued."[49] Gates's criticism of Casey came 10 years after such supporters of Casey as William Safire of the *New York Times*, Senator Paul Laxalt (R-NV), and Senator Richard Lugar (R-IN) called for Casey to resign. An old friend of mine, James McCullough, who was the director of Casey's executive staff, lamely explained that if Casey "had known that large sums of money ostensibly earmarked for the Contras had been piling up in a Swiss account . . . he would have taken steps to see that more of this money actually reached them."[50] This was McCullough's defense of his boss.

Gates never addressed his own role, including informal memoranda to Casey providing ammunition in support of those policies. Gates conceded that he missed the change of course in Soviet policy, but never acknowledged that he thoroughly erred on the biggest intelligence issues of the day, including Gorbachev's strategic retreat abroad and the destruction of the Soviet system at home. Gates was thoroughly wrong about the strength of the Soviet Union and the intentions of its leaders toward the United States and arms control.

Gates concluded that the confirmation process was "exhausting, insulting, humiliating and sometimes destructive."[51] Perhaps, but it was a procedure that prevented the confirmation of Robert Bork and John Tower, and should have prevented the confirmation of Clarence Thomas and Robert Gates. Several weeks after the Senate Select Committee on Intelligence mishandled the Gates confirmation, the Judiciary Committee mishandled Anita

Hill's sexual harassment charges against then Supreme Court nominee Clarence Thomas.

My testimony certainly caused greater division within the CIA itself. Many CIA personnel were upset to see their dirty linen washed in public and possibly shared Gates's view that it was inconsequential. I received support from colleagues, some of whom took risks to make sure that I got classified material. I will not embarrass these individuals by revealing their names, but they should all know that I was grateful. Naturally, there were those colleagues, including some longtime friends, who were bothered by my testimony or, in some cases, supported the testimony but believed that I should shut my mouth and allow the CIA to get its house in order. If I thought that the CIA would actually be doing some soul-searching, then I might have tempered my criticism.

The Senate confirmation of a CIA director tightly linked to the violence and deceit of the 1980s should have been anathema to an oversight committee. The integrity of senior and middle management is essential to any organization, particularly a secret one. There will always be temptations in any organization to engage in immoral and illegal acts, particularly in the field of secret operations, but there must be resistance from within. The controversial vote for confirmation indicated that too many senators decided to give Gates the benefit of the doubt, when it was the whistleblowers and the critics that should have been given that benefit.

SIX

THE CIA'S DOUBLE STANDARDS AND DOUBLE-DEALING

"In addition to bringing in staffers who have chips on their shoulders, the Office of the Inspector General also brought in people who had noticeable agendas. For example, one of the most senior officers on the staff was married to one of the Agency's most vitriolic external critics."
—Jose A. Rodriguez Jr., author of *Hard Measures*, 2012

The senior officer on the staff of the CIA's inspector general was Carolyn M. Ekedahl, the recipient of one of the highest honors that the Agency can bestow, the Distinguished Career Intelligence Medal, in 2005, as well as a special award from the Presidential Commission on Integrity and Efficiency in Government, which oversees all inspectors general in the intelligence community. Upon her retirement after more than 40 years of service, she was one of the highest-ranking women in the Agency. Ekedahl received special commendations for her work in directing CIA inspections, including hard-hitting reports on CIA failures in regard to 9/11; the downing of a missionary plane over Peru; and our nation's unconscionable detention, rendition, and interrogation programs.

212 | WHISTLEBLOWER AT THE CIA

Ms. Ekedahl is also my wife, and she is referenced in *Hard Measures: How Aggressive CIA Actions After 9/11 Saved American Lives* by Jose A. Rodriguez Jr. as one of the "most senior officers on the staff" who was also "married to one of the Agency's most vitriolic external critics."[1] Whenever I published an article critical of the CIA, she would be confronted with "pillow talk" accusations from one of her erstwhile colleagues from the Directorate of Operations. The truth was that she never shared classified information with me or anyone else outside her office.

If there were a compelling reason for being a CIA dissenter, it would be the double standard and double-dealing at the Agency. The absence of internal oversight from the Office of Inspector General, the absence of external oversight from the congressional intelligence committees, and the presence of corrupt CIA leadership have allowed continued improprieties and created a need to expose these activities.

There is no better example of the need for monitoring than the case of Jose A. Rodriguez Jr., the senior clandestine officer who destroyed more than 90 tapes of evidence documenting torture in the CIA's secret prisons. These tapes represented the best evidence of the sadistic nature of the "enhanced interrogation techniques," a term used by the Germans during World War II. There was no punishment for the destruction of the tapes, despite a White House directive not to do so. The act committed by Rodriguez constituted an obstruction of justice.

Rodriguez was investigated by a special prosecutor, John Durham, who reported directly to the deputy attorney general of the Department of Justice. (Several observers believed that the White House should have appointed an independent counsel, who would have reported to no one.) On November 9, 2010, which happened to coincide with the fifth anniversary of the destruction of the tapes, the Department of Justice announced that "Durham has concluded that he will not pursue criminal charges for the destruction of the interrogation videotapes."[2]

In 2013, Rodriguez got his revenge in a memoir that slandered the CIA's Office of Inspector General and its personnel. Rodriguez set the tone for his views by comparing undergoing the scrutiny of the inspector general to being a "test dummy at a proctologist's college."[3] It went downhill from there. The "personnel were flawed," according to Rodriguez, with people assigned to the Inspector General staff on a rotational basis, who would "not be missed" in their home offices. According to Rodriguez, this was like "middle school, where you give a few kids a reflective vest and badge and make them crossing guards. They can't wait to start blowing the whistle on their more popular friends."[4] In fact, the CIA's Office of Inspector General was made up of senior analysts and operatives who appreciated the important role of oversight. Many of my colleagues went to the Office of Inspector General in the 1980s to get away from the politicization of intelligence in the Casey-Gates era.

Rodriguez lauded the efforts of Dusty Foggo, the number three man at the CIA, to use the Office of Security to "scrutinize" the staff of the inspector general. In fact, the Office of Inspector General was investigating Foggo, who was eventually indicted in a contracting fraud case and sentenced to 37 months in federal prison. So much for Rodriguez's concern about "who investigates the investigators."[5] The FBI's investigation of Foggo inside the CIA building itself was unprecedented.

The CIA's torture program justified the need for dissidents and whistleblowers within the Agency, but the abuses that needed monitoring were there at the start. In the early 1950s, CIA director Allen Dulles regularly received reports on Project Artichoke, which involved a four-year effort to test heroin, amphetamines, sleeping pills, LSD, and "other special techniques" in CIA interrogations.[6] Dulles approved a program that gave LSD to prisoners in federal penitentiaries, and in 1953 the CIA slipped LSD to an army civilian employee who somehow fell from the window of a New York hotel. Richard Helms, who became CIA director in

1966, authorized the destruction of nearly all the records dealing with these programs.

In 1961, the President's Board of Consultants on Foreign Intelligence Activities concluded that CIA covert actions weren't "worth the risk of the great expenditure of manpower, money, and other resources involved."[7] The Board warned that the concentration on covert action distracted "substantially from the execution of its primary intelligence-gathering mission." The Board called for ending the role of the CIA director as leader of the entire intelligence community, which President Dwight David Eisenhower supported. The separation took place four decades later, but the Pentagon made sure that there would be no genuine reform of the intelligence community. Meanwhile, the CIA has become militarized, and the director at the time of this writing in 2016, John Brennan, has destroyed the bureaucratic wall between clandestine operations and intelligence analysis.

THE "DISAPPEARANCE" OF THE CIA'S INSPECTOR GENERAL

One of the reasons why the CIA cannot correct its past behavior is the demise of the Office of the Inspector General and the virtual disappearance of the statutory inspector general. The campaigns of the Bush and Obama administrations against the Office of the Inspector General must be understood in order to appreciate the decline of integrity and credibility throughout the intelligence community.

The CIA received its first inspector general in 1952, but until 1989 the inspectors general were appointed by the CIA director, had limited access to sensitive information, and had no more than a handful of professionals on its staff. The oversight committees, which were not created until 1977, were not given full access to inspector general reports until the 1990s, after I raised this issue in my testimony before the Senate Intelligence Committee. Not even the Department of Justice received all inspector general reports, including those that recorded suspected illegalities.

Statutory inspectors general—meaning they are appointed by the president—were instituted in 1978 at most government agencies as part of the post-Vietnam reform process, but the CIA was exempted from the law. The Church Committee favored a statutory inspector general for the CIA, but the Carter administration would not agree. The Pike Committee recommended the creation of an inspector general for the entire intelligence community, including the CIA, but this proposal was considered too radical.

I considered my exposure of the inability of the U.S. Congress to gain all inspector general reports to be one of the most important aspects of my testimony in 1991. I couldn't stop the confirmation of Gates, but I did ensure that the Senate Select Committee on Intelligence would have access to the internal oversight process of the Office of Inspector General. One of the major purposes for creating a statutory inspector general was to make sure that the intelligence committees would have a place to go for sensitive CIA documents. This was the key to the Senate Select Committee on Intelligence's preparation of the torture report two decades later.

CIA director Casey was particularly zealous in making sure that evidence of illegalities was kept from the attorney general. As a result, Senator Arlen Specter (R-PA) sponsored a bill in 1988 to create an independent statutory inspector general at the CIA appointed by the president of the United States. With the eventual bipartisan support of the Democratic chairman of the Senate Intelligence Committee, David Boren, and the vice chairman and ranking minority member, William Cohen, Specter was ultimately successful.[8] It was not an easy task.

The major opponent of a statutory inspector general for the CIA was its director, Judge William Webster, who feared interference with operational matters as well as an inspector general that he could not control. Webster also feared that the inspector general would become a source of leaks that would make potential sources reluctant to support the CIA. There have been no leaks from the Office of Inspector General at the CIA or the Departments of State and Defense, but Webster insisted there would be compromises of sources and methods.[9] Webster had the assistance of senior members of the CIA's Directorate of Operations who used congressional and media sources to lobby against creating a statutory inspector general.

Webster joined forces with Senator Boren, who believed an independent inspector general would be a rival to his intelligence committee on issues of oversight. This was particularly short-sighted on Boren's part, because the statutory inspector general virtually guaranteed that the intelligence committees would have access to sensitive intelligence and operational matters that the CIA would prefer to conceal. (Senate intelligence chairman Dianne Feinstein, D-CA, was similarly short-sighted, failing to protect the independence of the CIA's inspector general and allowing the Obama administration to marginalize the office.)

Specter's case for a statutory inspector general was strengthened by the poor track record of the CIA's Office of Inspector General throughout the 1980s, preparing reports that were analytically shoddy, failing to pursue key lines of inquiry, and failing to interview key witnesses.[10] My experience with the Office of Inspector General in 1987 was typical. In an inspection of the Office of Soviet Affairs where I worked, a number of us reported various examples of intelligence that had been corrupted for political ends. The charges were devastating, but they didn't appear in the final report. When I mentioned this to the interviewing officer from the Office of Inspector General, she stated that sensitive charges were not part of the written report, but were briefed orally to the director and deputy director of Central Intelligence. In fact, the charges went nowhere. She was simply covering up the inspector general's unwillingness to document bad news, thereby ensuring there would be no accountability. This cover-up contributed to my enthusiastic willingness to brief the Senate Intelligence Committee in 1991.

With the controversial confirmation of Gates, the intelligence committee, which had been hitherto bipartisan in its handling of sensitive matters, became as partisan and narrow-minded as other committees. This is a terribly worrisome aspect of Gates's legacy, marking the end of bipartisan oversight. At the same time, the Obama administration gutted internal oversight by leaving the position of the inspector general vacant for nearly two years in the president's first term, then in 2010 appointing a weak inspector general, who moved the Office of Inspector General out of the headquarters building in 2015. Oversight has become just that . . . oversight, and even the statutory inspector general resigned in 2014 to protest CIA efforts to block the Senate's torture report. Nearly two additional years passed before another inspector general was appointed.

The CIA began to push back against the Office of Inspector General during the Bush administration, a battle that was waged more aggressively and successfully in the Obama administration. The campaign against the inspector general was led by the senior leaders of the CIA's Directorate of Operations, who resented the criticism of inspector general investigations on 9/11, torture and abuse, extraordinary renditions, and the 2000 downing of a missionary plane that killed innocent civilians in Peru. These reports were hard-hitting and revealed a great deal of malfeasance and even a high-level cover-up in the case of the missionary plane. High-level members of the Directorate of Intelligence were also critical of the inspector general reports, including a former deputy director for intelligence, John Gannon, who told me the Office of Inspector General had become a "vindictive" institution.

As a candidate for the presidency in 2008, Barack Obama promised to protect whistleblowers because they were, in his words, "watchdogs of wrongdoing and partners in performance." As president, Obama emphasized the need for strong support for government workers who disclose government misconduct, and called for whistleblower protection in such legislative initiatives as the economic stimulus package, health care reform, and the financial reform bill. But national security and intelligence whistleblowers have been excluded from President Obama's so-called guarantees.

The Obama administration's policies toward national security whistleblowers were anything but sympathetic. President Obama called for aggressive prosecution of leaks and unauthorized disclosures; he used the Espionage Act of 1917 to prosecute more government employees than all U.S. presidents combined since the passage of the act. The Obama administration objected to reporters claiming a privilege not to reveal their sources, and used the subpoena to inhibit the work of the Associated Press, the *New York Times*, and Fox News. Most importantly, President Obama endorsed an overall weakening of the Office of Inspector General throughout the national security bureaucracy and undermined the work of individual inspectors general who are the best hope for internal oversight within the government.

The successful campaign of the White House and the CIA against the Office of Inspector General and the statutory inspector general meant there was no place for a contrarian or whistleblower to take his or her case inside the organization. This marked the failure of the CIA to protect its integrity as well as the failure of the congressional intelligence committees to conduct genuine oversight. The statutory inspector general post was finally created in 1989 because of political abuses (i.e., Iran-Contra) and the belief that an internal oversight body was needed within the CIA to ensure that laws were not violated and that the intelligence committees responsible for oversight had an Office of Inspector General to consult when an investigation was required.

The Senate Select Committee on Intelligence could not have issued its authoritative report on the CIA's torture program without the research and analysis conducted by the Office of Inspector General over a five-year period. The so-called Panetta Review, the key to the findings of the Senate's report, was based on work done in the Office of Inspector General; it served as a guide to the data dump of millions of pages of documents that the CIA hoped would stymie the work of the committee. Nevertheless, the report was published without support from Republican members, who blocked staffs from working on the document.

Senate Intelligence Committee chair Feinstein believed that the Panetta Review was deliberately placed in the documentation to be found by the congressional staffers, begging the question of whether a whistleblower was involved. I can't speak to that issue, but I had two meetings near Union Station with the two major drafters of the Senate report, Alyssa Stazak and Dan Ford, to urge them to gain access to the files of the Office of Inspector General. The current chairman of the Senate Intelligence Committee, Richard Burr (R-NC), blocked Stazak from confirmation as legal counsel for the Department of the Army.

The Senate Intelligence Committee hasn't protected the independence and integrity of the Office of Inspector General, which was essential to its work and the oversight process. The U.S. Congress has failed to deal aggressively with CIA directors who have lied in their testimony or in remarks to committee members. In 2014, CIA director Brennan joined an exclusive list of CIA directors and deputy directors who have lied to the U.S. Congress and the American people. Like Helms, Casey, Gates, and Tenet, Brennan received protection from a White House that ignored his deceit.

CIA directors, particularly General Michael Hayden and Leon Panetta, combined to neutralize the Office of Inspector General, demonstrating they had no respect for the political culture of the nation's key civilian intelligence agency. The Office of Inspector General was a central part of that culture, particularly its efforts to ensure that a secret organization was obedient to the laws of the land and the desires of the American people. Crimes committed by the United States during the Vietnam War led to the creation of congressional intelligence committees to conduct oversight of the intelligence community, and the misdeeds of Iran-Contra led to the establishment of a statutory inspector general, appointed by the president and committed to making sure that improprieties, let alone crimes, were scrutinized. The Bush and Obama administrations have reversed these successes.

The stated values of the CIA are well known, but the actual behavior of the CIA must be monitored and verified, which is the mission of the Office of Inspector General. Richard Helms claimed that "we are all honorable men," but we learned that was not the case. Gates said that he had no role in Iran-Contra, but that was not the case. Tenet said that the CIA didn't torture, but that was not the case. Brennan said that it was "beyond the scope of reason" to believe the CIA would hack into the computers of the Senate Intelligence Committee and its staffers, but in fact the CIA did exactly that.

There have been too many discrepancies between what CIA directors have said and what they have done, which will be discussed in the following chapter. Since there are few people in any organization who are willing to expose improprieties, we are dependent on the whistleblower, a rare breed, to make these discrepancies known. Political leaders must protect whistleblowers and must make sure that there is accountability in the process. If there are no individuals in an organization who can be counted on to tell truth to power in dubious circumstances, then that organization will fail tests of ethics and morality. I became a dissident and a whistleblower because of this failure.

No administration has done more damage to the institution of the inspector general than the Obama administration. There are 10 inspector general positions that were vacant for more than a year, which means there was no real accountability in these agencies and departments, particularly in the field of national security.[11] The State Department had no permanent inspector general during the entire tenure of Secretary of State Hillary

Clinton, leaving in place an acting inspector general with close ties to the Secretary and her husband. The Obama administration didn't nominate a permanent inspector general until Clinton left office. The five-year period at the Department of State without a confirmed inspector general was the longest such gap since the position was created in 1957. Since acting inspectors general don't feel empowered, there is no better way to prevent oversight than to leave the post of inspector general vacant.

THE CIA'S DOUBLE STANDARD: "TOO BIG TO JAIL"

The poster child for the CIA's double standard is former CIA director General David Howell Petraeus, who escaped a jail sentence despite providing eight notebooks of highly classified information, including names of covert operatives, to his biographer-mistress Paula Broadwell. In 2014, prosecutors from the FBI and the Justice Department recommended felony charges against Petraeus for providing classified and extremely sensitive documents to his lover.[12] The matter was on Attorney General Holder's desk for nearly a year, which speaks to the special treatment that political celebrities, let alone the preeminent military officer of this generation, received from the highest levels of the U.S. government. Broadwell has dropped out of sight, but Petraeus is earning a small fortune from lucrative speeches and a partnership in one of the world's largest private-equity firms, Kohlberg Kravis Roberts.

The fact that he lied to the FBI about providing classified information to his mistress should have drawn a prison sentence. In 1991, I was questioned by the FBI regarding the role Gates performed in the Iran-Contra scandal, and it was clear that the "truth and the whole truth" carried a special meaning. General Petraeus presumably understood this as well, but in a miscarriage of justice that my good friend Ray McGovern termed "too big to jail," the general was given a misdemeanor wrist-slap and a $100,000 fine, which the general presumably covered with one of his public speaking fees. Adding insult to injury, Petraeus remains an advisor to the White House.

Holder refused to discuss the matter, but FBI director James Comey said it best in response to queries regarding the extended delay in deciding on an indictment: "I can't say. I mean, I guess I could say, but I won't say." The Obama administration disingenuously concluded that secrets given to Broadwell by the general had no negative impact on national security. Former CIA operative John Kiriakou's actions certainly had no negative impact on national security; indeed, there was a positive impact. But Kiriakou served a jail sentence for his "indiscretion."

Meanwhile, McGovern, a CIA veteran and fellow dissident, was jailed for simply trying to get into a speaking event featuring General Petraeus at the 92nd Street YMHA in New York City on Halloween eve in 2014. McGovern was denied entrance to the YMHA despite having a ticket to the event; New York's finest were summoned and McGovern was dragged away and spent the night in jail. It is reasonable to assume that the government's monitoring of McGovern's Internet activity, which included the online purchase of the ticket, led to the encounter at the Y.

There is nothing new about the careful handling of Petraeus and the rough treatment given to his critics. Former CIA director Deutch placed the most sensitive operational materials of the CIA on his home computer, also used to view pornographic sites. Like Petraeus, Deutch agreed to plead guilty to one misdemeanor charge and to pay a modest $5,000 fine. Before the prosecutors could file the papers in federal court, President Clinton pardoned Deutch on his last day in office. Clinton's National Security Advisor Samuel Berger similarly pled guilty to a misdemeanor charge and received a $50,000 fine for stuffing his pants with classified documents from the National Archives in 2005.

Several years later, Attorney General Alberto R. Gonzales was not even charged—merely admonished—for keeping information about the NSA's surveillance program at home. Meanwhile, under the Espionage Act, NSA official Tom Drake was charged with violations for dealing with unclassified information. Other NSA officials were also harassed by the government for the handling of unclassified information, and one of them, Edward Loomis, faced a one-year government review of his book on NSA transgressions.

John Kiriakou, a CIA operative who revealed the CIA's torture and abuse program, was given a 30-month jail sentence for providing the name of a CIA operative to two journalists who never used the name in their stories. Meanwhile, the CIA cleared for publication the memoirs of three senior officers with more than 100 years of professional experience at the CIA who claimed there was no torture and abuse. John Rizzo, then acting General Counsel at the CIA and the author of *Company Man: Thirty Years of Confrontation and Crisis in the CIA*, took part in decisions that gave the green light to torture and abuse, and rationalized CIA wrong-doing at its "black sites."

Jose Rodriguez denied that the CIA conducted torture and abuse, hiding behind the so-called "torture memoranda" of the Department of Justice that provided legal cover for some—but not all—CIA practices. Even the major author of the torture memoranda, John Yoo, a faculty member at the University of California's law school in Berkeley, conceded that CIA officers went beyond the letter of the authorization and should be held accountable.

The most recent example of the CIA's double standard involves the publication of former acting director Michael Morell's book that defends the CIA's sadistic interrogation techniques and argues that waterboarding and sleep deprivation produced critically important intelligence.[13] Morell, who admitted to not reading the U.S. Senate report on torture and told Senator Feinstein, "I'm not in the weeds" on the details of the report, misrepresented various terrorist plots in order to make a specious case for CIA successes. He claims that Khalid Sheikh Mohammed, who was waterboarded more than 100 times, provided information on plans for future acts in the United States, although CIA interrogators stated that Khalid Sheikh Mohammed "held back."

The ghostwriter for the CIA authors (Morell, Tenet, and Rodriguez) has been Bill Harlow, who was instrumental in covering up the creator of the torture program—Tenet; the leading manager of the program—Rodriguez; and the leading denier of the program—Morell. Harlow, a public relations specialist and the CIA's spokesman in the 1990s, has been the grand strategist and apologist behind the Agency's defense of its shoddy record over the past two decades. He also coordinated the response of former CIA directors and deputy directors to the Senate's torture report that concluded CIA's interrogations were far more brutal than previously thought, failed to produce actionable intelligence, and were misrepresented to the White House and the Congress.

A colleague from the 1970s, Frank Snepp, wrote an important book with only unclassified information, but it wasn't submitted for Agency clearance. As a result, he had to forfeit his considerable royalties of hundreds of thousands of dollars for violating his obligation to submit such a manuscript. Nevertheless, former director Panetta submitted his memoir to his publisher in 2013 long before he passed the manuscript to the CIA, for security review, receiving no punishment whatsoever. Snepp's book was severely critical of the CIA and the U.S. government for leaving behind loyal Vietnamese in our withdrawal in 1975. Panetta had only great praise for the CIA. Moreover, Panetta used a ghost writer from the Los Angeles Times, who had no security clearances.

The CIA's Publications Review Board took more than a year to "review" this book, although two members of the Board acknowledged that it contained no sensitive information. My previous books, which number six, were reviewed between 1991 and 2013 in less than a month. If CIA analysts submit their books for review, then the CIA has no right to compromise our First

Amendment rights by slow rolling the review process. There was a circuit court decision in 1972 that mandated a response to submissions in 30 days.

The fines for the crimes of Petraeus, Berger, and Deutch must be compared to the jail sentences given low-ranking government officials and contractors who have mishandled classified information. Stephen J. Kim, a contractor, received a one-year prison sentence for disclosing information to a reporter for Fox News; the reporter was also charged for merely doing his job of investigative journalism. A former FBI technician received a four-year sentence for discussing classified information with the Associated Press. Jeffrey Sterling, a former CIA operative, received a lengthy prison sentence for discussing classified information with James Risen of the *New York Times*. Risen also faced serious charges, but in a sudden twist, former Attorney General Holder backed off, realizing that his controversial legacy at the Department of Justice shouldn't include the harassment of journalists.

BAMBOOZLING THE CONGRESS

Another reason for monitoring the CIA is to expose the long history of dissembling on the Hill. In 1973, CIA director Helms deceived the Senate Foreign Relations Committee, refusing to acknowledge the CIA's role in overthrowing the elected government in Chile. Helms falsely testified that the CIA had not passed money to the opposition movement in Chile, and a grand jury was called to see if Helms should be indicted for perjury. In 1977, the Justice Department brought a lesser charge against Helms, who pleaded *nolo contendere*; he was fined $2,000 and given a suspended two-year prison sentence.

Helms went from the courthouse to the CIA, where he was given a hero's welcome from the senior members of the CIA's Directorate of Operations and a gift of $2,000 to cover his fine. I was in the lobby of CIA headquarters as the senior operatives were gathering, so I hung around to observe the commotion. When Helms came through the door, he got a huge ovation. It was embarrassing; I returned to my desk to spread the word on the day's unusual activities.

The CIA violated its charter in the mid-1970s when it tried to block and discredit the work of the Church and Pike Committees that were investigating the crimes of COINTELPRO during the Vietnam War. During the hearings in 1975, the CIA station chief in Athens, Richard Welsh, was gunned down by a terrorist organization, and the CIA charged that the recklessness of the Committee's investigations were responsible for the outing of Welsh and the assassination. Welsh's cover had in fact been blown during his previous assignment in Lima, Peru, as well as in Athens, where he was living in a house linked to previous station chiefs. The *Washington Post* referred to the killing of Welsh as an "entirely predictable result of the disclosure tactics chosen by certain American critics of the Agency," thus doing the CIA's bidding.

One high-ranking CIA operative, David Atlee Phillips, left the CIA to organize retirees into an "independent" lobbying organization, the Association of Retired Intelligence Officers, which orchestrated supportive op-eds, letters to the editor, and speeches.[14] The CIA had circled the wagons because a former operative, Philip Agee, had published a long list of CIA agents working overseas as well as a list of covert actions that involved violence.[15] The retired officers' organization remains active on behalf of the Agency's clandestine operations, and has prevented me from taking part in its panels.

It took courage for Church and Pike to pursue their investigations. They received universal criticism, not unlike the criticism aimed at Senator Feinstein for orchestrating her committee's investigation into CIA's torture program. On the right, Governor Ronald Reagan, a member of the Rockefeller Commission, dismissed the congressional investigations as "much ado about—if not nothing, at least very little." According to Reagan, the CIA crimes were simply "instances of some wrongdoing with regard to keyhole peeking." On the left, Senator William Fulbright (D-AK), who had orchestrated the congressional criticism of U.S. policy in Vietnam 10 years earlier, proclaimed that, even if the charges against the CIA were true, "I have come to feel of late that these are not the kind of truths we need right now; these truths which must injure if not kill a nation." More recently, CNN's Wolf Blitzer said that Feinstein would have "blood on her hands" if Americans were killed in the wake of her report. No Americans were killed.

There is a more damaging comparison between the congressional investigations of the 1970s and the more recent report on torture and abuse. Just as Chairman of the Senate Intelligence Committee Richard Burr (R-NC) has killed any chance to get a release of the full Feinstein report, in 1976 the House of Representatives voted by more than two to one to suppress the report of the Pike Committee that it had authorized, which took a year and several hundred thousand dollars to produce. Feinstein's report took four years of preparation and tens of millions of dollars. Both reports documented despicable acts by the CIA.

During the Ford administration in the 1970s, the CIA provided phony intelligence to the Congress to get an endorsement for covert arms shipments to anti-government forces in Angola. The CIA lied to Senator Dick Clark (D-IA), the chairman of the Senate Foreign Relations Committee, who was a critic of the Agency's illegal collaboration with the government of South Africa against Angola and Mozambique. The Ford administration and the CIA's directorate of operations looked at Southern Africa as a zero-sum game; it believed that any gain for Soviet-backed forces in the region would be a setback for the United States, and had no concern for additional victims caused by increased arms deliveries. In this case, Agency briefers exaggerated the classification of their materials so that Senate and House members could not publicize their information.

In the 1980s, Casey and Gates lied to oversight committees about their knowledge of the Iran-Contra operations. Senator Moynihan believed they were running a disinformation campaign against the Intelligence Committee. Casey managed to alienate Senator Barry Goldwater (R-AZ), a pro-intelligence, conservative senator who always supported the CIA. As mentioned, Gates's lies regarding Iran-Contra led to the Intelligence Committee's unwillingness to approve his nomination in 1987, and when he was finally confirmed in 1991, an acrimonious hearing had produced significant evidence documenting how Gates tailored intelligence to fit Casey's biases. The Committee never took up my challenge to determine how much spurious intelligence from Gates was in CIA briefings to the Congress.

A trio of CIA directors—Gates, Webster, and Woolsey—failed to inform the intelligence committees of the most destructive traitor in the CIA's history, Aldrich Ames. For nearly a decade, Ames exposed every operational program against the Soviet Union and Russia, but these directors didn't inform the oversight committees of the serious counterintelligence problems that had been created. The chairmen of the Senate and House Intelligence Committees, Senator DeConcini and Representative Dan Glickman (D-KS), were furious with the deception tactics of CIA briefers. The CIA also falsely claimed credit for the discovery of Ames as a mole for the KGB, but in fact a highly placed defector from Russia in 1993 provided the necessary information.

The CIA's most extensive disinformation campaign on the Hill took place prior to the unprovoked U.S. invasion of Iraq in 2002–2003, when CIA director Tenet and his deputy, McLaughlin, made false reports suggesting that Iraq was training members of al Qaeda to use chemical and biological weapons as well as creating mobile labs to manufacture such weapons. Several days before the Congress voted on the authorization to use force, CIA senior analyst Paul Pillar delivered an unclassified memorandum to the Congress with false charges about Iraqi weapons of mass destruction. The memorandum was a direct violation of the CIA Charter prohibition of using intelligence information on U.S. soil to influence American citizens, let alone congressional legislation.

The memorandum and a phony National Intelligence Estimate were then used to write Secretary of State Powell's address to the United Nations in February 2003, only six weeks before the U.S. started its war. Powell's aide, Colonel Larry Wilkerson, told me that McLaughlin lied to Powell regarding various charges against the Iraqis, including the provenance and credibility of evidence for the most serious charges. McLaughlin gave a spurious briefing on Iraqi weapons of mass destruction—the so-called "slam dunk" briefing—to President Bush in January 2003.

In 2008, Representative Peter Hoekstra (R-MI), the ranking minority member of the House Intelligence Committee, documented the dissembling of the CIA to cover up the Agency's involvement in a drug interdiction program in Peru that led to the loss of innocent lives. Hoekstra claimed Tenet misled the Congress; Brennan was Tenet's chief of staff at this time, but was never questioned about this issue during his confirmation hearings in 2013. Brennan, a protégé of Tenet, was presumably witting of the cover-up.

The CIA still has not addressed the serious procedural and institutional illegalities that were exposed in the inspector general report on the Peru program, which concluded that Agency officials deliberately misled Congress, the White House, and the Justice Department. Hoekstra got no traction on this issue because none of his congressional colleagues endorsed the idea of an investigation or inquiry. If the missionary victims in the air attack had not been from Hoekstra's district in Michigan, there may not have been any protest from Hoekstra either.

More recently, the Director of National Intelligence, General James R. Clapper, lied to the Senate Intelligence Committee about illegal surveillance of American citizens. On March 12,

2013, Senator Ron Wyden (D-OR), one of the few watchdogs in the Congress for the intelligence community, asked Clapper, "Does the NSA collect any type of data at all on millions or hundreds of millions of Americans?"[16] "No sir," Clapper replied, "not wittingly." Several months later, Snowden's revelations revealed the extent of Clapper's dissembling. The general lamely explained that he was trying to give the "least untruthful" answer. Orwell would have been proud. In May 2015, a federal appeals court finally ruled that the NSA program to collect information on billions of telephone calls was illegal.

Former directors Brennan and Panetta consistently mouthed platitudes about the CIA's moral compass, but there were too many clouds on the horizon. Panetta stated on many occasions that "it was not CIA policy or practice to mislead Congress. That is against our laws and our values." Brennan once remarked: "If I did something wrong, I will go to the president and explain to him exactly what I did."[17] There is no indication that either Panetta or Brennan reported improprieties to the president.

Brennan told the chair of the Senate Intelligence Committee, Dianne Feinstein, that it was "beyond the scope of reason" to charge that the CIA was blocking the Committee's investigation of CIA torture and had hacked into the computers of the committee and its staff members. We learned later that Brennan not only knew about the obstruction of the congressional investigation, a violation of the separation of powers, but had ordered a CIA lawyer, Robert Eatinger, the acting general counsel, to conduct the search. Like Helms, Casey, Gates, and Tenet, Brennan got protection from the White House and got away with his duplicity.

Brennan established an accountability board to investigate the matter, consisting of three Agency officers and two outsiders, which recommended no punishment for the five CIA officials involved. According to the *New York Times*, the CIA's inspector general determined that the CIA improperly monitored the committee's activities and sent a criminal referral to the Department of Justice based on false information. Nevertheless, President Obama continues to refer to Brennan as a "patriot."

CIA MYTHOLOGY

A close look at the double dealing and double standards of the CIA reveals some of the myths that surround the organization. A major myth is the belief that the intelligence community is indeed a genuine community that fosters intelligence cooperation and the sharing of intelligence information. The intelligence community has rarely functioned as a community. With the exception of the production of National Intelligence Estimates, which are a corporate product of the community, there is not always sharing of the most sensitive documents collected by the various intelligence agencies, and very little esprit de corps within the community. The agencies are a team of rivals.

There have always been deep rivalries between civilian and military agencies, with the CIA and the State Department's Bureau of Intelligence and Research often lined up against the Defense Intelligence Agency and the four military intelligence branches. This division was particularly profound during the debates over Soviet military power and the verification of Soviet-American arms control agreements, with the military exaggerating the strength of the Soviet military and opposing the disarmament agreements of the 1970s and 1980s. The 9/11 failures also revealed a lack of cooperation within the community.

The intelligence community suffers from an inability to learn from its failures and successes. The CIA needs to emulate the U.S. Army, which routinely conducts after-action reports and boasts a Center for Army Lessons Learned at Fort Leavenworth, Kansas. The center has a small staff, uses teams of experts to investigate specific issues, and maintains a direct line of communication to senior military leaders for a response to their requirements. Conversely, the CIA has tried to cover up failure aftter failure, with no attempt to mend its ways.

Another myth is the belief that the creation of the Office of the Director of National Intelligence, which serves as the principal advisor to the president and the National Security Council on intelligence matters related to national security, was a major reform that instituted central control over the 17 agencies and organizations that comprise the U.S. intelligence community. The creation of a directorate of national intelligence in 2004 has worsened the malaise within the CIA, and has not led to reform for either the agency or the intelligence community. The fact that the president had to meet with more than 20 intelligence principals to discuss the failure to stop a would-be bomber from boarding a flight on Christmas Day points to the crazy-quilt bureaucratic structure created in the wake of 9/11, as well as the lack of centralized authority and responsibility within the community. The Pentagon has veto power over the director of national intelligence with respect to transferring personnel and budgetary authority from individual agencies into joint centers or other agencies. This undermines the possibility of any legitimate reform process.

The first director of national intelligence, John Negroponte, became frustrated and left suddenly in December 2006 for a lesser position at the State Department. His successors were retired generals and admirals until the appointment of former Senator Dan Coats in 2017. All of them had an inadequate understanding of the importance of strategic and long-term intelligence. The director of national intelligence spends too much time preparing for the daily briefing of the president, which should be in the hands of the CIA, and the issue of cyber-security, which should be in the hands of the NSA.

Instead of pursuing reform, the directors of national intelligence have built a huge, lumbering, and bloated bureaucracy that includes a principal deputy director, four deputy directors, three associate directors and no fewer than 19 assistant deputy directors. The Office of the Director of National Intelligence has a huge budget—over $1 billion—and has taken its management staff from the CIA and State Department's Bureau of Intelligence and Research, thus weakening the overall intelligence apparatus. There has been no real accountability for the directors of national intelligence, and congressional oversight committees took too long to limit his hiring of contractors with extravagant salaries.

The CIA is not a policy agency; it was chartered to provide objective and balanced intelligence analysis to decision makers without any policy axe to grind. This is possibly the most harmful myth of all, because covert action, which has registered a series of strategic disasters over the past 60 years, finds the CIA a major participant in the policy process. U.S. counterterrorism operations against countries with which we are not at war is a violation of international law and a violation of the sovereignty of those nations. Much clandestine collection over the years has been designed to collect information to support policy.

CIA covert action is a major part of the White House policy process. Presidents have authorized regime change in Iran, Guatemala, Cuba, the Congo, Chile, the Dominican Republic, and South Vietnam, with disastrous consequences for these nations, and the United States. The White House authorized assassination plots in Cuba, the Congo, and South Vietnam, and provided legal sanction for the CIA to create secret prisons, conduct torture, and pursue renditions, often involving innocent people without recourse to judicial proceedings. Former Supreme Court Justice John Paul Stevens believes that many of the prisoners being held at Guantánamo are entitled to reparations.

One of the greatest weaknesses in the CIA's Directorate of Intelligence is the lack of formal peer review of its publications. Unlike the academic, scientific, and medical communities, the intelligence community largely abhors the sharing, vetting, and reviewing of its finished intelligence. The isolation of the Directorate of Intelligence is another weakness, and the creation of "fusion centers" will increase the parochialism and isolation of CIA analysts.

Despite the myth of clandestine recruitment of assets, the Directorate of Operations has had mixed success in recruiting assets in the closed world of terrorism or in closed societies such as China, Iran, and North Korea. Many of the agents recruited from Cuba, East Germany, and the former Soviet Union were double agents reporting to their host governments. The suicide bomber in Afghanistan responsible for the deaths of seven CIA employees and contractors in 2009 was a double agent. The CIA's clandestine officers responsible for this costly tragedy ignored key aspects of tradecraft in allowing the bomber access to a sensitive facility without proper vetting.

The CIA often relies on foreign intelligence liaison sources for sensitive intelligence collection and the recruitment of foreign assets. There are few al Qaeda operatives who have been killed or captured without the assistance of foreign liaison. Humam Khalil Abu-Mulal al-Balawi, who carried out the devastating suicide attack inside the CIA's Forward Operating Base Chapman near Khost, Afghanistan, was recruited with the help of the Jordanian intelligence service, an extremely risky way to recruit assets; he was brought onto the base without proper inspection and met with more than a dozen officers.

President Truman's idea of a CIA outside the policy community telling truth to power in the form of objective and balanced intelligence has been replaced by a CIA as a paramilitary organization. The trend toward militarization of the entire intelligence community was strengthened by both the Bush and Obama administrations. Both presidents appointed general officers to run the CIA and the office of National Intelligence. In his first term, Obama appointed a retired admiral to be the director of national intelligence, a retired general to be national security advisor, a retired general to be CIA director, and retired generals to be ambassadors to key countries such as Afghanistan and Saudi Arabia.

By placing the position of the director of national intelligence in the hands of the military, the Bush and Obama administrations completed the militarization of the CIA and even the intelligence community itself, where active-duty and retired general officers typically ran the Office of National Intelligence, the National Security Agency, the National Geospatial Intelligence Agency and the National Reconnaissance Office.

The Pentagon is responsible for nearly 90 percent of all personnel in the intelligence community and 85 percent of the community's $75 billion budget. The absence of an independent civilian counter to the power of military intelligence threatens civilian control of decisions to use military power and makes it more likely that intelligence will be tailored to suit the purposes of the Pentagon. This is what President Truman hoped to prevent in creating a civilian intelligence agency that "was not intended as a 'Cloak & Dagger Outfit.'"[18]

I am using my national security project at the Center for International Policy to lobby for legislation that would create fixed terms for both the director of national intelligence and the director of the CIA. Fixed terms would take the selection of directors outside of the electoral process for new presidents and would promote honest reporting to the White House and the Congress. In the past, the turnover of intelligence directors at the start of presidential administrations has led to instability and intelligence failures.

Finally, the congressional intelligence oversight process must monitor the CIA's flawed intelligence analysis, and challenge the illegal activities of the CIA that are part of the policy process. The chair of the Senate Intelligence Committee sat on her hands while CIA director Panetta dismantled and marginalized the oversight responsibilities of the Office of Inspector General.

THE CIA AND THE DANGER OF WORST-CASE ANALYSIS

A major reason for creating the CIA was to end the Pentagon's monopoly on intelligence and its resort to worst-case analysis of international issues. The Pentagon was opposed to the creation of the CIA precisely because it didn't want to lose that monopoly and didn't want to encounter objective intelligence analysis. With the increased militarization of intelligence over the past two decades and particularly the creation of the Director of National Intelligence, the so-called intelligence tsar, the delivery of intelligence to the White House and the Congress has been in the hands of retired generals and admirals. Thus, there has been a return to worst-case analysis.

The best example of the worst-case point of view has been the briefings and testimony of the current intelligence tsar, General James Clapper. In February 2014, the general made his way to the Hill to deliver the annual worldwide threat assessment, which used to be delivered by the CIA director, relying on the analytic work of the CIA's Directorate of Intelligence. I contributed to many of these briefings over my 24 years at the Agency, and there was a serious effort to get the briefing right and to avoid worst-case views. Conversely, Clapper's threat assessment was designed to fill the committee room with dread. "Looking back over my more than half a century in intelligence," Clapper intoned, "I have not experienced a time when we have been beset by more crises and threats around the globe."[19] Very scary stuff, but bogus.

A year earlier, in February 2013, General Clapper told the committee that in "my almost 50 years in intelligence, I do not recall a period in which we confronted a more diverse array of threats, crises and challenges around the world. This year's threat assessment illustrates how dramatically the world and our threat environment are changing."[20] And the year before that it was "Never has there been, in my almost 49-year career in intelligence, a more complex and interdependent array of challenges than that we face today."[21] Such specious thinking has led the United States to spend more on its military and its intelligence community than the aggregate spending of the global community as well as to develop bases and facilities that allow the United States to intervene anywhere on the globe.

Does the intelligence tsar believe that the threat of nuclear holocaust during the Cold War era and the constant monitoring of U.S. borders by Soviet strategic bombers and submarines was less dangerous than dealing with such strategic backwaters as Iran, North Korea, and various terrorist organizations that couldn't, to paraphrase Lyndon B. Johnson, "piss their way out of a phone booth?" General Clapper described an "assertive" Russia; another description could be "enfeebled and corrupt." China is described as "competitive"; "economically and environmentally challenged" would be apt. Neither Russia nor China can be compared to the United States in terms of military or economic power; neither country has a power projection capability to threaten U.S. interests, let alone the United States itself. Clapper recited chapter and verse on the "lingering ethnic divisions in the Balkans; perpetual conflict and extremism in Africa; violent political struggles in Ukraine, Burma, Thailand, and Bangladesh." Does the intelligence tsar genuinely believe that any of these situations represent a "threat" to the United States? I hope not.

The fact is that the United States has never been in a more secure strategic environment than the one it currently faces, and, since the collapse of the Soviet Empire and the Soviet Union 25 years ago, the United States has been particularly safe. With oceans east and west, and friendly neighbors north and south, there is no threat to American territorial integrity, let alone survival. Terrorism will remain a concern, but it doesn't represent an existential threat. It is fear-mongering that is truly dangerous.

General Clapper's alarmist tone refers to the "scourge and diversification of terrorism" of the global jihadist and homegrown variety, but this is an example of worst-case analysis that finds the actual threat no match for the rhetoric. The former chairman of the Joint Chiefs of Staff, General Martin Dempsey, a former student of mine at the National War College, believes the present international situation represents the most dangerous era in his lifetime, which raised serious questions about the general's memory and acumen. General officers have muddied the waters of intentions vs. capabilities, which has always been a problem in dealing with military intelligence. One of the major reasons for the creation of the CIA was to learn to balance these two important areas in threat assessments.

The CIA has committed despicable acts throughout its history, particularly during the Vietnam War, and has conducted even worse activities during the current Terror Wars. The overuse of secrecy has limited debate on these policies; a culture of openness is needed to reverse the damage that has been done. As long as Congress defers to the president on the conduct of national security; the courts intervene to prevent any challenge to the power of the president in national security policymaking; and the media defer to official and authorized sources, the nation will need courageous whistleblowers to make sure that that CIA actions are legal, ethical, and moral.

President Truman never wanted the CIA to be an "agency to initiate policy or to act as a spy organization." President Carter signed the Foreign Intelligence Surveillance Act into law in 1978 to bring the CIA and FBI under control; Congress created the Foreign Intelligence Surveillance Court for the same reason. We now know, however, that judicial supervision failed and that the voyeurs of the National Security Agency and the CIA were not under control. Before 9/11, a warrant could only be issued under the Foreign Intelligence Surveillance Act if intelligence gathering was the primary purpose of an investigation; after 9/11, intelligence merely had to be a significant part of an investigation. Meanwhile, the intelligence community conducts illegal activities in the name of the American people, and if it weren't for the whistleblowers, we would all be in the dark.

SEVEN

CIA DIRECTORS AND DISSENT

"Every thing secret degenerates, even the administration of justice; nothing is safe that does not show how it can bear discussion and publicity."

—Lord Acton

"No nation could preserve its freedom in the midst of continual warfare."

—James Madison

The directors of the CIA have been a mixed lot. The first several were from the military, including General Walter Bedell Smith, who had the requisite qualities of truth and candor, and who ran the Agency with a firm hand. He replaced General Roscoe Hillenkoetter, who was thrown overboard for failing to predict the North Korean invasion of South Korea. Smith and the other general officers feared from the beginning that the "operational tail" of the CIA would "wag the intelligence dog," which became reality. Smith predicted it would be essential to "decide whether CIA will remain an intelligence agency or become a 'cold war department.'"[1] The current CIA is a paramilitary agency where worst-case intelligence, designed to exaggerate the threat, is back in vogue.

The second group of CIA directors included Allen Dulles, who was forced to resign because of the Bay of Pigs disaster, and John McCone, who chose to resign because the Kennedy administration ignored his warning about the introduction of Soviet missiles into Cuba. Admiral William Raborn was clearly not suited to run an intelligence organization. In a memorable briefing, he referred to Libya as land-locked, and one of my colleagues, Mark Sullivan, replied, "On three sides, Sir."

From 1966 to 1980, the CIA's directors were more capable and competent, particularly William Colby and Admiral Stansfield Turner. Colby stuck his neck out, providing sensitive documents—the so-called crown jewels of the CIA—to the Church Committee in 1975, which cost him his job. National Security Advisor Kissinger was furious with Colby's cooperation with the Committee; so was the senior management of the Agency's Directorate of Operations and Colby's patron—Dick Helms.

CIA directors in the 1980s and 1990s, particularly Casey, Gates, and Tenet, were unwilling to contradict the policy interests of the White House; they refused to give those in power information that they would not want to hear, and they lied to the U.S. Congress. Casey and Gates were dedicated to providing Ronald Reagan with the intelligence needed to advance his agenda and to defeat the détente policies of Secretaries of State Shultz and Baker. Neither Director Webster nor Director Panetta had the energy to manage the Agency, let alone the intelligence community. James Woolsey was unwilling to reform the CIA in the wake of the Aldrich Ames scandal that cost the lives of key CIA assets in the Soviet Union.

As mentioned my major reason for leaving the CIA to the corruption of the intelligence process by Bill Casey and his deputy, Bob Gates. My reason for becoming a dissident was the appointment and confirmation of Gates as director of the CIA in 1991, an act of Congressional cynicism. This chapter will discuss the CIA directors from 1981 to the present, except for Gates, who deserves his own chapter because of my ties to him from 1968 to the early 1980s.

The CIA that I joined was not the paramilitary organization it is today. When I joined its ranks, the CIA had neither the chain of command of the Pentagon nor the stiff formality of the Department of State. It was a secret agency, but it didn't have the stifling atmosphere of the National Security Agency (where NSA stood for No Such Agency until the revelations of Edward Snowden in 2013).

Even a new analyst at the CIA could write for the president, as I did after less than a year at the Agency, or meet with the CIA director to discuss substantive issues. This was a heady experience for a new hand only one year removed from graduate school, and it contributed to the esprit de corps that marked the CIA in the 1960s. The meetings with CIA directors offered the opportunity to assess these men (and for the past seven decades they have been men, with a woman briefly serving as deputy director in 2013).

My alienation from the CIA can be traced to the limitations of these leaders since 1981, and not simply to flaws in the intelligence process. There is no silver bullet of reform that will halt the steady decline of the CIA as long as U.S. presidents appoint individuals without the integrity and character the post demands. At least four CIA directors—Casey, Gates, Porter Goss, and George Tenet—directly corrupted the process of intelligence, with the low point being the selling of a preemptive war with intelligence and analysis, a war that has claimed the lives of thousands of U.S. soldiers, killed countless people in the Middle East, and directly led to the formation of virulent new enemies, particularly ISIS. The Congress requested the specious National Intelligence Estimate on Iraq in 2002 that very few senators bothered to read. The chairman of the Senate Intelligence Committee, Bob Graham, saw the product as corrupt, but he couldn't convince any colleagues to join his criticism.

A flawed congressional confirmation process took place in 2006, when President George W. Bush named General Michael Hayden to lead the CIA. The appointment of a controversial four-star general did not augur well for an independent intelligence agency that is supposed to be free from military or policy bias. General Hayden was the NSA director when the Bush administration began massive warrantless eavesdropping that broke federal laws and violated the Fourth Amendment of the U.S. Constitution. (The charges in the impeachment process for President Nixon in 1974 included the use of warrantless eavesdropping.) During his confirmation process, General Hayden was never asked about his role in the NSA's massive surveillance of U.S. citizens. A federal appeals court finally termed the massive surveillance illegal, and at the time of this writing in 2016, the issue is on its way to the U.S. Supreme Court.

In addition to CIA directors who politicized intelligence and general officers who brought a definite bias to political intelligence, there were leaders such as Gates, James Woolsey, and John Deutch who supported the militarization of intelligence in the 1990s. In the wake of the 2001 attacks on the Pentagon and World Trade Centers, the process of militarization spiraled out of control, with the CIA becoming a paramilitary organization in the ongoing Terror Wars. Former CIA director Brennan told the Senate during his confirmation process in 2013 that he would reverse this trend, but there was no sign of any reversal. Nor was the Obama administration willing to seek accountability for the use of secret prisons, torture, abuse, and extraordinary renditions that have occurred during the Terror Wars.

No large organization could survive mediocre leadership over such an extended period. Corrupt leadership is the major reason for the CIA's loss of credibility and influence as well as the reason that I—and so many others—decided to call it quits. Only a president can reverse this cycle, which a congressional oversight process must demand. Thus far, there is no sign of leadership in either branch of government, and no sign of dissent among the ranks.

Over the past 70 years, there have been 24 CIA directors.

There have been generals and admirals; clandestine operatives and even two intelligence analysts; congressional staffers and a former congressman; various political appointees; and one political ideologue. There have been political biographies of some of these directors. The best one has been Thomas Powers's *The Man Who Kept the Secrets*, which explains the political role of the CIA director. Overall, however, there is a dearth of reliable literature on the directors, which is needed to explain the relationship between policy and intelligence. Very few memoirs and biographies of presidents and Secretaries of State and Defense incorporate the impact of intelligence—both successes and failures—on policy.

President Truman created the CIA in the National Security Act of 1947 to end U.S. dependence on foreign intelligence, and to challenge the influence of J. Edgar Hoover's FBI and the Pentagon's Joint Chiefs of Staff on gathering and interpreting foreign intelligence. Truman understood the risks of permitting policy agencies such as the FBI and the Pentagon to dominate the field of political intelligence. In the wake of his decision to close down the Office of Strategic Services, which many felt to be premature and unwise, Truman favored the creation of a "broad intelligence service attached to the President's office."[2] Truman's successors, however, failed to understand the importance of appointing powerful men or women who could stand toe-to-toe with powerful leaders of the military and the FBI and defend the independence of the CIA.

In my 24 years at the Agency, I reported to six CIA directors, starting with the urbane and unflappable Richard McGarrah Helms and concluding with a dyed-in-the wool political operative, William Joseph Casey.[3] Helms was a skilled administrator and a professional insider; Casey was an ideologue who mismanaged the Operational and Intelligence Directorates of the CIA and put me on a path of dissent. Sandwiched between Helms and Casey were four very different directors: James Schlesinger, who was sent to politicize the CIA; Bill Colby, who gave up the Agency's "crown jewels" in order to save the Agency; George Herbert Walker Bush, who left very few footprints other than trying to calm the waters of an Agency in turmoil; and Admiral Turner, who was a good and decent CIA director but inexperienced in the ways of Washington.

Only Helms, Colby, and Turner respected the independent role of the intelligence analyst. Bush believed the stewardship of the CIA would end his political career; he couldn't have been more wrong. Casey institutionalized the corruption of intelligence and destroyed the CIA's moral compass.

I met with all these leaders except for Schlesinger, whose brief stewardship coincided with my sabbatical as a visiting professor of political science at the University of Connecticut, and Bush, who had no interest in meeting with intelligence analysts. The first meeting with Helms took place during the Six-Day War in the Middle East, when I was assigned to a task force to detail Soviet political and military actions in the region. The Six-Day War demonstrated the important role that the CIA performs in providing premonitory intelligence to U.S. decision makers as well as in offering timely estimates of war.

I soon learned that good intelligence analysis would not necessarily be well received at the White House, particularly if it didn't support a particular policy or point of view. President Johnson's national security advisor, Walt Rostow, didn't believe our intelligence on the Israeli preemptive attack in the Six-Day War, and President Nixon's national security advisor, Henry Kissinger, failed to exploit our premonitory intelligence that Egyptian President Sadat had decided to expel the Soviet advisory presence. Both of these administrations abhorred the CIA's intelligence analysis on Vietnam.

President Johnson probably said it best, comparing the role of the "intelligence guys" to getting a full pail of milk from one of his cows and then have the cow "swing her shit-smeared tail through the bucket of milk." According to Johnson, "that's what those intelligence guys do. You work hard and get a good program or policy going, and they swing a shit-smeared tail through it." The Johnson and Nixon administrations were furious with the pessimistic assessments of the CIA on the Vietnam War, with Nixon asking Kissinger, "What is it those clowns out at Langley do?"

Since I left the CIA in 1990, there have been 10 directors, and this motley group explains a major reason for CIA's decline. Webster and Deutch did not seek the job, and had to be persuaded to take it. No one wanted the post more than Gates, but his role in distorting intelligence in the 1980s should have disqualified him from consideration. Jim Woolsey, Porter Goss, and David Petraeus were poor fits, and all resigned in short order or were pressed to resign for different reasons.

George Tenet, Leon Panetta, and John Brennan have failed as stewards for intelligence. Tenet could have been a hero, but chose to say "slam dunk" when ordered to provide intelligence to help sell the Iraq war. Panetta was captured by the operational side of the Agency in the early going and never had the energy or ambition to put the CIA back on the track. Brennan lied to the Senate Intelligence Committee and its chair and should have resigned, but President Obama had his back, calling Brennan a "patriot."

The key to managing any large organization, particularly a secret agency such as the CIA, is based on the integrity and competence of its chief executive and its senior managers. An intelligence chief must be tough, candid, and honest; he or she must be willing to tell people in power things they may not want to hear, or be willing to step aside. Tenet failed this test in December 2002, when President Bush pressured him to conjure intelligence to dupe the nation into launching an unprovoked military invasion. Tenet should have said such intelligence did not exist and then stepped aside. Instead, he said it would be a "slam dunk" to provide such intelligence, assigning his deputy, John McLaughlin, to deliver the phony briefing to the White House in January 2003. Brennan's public service marked a despicable new low when he ordered CIA lawyers and technicians to break into the computers of a Senate Intelligence Committee engaged in conducting lawful oversight of the Agency.

Helms, the first CIA director that I served, was the polar opposite of Bill Casey. Casey was a bully who was rough not merely around the edges. He was gruff and ill-mannered; he made his expensive tailored suits look like off-the-rack models that were the wrong size. Helms was a public servant with nearly 30 years as an intelligence professional. He was urbane and sophisticated. Casey was a multimillionaire whose shady investments should have created problems at his confirmation hearings. Helms lived on modest government salaries his entire career, never capitalizing on his expertise to seek vast sums of money on Wall Street like Tenet or comfortable salaries in private enterprise like General Hayden or Jim Woolsey. He was pushed aside because he refused to cooperate with the Watergate cover-up and oversaw a series of estimates on Vietnam that failed to support Nixon's views.

Both Casey and Helms were World War II veterans of the Office of Strategic Services. Like the Agency's first director, General Wild Bill Donovan, the chief of the Office of Strategic Services during the war, Casey was a New York lawyer and a great believer in covert action. At the CIA, Casey was aggressive in pursuing covert action in order to bring down the Soviet Union. He was not interested in congressional oversight, independent analysis, or the rule of law.

One of my low points at the CIA occurred during the stewardship of Helms, on the heels of his testimony to the Senate in 1973 when he perjured himself regarding the Agency's role in subverting the Chilean government. Despite Helms's willingness to lie for the Nixon administration, Henry Kissinger and presidential aide General Alexander Haig were convinced that a left-wing cabal at the CIA had stood by while Salvador Allende emerged on the Chilean political scene as a strong presidential contender. Haig believed that covert action had failed in Chile because CIA operatives had let their political feelings "flavor their final assessments and their proposals for remedial action in the covert area."[4] He wanted to purge "key left-wing operatives under Helms" and conduct a "major overhauling of the means, the attitude, and the conceptual basis on which CIA's covert programs should be carried out."[5]

President Nixon distrusted the CIA, and fired Helms for refusing to impede the FBI investigation of the illegal Watergate break-in, the botched operation that led to Nixon's resignation. "Get rid of the clowns," Nixon told Schlesinger, referring to the CIA's staff. "What use are they? They've got 40,000 people over there reading newspapers."[6] What Nixon really meant was do something about the lack of intelligence support for his views, particularly in regard to Vietnam, where the CIA, with its 17,000 employees, had raised doubts about the U.S. war.

According to an oral history interview with a Nixon friend, Frank Gannon, President Nixon believed Helms was out to get him and that there had been a CIA conspiracy to remove him from office.[7] Nixon explained that it was "no secret that I was dissatisfied with the CIA, with its reports and particularly with their appraisals of Soviet strength and our other problems around the world." He admitted that he "wanted to get rid of some of the deadwood and so forth. And they knew it. So they had a motive."[8] Helms was fired at a short meeting at Camp David on November 20, 1972, and Schlesinger was named director of the CIA the following day.

Why Schlesinger? He was sent to Langley to complete the job that Kissinger and Haig wanted. Schlesinger did great damage to the institution in a short time, particularly to the Office of National Estimates, which had become too independent. According to Helms, Nixon was happy to "put his own man in—I mean one that really had R.N. tattooed on him—which was Schlesinger."[9] Schlesinger had orders to turn the place upside down, and he zealously carried out his instructions. He removed hundreds of analysts and operatives in his unprecedentedly short stewardship. When one subordinate said the mass firings appeared ruthless, the acerbic Schlesinger responded: "Ruthless? I'm just trying to clear the aisles so I can walk."[10]

Schlesinger had no experience in the world of intelligence, but he was well known for being a bureaucratic behemoth. His CIA service was short and stormy as he undertook comprehensive organizational and personnel changes. He became so unpopular at CIA headquarters that a security camera was installed opposite his official portrait because of fears that it would be vandalized.

Schlesinger did his best to tailor intelligence for political ends, but there was no institutionalization of this process until Casey and Gates arrived. Schlesinger centralized the production of intelligence by ending its separation into categories such as estimative, historical, and current. In doing so, it was easier to control the assessments that went to the White House where there was great discontent with CIA analysis on the Vietnam War, the Soviet Union, and arms control. The director of the CIA's Office of National Estimates, Abbott Smith, accurately stated that the weakening of the CIA's analytical function was a "turning point from which everything went down."[11]

As director, Schlesinger abolished the Office of National Estimates and the senior research staff, which were the most independent analytical parts of the Agency, the most difficult to influence even for the CIA director. The Office of National Estimates was replaced by a group of national intelligence officers who were appointed by the CIA director and thus beholden to Schlesinger's office at Langley. In the 1980s, the national intelligence officers for strategic weapons (Larry Gershwin), the Middle East (Graham Fuller), and the Soviet Union (Fritz Ermarth) were responsive to the dictates of Casey and Gates and politicized intelligence estimates in their areas of responsibility. Three decades later, Gershwin was still a national intelligence officer.

Schlesinger went further than simply abolishing the CIA's Office of National Estimates and senior research staff, summoning the senior Soviet analysts to his office on the seventh floor and telling them that they were to "stop fucking Richard Nixon." For the first time, I realized that the CIA's mission of objective and balanced intelligence had been compromised, and decided to look elsewhere within the intelligence community for a place to serve. The following year, an opportunity opened up at the Department of State's Bureau of Intelligence and Research, which placed me in a bureau that had maintained its independence and credibility even though it was located within a policy department. Director Schlesinger had damaged the CIA's moral compass, and 10 years later the atmosphere worsened.

Schlesinger did register a major accomplishment with regard to the crimes of Watergate that angered the White House. Upon learning that the CIA had offered technical assistance for the break-in at Daniel Ellsberg's psychiatrist's office in September 1971, he was furious and considered the break-in a violation of the CIA's charter, which prohibits the Agency from acting as a domestic police force, let alone a secret one.[12] He demanded all information about CIA illegal activities over the previous 15 years, which produced evidence of illegal spying against Americans, including antiwar protesters and journalists.[13] The Nixon administration was already unraveling as a result of the Watergate affair, and Schlesinger was soon dispatched to the Pentagon as Secretary of Defense to replace Elliot Richardson, who was moving to the Department of Justice after the resignation of scandal-plagued Attorney General Richard Kleindienst.

Reflecting on his career as director of the CIA, a cabinet secretary at the Department of Defense, the Department of Energy as well as chairman of the Atomic Energy Commission, which ran the Pentagon's nuclear weapons complex, Schlesinger conceded that he was "too self-righteous, a quibbler, stubborn. It took me a while to understand how hard I must have been to deal with."[14] There has probably been no more mellow a president in the White House than Gerald Ford, who found Schlesinger "aloof . . . arrogant. I could never be sure he was leveling with me."[15] With the exception of Casey, there was no CIA director more abrasive than Schlesinger, who wore out his welcome with three American presidents. Both were bureaucratic bullies.

An end to the senior research staff was a setback for the CIA's ability to produce strategic intelligence and to train new analysts. President Eisenhower's criticism of the Agency's lack of useful intelligence on the Soviet Union and on Sino-Soviet relations had led to the creation of the senior research staff. At the start of the Cold War in the late 1940s and early 1950s, U.S. policymakers were preoccupied with the threat of international communism, particularly the conspiratorial role of the Kremlin. Sino-Soviet collusion also was wrongly seen as responsible for the start of the Korean War in 1950, and exaggerated concerns about Sino-Soviet collusion also played a major role in the initial U.S. involvement in South Vietnam in the 1950s and 1960s. It was the senior research staff that developed the first evidence of the split in the Sino-Soviet relationship, which was not accepted within the policy community until the late 1960s when Nixon and Kissinger exploited the differences between Moscow and Beijing in order to improve Washington's strategic situation. The senior research staff did groundbreaking work on strategic issues that the CIA no longer studies.

President Nixon named William Colby to replace Schlesinger because he considered him weak and easily controlled, someone who would follow orders. When he was appointed to direct the CIA, Colby had three decades of experience with the Office of Strategic Services and the CIA. Nixon failed to recognize that Colby was a reformer and willing to cooperate with the congressional investigation in order to protect the CIA in the long run. Colby was a devout Roman Catholic, and his insider's knowledge of the crimes and calumnies of the CIA troubled him.

Colby was responsible for my most productive and enjoyable years at the CIA, where he turned the daily intelligence bulletin into a four-page newspaper with an editorial board that argued over articles and assessments. Colby, like Casey and Helms, was a veteran of the Office of Strategic Services; he was also a Helms protégé. Helms was responsible for all of Colby's major assignments that led him to the seventh-floor office as CIA director. Both Helms and Colby had long experience in clandestine operations, which gave them strong views on intelligence collection and the importance of covert action. In 1973, after Helms was forced to resign, Schlesinger named Colby deputy director for operations, a post he had coveted for many years, making him master of all clandestine operations.

The rungs of Colby's ladder included chief of station in Saigon; chief of the Far East division at the height of the Vietnam War; and then executive director–comptroller of the Agency, its third most powerful position. Colby was a Princeton University graduate in an Agency still dominated by patrician Ivy Leaguers.[16] He had fewer social connections than his Ivy League colleagues and didn't display the genteel snobbery of his peers; he was sub-dued and even scholarly in appearance. Helms and Colby had a falling–out during Colby's stewardship of the CIA because of Colby's opposition to Operation CHAOS in the 1960s, which was a surveillance and espionage operation against American cit-izens, and because of Colby's cooperation with the Church Com-mittee's investigation. Neither Helms nor any senior leader of the directorate of operations attended Colby's memorial service at the Washington National Cathedral in 1996.

No one survives a long career in clandestine operations with-out some black marks on his escutcheon, and Colby was no ex-ception. A World War II Resistance hero in France for the Office of Strategic Services, Colby was head of the Phoenix Program during the Vietnam War, a controversial CIA effort to neutralize the Viet Cong. The program was designed to destroy the Viet

Cong infrastructure through infiltration, abduction, terrorism, torture, and assassination and was responsible for the deaths of many innocent Vietnamese. Colby always denied that assassinations were part of U.S. operations, but he acknowledged that 20,000 Viet Cong had been killed.

On the basis of my conversations with Colby I concluded that he suffered from tremendous guilt, perhaps due to his Catholicism, in conducting the dark side of the Vietnam War. To assuage this guilt, Colby made public some of the most incriminating secrets of the CIA and supported the idea of the U.S. government paying $750,000 to the family of an intelligence officer who died as a result of the Agency covertly dosing him with powerful psychedelic drugs. Colby told the House Intelligence Committee about the CIA's role in the overthrow of the Allende government in Chile, violating a presidential directive to keep the matter secret and angering Kissinger. Colby's testimony demonstrated that his friend and rival at the CIA, former director Helms, had lied to the Senate Intelligence Committee.

As CIA directors go, Colby was a romantic; he was a committed liberal and anti-communist who parachuted into occupied France during World War II; directed a major effort in Italy in the 1950s to weaken the Italian Communist Party; and led a campaign in the 1960s to defeat the communist insurgency there. He was a contrarian in his own way, trying to work with Italian centrists to wean the socialists away from the communists and urging land reform and local self-government in South Vietnam as the best weapon against the National Liberation Front. He confronted U.S. ambassador to Italy Clare Booth Luce, who wanted to work with the political right and not the center, and he challenged the U.S. military in Vietnam, which was dismissive of Colby's "nation building." He opposed the Kennedy administration's campaign to oust the leaders of South Vietnam, and warned there were no alternatives to President Ngo Dinh Diem and his brother. Colby was more often right than wrong on all of these matters.

Colby believed that he could reform the clandestine culture of the CIA and provide the Congress with the "crown jewels"— the highly classified documents that described secret and illegal covert activities of the CIA in the 1960s and 1970s. These documents were a complete record of the CIA's domestic surveillance and disruption of antiwar groups; a mail-intercept program; the surveillance of journalists to identify leaks; experiments with mind-altering drugs; and a variety of assassination plots. His long time colleagues at the CIA were furious with Colby for providing these documents; a few even insinuated he was a Soviet mole trying to destroy the Agency. Colby believed that he was trying to save the CIA from the wrath and scrutiny of the new oversight committees created by the Church Commission.

As CIA morale plummeted, Colby was vilified and then pushed off the gangplank for cooperating with Congress. Before he was fired, he testified 35 times to various committees and opened the CIA to congressional scrutiny. Unlike such CIA directors as Helms, Casey, Gates, and Brennan, Colby did his best to accommodate congressional oversight and to set the record straight on the CIA's crimes. For the next two decades, Colby defended his reputation, promoted détente, and became an active supporter of the Nuclear Freeze Movement. Unlike too many of his contemporaries, Colby was embarrassed by the CIA's history of running operations against U.S. citizens who were engaging in activities protected by the Constitution.

Colby's death while canoeing in Chesapeake Bay in April 1996 remains a controversy. One of his sons believed his dad committed suicide and produced a documentary film to say so; one old friend was convinced that Colby was murdered. As with Gary Webb, we may never know how Colby died, but we should respect his efforts to balance secrecy and openness in a democratic society, a current controversy today, and his commitment to the need for limits on covert operations. Colby and Turner were the only genuinely honorable CIA directors during my 24 years there.

In October 1975, President Ford's key aides, Rumsfeld and Cheney, who led the Bush administration's sales pitch to invade Iraq three decades later, convinced President Ford to fire Colby and to name George H.W. Bush as CIA chief. For Rumsfeld, this would serve to get Bush out of the line of succession to the White House, although this was not the first time that the "best laid plans" of mice and men "gang aft a-gley" (oft go astray). Bush represented the unprecedented appointment of a partisan politician to run the nation's leading intelligence agency. Ironically, he thought it was the "total end of any political future," instead of one more rung in the ladder that led him to become the only Agency director to occupy the Oval Office.[17]

The removal of Colby and the appointment of Bush enabled Rumsfeld and Cheney to appoint a team (Team B) of neoconservatives, led by Harvard professor Richard Pipes, to move Agency analysis far to the right, particularly on matters dealing with the Soviet Union as well as arms control and disarmament. This was ironic, because many of Harvard's best and brightest had committed much of their energy to détente with the Soviet Union and to the Arms Control and Disarmament Agency. An anti-Soviet armchair warrior, Pipes assembled a group of like thinkers, including Paul Wolfowitz, William Van Cleve, and General Daniel Graham. One of my CIA colleagues noted that putting Team B outliers up against Team A insiders was like "putting the Washington Redskins against Walt Whitman High School," the school my children attended in Bethesda.

The clandestine operatives of the CIA were ecstatic over the selection of Bush, because they had never trusted Colby or Schlesinger and expected Bush to defend them on the Hill. The only other candidate to be considered was Elliot Richardson, but Henry Kissinger feared Richardson would be too independent and would reveal secrets that Kissinger wanted to remain hidden.

Bush did his best to block release of classified portions of the Pike and Church Committee reports, and pressed the media to withhold commentary of some revelations. He provided strong support for a bill that Cheney and Rumsfeld wanted to allow jail terms for government employees who disclosed intelligence "sources and methods." He also allowed the neoconservative Team B to do its best to push the CIA's Directorate of Intelligence analysis to emphasize worst-case assessments. A senior operative, Thomas Polgar, compared Bush's stewardship to the Queen of England's. "He ruled but he didn't govern," said Polgar.[18]

There was no chance that President Carter would keep Bush at the CIA; he selected Turner to provide the leadership of the Directorate of Operations that Bush disdained. Turner became CIA director in the wake of the investigations of the Church and Pike Committees and the Rockefeller Commission into CIA abuses during the Vietnam War. President Carter told Turner that he wanted to know if there were other abuses that needed to be examined, and Turner guaranteed that he would be cleaner than a hound's tooth. We were concerned about the appointment of a naval admiral, particularly one who brought along a military staff that included the director's son, but ultimately thrilled that a housecleaning would take place at the Agency. The straitlaced Turner was true to his word.

The response in the Directorate of Operations was far different, because Turner was charged with cutting back covert actions in the wake of the war. Most of the personnel cuts came from attrition; very few clandestine officers actually lost positions. But operatives went to the press with protests over personnel losses, particularly overseas. The media dutifully reported rumors from operatives, although few of them were true. Meanwhile, Turner briefed the White House in August 1977 on past CIA abuses and detailed the steps that would be taken to prevent recurrences.[19]

Turner was committed to cleaning up the CIA in the wake of the scandals, but he was naïve about the mores of Washington. I had a good working relationship with Turner, which continued after I joined the National War College, and I'm convinced he would never have supported the corruption of intelligence that Casey and Gates imposed on the Directorate of Intelligence or that Tenet and McLaughlin orchestrated to justify an unprovoked invasion of Iraq. Turner had too much integrity for that. CIA leadership has lacked such rectitude since he left in 1981.

Turner had no exposure to the political scene in Washington and no intelligence experience, which contributed to a perception of failure on his part. Yet he met more frequently with intelligence analysts than any other CIA director, enjoying the give and take that is part of the intelligence profession. Turner relished sitting around a table with analysts to discuss the nature of the Sino-Soviet dispute or Moscow's ambitions in the developing nations, and asking analysts to prepare assessments that incorporated the most important ideas of the day. We referred to these sessions facetiously as "bogsatt" (a "bunch of guys sitting around the table"), but we relished the task of preparing the assessment of the day for the Director of Central Intelligence.

No CIA director was as protective of his analysts as Stansfield Turner. In 1978–1979, the Intelligence Directorate registered one of its worst intelligence failures, the lack of warning on the fall of the Shah of Iran and the emergence of Islamic fundamentalism. In 1978, while the Shah was still in power, Turner received a scathing memorandum from President Carter (that had been drafted by National Security Advisor Brzezinski) complaining about the CIA's inadequate reporting on Iran. Turner shielded the analysts from the memorandum by keeping it in his desk, but Brzezinski leaked it to the press. (Two decades later, the National Security Council had to prod the CIA on the importance of tracking non-state terrorist organizations, such as al Qaeda, as opposed to the state terrorism that preoccupied CIA analysts. But National Security Council directors Tony Lake and Sandy Burger didn't go public to embarrass the CIA chief or his analysts.)

Unlike subsequent CIA directors, Turner was willing to get

into the Pentagon's rice bowl and investigate topics that required sensitive information on military deployments and exercises. Successors to Turner, particularly Gates and Woolsey, were intimidated by the Pentagon and yielded key topics, such as order of battle analysis or the analysis of satellite photography, to the Pentagon. Turner knew that a major CIA weakness was lack of access to information about U.S. military capabilities, let alone war plans, making it difficult to prepare net assessments to compare Soviet and U.S. military capabilities. It would have been possible to anticipate Soviet naval maneuvers in the Mediterranean Sea and Indian Ocean, for example in the 1970s, if CIA had been witting of prior U.S. deployments.

The Pentagon fought the creation of the CIA, and worked to prevent civilian agencies from challenging military assessments. There were significant differences between the Defense Intelligence Agency and the CIA on estimates of Soviet strategic forces, with the military exaggerating Soviet capabilities in order to make a stronger case for U.S. defense spending. The military's control of intelligence collections directed by the National Security Agency or the National Reconnaissance Office tilts collection in favor of support for the warfighter and creates serious problems for producing strategic intelligence.[20]

In one of Turner's first congressional briefings, he was asked to describe the damage that Soviet long-range nuclear missiles could do to U.S. cities and military sites, a reasonable line of inquiry. Turner asked the Intelligence Directorate to calculate how much of the U.S. strategic force would survive an all-out nuclear attack. The Pentagon was furious with this line of analysis and accused the CIA of compromising the Pentagon's domination of war modeling. The CIA was unable to assess Soviet anti-submarine capabilities because the Pentagon would not tell the Agency where U.S. subs were located. The Pentagon feared any intelligence assessment that might encourage Congress to cut defense spending.

Turner was popular in the Intelligence Directorate because he challenged the plans and personnel of the Operations Directorate. He was appalled to learn that two operations officers had assisted Edwin Wilson, a former operations officer, in providing intelligence and military assistance to Libya.[21] Turner immediately called the Agency's inspector general and demanded an investigation that determined the guilt of the operatives. Senior members of the Operations Directorate favored moderate punishments so that careers would not suffer. Turner fired them both and courted a potential mutiny in the Directorate.

Turner's tough handling of the Operations Directorate led operational officers to whisper to the press that the Agency's new director was inept and inexperienced. Operatives were not accustomed to being scrutinized by the Agency chief: they called Turner smug and self-righteous. These views found their way into the press, which branded Turner unfairly as incompetent. As a naval admiral, moreover, Turner was accustomed to quick and direct responses to his inquiries; instead, he found himself stonewalled by senior operatives.

CIA operatives were delighted with Ronald Reagan's defeat of Jimmy Carter in 1980, which was the first time that CIA leaders overtly pulled for a presidential candidate. Leaders from the Directorate of Operations knew that Reagan would end Turner's stewardship, although it couldn't have known that it would lead to the appointment of Casey, a right-wing ideologue. Thirty years later, the victory of the Directorate of Operations was complete when it targeted the CIA's Office of Inspector General to bring an end to its investigations that criticized operations officers and, in the case of the 9/11 failure, even the director and deputy director of the CIA.

President Reagan wasted no time in naming Casey, his national campaign manager, as CIA director. Prior to Carter's election in 1976, newly elected U.S. Presidents did not feel the need to appoint their own CIA directors along with their cabinet appointments. President Eisenhower chose a new CIA chief, but he had been the Agency's deputy director in the Truman administration. Presidents Kennedy, Johnson, Nixon, and Ford kept the CIA directors they inherited; both Presidents Bush did the same. Presidents Clinton and Obama appointed their own CIA directors, and neither Woolsey nor Panetta distinguished themselves in the job.

President Reagan's appointment of Casey, a dyed-in-the-wool political ideologue, harmed the mission and credibility of the CIA, sending shock waves throughout the intelligence and policy communities. Reagan wanted to unleash the CIA, and in choosing Casey, he got someone devious and crass enough to do the job. Casey pushed CIA analysis to the right and demanded covert actions in every CIA station. His deputy, Gates, acted as a filter on intelligence production to make sure that it suited Casey's whims. Some of Casey's operatives, as well as Gates, were caught up in the Iran-Contra scandal in the mid-1980s, but the operatives involved were pardoned by President Bush in 1992.

Casey, the worst political appointee at the CIA, was joined by Haig at the State Department, Weinberger at the Department of Defense, and Richard Allen at the National Security Council, which offered few opportunities for objective intelligence on the Soviet Union or arms control.[22] Casey was the first CIA head to be named to the president's cabinet, a violation of the principle of keeping the CIA director outside the policy process.

In his aptly titled memoir *Company Man*, former acting general counsel of the CIA John Rizzo described Casey as the "toughest, smartest, most complex, and most enigmatic of the dozen CIA directors I served under."[23] Only a company man could describe Casey in such fashion. Casey was a bully and a slob, often incoherent and extremely contemptuous of those who were not willing to do anything—even break the law—for the United States. He wore expensive tailored suits but looked as if he had slept in them. If you happened to see Casey after lunch, you could tell the menu from the crumbs on his collar. He was an embarrassment, but only Nancy Reagan could tell her husband that Casey needed to be replaced because he didn't suit the image of the Reagan administration.

Like William ("Wild Bill") Donovan, Casey was a World War II veteran of the Office of Strategic Services; he was also a New York lawyer, and a great believer in the role of clandestine operations. Casey wanted the CIA to be aggressive in promoting covert action to bring down the Soviet empire, and he was hostile to the notion of congressional oversight and the rule of law. He ran the CIA in the authoritative way that Donovan ran the Office of Strategic Services; Casey looked at the Soviet Union in the same way that Donovan perceived Nazi Germany. Casey's aggressive tactics coincided with the emergence of Soviet leaders who reduced the growth of defense spending and favored a stable and peaceful Soviet-American relationship. Casey rejected this approach, and Gates pandered to the boss's hard-line views. An intelligence assessment without a hard line toward Moscow never left Gates's desk.

Gates, like his mentor Casey, had the simplistic ideological view of the Soviet Union that had dominated strategic thinking during the Cold War: Soviet forces in the Middle East and Southwest Asia threatened the Western supply of oil; a Soviet presence in Afghanistan could threaten interests in Iran; Soviet-supported rebels were active in Central America and posed an imminent threat; and Moscow supported Cuban mercenary armies in southern Africa. In other words, the Soviet threat was not just a nuclear one, but also one of proxy warfare and guerrilla insurgency.

They believed that Mikhail Gorbachev was a poseur and that his international agenda was a sham. As a result, the CIA recorded a catastrophic intelligence failure that its high-level officials continue to deny. Casey and Gates did their best to block Secretary of State Shultz's détente policy, leading to the worst relations that ever existed between CIA and State. Secretary Shultz's memoir documented the CIA's failure to track changes in Soviet policy.

Casey's single-minded aggressiveness as CIA chief contributed to the Iran-Contra scandal, which could have led to the impeachment of President Reagan for violating the laws of the land. The U.S. Congress had passed the Boland Amendment to outlaw funding for the overthrow of the Sandinista government in Nicaragua, but CIA director Casey ignored the law. A colleague of mine at the National War College, Commander Paul Thompson, who was a lawyer at the National Security Council in the 1980s, told me that Casey passionately argued that the amendment's restrictions applied to the CIA, not to the National Security Council.

Members of Congress were furious to learn that the U.S. had planted explosives in Nicaragua's harbor of Corinto, an unsanctioned act of war, and would have fired Casey if they had the power to do so. President Reagan laughed off the issue, remarking that if anyone in his administration pursued such an initiative "no matter what time it is, wake me, even if it's in the middle of a Cabinet meeting."[24] Acquiring money from foreign countries to fund the Contras was a violation of U.S. law, and therefore an impeachable offense. Selling weapons to Iran, a supporter of terrorism against the United States, was a violation of principles for dealing with terrorists.

I was a Soviet analyst at the State Department's Bureau of Intelligence and Research in the early 1970s when Kissinger was named secretary of state. In making the rounds of the building, Kissinger encountered Casey's name plaque as undersecretary of state for economic affairs. Kissinger was incredulous that Casey was in the building, let alone in a policy position as an undersecretary. "What is he doing here?" Kissinger asked. The question couldn't be answered, nor could the escort officer do anything about Kissinger's order to "get him out of the building." "He's senile," Kissinger added.

Casey was brusque and blunt, probably senile. The problem in judging Casey's acumen was that he could barely be understood. There were several occasions when we met with Casey and received instructions on what needed to be written, but no one understood what he said. On one occasion, we followed him to his personal elevator to get further instructions. We failed and were left looking blankly at each other as the elevator doors shut. One wag, after listening to Casey at his confirmation hearings, remarked that this was a CIA director who would not need a scrambler telephone. He was incomprehensible.

When Gates couldn't convince the Senate Intelligence Committee that he had nothing to do with the illicit Iran-Contra operations, the Reagan administration appointed someone with impeccable credentials, Judge William Webster. Webster had no background or interest in intelligence, but he had the judicious personality and professional experience to convince the congressional intelligence committees that he could do the job. Like Panetta two decades later, Webster lacked the stamina and focus that the task required and essentially allowed the CIA's Directorate of Operations to run the Agency. He dozed off during a sensitive briefing from the directorate on Aldrich Ames, the most notorious CIA double agent in history. I resigned from the CIA during Webster's stewardship, and he refused to grant me the exit interview that is customary for a member of the senior intelligence staff. His deputy, Dick Kerr, had informed Webster that I was a critic.

No U.S. president had more difficulty finding an acceptable CIA director than Bill Clinton, which spoke to his lack of interest in the world of secrecy and intelligence. He appointed a mediocre national security team that included Secretary of Defense Les Aspin, Secretary of State Warren Christopher, National Security Advisor Tony Lake, and CIA director Woolsey. Woolsey was the worst of the bunch and the first to go. Perhaps few presidential appointments could seize defeat from the jaws of victory like Woolsey, who spent most of 2015–2016 as an "intelligence advisor" to the Trump campaign. Only Gates, who logged in 14 months as director, and Schlesinger had a shorter tenure than Woolsey, who recorded 22 months on the job. Gates cracked that it took less time in 1991 for the Soviet Union to fall apart than it did for him to get Senate confirmation.[25]

Woolsey's hard-line views and close ties to neoconservatives should have ruled him out of any national security position, but President Clinton wanted one conservative advisor and Woolsey was his man. Like Obama in 2009, an inexperienced Clinton got less than he bargained for in creating his national security team. Pundits have overused the term "team of rivals" in describing national security appointments; the rivals in this case never performed as a team, and the first terms of both Clinton and Obama displayed examples of dysfunction. Only one national security appointment in either administration—the secretary of state—lasted for the first full term.

President Clinton was close to appointing an excellent candidate for the position of CIA director, Ambassador Thomas Pickering. But Clinton was so impressed with Pickering, an outstanding diplomat and a strategic thinker, that he decided to send him to Moscow as ambassador to help forge the close personal relationship that Clinton favored with the mercurial and unpredictable Boris Yeltsin. It could have made a huge difference if a serious candidate, such as George Kennan in the 1950s, Tom Pickering in the 1990s, or former deputy secretary of state William Burns more recently, had become CIA director and led the preparation of strategic intelligence.

But Woolsey was well-known to conservative Democrats such as Admiral William Crowe, former chairman of the Joint Chiefs of Staff, and it was Crowe who made the winning case to Clinton on behalf of his good friend. Some members of the Clinton team were drawn to Woolsey because of his reputation as the "Republicans' favorite Democrat." In fact, Woolsey was an unreconstructed "cold warrior," which did not hurt him during the confirmation process that led to a unanimous decision. President Clinton's press secretary, Dee Dee Myers, greeted Woolsey in their first meeting as "Admiral Woolsey, quite a promotion for someone who never rose above the rank of Army captain."[26]

Within months, Woolsey antagonized virtually every key member of the Senate Intelligence Committee, particularly Chairman DeConcini, as well as officials in the White House and the chairman of the Office of Management and Budget, former congressman Leon Panetta, who became CIA director in 2009. One of Panetta's senior staff officers commented on Woolsey's approach in dealing with the Office of Management as "graceless stonewalling."[27] No matter the issue, Chairman DeConcini said that "Woolsey felt he knew best, and nobody could tell him otherwise."[28]

One of Woolsey's major problems at the CIA was his management style, barricading himself behind closed doors, with little access for top managers. He had no strategic views for a post–Cold War world and no ideas for reforming the intelligence community. Woolsey could have compensated for some of these limitations if he had developed a political relationship with President Clinton, but he had never met Clinton before being nominated CIA director and never forged a relationship with anyone in the White House. When a Cessna aircraft crashed into the White House in 1994, pundits cracked that Woolsey was the pilot, merely trying to get an appointment with President Clinton.

Like a predecessor, Gates, and his immediate successor, Deutch, Woolsey thought that a greater role for the secretary of defense in the intelligence community would serve his role at the Agency. During Gates's tenure, the Defense Intelligence Agency was given control over order-of-battle intelligence that detailed foreign troop strength, which led to an exaggeration of the threat. During Woolsey's tenure, the Department of Defense gained control over the analysis of satellite reconnaissance, which also led to greater threat exaggeration. The actions of all three directors served to advance the militarization of intelligence, which triumphed 10 years later when Secretary of Defense Rumsfeld created the post of undersecretary of defense for intelligence, thoroughly weakening the authority of the director of National Intelligence.

During my 24 years at the CIA, there were serious espionage cases, but none compared to Aldrich Ames's 10 years of spying for the Soviets and Russians, which cast a shadow over Woolsey's stewardship of the intelligence community and forced his resignation in 1994. Woolsey refused to fire or even demote any of the 11 senior officers who were responsible for allowing an incompetent alcoholic like Ames to rise through the CIA bureaucracy, where he could expose every clandestine program involving the Soviet Union as well as every U.S. asset in the Soviet Union. Woolsey had no idea how much damage Ames, and the inability to find Ames, did to the CIA. Like the intelligence failures preceding the collapse of the Soviet Union, the 9/11 attacks, and the systematic falsification of information used to pitch an unprovoked U.S. invasion of Iraq, it was one more missed opportunity to reform the CIA.

I didn't know Ames, but I knew several members of the Mole Team that caught him and several members of the Operations Directorate who received letters of reprimand for allowing Ames to move through the bureaucracy. The letters of reprimand went to major players in the directorate who were central to operations against the Soviet Union throughout the Cold War. The list included Clair George, the director of covert operations; Gus Hathaway, the first chief of the Counterintelligence Center; and Burton Gerber, the Soviet division chief in the Operations Directorate. These letters didn't prevent the clandestine officers from retiring with high honors; meanwhile, the mole hunters were criticized by congressional committees for taking nearly a decade to uncover an agent as sloppy and careless as Ames.

Woolsey's defense for merely issuing bureaucratic reprimands was, "Sorry. That's not my way. And in my judgment, that's not the American way and it's not the CIA's way."[29] The chairman of the House Intelligence Committee, Dan Glickman (D-KS), identified the decline of the CIA in the wake of the Cold War when he remarked, "The question is whether the CIA has become no different from any other bureaucracy, if it has lost the vibrancy of its unique mission."[30] His counterpart, Senate Intelligence Committee chairman DeConcini, was more harsh, calling Woolsey's statement an "inadequate response to negligence in the biggest espionage case in the CIA's history."[31] Glickman concluded that it would take "dramatic reorganization to change the culture, the good old boys' club that protected this guy, promoted him, and gave him sensitive positions."[32]

Following Woolsey's resignation, President Bill Clinton nominated the failed director of his National Security Council, Anthony Lake, for the job. The bipartisan opposition to this selection led Lake to bow out before he could face the intelligence committee that was poised to reject him. Lake's failure was reminiscent of President Carter's nomination of Theodore Sorensen, also well known for liberal politics. What was less widely known was Sorensen's status as a conscientious objector, which made his nomination bizarre. Sorenson was at the CIA director's desk in the CIA building when a colleague brought him the wire service report that President Clinton had withdrawn his name from the committee. Sorensen had been given no advance warning; he quietly packed his bags and left.

The Clinton administration went from the frying pan into the fire by naming Air Force General Michael Carns to be the CIA's new chief. Carns, for good reason, wasn't even mentioned in Clinton's autobiography. Carns had violated labor and immigration laws, and was merely one in a series of failed and bungled nominations by the administration.

John Deutch was next. He didn't want the job, and had previously turned it down. Deutch feared that accepting the position of CIA director would compromise his chances of becoming president of the Massachusetts Institute of Technology. Nevertheless, he also thought it could be a stepping-stone to the job he desired—secretary of defense—and that he could follow the career path of Jim Schlesinger; Gates and Panetta traveled the same path two decades later.

When Senator William Cohen (R-ME) was selected to replace William Perry as secretary of defense in 1996, a disappointed Deutch immediately resigned from the CIA and returned to MIT—but not to the presidency of the august institution. Deutch's resignation was surrounded by scandal, including the possible compromise of the CIA's most sensitive operational intelligence, which ended any opportunity for leadership at MIT, thus completing his self-fulfilling prophecy. The penalty for compromising sensitive operational data on a home computer that was also used to view pornography websites? There was no penalty. President Clinton pardoned Deutch before any fine could be paid.

Like Woolsey, another member of the policy community picked to head the Agency, Deutch was uninterested in the professional problems of operatives and analysts and became extremely unpopular in the CIA as well as on the Hill. Several staff members told me that the Senate Intelligence Committee regretted its confirmations of Casey, Deutch, and Goss, who were temperamentally and professionally unsuited to be the CIA's top leader.

Deutch's short stewardship included a major contribution to the decline of the CIA and the militarization of the Agency. In 1996, he brokered the creation of the National Imagery and Mapping Agency (which became the National Geospatial Intelligence Agency in 2003). Mapping had always been done chiefly by the Pentagon's Defense Mapping Agency, but imagery had belonged to the CIA because of the sensitive nature of satellite imagery and the need to analyze it outside the government's policy bureaus.

In creating the National Imagery and Mapping Agency,

Deutch abolished the CIA's Office of Imagery Analysis, which had monitored key arms control agreements in the 1970s and 1980s, enabling ratification of the SALT and ABM treaties in 1972 as well as the Intermediate Nuclear Forces agreement in 1987. Deutch also abolished the joint CIA-Pentagon National Photographic Interpretation Center, which started as an Agency center in the 1950s, but became a joint operation in 1961. In losing both the CIA's Office of Imagery Analysis and the Pentagon's National Photographic Interpretation Center, the CIA lost imagery analysis as an intelligence function, despite the critical roles it played during the Cuban missile crisis as well as in arms control.

I wrote several editorials against Deutch's maneuvers and lobbied congressional offices about the militarization of a sensitive intelligence collection. Dick Helms wrote a letter to Deputy Secretary of State Strobe Talbott to alert the Department of State that important policy interests would be compromised if imagery analysis were given to the Department of Defense. "That big gorilla [the Department of Defense] controls enough assets," Helms wrote, "and needs no addition to its large Intelligence Community holdings. I watched for several years as the secretary of defense outgunned the secretary of state in White House meetings because he had more information sooner and in greater depth and I think State's position would be sounder if the CIA performed the service of 'common concern' as indicated in the National Security Act of 1947."[33] Helms was spot-on, as the State Department and the CIA were typically lined up against the Pentagon and the Defense Intelligence Agency in policy debates with the former supporting arms control and the latter opposed. President Clinton made matters worse in 1999 when he bowed to right-wing pressure and eliminated the Arms Control and Disarmament Agency, making arms control a continuous uphill battle.

The CIA hit bottom under George Tenet—one of the longest-serving directors in the Agency's controversial history. Tenet could have been a hero deserving of his Presidential Medal of

Freedom, which he received to assure his silence over White House pressure on CIA intelligence. Tenet merely had to tell the president that there was no reliable intelligence to support accusations regarding Iraqi weapons of mass destruction and that there was credible intelligence that such weaponry did not exist.[34] After all, the intelligence collection was that good. Instead, he and his deputy McLaughlin took part in the systematic campaign of the Bush administration to dupe the American people and our closest allies that a preemptive war against Iraq was required in order for the United States to protect itself. How many young American men and women actually entered the military in 2001 to fight in Iraq, where more than 4,500 Americans have been killed, believing they were avenging the losses of 9/11?

There has never been more of a "good old boy" heading the good old boys' club than Tenet, who laced his conversation with profanity and had a seven-year tenure at the CIA, which previously had four directors in seven years. Tenet's professional life up to then had been as a congressional staffer; he was hardworking, but, like Gates, much too eager to please. Tenet's loyalty to President Bush trumped his loyalty to the CIA, let alone his loyalty to the Constitution.

Perhaps Bush Jr. believed he owed something to Tenet, who renamed the CIA campus the George H.W. Bush Center for Intelligence to honor a CIA director who served in the post for one year but became president. Tenet was one of the most political directors in the CIA's history, and perhaps he saw the name change as political insurance in case a Republican administration succeeded President Clinton. Naming the CIA building after a U.S. president who had been a mediocre CIA director was an embarrassment. In any event, Tenet was off to New York City to make his fortune with Allen and Company, a secretive investment bank, and there was a new CIA chief, Porter Goss.

Goss was a Bush loyalist tasked with covering up the inspector general's devastating report on the CIA's failures to anticipate the attacks of September 11, 2001. For good measure, Goss got rid of officials who were suspected of disloyalty and even distributed a chilling message to all employees after Bush's reelection in 2004 that their job was to "support the administration and its policies in our work." Goss was neither the first nor the last CIA director to tailor the intelligence, but he was the only one to announce his plans publicly. In doing so, he essentially endorsed the corruption of intelligence and the CIA's inability to provide truth to power.

Goss, a former journeyman operative, had chaired the House Intelligence Committee. He was responsible for the greatest personnel turbulence in the CIA's history. Goss's executive secretary was forced to resign, and the FBI searched his office for evidence of criminal behavior, hardly an everyday event at CIA headquarters. Both Goss and Tenet came from Capitol Hill and both were major players in the distortion of intelligence, which should not have been a surprise. The political processes on the Hill do not offer the best training ground for senior positions in the intelligence community. The Hill is an institution of compromise and even caprice; the CIA demands principle and the ability to tell truth at all levels.

Goss had been a mediocre operative in the late 1950s and early 1960s under Dulles, McCone, and Helms, serving in the Latin American division for less than a decade. He contracted a serious infection while serving overseas and had to resign for medical reasons. Several months before his appointment as director, Goss conceded that "I couldn't get a job with CIA today. I am not qualified."[35] He was spot-on in that assessment, but it didn't stop President Bush from sending him to Langley and then demanding that he support the president and his policies. When the inspector general's critical analysis of the CIA's performance prior to 9/11 crossed Goss's desk, he did his best to make sure it went no further.

Presidents Bush and Obama appointed general officers to head the CIA who were inappropriate for the position. A military background rarely includes an interest in strategic intelligence, and Generals Hayden and Petraeus were unsuited to lead the CIA. Hayden was in the unusual position of having broken constitutional amendments at two intelligences agencies. At the National Security Agency, Hayden broke the Fourth Amendment against illegal searches and seizures when he used a massive surveillance program against Americans. At the CIA, he directed a program of torture and abuse in violation of the Eighth Amendment. At the time, a former student of mine at the National War College, Admiral Mike McConnell, was the intelligence tsar, meaning two general and flag officers were condoning waterboarding, a torture technique that simulates drowning. McConnell facetiously acknowledged that waterboarding would be torture if applied to him, but only "because of his delicate sinuses."[36] President Obama was also unsuccessful in selecting CIA chiefs, considering the disappointments of Panetta, Petraeus, and Brennan, who lied to the chair of the Senate Intelligence Committee. Panetta was a part-time director, traveling on Agency aircraft every weekend to join his family in California. He brought his dog to work on a regular basis, and his antics led operatives to refer to him derogatorily as "Uncle Leon." Panetta left the CIA in 2011 to become the secretary of defense. He continued to fly home nearly every weekend and to bring his dog to work.

President Obama demonstrated no interest in restoring the CIA's moral compass. In his first term he left a vacancy for more than 18 months in the post of inspector general; in the second term there was a vacancy of nearly 24 months. If President Obama had wanted to roll back the misdeeds of the Bush administration, restore the rule of law at CIA, and create the change that Americans wanted, he wouldn't have relied on senior officials who endorsed the shameful acts of the past. The American people need to know the complete story of the CIA's role in the Terror Wars, and recieve assurance that there will be no roadblocks facing oversight from the Congress.

Brennan's confrontation with the chair of the Senate Intelligence Committee, Dianne Feinstein, meant a refusal to accept the oversight role of the Senate. Recent history tells us that when a CIA chief is in the crosshairs of the Committee, that's when it is time to go. In the 1980s, when CIA director Casey lied to the Committee on Iran-Contra, its Republican members, such as Senator Goldwater, wanted Casey to resign. In the 1990s, CIA director Woolsey angered Senate Intelligence Committee chair DeConcini and other key members, and the Clinton administration forced Woolsey to resign. Brennan's resignation would have provided an opportunity to release the committee's report on the CIA's torture and abuse.

The fact that Brennan has crossed swords with the chair of the Committee, who had been an advocate for Brennan and the CIA at his confirmation hearing a year earlier, was sufficient reason for Brennan to go. Feinstein's advocacy included defense of massive surveillance, the use of drones and the misuse of the USA PATRIOT Act. There had never been a chair of the Senate Intelligence Committee more supportive of the intelligence community than Feinstein until Brennan tried to block the Committee's oversight functions.

Brennan never should have been appointed CIA director in the first place. During his campaign for the White House in 2007–2008, Obama spoke out against the militarization and politicization of U.S. intelligence, and indicated that he would demand more transparency and an end to abuse. Even before his election, however, Obama appointed an intelligence advisory staff that was headed by former associates of George Tenet, whose failed stewardship of the CIA included phony intelligence in the selling of the Iraq War and the cover-up of intelligence failures regarding 9/11. Tenet's deputy, John McLaughlin, who supported CIA torture programs and managed the preparation of Secretary of State Powell's phony speech to the United Nations, was part of the advisory group.

Immediately after the election, Obama appointed one of Tenet's protégés, Brennan, to head the transition team at the CIA. Tenet and Brennan were assigned to the National Security Council in President Clinton's first term, where they developed close personal relations. When Tenet was made the CIA's deputy director, he brought Brennan back as his chief of staff, which meant that Brennan was part of the corruption and cover-up at the CIA. Brennan often claimed that he was not in the chain of command for decisions involving secret prisons, torture, and abuse, but he became a cheerleader for those policies, which is worse. Tenet promptly promoted Brennan several levels in order to make him the chief of station in Saudi Arabia, an unprecedented jump for a career intelligence officer and one that was thoroughly deplored throughout the CIA's Operations Directorate.

Brennan had to remove his name from consideration as CIA director when it was certain he would have difficulty in the confirmation process due to his support for torture and abuse, as well as mass surveillance. Like Gates, who had to withdraw his nomination in 1987 because of his dissembling over Iran-Contra, but then laundered his credentials to become confirmed four years later, Brennan repackaged his credentials for a successful bid to become director of the CIA in 2013.

Brennan tried to hide the true history of the torture of more than 100 people at CIA secret prisons or "black sites" in Eastern Europe, Afghanistan, and Thailand between 2002 and 2006, many of whom were totally innocent of any wrongdoing. The congressional report and the CIA's initial review of the interrogations program, the so-called Panetta Review, established that no worthwhile intelligence was gained from torture. These documents demonstrated that the CIA openly and formally lied about the true nature of its secret prisons as well as the fact that innocent victims were tortured and abused.

Brennan's efforts to block the Senate Intelligence Committee's report on torture and abuse had support from the White

House. The Agency's director alerted President Obama's chief of staff, Denis McDonough, that CIA agents were hacking into Senate computers and that the CIA's inspector general, David Buckley, was filing a crimes report with the Department of Justice. The White House made no attempt to turn off Brennan's interference and allowed the CIA to make significant redactions in the Senate's report. Senator Feinstein appealed to the White House to end CIA redactions of its own questionable actions, but got no response from President Obama.

Brennan established an accountability board to examine Buckley's charges, but the board was unlike any other internal investigation at the CIA. Accountability boards are rare, but typically established to examine the charges of the Office of Inspector General in order to recommend disciplinary actions. In this case, however, Brennan's Board discredited the work of the inspector general, who soon resigned. Meanwhile, relations between the CIA and the Congress, which had turned sour during the Bush administration, significantly worsened.

The dearth of leadership at the CIA means the need for whistleblowers continues. As long as the U.S. intelligence community refuses to obey the law, refuses to report honestly to Congress, and refuses to advise the president without fear, there will continue to be an urgent need for dissidence. If the position of CIA director had a fixed term of five years, which would not coincide with the start of a presidential term, then it would be more difficult for an incoming president to appoint a compliant political crony to head the Agency. President Obama's legacy will include leaving torture and abuse on the table as a policy option for future administrations due to the lack of accountability.

The Senate Intelligence Committee had to investigate CIA torture because the Obama administration refused to do so. Meanwhile, the CIA refused to acknowledge that sadistic torture failed to produce valuable intelligence, and the Justice Department refused to read the report. As a result, barbaric practices are not considered illegal and no one is held accountable. FBI director James Comey told Congress that he didn't believe the Bureau could learn anything from the torture report.

The poor leadership at the CIA explains the bleeding of experience that has been taking place for 25 years. Greatness is an elusive quality, especially when trying to assess it through leadership, but I believe it is fair to say that no CIA director has had the vision and principles to qualify for greatness. For the past several decades, there has been no sound moral grounding among those who have endeavored to serve the nation as CIA director.

My decision to leave the CIA, probably too belatedly, had much to do with the shortcomings of the Agency's directors: the corrupting influence of Casey and Gates, the weakness of Webster, and even the clandestine legacy of Dulles and Helms. There is a case to be made for "starting over" at the CIA, and the loss of experience due to feckless leadership is now part of our national history. The Agency is currently experiencing another reorganization, but, without stable and scrupulous leaders, the CIA will continue to flounder.

EIGHT

MELVIN GOODMAN VS. BOB GATES

"A man does what he must—in spite of personal
consequences, in spite of obstacles and dangers, and
pressures—and that is the basis of human morality."
                              —President John F. Kennedy

One CIA director deserves special attention: Bob Gates, who
led the CIA from November 1991 to January 1993, one of the
shortest stewardships of any director of central intelligence. I
met Bob Gates on his first day at the CIA in August 1968, when
he reported to the Soviet Foreign Policy branch in the Office of
Current Intelligence. I had joined the office two years earlier and
remembered feeling lost in a vast bureaucracy, so I made it a habit
to take new analysts to lunch in the cafeteria to give them a sense
of what the Directorate of Intelligence was about. Doing so gave
me an introduction to our new analysts.

I knew from that first lunch that those of us in the foreign
policy branch would one day be working for Gates, and I spread
this view to my colleagues. I had never met anyone so ambitious,
who seemed to have no interests outside of work, who was prepared to work beyond any reasonable call of duty to achieve success. I was wrong about the timing of such a transition, because
I had no idea that, in less than 13 years, Director Casey would
name Gates as the deputy director for intelligence. I also didn't

predict the personal and professional compromises that Gates would make to succeed.

From 1968 to 1981, Bob Gates and I were colleagues and developed a close friendship. Both of us were accidental intelligence officers. We were graduate students at Indiana University, where we dropped in on CIA recruiting officers. Both of us pursued the recruitment pitch. I did so because I was getting restless in Bloomington, Indiana, and the recruitment process involved free trips to Washington for interviews and a polygraph examination. Both of us earned PhDs in history while we were working at the CIA, with Gates pursuing his course work at night at Georgetown University in addition to completing his doctoral dissertation.

When I took a sabbatical to teach at the University of Connecticut in 1972–1973, Bob Gates was the only CIA colleague I invited to Storrs to lecture to my undergraduate classes. When Bob began the first of his White House tours in the 1970s, I was one of two friends he invited to the White House mess for lunch and an opportunity to schmooze among the "best and brightest." Bob and I and our spouses went to dinner from time to time, and attended such events as Leonard Bernstein's *Mass*, which opened the Kennedy Center in 1971. We took an after-work tennis clinic in the 1970s with the understanding that we would play a match at the end of the clinic to establish bragging rights. I won the match and the bragging rights; Bob never played tennis again.

Bob and I were on opposite sides of the net on the role of the intelligence analyst in the production of intelligence. I came from the traditional school dominated by Professor Sherman Kent, who served in the Office of National Estimates from 1952 to 1967. Kent, whom many considered the "father of intelligence analysis," demanded a wall between the analyst and the policymaker so that policy views didn't affect intelligence analysis. Gates did not believe that intelligence was relevant unless it could be tied to a specific policy, meaning support for policy. To Gates, it was policy support that made intelligence relevant. To me, intelligence had to be neutral, pointing the way to opportunities and challenges for the policymaker but avoiding policy advocacy.

Gates's frequent memoranda to Casey emphasized that analysis generated by the CIA's Directorate of Intelligence was too tame and too non-controversial. He told Casey, "If no one gives a shit about what the intelligence analysis was saying, there would be no controversy, no pressure."[1] Gates believed that controversial intelligence analysis would attract the attention of policymakers and enable analysts to decipher what kind of intelligence policymakers desired. In a speech in 1989, Gates advocated the "aggressive use of intelligence. We in intelligence must think offensively. . . . We in intelligence are the shock troops of low-intensity conflict."[2]

Over a period of time, Gates found himself in positions in the 1980s as a deputy director for intelligence, chairman of the National Intelligence Council, and ultimately deputy director of the CIA, where he could indulge his fantasies of intelligence advocacy. Iran-Contra turned out to be the greatest fantasy of all. Gates had his acolytes in the 1980s, and there are still too many CIA intelligence officers who are unwilling to tell truth to power, including some who were responsible for the phony intelligence that paved the way to the invasion of Iraq in 2003.

My problems with Gates were professional and not personal. Serving as both the deputy director for intelligence and head of the National Intelligence Council, Gates began to corrupt the process and ethics of intelligence analysis in order to pander to the director of central intelligence and the White House. Casey's hard-line ideological views were well known, and it was not difficult to determine Director Casey's position on any given intelligence issue. For accommodating Casey, we began to refer to Gates as the "windsock."

Even before Casey came on board in 1981, Gates was named the national intelligence officer for the Soviet Union. Soon after Casey arrived, Gates requested a National Intelligence Estimate on Soviet policy in Africa, giving the task to a very malleable analyst, Grey Hodnett, who produced an execrable draft. I was the representative of the CIA's Directorate of Intelligence on that National Intelligence Estimate, and advised Hodnett and Gates that I would be taking a critical view of the product. The paper was extremely one-sided and gave no attention to the political and economic problems that the Soviets faced on the continent of Africa. Hodnett's response was typical of those who were willing to tailor intelligence. "Your problem isn't with me," he responded. "I was just a 'hired gun' on this paper." I asked: "Who hired you?" He responded, "Bob Gates."

So I took my problem to Gates, which led to the first of many acrimonious exchanges I had with someone who had been a friend since 1968. A key encounter on the issue of integrity and the intelligence process became a marker in our relations. He bridled over the use of the "I" word (i.e., integrity, not intelligence). I made my points at the meeting to coordinate the draft, but if anything, the final estimate was worse than the initial draft because of interventions from Gates. My final exchange with Gates over this issue brought an important rejoinder from the national intelligence officer: "This is the paper that Casey wants, and this is the paper that Casey is getting."[3] There is no better epitaph for the role Gates played at the CIA in the 1980s.

Several months later, Bob Gates became Casey's chief of staff. In addition to providing his boss with the hard-line intelligence that he wanted on the Soviet Union, Gates sent a stream of memoranda to Casey to establish himself as a critic of the Operational and Intelligence Directorates. The CIA's intelligence analysis, according to Gates, was feckless and wrong-headed; its operational culture was feckless and cautious. Gates was preaching to a one-man choir, and eventually the technique paid off. For Casey and Gates, it was love at first sight; Gates succeeded beyond his greatest dreams.

Very soon after becoming chief of staff, was Gates not only

Casey's executive assistant, but he was named to head the Office of Policy and Plans and to chair the Executive Career Service. Casey also kept Gates as the national intelligence officer for the Soviet Union because Casey was so paranoid he didn't trust anyone else to take the position. As for Gates, he considered Casey "intellectually. . . the most stimulating man I ever met."[4] A decade earlier, Secretary of State Kissinger had driven Casey out of the Department of State because he was convinced the old man was senile. Kissinger nailed it.

By the end of the year, Casey had become fed up with the deputy director for operations, John McMahon, whom he considered far too cautious to run the aggressive covert operations that Casey, a veteran of the Office of Strategic Services, favored. McMahon was an extremely popular CIA veteran, a genial and open-minded Irishman who had been successful in the Directorate of Science and Technology over the years. He was a gentleman's gentleman; Casey wasn't and soon replaced McMahon with an outsider, Max Hugel, a foul-mouthed businessman who was forced to resign in less than two months due to his boorish and clownish behavior. CIA Directorate of Operations agents leaked many stories to the *Washington Post* and the *New York Times* about Hugel and his bizarre-fitting toupee; Casey realized he had selected a loser.

In the meantime, McMahon was named the deputy director for intelligence and given the mandate to shake things up. McMahon created a good deal of bureaucratic turbulence in the process, but his essential decency and honesty contributed to his continued popularity within the Intelligence Directorate. I had never worked for a more accessible chief of the CIA's Directorate of Intelligence.

In a matter of months, McMahon, like Deputy Director Bobby Inman, grew disgusted with Casey's antics; he retired and moved to California. This opened up the position of deputy director for intelligence to Gates, who had grabbed Casey's attention with obsequious memoranda comparing the CIA to the

Department of Agriculture with an "advanced case of bureaucratic arteriosclerosis." According to Gates, the halls of the CIA were filled with "plodding mediocrities counting the days until retirement," which he called the major cause of the "decline in the quality of our intelligence collection and analysis over the last fifteen years," the very period that had been a source of some pride to me and others.[5] Like so many of my colleagues, I considered the promotion of Gates a disaster.

On January 4, 1982, Casey promoted Gates to the Agency's number two postion—deputy director for intelligence. According to Casey's biographer, Joseph Persico, Casey "untangled a bureaucratic knot" by making Gates the chief of the National Intelligence Council as well as the deputy director for intelligence. Persico naïvely believed that having two different directors as the deputy director for intelligence and the National Intelligence Council led to "duplication and confusion," with intelligence analysts in the "classic job hell of trying to serve two masters."[6] Persico's uninformed views are typical of outsiders who know little about the CIA's Directorate of Intelligence and rely on the views of insiders such as Bob Gates, the author's obvious source.

The separation of the offices of deputy director for intelligence, which is responsible for the analysis of current intelligence, and head of the National Intelligence Council, which is responsible for estimative intelligence, guaranteed competition and rivalry between the two disciplines, making it harder to politicize intelligence. Giving both positions to Bob Gates made it easy for him to manipulate the final intelligence product, and that is what Gates did with intelligence presented to the White House in the form of the President's Daily Brief; current and premonitory intelligence to the policymaking community; and estimative intelligence to the Departments of State and Defense. Bob Gates was positioned to create the very "job hell" that Persico incorrectly described. Persico was right about one thing, however: "Casey now had the machinery in place."[7]

There had always been turbulence in the CIA with the arrival of a new director or a new deputy director, but the combination of Casey and Gates led to a new level of change—unacceptable change—that institutionalized the tailoring of intelligence to please and satisfy the agenda of Ronald Reagan and the White House. Intelligence analysts, like all government bureaucrats, complain about change, but they typically adapt to new ways of operating. Life under Casey and Gates, however, became capricious, inconsistent, and totally biased. Too many analysts began to write for their new bosses: it was easy to produce intelligence if they took certain postures toward the Soviet Union, the leftist governments in Central America, or the "success" of U.S. efforts in Afghanistan. If you refused to accept these frameworks as a given, then you were taking on Gates personally, and were treated to his ad hominem attacks in the form of cover sheets attached to intelligence products. I garnered my share of them.

Soon after becoming deputy director for intelligence, Gates addressed his analysts in the auditorium and declared his new approach, the Genghis Khan school of management. Gates had virtually no experience as a manager when he took over the CIA's Directorate of Intelligence; his talk was widely discussed. He described the Directorate's analysis as "irrelevant or untimely or unfocused, or all three." He described analysts as "close-minded, smug and arrogant." He described their thinking as "flabby and complacent," lacking tolerance of the views of others. As for their writing, Gates called it "poor and verbose," and avoiding issues "germane to the United States" and its policymakers. He said the analysis was "often proved inaccurate," but it was "too fuzzy to judge whether it was even right or wrong."

Gates said that Casey was "deeply concerned about the quality of the Directorate's work," and that he had a mandate to "implement far-reaching changes in the way we went about our business." Later on, he conceded that some managers and analysts had been offended by his talk, but he argued that it was simply resentment over the "obvious intent to diminish their autonomy" and "the idea of accountability." Many of us walked out of the auditorium that day believing we had just reported for duty on Captain Philip Queeg's USS *Caine*.

Gates had previously made damaging charges. In 1973, still a relatively junior analyst, he wrote an article for *Studies in Intelligence*, the CIA's in-house journal, that criticized Soviet political analysis. After spending much of the 1970s on the staff of the National Security Council, Gates called the CIA's work "flabby" and far too charitable of Soviet foreign policy goals. We thought Bob Gates had become star-struck by his tours at the National Security Council and saw much to be gained in tough talk that separated himself from the Directorate.

Many analysts realized Gates was playing an ideological game to suit the interests of Casey and the hard-liners in the Reagan administration, but there were many careerists and company men who had no difficulty toeing his line. Supervisors and managers appeared to be competing for the role of truckling to the new deputy director for intelligence. This worked particularly well for Casey and Gates in support of a Reagan administration that viewed the Soviet Union as an "evil empire."

The departure of Secretary of State Alexander Haig from the Reagan administration and the arrival of Secretary of State George P. Shultz, however, brought "new thinking" and a new policy on the Soviet Union. As a result, Casey and Gates had to step up their game to resist the détente policies of the Department of State. Casey and Gates did their best to subvert the intelligence process in order to defeat the policy initiatives of Shultz and Jack Matlock, a foreign service officer assigned to the National Security Council. Secretary Shultz knew that as well.

Gates gave a particularly outrageous speech in January 1987, when he ignored the intelligence assessments of the CIA and relied on disinformation from the Defense Intelligence Agency and the *Washington Times* in order to make a case for President

Reagan's Strategic Defense Initiative, better known as Star Wars. Secretary of State Shultz thoroughly disagreed with the idea of Star Wars, but Gates argued that Reagan's Star Wars concept was essential to protect the United States from Soviet development of lasers and particle beam weaponry, the stuff of science fiction. Like Professor Richard Pipes and Team B, Gates stated that the Kremlin was "working to eliminate its own vulnerability and consolidate a unilateral advantage." Gates moved to the right of the Reagan administration, arguing that abandoning Star Wars would "preserve Moscow's monopoly in strategic defense" and mark a "key indicator of a loss of U.S. will to compete militarily." Secretary of State Shultz was furious, and made his anger known to Gates.

The success of Shultz and Matlock in getting President Reagan to turn to détente toward the Soviet Union in his second term was too much for neoconservatives to bear, including Casey and Gates. There were high-level resignations from the Department of Defense, including Secretary of Defense Weinberger and his assistant secretary of defense for policy, Richard Perle, the Prince of Darkness. Bob Gates was not about to resign, and Casey's sudden death in January 1987 nearly made him the CIA chief. Gates's involvement in the Iran-Contra scandal cost him confirmation, and the eventual successor to Casey, Judge William Webster, brought a new fairness and objectivity to the CIA. I was teaching at the National War College during his tenure.

By 1989, Gates left to become a deputy national security advisor to Brent Scowcroft at the National Security Council. My former bosses at the CIA, including Doug MacEachin, did their best to get me to return to the Agency, but I was happy at the National War College and was convinced that the days of politicization were not over. I was right about that one.

A major problem in battling Bob Gates over politicization was the difficulty of explaining the issue outside the world of intelligence, where many believe that everything in Washington is politicized. Since there will always be differences in judging and assessing Soviet or Russian policies and behavior, political differences are considered to be part of the game. There are also ideological differences and philosophic differences in explaining the Soviets. There were ideological roots in the differences between policymakers such as George Kennan and Paul Nitze, and between Democrats and Republicans. The intelligence analysts who best serve their country find ways to ignore the pressures that would have them arrive at ideological conclusions.

A complication in explaining our differences was the plethora of controversial issues in tense Soviet-U.S. relations. Most CIA resources for collection and analysis were devoted to the Soviet Union for more than four decades. Détente had gradually unravelled in the late 1970s and early 1980s, particularly because of the Soviet invasion of Afghanistan in December 1979, and the election of an ultra-right-wing president in November 1980. President Reagan received tremendous support for his glib remark that he "wanted to deal with the Soviets, but they kept dying on me." The deaths of Brezhnev, Andropov, and Chernenko in a three-year period were indeed a factor, but there was no indication in Reagan's first term that he had any interest in dealing with them. Mikhail Gorbachev changed all that, but Bob Gates—the deputy director for intelligence—disagreed.

Casey and Gates were never committed to providing objective intelligence on the Soviet Union. Their chief interest was in serving their master, President Reagan, and the attitude on the seventh floor of the CIA building, according to Hal Ford, was "the Russians are coming, the Russians are coming." Casey totally disparaged the work of CIA analysts on the Soviet Union, and Gates devoted himself to reifying Casey's opinions. The senior leadership of the CIA, particularly in the National Intelligence Council and the Directorate of Intelligence, bought the ideological line, but one national intelligence officer, John Horton, resigned in 1985 because he would not follow the line that Mexico was ripe for a revolution and vulnerable to the influence of the Soviet Union. When Horton left, Gates appointed Bryan Lytell to be national intelligence officer for Latin America, and Lytell produced the analysis that Casey and Gates wanted. If there had been serious oversight from Congress in the 1980s, Horton would have been subpoenaed to testify on the corruption of intelligence.

Casey and Gates took hard-line positions on every issue that involved Soviet foreign policy in the Third World and justified the CIA's covert action. Gates ignored ample evidence that the Soviet Union was retreating from the Third World, which Lyn Ekedahl and I documented in various assessments, and argued that Mikhail Gorbachev was continuing the Soviet commitments to Angola, Nicaragua, Cuba, Vietnam, Laos, and Cambodia. He completely dismissed Gorbachev's emphasis on détente, arguing that Moscow was merely trying to lock in "Soviet strategic gains of the last generation."

When it came to the possibility of Moscow basing military fighter jets in Nicaragua, he wanted an assessment that argued for deployment, which would have meant ignoring evidence to the contrary. When it came to the possibility of a Soviet retreat from the Third World, for which there was sufficient evidence, Gates stopped any assessment that made such an argument. I wrote my first book on the Soviet retreat from the Third World, which surfaced evidence that Gates rebuffed. My colleague and future wife co-authored a book on the Soviet retreat, along with an academic in residence, after Gates killed their paper on the subject.

Gates violated the CIA's charter against policy advocacy, pitching a bombing campaign in 1984 to "bring down" the leftist government in Nicaragua. In an incendiary memorandum to Casey on December 14, 1984, several weeks after the election of Daniel Ortega to the presidency, Gates argued that the Soviet Union was turning Nicaragua into an armed camp that would become a second Cuba. The rise of the communist-lean-ing Sandinista government, according to Bob Gates, threatened to destabilize Latin America. This message echoed the view of the neoconservatives who incorrectly predicted a communist takeover of the region. Gates's memo to Casey on Nicaragua and many other conflicts resembled the arrogance and hubris found in the notes, known as "snowflakes" from Secretary of Defense Rumsfeld decades later that helped pave the way for the catastrophic invasion of Iraq.

Bob Gates argued that the "only way that we can prevent disaster in Central America is to acknowledge openly what some have argued privately: that the existence of a Marxist-Leninist regime in Nicaragua closely allied with the Soviet Union and Cuba is unacceptable to the United States and that the United States will do everything in its power short of invasion to put that regime out."[8] Gates was particularly zealous in touching nerves associated with Cuba in order to gain an audience for his hard-line views.

When there were signs of Soviet interest in withdrawal from Afghanistan, which began to appear within months after Gorbachev's ascent to power, Gates laughed at our conclusions and lectured us on our naïveté. Some of us made money on this one because Gates and his hand-picked national intelligence officer for the Soviet Union, Fritz Ermarth, took bets against any Soviet military withdrawal. Lyn Ekedahl won a bottle of champagne from Ermarth on it, although he never paid off. When we showed Gates and Ermarth a copy of Gorbachev's first major Politburo speech on Soviet policy, which referred to Afghanistan as a "bleeding wound," they found nothing remarkable about the new Soviet line. Once again, Gates was wrong and made all of us look wrong.

Gates played the key role in developing a National Intelligence Estimate in May 1985 to justify the ill-fated deals known as Iran-Contra. He was totally dismissive of the much publicized investigations of Iran-Contra, calling hearings on the subject "bureaucratic bullshit" that Casey was determined to evade.[9] Just as falsified intelligence was cooked up to help sell the notion of sending thousands of U.S. soldiers to invade Iraq in 2003, phony intelligence had been created two decades earlier to justify selling arms to a regime that was supporting terrorism (Iran) and to use the profits of the arms sales to illegally fund a counterrevolutionary group in Nicaragua (the Contras).

In 1985, Iran-Contra was in the planning stages at the CIA and the National Security Council. In order to pursue controversial policies, administration hard-liners wanted "intelligence" to argue (falsely) that Iran had ended terrorism and that the Contras could overthrow the Sandinista government if given financial and military support. Gates was the intermediary between the national intelligence officer, Graham Fuller, at the CIA and the national security staffer, Howard Teicher, who argued that the Soviet Union was on the verge of improving relations with Iran and that the race between the United States and the Soviet Union "for Tehran was on, and whoever gets there first wins all." The problem for Gates, Fuller, and Teicher was that no Soviet analyst at the CIA or the State Department believed this Cold War hyperbole. The U.S. intelligence community had consistently taken the position that Iran was still resorting to the use of terrorism and that the Soviets had no chance to ingratiate itself with Ayatollah Khomeini.

It was obtuse to argue that Soviet-Iranian relations had improved, in view of the Iranian government's repression of the communist Tudeh Party; the expulsion of all Soviet economic advisors and numerous Soviet "diplomats" who were KGB officers; and Tehran's reference to Moscow's "godless" communist regime as the "Second Satan." Bob Gates blocked language in the analysis that reflected the views of the Soviet analysts regarding the unlikelihood of a Soviet-Iranian détente and inserted language that concluded Iran had given up terrorism as an instrument of policy. Gates was wrong on all counts, and the White House preoceeded to pursue weapons sales to Iran and channel cash and resources to the Contras.

There was considerable intelligence on important issues that didn't support the Reagan administration's interests, particularly with regard to providing military equipment to Iran to get the release of hostages. We had taken strong analytical positions on Iran's continued support for terrorism; the lack of a moderate faction in Iran's political scene; the fact that Iran was not seeking ties or the reopening of relations with the United States; the decline in Soviet arms to Iran; and the decline in the Soviet position in Iran. But Gates was the only CIA leader in history who banned footnotes (i.e., dissent) from Agency estimates in order to make sure the policy community was deprived of such dissent.

In order to justify the opening to Iran, the CIA supporters of Iran-Contra such as Casey, Gates, and Fuller had to argue the opposite on all these accounts. They introduced language that stated Iran's support for terrorism had diminished; there was a moderate faction in Iran favoring ties with the United States; the Soviets were building up their position in Iran; and Moscow was on the verge of a breakthrough in its relations with Iran as a result of its military assistance. These positions were taken in the spring of 1985 before the first delivery of Hawk surface-to-air missiles to Iran. My colleagues at the State Department Bureau for Intelligence and Research disputed these positions, but Gates stated in his testimony that he persuaded the Bureau's director, Morton Abramowitz, to drop the State Department's dissents, arguing that the "difference of view represented by the footnote was so scant that it was unwarranted."[10]

In addition to the analytical machinations of Gates and Fuller, the CIA's Directorate of Operations was used to slant the analysis of the Intelligence Directorate and thus provide the White House with views and recommendations favored by the Reagan administration or orchestrated by Casey. When National Security Advisor Robert McFarlane made his secret trip to Tehran in 1986, he was accompanied by a senior operative, George Cave. Upon return, Cave sent a typescript memorandum to the National Security Council on Iranian politics that was not coordinated with the Intelligence Directorate. The memo argued that there was a moderate faction in Iran that favored contacts with the United States, a notion created out of whole cloth. This report was cited in the President's Daily Brief, which was not coordinated with the Iranian analysts in the Intelligence Directorate. Cave also briefed the National Security Council on the basis of clandestine reporting at variance with other evidence.

The White House received specious intelligence from two National Intelligence Officers, Fuller, a specialist in the Middle East and a former clandestine operative, and Charlie Allen, a controversial CIA careerist who was the National Intelligence Officer for counterterrorism. Their reporting reified the notion there were moderates in Iran with sufficient political clout who were waiting for a U.S. emissary to improve bilateral ties. Allen, like Cave, also briefed the National Security Council on Iranian politics, although he had no background in this area. As Deputy Director for Intelligence, Gates coordinated the effort to provide sensitive intelligence on Iran that was not supported by analysts from the Directorate of Intelligence and was totally at odds with the evidence.

This was a serious violation of intelligence ethics, an effort to provide uncoordinated intelligence to the President of the United States to support dubious covert actions in Iran and Nicaragua. So when President Reagan explained to the nation that he believed he was dealing with a moderate faction in Tehran interested in reopening ties to the United States, he could claim to be acting on the basis of CIA analysis. The question that remains unanswered to this day is whether the President was a victim of CIA disinformation.

In any event, Gates was spinning intelligence to provide propaganda for the government to use with Congress and the American people. Presumably the Reagan administration would have pursued selling weapons to Iran regardless of what was said in the finished intelligence of the CIA, but the coordinated assessment of the intelligence community made it easier to claim legitimacy for the Iran-Contra operation. When Bob Gates told the Senate Select Committee on Intelligence that he was unaware of any disagreement among intelligence analysts, he was lying. Accurate intelligence could have bolstered policymakers who disagreed with the false sense of urgency regarding Iran-Contra.

Key members of the Senate Select Committee on Intelligence were quite familiar with Gates's glib and smug testimony on substantive issues. In 1986, Senator Bradley asked Gates, then the CIA's deputy director, whether there would come a time when the Soviet Union might be open to "fundamental change." It was an excellent question that reflected the committee's oversight responsibilities for CIA, and Gates's answer was revealing. "Quite frankly, and without any hint that such fundamental change is going on, my resources do not permit me the luxury of sort of just idly speculating on what a different kind of Soviet Union might look like," Gates replied.[11] This answer testified to Gates's inability to direct intelligence requirements and analysis at the CIA.

Bob Gates dwelled on the prospect of Moscow's ability to steal a march on the United States in a sensitive country such as Iran, despite the lack of evidence to support his assumptions, and made sure that the director of Soviet analysis, Doug MacEachin, a sycophantic supporter of Gates at the hearings, went along. MacEachin conceded in a classified memorandum of January 28, 1987, that the Gates-Fuller Estimate of 1985 suffered from a "swerve" in warning of growing Soviet influence in Iran and the potential for Soviet military pressure on Tehran.[12] He acknowledged that Fuller "made significant changes" in the estimate, adding for example that Gorbachev would "see Iran as the key area of opportunity for Soviet foreign policy in the next year" and would renew Soviet arms sales to Iran. In doing so, MacEachin ignored his Soviet analysts, who believed "their judgments in 1985 were overruled," although he acknowledged their judgments were "subsequently demonstrated to have been correct."

Gates dropped a key judgment from Soviet analysts that Moscow was "extremely unlikely to sacrifice good ties with Baghdad for uncertain gains in Tehran while an Islamic regime mistrustful of the USSR and Communism rules Iran."[13] There was evidence that Moscow had set certain conditions for improved relations with Tehran, including a requirement that Iran reduce its anti-Soviet rhetoric, end its support for rebels fighting the Soviet army in Afghanistan, allow the return to Tehran of expelled Soviet diplomats, and stop repression of the pro-Soviet Tudeh Party.

In a closed session in the evening of September 25, 1991, Jennifer Glaudemans, a key dissenter on the Iran estimate, told the Senate Intelligence Committee that Gates's "heavy-handed" supervision of the CIA's Intelligence Estimates had "tragic consequences" for American policy. Glaudemans, who eventually left the CIA to go to the State Department's Bureau of Intelligence and Research, described the "atmosphere of intimidation in the office of Soviet analysis" as well as the "under-handed efforts to reverse or to impose analytical conclusions."

In addition to tailoring the intelligence on Nicaragua and Iran, Gates supported the Reagan administration's decision not to inform Congress of the arms shipments going to Iran to gain release of U.S. hostages in Lebanon. Like Helms a decade earlier in the covert action against Salvador Allende, Gates knew that it was politically suicidal not to inform Congress. He chose to go along with a policy that he knew was wrong and remain on track to become the first intelligence analyst to be named director. Gates remained silent; he would not let principles stand in the way of professional advancement.

Casey was engaging in poor tradecraft by mingling two covert actions—one regarding Iran, the other dealing with Nicaragua.

Gates knew that laws were being broken and the consequences could be disastrous. In clear violation of federal law, a government agency, the Pentagon, was selling surface-to-air missiles to the government of Iran for a profit, and using the money to fund violent operations against the leftist Sandinistas in Nicaragua. Profits had to be turned back to the U.S. Treasury. Bob Gates's silence on these matters cost him the position of director of central intelligence in 1987; it could have cost Ronald Reagan the presidency.

Casey and Gates worked in tandem on other policy issues in which the intelligence wouldn't support Reagan's policies. They distorted intelligence to create a false sense of Soviet manipulation of leftists in Central and South America, and to create a picture of Soviet orchestration of terrorist organizations. Gates argued that Nicaraguan anti-communist forces (the Contras) would collapse within one or two years without U.S. funding, but that "new funding" was insufficient. He wanted to go beyond the tactical operations of Iran-Contra in supplying assistance to the Contras. He advocated that the United States withdraw diplomatic recognition of the Sandinista government, provide overt assistance to a government in exile, impose economic sanctions or a quarantine, and use air strikes to destroy Nicaragua's "military buildup." The recommendation for the use of air strikes was unprecedented for a CIA official.

The Reagan administration ignored Gates's recommendations, and none of his predictions panned out. Nicaragua didn't become a communist dictatorship, and the Sandinista regime didn't lead to the fall of U.S.-backed death squad governments in El Salvador, Honduras, or Guatemala. In fact, the Sandinistas and Ortega were voted out of power in 1990, and the Soviet Union ceased to exist a year later. Two decades later, President Obama ignored Secretary of Defense Gates's recommendations to increase the U.S. military presence in Afghanistan.

Before his recommendation to use force against Nicaragua, Gates wrote a paper for Casey that argued for cooperation between the United States and Egypt to work together against Libya to "redraw the map of North Africa." This paper got to Deputy National Security Advisor John Poindexter, who used it to promote a joint U.S.-Egyptian invasion of Libya. Fortunately, saner minds in the Reagan administration prevailed, and Gates's bellicose language was ignored.

Gates was a master at cherry-picking intelligence to serve Casey's views. Long before I had the opportunity to testify before the Senate Intelligence Committee, I collected evidence on the false assessment that linked Moscow to the Papal assassination plot in 1981. Casey and Gates had cherry-picked a clandestine report from a third-hand source, a Bulgarian, whose previous information lacked credibility. The Operations Directorate was not even planning to issue the report or circulate it in any fashion, but Casey—unlike other CIA directors—saw clandestine reporting in its raw form before it was circulated to the intelligence community. The Bulgarian was a member of the GRU—his country's military intelligence—and not connected to the KGB. If the Soviets had been involved in the Papal Plot, then it would have been a KGB operation, not GRU. As a result, a third-hand source, and an unreliable one, got to be the sole driving force behind one of the most dishonest intelligence assessments ever designed to manipulate a President of the United States.

Casey wanted an assessment for the White House; Gates saluted and selected three reliable drafters to prepare the product *in camera*. I found a draft copy of the memorandum on the desk of one of the authors, Kay Oliver, took it to the nearest Xerox machine; at the CIA no one was far from a photocopy machine. I confronted my boss at the time, MacEachin, but got nowhere, as he threw up his hands and said that he had to follow the bosses' orders. I knew then I would leave the CIA at the first opportunity.

So I went to his boss—and my boss—Bob Gates. Gates was a master of what is called in Baltimore "judge shopping in the courthouse." If a court wanted a specific sentence, it knew which judges to assign to a particular case; when Gates wanted a specific intelligence outlook, he knew which analysts to commission. I told Gates I found the draft document on the desk of one of the co-authors, who had a reputation for providing politically correct answers to intelligence questions, and that analysts responsible for international terrorism had not been consulted. In the course of the conversation, I again used the "I" word that raised Gates' hackles: "integrity:" and his lack of it.

Gates could never handle personal confrontation, which is not unusual in the case of bullies; the conversation was tense. His anger was revealed later that night in a phone call to my home. Several months later, I was removed as the Division Chief for Soviet Policy in the Third World. MacEachin delivered the message, showing me the email from Gates that ordered my removal. Six years later, I found myself in Room 211 of the Hart Senate Office Building, just to the north of the Capitol, to testify against Gates's confirmation as director of central intelligence, using the phony "Papal Plot" memorandum as a key document in the case against him. Testifying on behalf of Gates was MacEachin, who falsely claimed that it was his idea to remove me as a division chief.

In his memoir on his Agency years, *From the Shadows: The Ultimate Insider's Story of Five Presidents and How They Won the Cold War*, Gates described me as "one of his oldest friends in the Agency," although our friendship had virtually ended several years before his appointment to run the Directorate of Intelligence.[14] In his typically self-serving way, he wrote that he was "stunned and sickened" by my testimony against him, because I had never "come to [him] to express concern or disagreement." He took credit for promoting me and said he "certainly had no sense [Goodman] bore me ill will."[15] Well, Bob may have a wonderful memory, but he forgot our encounters in his office over the issue of integrity, and that he removed me as chief of the Soviet–Third World branch for arguing that the new Soviet president, Mikhail Gorbachev, was reducing the Soviet presence in the Third World in part to improve bilateral relations with the United States. Of course, this view was inconsistent with President Reagan's "Evil Empire" doctrine and the ideology of Bill Casey and Bob Gates.

One of the interesting twists of the Papal Plot exercise was that MacEachin—who was not an ideologue but simply too weak to stand up to any superior, particularly Gates—was fearful of a wider distribution of the phony assessment that would prove embarrassing. So at the last minute he asked a senior intelligence official, John Hibbits, to prepare a quick assessment of the memorandum's case for Soviet involvement, suggesting he was unhappy with the thrust of the paper. Hibbits told me the critique was MacEachin's idea, a cover-your-ass assignment that would offer some protection to those intelligence officials who were not involved in the exercise but tried to limit distribution and exposure of the paper. Hibbits, an old friend and close colleague, was chosen for the assignment because he was chief of the Foreign Activities Branch of the Office of Soviet Affairs, and had a reputation for objective and hard-hitting analysis.[16]

Hibbits viewed the paper on the Papal Plot as an effort by Casey and Gates to push the case for Soviet involvement much further than the evidence warranted. He knew that policymakers would quickly read nothing more than key judgments, and come away with the view that Moscow was behind the shooting of Pope John Paul II. The paper was speculative at best. Gates added to that impression by placing his own specious covering note on the paper to state that it was the most thorough work the CIA had ever done on the subject. The paper ignored Gates's demands for alternative scenarios or analysis, which became his mantra for killing assessments that didn't meet his ideological point of view. The key judgments made no attempt to be fully representative of the paper itself. Two years later, a National Intelligence Estimate concluded that the United States still had no conclusive evidence of any Soviet involvement in the unsuccessful assassination attempt of May 13, 1981. The recent opening of Soviet and East European intelligence archives after the dissolution of the Soviet Union similarly produced no evidence of involvement.

I was a major burr under Gates's saddle, and there were two others who had to be removed.[17] Douglas Garthoff, who headed the Soviet-U.S. branch and correctly recorded Gorbachev's interest in détente and arms control, was transferred. The other supervisor who was axed was one of the Agency's leading economic analysts, James Noren, who monitored the decline of the Soviet economy and its increasing irrelevance in the international arena. The three of us were given less influential positions in the Office of Soviet Affairs, so that in Gates's words we could not "poison" the intelligence message. I left in 1986 to join the faculty at the National War College. If the three of us had been left in our management positions, the CIA would have correctly advised the White House of the decline of the Soviet Union.

At that point, the three of us had more than 70 years of combined experience in assessing the Soviet problem. We had been accustomed to new directors and managers in the CIA instituting new ideas for producing intelligence. William J. Colby's stewardship as CIA director introduced the idea of a daily newspaper to display current intelligence; Turner favored a roundtable of analysts to discuss difficult issues, then assigning one of the participants to produce an assessment; John McCone allowed analysts to have their say, but when he didn't agree that the Soviet Union would introduce short-range missiles into Cuba, he told the president—and, as we soon learned, he was right. But Casey, with the devoted assistance of Gates, became the first director to rigorously subvert and tailor intelligence. Neither Casey nor Gates had any interest in producing balanced intelligence that offered opposing views and alternative scenarios. They combined forces to shatter the CIA's moral compass in the field of intelligence, paving the way one day at a time to the CIA producing phony analysis to sell a preemptive war. Schlesinger, Goss, and Petraeus similarly threatened to toughen the intelligence product, and might have done so if they had stayed around.

The removal of three experienced Sovietologists was not the only impact that Gates had on the CIA's Directorate of Intelligence and Office of Soviet Affairs. Intelligence analysts soon realized that certain types of papers, particularly those that didn't support his ideological positions, would be rapidly returned with gratuitously harsh criticism of both style and substance. CIA analysts were no different from other bureaucrats throughout the government; they soon understood what would get through the ideological filter that Gates had established and what wouldn't. As a result, there was a great deal of self-censorship of "unpopular" notions; analysts outside of the Office of Soviet Affairs decided to write about Soviet matters with a gratuitously hard-line view to please their bosses. As a result, there was an expansion of politicized intelligence designed to appease Casey and Gates.

Director of Intelligence managers also worked the system, pushing the ideological line far to the right to meet the policy demands of the Reagan administration. Hibbits's memorandum recorded a typical example of self-censorship in the Office of Soviet Affairs. In planning its research program, Office of Soviet Affairs managers killed a paper on Soviet opposition to the use of chemical agents in the Third World, because that was the type of paper that drew Gates's wrath. The senior analyst who wanted to write on the subject was told to try another project.[18] Gates, like Secretary of Defense Rumsfeld in the run-up to the Iraq War, considered the absence of evidence as evidence itself.

More recently, Gates produced a second memoir that revealed his self-aggrandizing personality. It was mean-spirited and angry, the type of memoir that the Washington press corps savors because it seems vivid, colloquial, and straight-from-the shoulder, which lends itself to reportage.[19] The memoir was also self-serving, duplicitous, and arrogant, but understanding this requires the kind of analysis that the media often abhor. Written three decades after his mismanagement of the CIA's Intelligence Directorate, the memoir conveys many of the characteristics that Gates displayed at the CIA.

The memoir indicates that Gates realized he had become an outlier in the Obama administration—just as Vice President Cheney had become an outlier in the Bush administration. In the last year of his administration, President Bush ignored Cheney's attempt to pressure him on the use of military force in Iran and Syria, as well as on the pardoning of his aide, Lewis "Scooter" Libby. In Gates's last year as secretary of defense, President Obama was no longer taking Gates's recommendations on Afghanistan, Libya, the raid against Osama bin Laden, the insubordination of General Stanley McChrystal, or the timing for ending "don't ask, don't tell." Gates was particularly agitated by Vice President Biden, who was coaching the president on dealing with the military and criticizing the ineptitude of President Bush on policy issues.

Gates was most resourceful in using the memoir to launder his own credentials, referring to the fact that he "witnessed" the Iran-Contra disaster in 1986–1987. In fact, as we have seen, he had to withdraw from the confirmation process for director of the CIA in 1987 because the intelligence committee didn't believe his denials of prior knowledge. Two of my former CIA colleagues, including Gates's deputy, Dick Kerr, had briefed him on the sale of missiles to Iran and the diversion of profits to the Contras. The "case officer" for Iran-Contra, Marine Colonel Oliver North, briefed Gates on the Swiss bank accounts where the money for the Contras had been kept. Senator Boren even called Lawrence Walsh, the independent counsel investigating Iran-Contra, to ascertain whether Gates would be indicted. Walsh "doubted Gates' veracity," but said he would "probably not" be indicted. He warned Boren, however, that there were still troubling areas suggesting Gates had falsely denied knowledge of North's Contra-support activities.

The issue that sank Gates's nomination in 1987—Iran-Contra—was the issue that should have been vetted in 1991 and could have precluded confirming Gates as CIA director. Gates, who pretended to be an innocent bystander in the Iran-Contra crisis, was actually on center stage at an important decision-making juncture.

Gates's effort to craft his own legacy as secretary of defense fell victim to the same gap between his rhetoric and his actions. He claimed to want a debate on defense spending, referring to wasteful and unnecessary weapons systems, but dodged the issue when appearing before Congress. He consistently lobbied the Congress in favor of modernizing key systems, including those for nuclear weapons and regional missile defense. Gates takes credit for the idea of a regional missile defense in Poland and the Czech Republic to "better defend the United States against Iranian ballistic missiles," which made no strategic sense. According to the Pentagon's Selected Acquisition Reports, the number of weapons programs increased under Gates, and nearly all of the so-called savings in the defense budget were shifted to other programs as the budget increased in his last two years at the Pentagon.

Gates constantly contradicted himself. He asked the annual Navy League convention in 2010 why the United States Navy needed 11 carrier battle groups, garnering headlines in the media. But he gave an emphatic "no" in congressional testimony regarding the possibility of eliminating even one carrier group. Gates may have been the first secretary of defense to acknowledge publicly that the United States was spending too much on the military and needed to spend more on diplomacy, but he gave another blunt "no" to the idea of transferring funds from the Defense Department to the State Department. He loved to cite the fact that there were more members of military bands than there were Foreign Service Officers, but he wasn't willing to do anything about it.

Gates disingenuously emphasized that U.S. defense spending did not contribute to the deficit and should not be part of any deficit-reduction program. He told the American Enterprise Institute in 2011 that "we're not going to see a return to Cold War defense budgets."[20] Months before he announced his retirement, Gates told close colleagues that he was leaving Washington because he couldn't "imagine being part of a smaller military that would go to fewer places and do fewer things." Ever since, he has maligned the Obama administration, and argued that cutting defense spending "sends a signal that we are not interested in protecting our global interests.[21]

The fact is that the United States is spending far more on defense than it did during the worst days of the Cold War. During his five-year tenure as defense secretary, defense spending shot from $350 billion to $680 billion. A return to Cold War spending would save the United States around $100 billion annually. As defense strategist Anthony Cordesman noted, "Gates never came to grips with the challenge of tying strategy to force plans and procurement plans or shaping U.S. deployment to available resources."[22]

Gates bears some responsibility for the fact that the defense budget is 40 percent higher than it was on 9/11, nearly equaling the defense spending of all other nations. Gates did not address the problem of cost overruns, which now finds 85 acquisition programs with overages of more than $400 billion. The Pentagon will never be satisfied with any level of defense spending, and it is the job of the secretary of defense to bring spending under control.

The memoir gives a free pass to President Bush and aims excessive criticism at the Obama administration. Gates is the consigliere of the Bush family, a story that has been well documented by investigative journalist Robert Parry.[23] Gates cannot criticize the Bush family because he is a creation of Papa Bush, who made

Gates the director of central intelligence in 1991 and the director of the George H.W. Bush School of Government and Public Service at Texas A&M in 1999, which led directly to Gates becoming president of the university in 2002. Bush Jr. made Gates the secretary of defense in 2006. Gates never questions the intelligence process in the run-up to the invasion of Iraq in 2003, which has destabilized the region, caused mass death and destruction, and directly contributed to the emergence of ISIS and sectarian conflict.

Gates ignored the role of the United States in terrorizing and destabilizing the Middle East in order to whitewash his own legacy as well as that of the Bush administration. Similarly, he failed to acknowledge the interlocking roles of the U.S. intelligence and military institutions, which have contributed to the creation of a national security state. Founding Father James Madison as well as President Eisenhower warned against such developments in an era of permanent war, which have now preoccupied the United States since 2001.

Conversely, Gates gratuitously criticized members of the Obama administration, such as Vice President Biden, who voted against his confirmation as CIA director in 1991 and warned against undue military influence on U.S policy. Biden told President Obama that he was getting the "bum's rush from the military" on Afghanistan. Gates labeled Biden "wrong on nearly every major foreign policy and national security issue over the past four decades."[24] In fact, Gates and Biden were together on many issues, including U.S. policy in the wake of the Arab Spring and the bin Laden raid. Gates even concluded his memoir with the view that "on issue after issue . . . the president, the vice president . . . and I were usually on the same page."[25] As is often the case with Gates, it is not easy to determine which version of his contradictory statements he believes.

More significantly, it is Gates who was wrong about so many intelligence and policy issues, including the central policy and intelligence issues of the 1980s dealing with Soviet-American relations and Mikhail Gorbachev. He refused to recognize Gorbachev as a reformer; he was among the first to argue that he would be ousted by neo-Stalinists, and said so in the *Washington Times*. Gates missed not only Gorbachev as a reformer, but Boris Yeltsin as a reformer as well. Even worse, and the reason he was so strongly criticized in 1991, is that Gates's politicization of intelligence throughout the 1980s made CIA analysts on the Soviet Union get it wrong as well.

Finally, it is ironic that as secretary of defense, Gates's greatest achievement was arguably his role in advancing the mine-resistant, ambush-protected vehicle—but it was Senator Biden who introduced the successful amendment to provide additional funding for the military vehicle more than a month before Gates's decision.

If the mine-resistant vehicle was his greatest success, then Gates's greatest failure as secretary of defense was exacerbating dangerous tensions between the Obama White House and the Pentagon, contributing to a flawed civilian-military relationship that had begun during the Vietnam War. Time and again, the Pentagon's senior leaders, particularly Admiral Mike Mullen and Generals Petraeus and McChrystal, made public comments or leaked controversial statements that were designed to garner greater deployments to Afghanistan, when it was clear that President Obama was committed to moving U.S. off the battlefield. Gates was unwilling to accept that President Obama's policy toward Afghanistan had changed; he even led his own campaign at the Pentagon and on the Hill to "win" a war that wasn't winnable.

As a result of his frustration over this decision-making, Bob Gates asserted that President Obama did not have his heart in the Afghan War, which could only have a devastating impact on the troops to whom Gates has dedicated his book. Similarly, his charge that President Obama "can't stand" Afghan President Hamid Karzai added one more irritant to the conclusion of a status-of-forces agreement with Kabul that would have determined the level and conditions of the U.S. military presence in Afghanistan. Gates's defiant posture toward President Obama included dragging his heels on ending the cynical policy of "don't ask, don't tell," and allowing senior general officers to campaign publicly for additional U.S. forces long before any decision was actually made. In instructing one of his senior generals to tell a senior member of the National Security Council to "go to hell," Gates was demeaning the entire White House.

There is no more important task in political governance than making sure that civilian control of the military is not compromised and the U.S. military-surveillance grid remains fully subordinate to our political democracy. President Obama initially demonstrated too much deference to the military, even retaining the Bush administration's secretary of defense as his own, and appointing too many general officers to key civilian positions such as National Security Advisor and intelligence tsar. Gates's memoir is an intentional slap in the face to his former Commander in Chief, Barack Obama. It also reflects a notable ignorance of the dangerous imbalance in civilian-military influence that is more threatening to the national interests of the United States over the long term than are developments in a strategic backwater like Afghanistan.

If the Senate Intelligence Committee had done its job in 1991, Gates would have been defeated for the position of director of central intelligence and probably wouldn't have been a candidate for secretary of defense in 2006. If President Obama had pursued his own secretary of defense instead of reappointing Gates in order to appease the Pentagon and the conservative right wing in this country, then the United States would have been spared Gates's machinations. In *Duty*, Gates accurately describes the unacceptable tension between the White House and the Pentagon, but he ignores his role in fueling the conflict. In the tense moments when Obama was deciding to increase military forces in Afghanistan, the military high command, including General McChrystal, the field commander, leaked a Pentagon report to *Washington Post* writer Bob Woodward that urged a long-term, 10-year counterinsurgency commitment to Afghanistan, which no one in the White House supported. In a speech in London, McChrystal stated that he could not support a policy that didn't rely on a long-term presence, which he knew Vice President Biden opposed. A year later, McChrystal and members of his staff used an interview with Michael Hastings of *Rolling Stone* magazine to trash Biden and other senior members of the Obama White House.

This is not ancient history. Indeed, it would be wrong and even cynical to believe that the fight with Gates that began in the mid-1980s should be discontinued in the twenty-first century. U.S. policymakers, including Secretary of State Shultz, were poorly served in the Reagan administration when Gates tailored intelligence to block Shultz's efforts to improve relations with the Soviet Union. Shultz concluded that the "CIA's intelligence was in many cases simply Bill Casey's ideology."[26] Gates made similar efforts to block Secretary of State Baker's efforts to improve relations with Moscow. President Obama certainly wasn't helped by the opposition of the professional military encouraged by his secretary of defense.

All Americans, moreover, were poorly served in the 1980s when the defense budget was doubled because of a conjured image of an all-powerful Soviet Evil Empire that was really on its last legs. Two decades later, the United States invaded Iraq on the basis of false information fabricated by the CIA; in some cases, it was provided by former acolytes of Gates such as CIA deputy director McLaughlin. Ironically, when Bob Gates took over the Department of Defense in 2006, he was surrounded by three- and four-star general officers who occupied key positions in the world of intelligence that once had been occupied by civilians: the director of the CIA, the undersecretary of defense for intelligence, the Department of State's director of counterterrorism programs, the Pentagon's deputy undersecretary for intelligence, the director of national intelligence, and finally, a two-star general running spies at the CIA.

As my former colleague Jennifer Glaudemans argued, the battle Gates waged was not with one or two analysts who happened to get it right, but with a number of "people who looked at all the available evidence, without much bias one way or another, and who had been to the USSR and witnessed its hollow political and social structure, seeing not an omnipotent superpower but a clumsy, oafish regime often stumbling over its own feet."[27] If the Senate had done its job in 1991 and rejected the Gates nomination as it was prepared to do in 1987, and if the Senate Intelligence Committee had followed up the warnings regarding the corruption of intelligence that it received in the mid-1980s, then perhaps it would have been more difficult to falsify intelligence and get away with it, as occurred when right-wing forces colluded to invade and occupy Saddam Hussein's Iraq. Elected officials, particularly U.S. Senators, should have been more diligent in auditing what we now know was false intelligence cooked up by leadership at the Central Intelligence Agency.

My warnings to the Senate Select Committee on Intelligence in October 1991 went unheeded. I made the strong case that Casey and Gates had managed to inextricably link policy and intelligence. I emphasized that, in confirming Gates as director, the committee would be sending him to the politicized environment that he had created on behalf of Casey. I asked the committee to consider the "effect this would have on the standards of others at the CIA to be led by someone so lacking in vision, integrity, and courage." Thirty-one senators heeded these warnings and voted against the confirmation of Gates; 64 senators, including all Republicans, supported a president who was Gates's patron.

Several years after the hearings, I received an authoritative endorsement of my testimony against Gates from former secretary of state Shultz. Shultz, one of the most formidable public figures of contemporary times, produced a memoir, *Turmoil and Triumph: My Years as Secretary of State*, that confirmed my charges of politicization. Shultz was known to the Washington community as tight-lipped and discreet, and his memoir recorded his numerous fights with neoconservatives at the National Security Council and the Pentagon as well as his cold fury at the CIA, which he knew to be incompetent and out of control under Casey and Gates. If Shultz had expressed these views during the hearings, as he was asked to do, his remarks could have been a game changer in the committee's vote. Shultz was that powerful and that credible.

In his memoir, Shultz recorded his remarks to Gates when Gates became acting director. "I wouldn't trust anything you guys said about Iran no matter what. I feel you try to manipulate me. The DCI [director] should not be part of the policy process," which is exactly what President Truman had intended in the National Security Act of 1947.[28] In addition to Iran, Shultz made it clear that the CIA could not be trusted on Central America, Southern Africa, Afghanistan, and the Soviet Union, the same regions and countries I cited in my testimony.

His credibility within the Reagan administration and his eventual dominance over the foreign and security policies of the United States were so great that Shultz's threat to resign occasionally reversed policy. When the Reagan administration wanted to subject all leading officials within the national security establishment, including the Department of State, to polygraph or lie detector tests, Shultz threatened to resign, and the White House capitulated. When he privately threatened to resign because of obstacles to his détente policy from a National Security Council staff "operating on the fringes of loyalty to the president and . . . common sense," he got a signal from the White House to continue his high-level dialogue with the Soviets. If he had threatened to resign over Iran-Contra, the United States would have been spared the embarrassment of linking policy toward non-existent Iranian "moderates" to Nicaraguan counter-revolu-tionaries. If only he had opposed the nomination of Gates.

Shultz documented my key charge at the confirmation hear-ings regarding Gates's role in manipulating intelligence, par-ticularly the failure to track changed in Moscow's disarmament policy. On several occasions, Shultz was caught off guard in high-level meetings with Soviet President Mikhail Gorbachev and Foreign Minister Eduard Shevardnadze because he was surprised by the Kremlin's willingness to accept intrusive on-site inspec-tions, asymmetric agreements, and even unilateral reductions. American negotiators, according to Shultz, were unprepared for Gorbachev's flexibility and conciliation at talks in Geneva, Reyk-javik, and Vienna.

There was intelligence that provided evidence of Soviet moderation, but such intelligence wasn't allowed out of the build-ing because Gates believed Moscow was exploiting disarmament issues to weaken the West. Just as Gates used a national intelli-gence officer on the Middle East, Fuller, to politicize intelligence on Iran, he used a national intelligence officer on strategic mat-ters, Larry Gershwin, to politicize intelligence on arms control.

Shultz charged Gates with "manipulating" him and re-minded the former Soviet analyst that he was "usually wrong" about Moscow, having dismissed Gorbachev's policies as "just another Soviet attempt to deceive us."[29] He accused Casey of providing "bum dope" to the president. Shultz was, of course, spot-on; Casey and Gates were using assessments to pander to Reagan's ideologues and to build support for aggressive policies.

It would have helped if Shultz had recorded these views in the *Washington Post* or the *New York Times*, but he refused the im-portuning of one of my colleagues, Ray McGovern, to do so. Mc-Govern was well known to Shultz because he was the secretary of state's briefer during the tumultuous days of the mid-1980s, when Shultz was trying to move Reagan toward improving U.S.-Soviet relations but found his efforts undercut by Casey and Weinberger. McGovern carried intelligence items to the secretary that described the new Soviet leadership's interest in détente; these were items that Gates kept out of the President's Daily Brief. I had a hand in making sure that certain Soviet items got to Mc-Govern, an old friend and colleague since the day I entered the CIA. When my boss, MacEachin, learned that I was passing boot-leg copies of sensitive intelligence to McGovern, he summoned me and made it clear that passing information to McGovern was risky. But he didn't ask me to stop doing it, and I didn't.

Shultz understood Gates's game, which was to dismiss the emergence of policy change under Gorbachev as "just talk"; that the Soviet Union was a "powerfully entrenched and largely successful system that was incapable of change"; and that Gorbachev would fail. When the changes took place, the "CIA line was that the changes wouldn't really make a difference."[30] This is the most authoritative description you will find of the role of Casey and Gates in the mid-1980s, loyally assisted by such intelligence apparatchiks as MacEachin, George Kolt, Gershwin, Kay Oliver, and Grey Hodnett.

Shultz emphasized that he had been kept out of the loop by the CIA.[31] When Frank Carlucci, a former deputy director at the CIA, was named to head the National Security Council to replace Admiral Poindexter in 1987 because of Poindexter's involvement in Iran-Contra, Shultz told Carlucci that he had been "misled, lied to, cut out" by the CIA.[32] Shultz emphasized that "CIA analysis was distorted by strong views about policy," particularly its inability to recognize that Gorbachev's accession to power and his pursuit of glasnost and perestroika—openness and restructuring—marked a transformation of Soviet society and political structure.

The next day, Gates, who had just been named acting director of the CIA, called Shultz to discuss the remarks that Carlucci had passed on, giving Shultz an opportunity to repeat the message:

"I don't have any confidence in the intelligence community. I feel you all have very strong policy views. I wouldn't trust anything you guys said about Iran no matter what. I feel you try to manipulate me. So you have a very dissatisfied customer. If this were a business, I'd find myself another supplier. I feel bad about my state of mind, as I have historically been a supporter of the agency. Now I feel that the CIA is an alternative State Department with its own strong policy views. I want to have my confidence rebuilt. The director of central intelligence should not be part of the policy process; heavy involvement just can't help but influence you. In the policy business you develop a bias. The CIA should be objective, and if it is not, that means what you say must be discounted."[33]

There has never been a better description and confirmation of the deterioration and corruption of the CIA than the one provided by Shultz. Two years after Shultz told Gates, "You have a big, powerful machine not under good control. I distrust what comes out of it,"[34] Secretary of State Baker threatened to go to his president to stop Gates from delivering a speech that would have compromised Baker's diplomatic initiatives.[35] National Security Advisor Scowcroft got the message from Baker and turned off Gates's speech.

When my wife and I interviewed Shultz several years later for our political biography of Soviet Foreign Minister Shevardnadze, Shultz was still angry over the role of the CIA in the 1980s and, seemingly, our association with the Agency. The fact that we were strong-willed dissidents and whistleblowers was lost on him. I am still angry about Shultz's unwillingness to speak out in 1991. It was unfortunate that Shultz didn't make his strong views on Gates available to the members of the Senate Intelligence Committee; two years later, when it would have no impact on events, Shultz did so in his memoir.

There will always be major analytical differences in the production of intelligence, but these differences should involve interpretations of evidence, and not differences in agendas for the manipulation of policy. Ideological differences can block objective and balanced intelligence. It is up to the intelligence professional to find ways to avoid ideology and to fight politicization, which is corruption. My dispute and falling-out with Bob Gates was not personal; it was a battle between the need for objective and balanced intelligence analysis versus the manipulation of evidence for preconceived ends.

NINE

THE PRESS AND THE WHISTLEBLOWER

"Opinions that we loathe should not be suppressed."
—Justice Oliver Wendell Holmes

"They that can give up essential liberty to obtain a little temporary safety, deserve neither liberty nor safety."
—Benjamin Franklin

The U.S. Constitution was drafted in secret sessions, and the Congress was allowed to resort to secrecy in some matters. But the Founding Fathers emphasized openness over secrecy and were concerned with any threat to freedom of the press. For that reason, the First Amendment dealt with press freedom. James Madison argued that the "censorial power is in the people over the Government, and not in the Government over the people."[1] With the creation of the CIA and the NSA, the role of secret government made it essential for American democracy to monitor secret activities of these powerful arms of American government.

My experience demonstrates that the press has not been willing to adequately question and investigate government, particularly in the realm of national security where journalists become beholden to official sources and are rarely supportive of contrarians, let alone whistleblowers. There are exceptions to the rule, and the work of Seymour Hersh, James Risen, and Eric Lichtblau is scrupulous. They are rigorous journalists who go to any lengths to protect sources. But more watchdog journalists are needed to keep secret government in check. More often than not, the press is quick to marginalize a whistleblower, and unwilling to do the hard work of understanding arcane aspects of the intelligence community.

One of the greatest enemies of press freedom and the people's right to know has been the incestuous relationship between the White House, the CIA, and the media. This hasn't always been the case, particularly during the administrations of Eisenhower and Carter. During the Kennedy and Johnson administrations, however, the close contacts between CIA directors such as Allen Dulles and Richard Helms, key journalists such as Joseph Alsop, Drew Middleton, and Joseph Kraft, and officials at the National Security Council such as William and McGeorge Bundy and Walt and Eugene Rostow created inaccurate and distorted portraits of the Soviet Union and Vietnam.

The *New York Times* encouraged writers such as Les Gelb and Richard Burt to develop close relations with national security advisors Kissinger and Brzezinski and to carry the administration narrative on foreign policy and arms control. When Gelb left the *Times* to join the Carter administration, a *Times* editorial boasted that Gelb "stepped down." The *Washington Post* throughout the Cold War carried White House charts that gave a distorted portrayal of the strategic balance between the United States and the Soviet Union. The writings of David Ignatius and Walter Pincus in the *Post* give the benefit of the doubt to the intelligence community and marginalize whistleblowers.

The media did a particularly poor job of reporting and analyzing key issues in the confirmation hearings for Gates. The media made little effort to understand or investigate how the tailoring of intelligence throughout the 1980s affected the country. More recently, the press assumed an almost Orwellian support for authority when another Republican White House insisted that intelligence be generated to support its obsessive march to invade Iraq in 2003. Too often the benefit of the doubt went to decision makers in the Reagan administration who dominated the field of strategic intelligence, and not to the contrarians. Currently there is unacceptable ridicule of whistleblowers, who are essential to both investigative journalism and democracy. Finally, there is the double standard within the CIA that allows its leaders and operatives to communicate with the press while keeping dissenting intelligence analysts at arm's length.

The media missed the intelligence story unveiled at the confirmation hearings for Gates because they were primarily interested in the personalities of those involved in challenging authority, instead of the national policies that were compromised by the corruption of the intelligence process. There were at least three substantive issues that the press should have examined, but journalists were too dilatory at the hearings or simply failed to understand the policy implications of tailored intelligence. The substantive issues, as we have seen, dealt with Soviet strategy in the Third World; the shooting of the Pope; and collusion in the Iran-Contra operations. My testimony led to the declassification of many assessments on these subjects, but no journalist asked me about them and very few examined them.

The media played their usual game of false equivalence by conceding that Gates went beyond normal editing to slant assessments in a "heavy-handed and underhanded" way, but propounded the notion that such interventions were merely an attempt to challenge stodgy and smug analysts. The evidence in favor of Gates's tampering with intelligence for political ends was far stronger than the evidence for business as usual in the intelligence community, and the media never acknowledged that too many senators had been misled by these assessments over the years.

In 1981 my office prepared a National Intelligence Estimate that concluded Soviet influence was waning in the developing world, which challenged Casey's advocacy of covert operations to counter supposedly increased Soviet intervention. The press should have taken a hard look at the competition between the United States and the Soviet Union in the developing world, but neglected to do so. In his Congressional testimony, Gates argued that, as deputy director for intelligence, he was in "no position to bureaucratically kill a National Intelligence Estimate."[2] The fact is that Bob Gates wrote a damning memorandum that killed the CIA's draft estimate, and hired a professor from Rutgers University without experience in the intelligence community to whip up the assessment he desired to justify greater covert action on a global basis.

The press needed to scrutinize the CIA's examination of the shooting of the Pope in 1981, which Gates ordered as the "case for Soviet involvement." He wanted the assessments to derail the momentum for improving US-Soviet relations that Secretary of State Shultz had created inside the Reagan administration. Casey and Gates wanted to end any interest in disarmament talks with the Soviets, just as Cheney and Rumsfeld had wanted to block Secretary of State Kissinger in the Ford administration in 1975.

Bob Gates told me that "Casey was convinced of Soviet involvement in the Papal Plot," but said, "I'm agnostic and I expect [the drafters] to be agnostic also."[3] Neither the draft nor the deputy director was agnostic, however. The draft concluded that "since the Soviets haven't been blamed by world opinion, they are more inclined to take adventurous actions."[4] Gates added a cover note for Vice President Bush that called the report "comprehensive," which it wasn't. The job of intelligence analysis is to explain complicated issues, not to play devil's advocate for unlikely scenarios. An internal CIA review concluded that the paper on the shooting of the Pope "stacked the deck," and blamed senior management for having anointed one group of analysts to conduct the stacking and having "discouraged others from taking the initiative."[5]

Among the declassified documents that the press ignored

was Gates's secret memorandum to Casey exaggerating the Soviet and Cuban role in Nicaragua and recommending the use of military force against Nicaraguan leftists, the Sandinistas. His memorandum on Nicaragua was an example of policy advocacy, which is forbidden by the Agency's charter. Never before had a deputy director of the CIA lobbied for U.S. military action against a foreign nation.

Gates's memorandum to Casey recommended a bombing campaign against Nicaragua in 1984 to "bring down" the leftist government. I made sure that the memorandum got to the Senate Intelligence Committee in order to declassify it. The document was an example of Gates at his worst, arguing that the Soviet Union was turning Nicaragua into an armed camp that would become a second Cuba. There was no intelligence evidence to support either assumption. I failed to get journalists to write about this issue, and couldn't convince them of the danger of policy advocacy.

One week before his memorandum, Gates killed my assessment that argued "disincentives outweigh the incentives" regarding any potential Soviet delivery of MiG-21 fighter aircraft to Nicaragua. His rejoinder to the chief of my office coyly concluded that my conclusions were "unhelpfully leading with our chin to make a prediction when we really don't have anything to go on," which simply wasn't true: Intelligence indicated that the Soviets would not supply the Sandinistas with sophisticated military aircraft. Sensitive State Department cables made it clear that the Kremlin had high hopes for reopening arms control talks with the United States, and that providing fighter jets to Nicaragua would be counter-productive. But Gates found these arguments "very loose, analytically and editorially." I didn't know at the time that Gates was preparing a memorandum for Director Casey that made the case for "bringing down" the Sandinista government.

My arguments weren't loose, and the Soviets never sent MiG aircraft to Nicaragua. Moscow was playing a clever game in supplying the Sandinistas, making sure that small arms deliveries arrived on ships flying flags other than that of the Soviet Union. If they were to supply MiG aircraft, the Soviets would have had to use their own carriers. Even the aircraft the Soviets may have considered sending—the modest Czech-built L-39 jet trainer—sat at a Bulgarian airfield for months before returning to the Soviet Union.[6]

I was furious with the tone and the substance of Gates's refutation of my assessment. His provocative and gratuitous political memorandum to the director incorporated false assumptions and allegations. Gates was not going to allow his analysts to publish an item that indicated that the Soviets were going to be very careful in Nicaragua and had bigger fish to fry with the United States, such as the resumption of the strategic disarmament dialogue.

The top-secret Nicaragua memoranda started out in typical self-serving Gates fashion ("It is time to talk absolutely straight about Nicaragua"), with the "straight" talk ignoring the intelligence and exaggerating the role of Soviet and Cuban military aid. With language such as "The Soviets and the Cubans are turning Nicaragua into an armed camp with military forces far beyond its defensive needs in order to intimidate and coerce its neighbors," Gates described a Nicaraguan government that had an avowed aim to "spread further revolution in the Americas."[7] He argued that Honduras would be forced to "accommodate" the Sandinistas, and that there would be a "complete reopening of the channels of arms support to the Salvadoran insurgency." In doing so, Gates begged comparisons with Castro's Cuba as well as the infamous "domino theory" of years gone by that had led the United States into Vietnam. Gates lacked evidence for these allegations, so he cited the views of a CIA station chief in Central America for support. None of these leads seemed to spark enough interest in the press to warrant further reporting.

The media never linked the fact that, shortly before the U.S. placed mines in a Nicaraguan harbor in December 1984, Gates had made the recommendation to pursue "all necessary measures to bring down the regime," including "air strikes to destroy a considerable portion of Nicaragua's military buildup."[8] "Putting our heads in the sand," Gates concluded, "will not prevent the events that I outlined" and would lead directly to a "second Cuba in the Western Hemisphere." He castigated Congress for cutting off aid to the Contras (in effect advocating that Congress ignore the Boland Amendment) and for using "half measures, half-heartedly applied" as in Vietnam (where we dropped twice as much ordnance as had been used over Germany in WWII).

Then the media ignored the fact that, the following year, Gates and Graham Fuller colluded in preparing a National Intelligence Estimate to justify arms sales to Iran and to warn of a non--existent Soviet threat to Iran. The estimate falsely charged that the Iranian government was moderating its policies, including reducing support for international terrorism, and that the Soviet Union was gaining influence in Tehran.[9] Fuller warned that "the U.S. position seems roughly akin to someone lying immobilized watching a snake crawl towards him: we know the snake is coming, it's just a matter of time. The critical issue is whether we can do anything about it."[10]

When I accepted a faculty position at the National War College, my first months at the college found me watching the congressional investigation of the Iran-Contra scandal with Rudy Enders, the operations officer who led the illegal mining of Corinto, Nicaragua, that Casey and Gates supported. I was the Intelligence Directorate's representative on the college faculty, and Enders was the representative from the Operations Directorate. I should have recorded our sub rosa comments during the hearings, because they reflected the cultural and political differences between the two directorates and their senior officers. Enders conceded that if he had not been on the college faculty, he would have been called to testify. Senator Rudman, the co-chairman of the committee, should have subpoenaed Enders in order to expose the laws that were violated by the Iran-Contra operations.

In explaining their votes to confirm Gates, a Senate majority conceded there had been manipulation of intelligence at the CIA on key issues. At a moment of historic change for the CIA, the media ignored Gates's role in tampering with intelligence. A decade later, CIA director Tenet, the former staff director of the Senate Intelligence Committee who managed Gates's confirmation process, manufactured intelligence to coerce the country to send thousands of U.S. soldiers to their death in a preemptive invasion of Saddam Hussein's Iraq. Again, the press was silent.

Nowhere in the mainstream media did anyone point out that, in the case of Nicaragua, the country didn't become a communist dictatorship and the Sandinista regime didn't precipitate the fall of the brutal U.S.-backed death squad governments in El Salvador, Honduras, or Guatemala. President Obama has ordered the declassification of secret CIA documents dealing with the right-wing regimes in Argentina and Chile, but the documents dealing with the death squads in Central America remain out of sight. By 1990–1991, the Sandinista government was voted out of power, and the Soviet Union ceased to exist. Meanwhile, Gates was confirmed as director of the CIA despite his politicization of intelligence on both events.

When the U.S. Congress is deaf to the importuning of government whistleblowers, the press is the only outlet for a dissident attempting to deal with improprieties in the national security arena. I regret not being more aggressive in using the press to make my case against the confirmation of Gates. I had no intention of talking to reporters until I learned that the White House was distributing scurrilous material about me that even CIA officials had repudiated. It was at that point that I began to call Elaine Sciolino of the *New York Times* and Benjamin Weiser of the *Washington Post* in an effort to set the record straight. Gates was involved in the White House campaign, and he even had the effrontery to have his wife, Becky, call my former wife to gather gossip on our separation.

Most of the establishment press sat together at the hearings, and it was obvious that journalists such as Roger Mudd of PBS and the late Mary McGrory, a syndicated columnist with the *Post*, were supportive of Gates and sought to ridicule and marginalize those who questioned his record. Mudd, a close friend of McGrory, used his PBS broadcasts on the confirmation hearings to support the CIA's defense and to pillory its critics. Both worked closely with Senator Bill Cohen (R-ME).

At the same time, there were important columnists, such as the peerless Anthony Lewis of the *New York Times*, and excellent beat reporters, such as Haynes Johnson of the *Post*, who understood the issues and didn't resort to the false equivalence that most journalists adopt. They cited the comments of those who questioned Gates's record.

The commandant of the National War College, Major General Stadler, who did his best to block my testimony, warned me not to "go out on a white horse" and carry my case to the media. He seemed genuinely afraid that I would do so, bringing negative publicity to the college and the Department of Defense. It made the General nervous to see one of his own faculty members trying to block the president's nominee for a key national security position. On the other hand, the military establishments ultimately allowed a civil servant to testify in front of a national television audience and the national press corps.

Both Sciolino and Weiser (of the *Times* and *Post*, respectively) were initially receptive when they were on the listening end of my accounts of the first closed session. They understood that the confirmation was Gates's to lose when the hearings started, but that the game had suddenly changed. After two days of testimony, however, it appeared that although Gates was heavily bruised in the hearings, that he was going to be confirmed. At that point, Sciolino's coverage tilted heavily toward confirmation of Gates in order to protect her access to a future director.

Several weeks after the hearings, I arranged lunch with Sciolino to pursue a simple agenda. What was her explanation for being even-handed at the start of the confirmation hearings, but then being biased in favor of Gates at midpoint? Her answer revealed a fundamental conceit of the Washington press corps. Sciolino appreciated the material I brought to her and initially reported it factually and fully. But when she determined that Gates would be confirmed regardless of the testimony, she knew she had to "choose between the revelations of a Gates critic who would soon return to the faculty of the NWC [National War College], and Gates who was about to become the CIA director."[11] She added unselfconsciously that "you would probably never be a source for a future story, but Gates could be a key source for many important stories."

Weiser was even-handed throughout, although his paper the *Post* politicized the hearings. The two leading reporters from the *Post* on national security were longtime veterans, Walter Pincus and George Lardner. I met with Pincus and Lardner several times, including brunch at Pincus's house during the hearings. At brunch, Pincus confessed that he and Lardner opposed the confirmation of Gates, and had drafted a long editorial piece for the paper's Sunday Outlook section making the case against him.[12] Their argument was simple: Gates was a liar and could not be trusted to head the CIA. The story never ran, because the editor of the Op-Ed section, Meg Greenfield, along with the paper's editor, Katherine Graham, were favorably disposed toward the Bush administration and Gates, and would not permit a critical story by two of their most influential writers.

This experience with the press demonstrated that contrarian views in Washington, particularly in the national security area, are easily marginalized. It is a rare journalist willing to pursue the ethical arguments of the contrarian or to challenge conventional wisdom. Sciolino conceded that contrarians make good sources only in the short run, but journalists rely on policymakers for long-term access, and run a risk when offending high-level bureaucrats. This is the best explanation that I've ever received for the conventional analysis of the media and their unwillingness to challenge high-level sources.

There are, of course, exceptions to the rule. Although most of what you read in the press comes from official sources, reporters exist who dig for the truth and take risks. At the *New York Times*, there are several reporters I would recommend to any whistleblower who needed guarantees that his or her identity would be protected and the story handled fairly. The *Times*'s James Risen faced possible prosecution for protecting a CIA source for a sensitive CIA operation in Iran that ran aground, but he never buckled. Two additional writers from the *Times*, Eric Lichtblau and Charlie Savage, take risks in protecting sources, as does Greg Miller of the *Washington Post*. Doug Jehl, a former *Times* national security writer and now the foreign editor of the *Post*, was scrupulous in protecting sources, and the late Anthony Lewis of the *Times* was one of the brightest, toughest, and most honest writers I ever encountered.

Lewis's only rival in that department is Seymour Hersh of the *New Yorker* magazine. He has a well-deserved reputation for breaking key stories dealing with My Lai, KAL 007, and Dick Cheney's "dark side." I had several meetings with Hersh during the confirmation hearings, and at one of them he noted that the difference between the two of us was that "you want to keep Gates from becoming director of the CIA, whereas I want to put Gates in jail." The only man who could have done that was Lawrence E. Walsh, the chief prosecutor of the Iran-Contra investigation, but even if Gates had been found guilty and sentenced, Bush Senior would have pardoned him, as he did with the other criminals. Even Walsh, with significant legal leverage, found that he could be stonewalled by the White House.

The media ignored the many Houdini-like maneuvers Gates used to escape responsibility while testifying before the committee. His greatest dodge was his claim that he could not remember various aspects of the Iran-Contra operations, including his active role in preparing the specious testimony of CIA director Casey and encouraging the director's militant hard-line views toward both Iran and Nicaragua. Everyone who knew Gates, including members of the Senate Select Committee on Intelligence, knew that his memory was superb. His momentary lapses in front of the committee were risible to those who knew him best. The media made no attempt to explore this issue or challenge his performance.

Just as Congress neglected its watchdog role regarding the CIA, so too have the media neglected their role investigating improprieties at the Agency. When Attorney General Holder decided to name a special counsel to examine law-breaking by CIA interrogators, the *Washington Post* crucified him. David Ignatius has been a longtime apologist for the CIA, and he has had help from the editor of the editorial page, Fred Hiatt, and such op-ed writers as Richard Cohen and the late David Broder.

Pincus was the apologist-in-chief, defending operatives against accountability for violence, torture, and abuse by citing Department of Justice memoranda "legalizing" the techniques. Mafia lawyers couldn't have done a better job than the authors of these memoranda, Jay Bybee and John Yoo. Pincus used to exercise some independence in these matters, but too often he resorted to doing the CIA's bidding. In January 2015, he wrote a long article comparing the importance of the CIA's torture program to the U-2 program in the 1950s.[13]

Several journalists for the *Post* and the *Wall Street Journal* even defended flawed CIA operations, such as the disastrous failure to prevent Humam Khalil Abu-Mulal al-Balawi's suicide attack against the Agency facility inside Forward Operating Base Chapman in eastern Afghanistan on December 30, 2009. The *Journal* cooperated with the CIA by posting CIA director Panetta's op-ed that ignored the failure in clandestine tradecraft and praised the operatives in the field. The *Post* fully supported drone attacks even when President Obama announced in April 2015 that an operation in the Afghan-Pakistan border region had killed innocent civilians, including an American hostage.

There are other examples of the double standard that rules the CIA. Theoretically, no CIA official can deal with the press without reporting it to the Office of Security. One of the first questions in the counter intelligence polygraph to review security clearances deals with such contacts. In practice, however, analysts are held to a much higher standard than operatives.

In 2006, a CIA analyst in the Office of Inspector General, Mary McCarthy, was marched out of the building because of suspected contacts with a *Washington Post* reporter, Dana Priest. She was forced to resign in 2006 when a polygraph examination revealed "unauthorized contacts with the media," which clandestine officers often have. But McCarthy was a regular contributor to the Democratic Party and a critic of the U.S. bombing of the civilian pharmaceutical factory in Sudan in 1998, and her previous job at the National Security Council required regular contacts with key journalists. She knew Priest, but never revealed sensitive information. I learned from a source close to Priest, moreover, that her story on the CIA's secret prisons relied on sources in Europe, not Washington.

McCarthy denied being the source of press stories, but she was the target of a "witch hunt" to allow the CIA to march someone, indeed anyone, out of the building to make sure disgruntled employees didn't talk to the press. The campaign against McCarthy—an example of the harassment and intimidation that occurs at the CIA—was designed to warn staffers in the Office of Inspector General that there would be a price to pay in dealing with the media.

Agents in the Directorate of Operations deal with reporters overseas and contact them when they return home. As a result, the media tend to deal gingerly with issues that involve clandestine operations in order to protect these sources. David Ignatius is a case in point. He had a long-term relationship with one of the CIA's best operatives, Robert Ames, who was killed in the attack on the U.S. embassy in Lebanon in 1983. Ignatius wrote a highly regarded spy novel, *The Agents of Influence*, that dealt with clandestine tradecraft; the source for the tradecraft was Ames. As a result of such contacts, Ignatius has given the clandestine service the benefit of the doubt on most issues.

During the Vietnam War, influential journalists such as Joseph and Stewart Alsop and Joseph Kraft were able to contact high-ranking officials from the State Department and the CIA to obtain classified information on the war. *Washington Post* reporter Carl Bernstein reported in *Rolling Stone* magazine about the longtime collusion between the CIA and key reporters whom the CIA considered "known assets."[14] Joe Alsop was particularly unapologetic about doing the bidding of the CIA, noting that he was proud to be asked and to comply. According to Alsop, the "notion that a newspaperman doesn't have a duty to his country is perfect balls."[15] And I was meeting with the national intelligence officer for the Soviet Union on one occasion when the secretary broke in to tell the officer, "Joe Kraft is ready to see you now." That was in the CIA building.

Most CIA directors mingled extensively with members of the so-called Georgetown set that once dominated the decision-making community. Former CIA director Helms was a reporter for a wire service before he entered the secret world of intelligence, and he used his urbanity to advantage in dealing with journalists. He was a regular at social functions in Georgetown that allowed him to make his case for the CIA. Other leading operatives also have close relations with journalists.

Close ties between clandestine operatives and the press are a legacy from the days of the Office of Strategic Services, a precursor of the CIA that sent many of its leading members to the Agency, including CIA directors Dulles, Helms, Colby, and Casey. Some critics remarked that Office of Strategic Services actually stood for "oh-so-social" because of the close ties between the upper-class members of the Office of Strategic Services and the press, such as the Alsop brothers. The Alsops, like so many leading journalists, favored the creation of the CIA because they wanted to get counterintelligence and intelligence collection out of the hands of the FBI's J. Edgar Hoover, who intimidated journalists. They thought it would be easier to get information out of the CIA than the FBI, and they were right.

A key aspect of the polygraph exercise is to find out if anyone met with journalists for any reason. My former father-in-law was an editor with the *New York Times*, and my contacts with him came up in my polygraph sessions. My wife's uncle, long deceased, was a professor of journalism at the University of Montana, and this was explored in her polygraph test for a security review.

The CIA's Publications Review Board censors the writings of former employees who criticize the Agency, but is lenient in approving works that favor it. As mentioned earlier, an excellent example is the recent work by Jose Rodriguez, a former CIA agent who destroyed the tapes that recorded the CIA's sadistic brutality against people held in their secret prisons. No charges were filed, and Rodriguez published a book and a *Washington Post* article in 2014 denying that any illegal activity took place.[16] The *Post* has been cooperative in allowing CIA officers to praise the work of the Agency, even running an article in 1985 by Harry Gelman, a former CIA analyst who supported the case for Soviet involvement in the plot to assassinate the Pope. My own submissions to the *Post* on the myths that surround the CIA and the intelligence community were not accepted.

The Review Board allowed Rodriguez and the CIA's chief legal counsel, John Rizzo, to publish books that falsely justified the torture of Abu Zubaydah, who was not a senior al Qaeda operative, who did not provide sensitive information on the 9/11 attacks, and who suffered solitary confinement for years without any charges from the U.S. government. Rodriguez destroyed the tapes of the torture of Zubaydah, and Rizzo explains that it was necessary to protect the identities of CIA officers who conducted the torture that had been approved by Justice Department memoranda. In fact, the torture techniques went far beyond the recommended guidelines, and the torturers were hooded and could never have been identified from the videotapes. The useful information that was obtained from Zubaydah was elicited by FBI officers who used traditional techniques of interrogation that had nothing to do with torture and abuse.

The CIA manipulated the U.S. Congress and the American public in the 1990s in order to conceal its failure to anticipate the decline and fall of the Soviet Union. No one inside or outside the CIA warned of the collapse of the Soviet Union, but anyone who watched the news regularly understood that the Soviet Empire, including the Soviet Union itself, was in decline. The CIA went to great lengths to argue that it had gotten it right all along, even though former CIA director Turner called the failure a "corporate" one for the entire Agency, and former chairman of the Joint Chiefs of Staff Powell expressed incredulity at the Agency's failure.

In order to get a proper academic imprimatur on the CIA's track record in regard to the nation's greatest geopolitical threat and superpower rival, the Agency entered into a cooperative venture with the John F. Kennedy School of Government at Harvard University to prepare a case study to conclude that the CIA "got it right." The title of the case study was dispositive: *The CIA and the Fall of the Soviet Empire: The Politics of "Getting It Right."* Just suppose that the Kennedy School was preparing a case study on the tobacco industry, funded by the tobacco industry, based on a small number of documents carefully selected by the tobacco industry, with a preponderance of testimony taken from senior officials of the tobacco industry. Now, that would be ethically questionable. Well, an equivalent scenario is what the contractual arrangement between the CIA and the Kennedy School put into play for CIA officials and CIA documents. The *modus operandi* was simply wrong, and ethically offensive.

Harvard's Kennedy School made no attempt to "get it right," and as a result the CIA could go to the media and the American public with the imprimatur of Harvard to make its case. Harvard ignored the three former officials at the CIA who testified to the Senate Intelligence Committee and could have helped draft a balanced report. There were many sworn affidavits from CIA officials who opposed the nomination of Gates and could have been interviewed; no one was. Moreover, the three officials who testified against Gates had a combined 70 years' experience with the CIA, but were dismissed in the case study as "disgruntled" and "unhappy analysts," who were "young" but "allowed to vent their anger against Gates." I liked the "young" part at my own age of 53 at the time.

I recorded my opposition to the case study in an article published in *Foreign Policy* that drew an angry response from the directors of the Harvard Intelligence and Policy Project, Philip D. Zelikow and Ernest R. May, whose academic works were known for giving the United States the benefit of the doubt.[17] Zelikow ran the investigation of a more significant intelligence failure—9/11—and succeeded in downplaying the CIA's failures there as well. In my response to Zelikow and May, I noted that my last position at the CIA in 1990 was as director of the Center for the Study of Intelligence, where I was the coordinator of all dealings and contracts with the Kennedy School. At the time, I questioned the ethics of CIA relations with the Kennedy School, just as many Harvard professors have questioned their links to the CIA and tried unsuccessfully to kill the program.

In addition to the Kennedy School contract, the CIA sponsored academic exchanges on the end of the Cold War and the Agency's track record. These symposia were held at Texas A&M University and Princeton University. Similar to the Harvard contract, the CIA carefully selected the documents that would be released and controlled the speakers to be invited. On both occasions, I was told by the directors that I would be invited to speak, but on both occasions I never received a formal invitation and was told that I could attend only as an observer. Interestingly enough, the CIA officer vetting the invitation list was a CIA operative, Lloyd Salvetti, an erstwhile colleague of mine at National War College and a member of Zelikow's "truth" commission on 9/11. Truth is elusive, but the best way to obtain truth on the CIA's analytical record is to ensure there is an outside institution—not paid by the CIA—that searches for answers.

There was one more experience with Harvard's Kennedy School that turned out to be preposterous. A longtime friend and confidant, James Worthen, was on a sabbatical from the CIA teaching a course on intelligence at the Kennedy School. Jim and I had engaged in many conversations about the rampant manipulation of intelligence and the corruption of intelligence under Casey and Gates, so he invited me to speak to his classes. I reviewed the dangers of producing biased intelligence and the heavy role that Gates had played in the process, which Worthen found embarrassing to him as a senior manager in the Intelligence Directorate. We discussed the problem over lunch.

Three years later, the CIA's in-house publication, *Studies in Intelligence*, featured an article by him that completely endorsed the views of those testifying on Gates's behalf at the hearings. Worthen resorted to the "we are all honorable men" defense, in the best tradition of Richard Helms in the wake of his sentencing in the 1970s, and attributed the criticism of Gates to misperceptions or base motivations. He totally ignored the institutionalized effort by Casey and Gates to slant the intelligence product to support the right-wing agenda of Ronald Reagan. Worthen accused Gates's critics with having "hurt feelings and damaged egos" in order to close the book on the issue and deter further comment. This was the same argument that the White House sold to many Republican members of the Senate Intelligence Committee in 1991.

The self-serving and one-sided article by Worthen, which truckled to CIA leaders, required a rebuttal. When no one stepped up, Lyn Ekedahl submitted a response to document Worthen's total lack of analytic objectivity, although objective analysis was the major reason for the CIA's existence in the first place. Ekedahl documented efforts to slant analytical conclusions from *outside* the CIA over the years, as well as how Casey and Gates were the first to manipulate evidence and assessments from *inside* the CIA.

In addition to using Harvard to create an impression of analytical success, the CIA has a long history of leaking classified material to key reporters to manipulate public opinion about clandestine programs. There are laws to protect U.S. citizens from being subjected to propaganda from their government, but these laws are observed in the breach. The Agency manipulated information during the Cold War in the 1950s and 1960s, and it did so more recently with its interrogation program. In 2002, the CIA convinced the *New York Times* to withhold a story about a secret CIA prison in Thailand. The CIA worked with Tom Brokaw of NBC news on key stories, and with author Ronald Kessler for his books on the CIA.

The *Washington Post* has a long history of cooperating with the CIA that began in the 1950s when Philip Graham was close to the Georgetown set and CIA directors such as Richard Helms and Allen Dulles. It continues to bend over backwards for the CIA. PBS has avoided opportunities to interview Agency critics, and allows former CIA deputy directors John E. McLaughlin and Michael Morell to defend the Agency without providing alternative views. Morell, hoping for a return to the intelligence community in a Hillary Clinton administration, was a regular spokesman for CBS. It is for good reason that television news has become the great wasteland.

Washington Post writer Bob Woodward is a major beneficiary of the double standard. He regularly drafts insider accounts based on classified information from high-level national leaders, including presidents and secretaries of state and defense, but no concern is expressed regarding compromise of security. After all, the United States is the ship of state that leaks from the top. Lower-level government employees who challenge authority or disclose documents revealing illicit activity, such as surveillance of the general population, torture, and abuse, can find themselves not only indicted and prosecuted, but sent to federal prison.

I've briefed journalists discreetly about the CIA and its politics and policies. I have never revealed classified information in these discussions, and a CIA spokesman acknowledged this. I've always gone on record to identify errors in media coverage of the CIA and the intelligence community. In a favorable review of one of my books in 2008, Spencer Ackerman, writing in *The Nation*, credited me with serving a "particular function to Washington national security reporters and CIA officials."[18] I don't know Ackerman, and he clarified that he had "never spoken" with me. It was obtuse, however, for him to describe me as an "intermediary to pass messages between active-duty colleagues, who are not authorized to speak with the press without official permission, and journalists seeking to discover the agency's inner workings." I have never been a conduit for stories or a mouthpiece for anyone. I found Ackerman's remarks insulting. Why would a journalist try to compromise any member or former member of the intelligence community willing to speak to the press, particularly when such analysts are so few?

Even Steven Colbert (or his lawyers) lost his nerve in deciding whether to feature my book, *The Failure of Intelligence: The Decline and Fall of the CIA*, on *The Colbert Report*. I had several pre-interviews with the show's producer, and things were moving in a favorable direction. In the last conversation, however, Emily Lazar, producer for author segments and co-executive producer of the show, said she had some final questions from the show's lawyers. They wanted to know if the book had been cleared by the CIA and expressed concerns about my identification of CIA officers. I told them that the book had been submitted for clearance, but that I had filed a *reclama* and rejected the CIA's "recommendations." I couldn't assuage their concerns about the names that I mentioned, even though all of them were CIA bad guys whom Colbert could have defended in his persona as head of the ultra-conservative Colbert Nation. *C'est la guerre.*

The inept performance of the media regarding the confirmation hearings of 1991 convinced me that I should pursue my own communications with the press corps and write my own op-eds. In addition to Doug Jehl, an outstanding writer with the *New York Times* who is now foreign news editor of the *Washington Post*, and Seymour Hersh of the *New Yorker*, I dealt with John Crewsdon of the *Chicago Sun Times* and Knut Royce of the *Long Island Newsday* from time to time. I always spoke on the record, and I never violated my security oaths to the CIA or the Department of State. Because I am quoted from time to time in various newspapers and magazines, I continue to receive calls from journalists on the national security and intelligence beat who seek an insider's view of the CIA and its successes and failures. I also remain active on what is left of progressive radio around the country.

One of the reasons intelligence officers are hesitant to talk to journalists is that they are never sure who is trustworthy on sensitive matters, who will protect sources regardless of political pressure, and who understands the mechanics and ethics of the intelligence world. There is a small band of national security correspondents who excel at what they do and have a moral compass for protecting sources, but there are too many like Elaine Sciolino, who want to protect access to political officials above all else. The result is the kind of toothless, self-censoring journalism that is incapable and unwilling to investigate, critique, and question authority. When Tim Weiner wrote for the *Times*, he spent more time promoting his own writing than making sure he accurately transcribed information from his sources.

Colbert was spot-on with his remarks at the White House

Correspondents' dinner in 2006 when he lambasted President Bush but also skewered the Washington press corps for failing to report the excesses of the Bush administration. Colbert lauded the press corps for "being so good—over tax cuts, weapons of mass destruction, and the effects of global warming. We Americans didn't want to know, and you had the courtesy not to try to find out."[19] In fact, the Washington press corps knows a great deal more than it is willing to publicly share, because it doesn't want to bite the "official sources" hand that feeds it; there is even more information that it does not pursue. Too many correspondents from major newspapers and news magazines prefer "room service," having the story brought to their door on a silver platter.

I did my best to place an important story about the intelligence community on such a silver platter and take it to Scott Shane of the *New York Times*. In 2010, I had lunch with Shane, and I had an agenda: I was there to expose the successful efforts of the Bush and Obama administrations to compromise the role of the statutory inspector general at the CIA and effectively neuter the Office of Inspector General. Shane either didn't understand the importance of the role of the inspector general or was unwilling to pursue supportive sources or materials.

The CIA began to push back against the Office of Inspector General during the Bush administration, a battle that was waged more aggressively and successfully in the Obama administration. The campaign against the inspector general was led by the senior leaders of the Operations Directorate, who resented the criticism of inspections and investigations on 9/11, torture and abuse, extraordinary renditions, and the shoot-down of the missionary plane over Peru in 2000 that killed innocent civilians. These reports were hard-hitting and revealed a great deal of malfeasance and even a high-level cover-up in the case of the missionary plane. High-level members of the Intelligence Directorate were also critical of the inspector general reports, including a former deputy director, John Gannon, who told me the Office of Inspector General had become a "vindictive" institution.

Journalists fail to appreciate that the CIA has the upper hand in all matters that deal with public disclosure of intelligence information and that insiders are rarely willing to criticize or expose the foibles of others. When Larry Summers was advising Elizabeth Warren to become an insider in the Obama administration, he warned her that, once on the "inside," she could no long criticize other insiders. The CIA's Publications Review Board is designed to make sure that CIA "insiders" don't criticize other insiders. It protects classified information, but its review is far less rigorous for praise of Agency practices than it is for criticism. An important mission of the Publications Review Board is to keep embarrassments, not just secrets, out of the press.

My exchanges with the Review Board over the writing of six books have been risible, because it is obvious that the office has no idea what actually constitutes a classified statement. On several manuscripts, I was told that I could not use the term "station chief" because the posting of senior CIA officers overseas is classified. The Publications Review Board finally backed off when I produced a series of books by former CIA directors who used the term "station chief" with impunity.

Of course, there is another double standard at work: former CIA directors don't get the heavy review that critical officers receive. When I asked about the security review for the two memoirs of former director Gates, I was met with silence. There is also the example of former director Panetta, who submitted his book to his publisher long before giving it to the Publications Review Board. There were no consequences for Panetta, who produced a book that said nothing critical. Whenever George Tenet ran into opposition from the Review Board, he simply turned to a senior CIA official, Mike Morell, to intervene and make sure there was no need to drop information from the manuscript.

The media have been complacent about restrictions on personal and civil liberty, except when journalists are targeted aggressively for leaks. The Associated Press was targeted in 2012, when it reported that the CIA had stopped a terrorist plot to blow up an airliner. The Department of Justice ignored the fact that the Associated Press, at the request of the CIA, had held the story for several days so that the Agency could target an al Qaeda official on the basis of information from an infiltrator of the terrorist organization. As a result of the Associated Press story, the FBI secretly perused phone calls made over a two-month period by nearly 100 Associated Press editors and reporters in Washington and New York. (The right of journalists to protect their sources exists in state law—with the exception of Wyoming—but not in federal law. In its 1972 ruling in *Branzburg v. Hayes*, the Supreme Court failed to find such a right in the Constitution.)

In 2013, the FBI seized the email records of Fox News reporter James Rosen, who reported that North Korea was preparing to test a nuclear weapon. In this case, the Obama administration labeled Rosen an "aider, abettor and/or co-conspirator" in violation of the Espionage Act of 1917. Rosen was not indicted, but he was targeted for following his journalistic instincts to report a story that could have been a surprise to no one following events on the Korean peninsula. In both cases regarding the Associated Press and Fox News, the government clearly had a right to stop the leaks of classified information, but, if the First Amendment right of the free press means anything, then journalists have the right to investigate stories concerning national security. The media were outraged by the government's campaign against Rosen and the seizure of his phone records and emails.

In 2011, federal prosecutors conducted similar actions against James Risen of the *New York Times* on the CIA's role in providing faulty nuclear blueprints to Iran. The Justice Department obtained Risen's credit reports from three major commercial agencies, individual credit card bills, bank records, and air travel documents in an effort to expose his sources. The Department of Justice made special efforts to get Risen to give testimony to a grand jury and to the jury for the trial of CIA agent Jeffrey Sterling indicted for providing information to Risen. The case against Risen continued until December 2014, when the Department of Justice finally dropped the matter to avoid embarrassment.

With the exception of the government's attacks on Risen, Rosen, and the Associated Press, which raised hackles in the press community, the media's attitude toward actual whistleblowers has been one of disdain and borderline contempt. Glenn Greenwald, used to write for the U.K. *Guardian* and reported the Snowden revelations, was asked by NBC's David Gregory, "To the extent that you have aided and abetted Snowden, even in his current movements, why shouldn't you, Mr. Greenwald, be charged with a crime?"[20] At least Gregory is no longer host of *Meet the Press*.

The press has been particularly snarky in dealing with contrarians who take on the government and conventional wisdom. The editorial pages of the *Washington Post* outdid themselves in condemning the whistleblowing of Snowden and Manning. Walter Pincus typically rose to the defense of the intelligence community, and made a series of errors in his columns that had to be corrected on the *Post* website. David Ignatius, an apologist for the CIA for the past three decades, charged that Snowden looked "more like an "intelligence defector . . . than a whistleblower."[21]

So-called liberal pundits piled on. Richard Cohen, who beat the drums for war against Iraq a decade ago, called Snowden a "cross-dressing Little Red Riding Hood."[22] Ruth Marcus, another liberal editorial writer with the *Post*, not only referred to Snowden's "unattractive personality," but gratuitously maligned all whistleblowers who "tend to be the difficult ones, the sort who tend to feel freer to speak out precisely because they don't fit in."[23]

Marcus and her colleagues do not recognize that the oversight system is broken; if it were functional, there would be less need for whistleblowers—who operate in every facet of American life, not merely in the field of national security. Last year, for example, over $400 million was awarded to whistleblowers in private industry who reported varieties of fraud and misbehavior. There are no financial rewards for whistleblowers in the intelligence community, although the improprieties they report are often more costly to U.S. citizens than those that take place in the marketplace. The fabrications surrounding the existence of weapons of mass destruction in Iraq would be a prime example.

Nevertheless, the media are quick to criticize whistleblowers for a variety of perceived faults. The press has been particularly critical of Snowden for fleeing to Russia, but that was never his intention, and the political irony is that he is far safer in Moscow then he would be in facing the judicial system in the United States. The treatment of whistleblowers such as Tom Drake and Chelsea Manning speaks to the caprice of U.S. jurisprudence in the wake of 9/11. Yet Marcus believes that Snowden should have "stuck around to test the system the Constitution created" and dealt with the consequences of his actions, which would mean many years in prison and even the possibility of solitary confinement.

The overarching lesson is the profound value of skepticism. Skepticism on the part of the overall citizenry, the press, and the intelligence analyst. I'm not talking about cynicism, which is a corrosive attitude that justifies standing on the sidelines because of the belief that there is no possibility of correcting mistakes or challenging conventional wisdom. I favor skepticism and the need for scrutiny of government claims. As a lawyer in Chicago, Barack Obama represented defendants trying to maintain their whistleblower protections. As president, Obama seems intimidated by a national security arena that equates legitimate leaks and whistleblowing with espionage.

No event brought home the need for whistleblowing like the false and absurd report that Secretary of State Powell delivered to the U.N. Security Council on February 5, 2003, only six weeks before the invasion of Iraq. Secretary Powell broke every rule regarding policy statements. He ignored his advisors and spent several days at the CIA overseeing the drafting of the speech. No secretary of state had ever done this in crafting a speech. There wasn't an accusation in the speech that could have survived scrutiny from an interested punditry or public. Powell now realizes that he was bamboozled by CIA deputy director John McLaughlin.

Nevertheless, numerous editorials from the media bought the speech—hook, line, and sinker—and never warned readers that Powell's performance rested on suspect sources lacking corroboration. A good investigative reporter wouldn't advance a story that depended on a single source. Neither should an intelligence analyst or a secretary of state. But Powell gave a speech at the UN that depended on single sources, including sources such as Curveball, an alcoholic with a reputation for lying whose "information" was made out of whole cloth.

The *Washington Post* never noted that Powell had embellished some of his so-called facts, and its editorial writers didn't do the homework that would have meant comparing actual evidence to Powell's statements. The *Post* ran an editorial and five op-eds in support of the speech the following day, led by Mary McGrory's article "I'm Convinced." The writers claimed that Powell had made a "strong, credible and persuasive case," a "powerful case," and a "compelling case." "Only the most gullible and wishful thinking souls," according to the *Post*, could "now deny that Iraq is harboring and hiding weapons of mass destruction."[24] I looked for signs of skepticism in the national press; there were few.

I provided ample warning to numerous journalists, but with the exception of Warren Strobel and Jonathan Landay of the *Philadelphia Inquirer*, no one was prepared to step back and stop the rush to judgment. Joseph Stalin referred to agreeable journalists as "useful idiots" when they served the interests of the Soviet state. The Bush administration had a stable of "useful idiots" to help make its case. I had a similar experience dealing with the British press. I provided my argumentation against Iraq's so-called weapons of mass destruction to Ed Vulliamy of the *London Observer*, but the paper had taken a pro-war editorial position based in part on disinformation supplied by CIA operatives assigned in European capitals.

Most of what appears in the media on international security reflects what the government wants you to read. The run-up to the war in Iraq was the classic example of that behavior. George Tenet and John E McLaughlin, the director and deputy director of the CIA, led the way in accommodating the policy preferences of President Bush and Vice President Cheney. They released spurious judgments and executive summaries of intelligence products, and didn't stop a maverick intelligence operation at the Pentagon that circulated "intelligence" that even the CIA wouldn't touch. Intelligence has been tailored to support our wars in the past, but nothing compared to the politicized intelligence that made the case for war against Iraq. There has rarely been more need for whistleblowers.

The critical voice of the nation's press is rarely turned inward, so it was probably naïve to expect editorial leaders of the media to concede their shortcomings over the issue of politicization of intelligence in 1991 and the run-up to the Iraq War in 2002–2003. Finally, in January 2015, the executive editor of the *New York Times*, Dean Baquet, told a German magazine, *Der Spiegel*, that his newspaper (as well as the U.S. mainstream media) "was not aggressive enough after 9/11, was not aggressive in asking questions about the decision to go to war . . . [and] in asking the hard questions about the war on terror."[25] Interestingly, Baquet chose a foreign audience and a foreign publication to raise an issue that should have been debated in the United States.

Baquet conceded that "it hurt a lot" on both a moral and professional level that Snowden gave his story to the U.K. *Guard-*

ian. "Morally," according to Baquet, "it meant that somebody with a big story to tell didn't think we [the *New York Times*] were the place to go, and that's painful."[26] It also meant that "on what was arguably the biggest national security story in many, many years," Snowden went to the *Guardian* and to the *Times*'s most important rival, the *Washington Post*, which was "really, really, really painful."[27] It was obvious that the failure of the *Times* to publish the initial research about the NSA's massive surveillance in 2004 convinced Snowden that the paper was not trustworthy. I personally doubt that the *Times* would have had the courage to print Snowden's revelations, in view of its timid handling of stories from their own reporters.

This is exactly the lesson that James Risen has been trying to impart to his paper and to the media. In 2003, Risen prepared a story about a covert CIA effort to undermine Iran's nuclear program, but CIA director Tenet persuaded the *Times* to withhold publication because it would "compromise national security."[28] The following year, Risen and a colleague, Eric Lichtblau, developed a story about NSA's massive violation of American privacy. Again, the Bush White House engaged in an intense lobbying effort, and the Old Gray Lady bowed to the pressure. The following year, when Risen planned to publish both stories in his book-length manuscript, the paper's leadership finally ran the NSA story, which won a Pulitzer.[29]

The Bush administration refused to indict Tom Drake for his information on NSA; it was the Obama administration that did so. The Bush administration refused to go after Risen; again, it was Obama who decided to ignore the Constitution's First Amendment and the rights of journalists. Although Attorney General Holder ultimately dropped the case against Risen, his legacy will sadly include the criminalization of professional reporting on national security issues. Once again, potential whistleblowers have learned that they will get no hearing from their inspectors general, from congressional intelligence committees, or from the Department of Justice. This is why whistleblowers often go directly to the media.

The Founding Fathers intended for the press to serve as a check on government power, making freedom of the press the very first amendment. When Thomas Jefferson was asked if he had to choose between a free press and the government, he chose the press. The Congress and the press failed to sufficiently examine the phony intelligence used to coerce the country into a disastrous and unnecessary war. The press not only failed in its function to scrutinize such intelligence, but two journalists from the *New York Times*—Judith Miller and Michael Gordon—were derelict in their handling of intelligence issues. Miller served time in prison for refusing to testify about her sources for the phony intelligence; her real crime was misleading Americans about Iraq.

The public needs an informed debate about the key issues of national security, particularly issues of war and peace, but this cannot happen without information the government keeps secret. Our government often classifies information to prevent embarrassment; conversely, almost everything we read in the press comes from official sources. It is very difficult for a dissident to get his or her views into the press, particularly influential op-ed pages. If sources cannot speak out with the confidence that they will receive protection, the information itself will dry up and the nation as a whole will be the loser. Lucy Dalglish, the dean of the University of Maryland journalism school and formerly the executive director of the Reporters Committee for Freedom of the Press, said that the "public is in danger of learning only what the administration wants them to know."[30]

The lies of too many administrations fell into a demilitarized zone where the press feared to tread. It took whistleblowers, or "lawbreakers with a conscience" like Daniel Ellsberg, to expose the lies of the Vietnam War; the gang of eight in Media, Pennsylvania, to expose the violations of COINTELPRO; Chelsea Manning to disclose the extent of U.S. war crimes being committed in Iraq; and Edward Snowden to reveal the massive surveillance of the NSA in violation of the Fourth Amendment of the Constitution.[31] My own efforts to expose the CIA's politicization of intelligence does not rank with the courageous efforts of these patriots, but it surfaced the dangers of ignoring oversight of secret agencies.

There are too few truth-tellers in our society. Just as we need poets to reveal beauty and satirists to point out our flaws; we need truth-tellers within government to expose official crimes and improprieties. Likewise, we need a press that is truly free and independent enough to investigate and report the facts, no matter how far up the bureaucratic ladder the implications take them. Atrocious misconduct in the terror wars has demonstrated U.S. deviance from rules and standards that once governed American foreign policy and warfare. In the absence of an official system of accountability capable of upholding such standards, those in power can be expected to continue to play by their own rules and lie to the American public along the way. The openness and accountability that makes our nation an authentic democracy thus depends on truth-tellers to expose official corruption and a justice system that holds everyone equal before the law.

TEN

CONCLUSIONS:
MAINTAINING THE PATH TO DISSENT

"A people at war become in the most literal sense
obedient, respectful, trustful children again, full of that
naïve faith in the all-wisdom and all-power of the adult
who takes care of them."
                                        —Randolph Bourne

"Dissent is the lifeblood of democracy."[1]
                                        —John Raines

On too many occasions in U.S. history, the use of force has been
justified with either corrupt intelligence or just plain lies. Such
was the case in the Mexican-American War, the Spanish-American War, the Vietnam War, and the 2003 Iraq War. The checks
and balances that were needed to prevent the misuse of intelligence were not operative, and manipulative presidents such as
Polk, McKinley, Johnson, and Bush deceived the American people, the U.S. Congress, and the press. The loss of thousands of
U.S. soldiers and taxpayers' treasure in these cases was massive,
and the resulting threats generated by the chaos of war truly in-
calculable. Have we learned from the catastrophes for which we,
as a nation, are responsible?

Because secret intelligence agencies operate outside—and

in many ways *against*—the process of democracy, we are usually unaware of the costs and consequences of corrupt intelligence. The increasing power of secret government limits debate on foreign and domestic policy and deprives citizens of their right to information requisite to be fully engaged in the political process. A counter-culture of openness can reverse the damage, but oversight has languished and the intelligence community has been difficult to monitor, let alone control. As a result, there is no more important check or balance than the act of whistleblowing, particularly in dealing with the CIA where the path to truth and dissent can be tortuous.

A dissenter can make a huge difference in righting wrongs. In the 1970s, before Richard Nixon resigned the presidency, he tried to destroy White House records, leading to a legal challenge that convinced the National Archives to take control of his papers and tapes. The challenge was led by Robert E. Herzstein, a Washington lawyer, who sued on behalf of a group of historians and overturned Nixon's deal with the General Services Administration. Herzstein got a restraining order from a federal judge, Congress passed legislation to revoke the agreement with the General Services Administration, and the Justice Department reversed itself. These actions historically preserved 42 million pages of documents and 880 recordings.

At the CIA, in the 1970s, one person attempted to stop some of the worst aspects of Watergate. In August 1971, before the break-in at the Watergate, Karl Wagner, the executive assistant to the CIA's deputy director, learned that a former agency operative, Howard Hunt, had met with Deputy Director Robert E. Cushman Jr. to obtain clandestine materials for the break-in of the office of Lewis Fielding, the psychiatrist for Daniel Ellsberg. Ellsberg was the former Pentagon official who leaked the Pentagon Papers, the top-secret history of the U.S. war against Vietnam.

Wagner wrote a memorandum to Cushman, a retired Marine general, that questioned the legality of the Agency's involvement in domestic clandestine activity. "Hunt's use of unique clandestine equipment in domestic activity of an uncertain nature," Wagner wrote, "has potential for trouble."[2] Wagner then instructed the CIA's technical division to ignore Hunt's further inquiries, and urged Cushman to contact the White House to "obtain assurance that Hunt's latest caper is OK."[3] Cushman did so, and received assurances from White House advisor John Ehrlichman that he would handle Hunt and "call a halt to this."[4]

In 1974, the CIA awarded Karl Wagner the Intelligence Medal of Merit for his "personal integrity" and his "exceptional perception and courage of action under very awkward circumstances . . . to bring about the cessation of support to an operation which proved to be beyond the jurisdiction of the Agency."[5] In this case, a whistleblower stepped up and was honored for protecting the integrity and professionalism of his agency. Such an award is unusual, because whistleblowers typically pay a high price for being right at a time when a presidential administration or a government agency, such as the CIA, is anxious to do wrong.

But whistleblowers, dissidents, and leakers are rarely honored. Although whistleblowers are often vindicated both legally and morally for their revelations, they are typically ridiculed, vilified, and subjected to retaliation. CIA officers who submitted sworn affidavits in support of my testimony against Bob Gates in 1991 were summoned for polygraph examinations, an act of harassment and intimidation. Other officers were warned not to cooperate with the Senate Select Intelligence Committee. This was the kind of action that the chairman of the committee had warned Gates to prevent and that his committee would not tolerate.

When Senator David L. Boren said he would protect CIA employees who testified against Gates, he had to know he was powerless to do so. Indeed, there was shock within the committee when Boren made this commitment; his colleagues knew they had no recourse to CIA retaliation or intimidation, which is what the agency pursued.

Whistleblowers at the Department of State have also suffered for their efforts to expose U.S. support for the criminal actions of its allies. In 1971, Archer Blood, a senior foreign service officer serving in East Pakistan, informed the Department of State of the war crimes being committed in East Pakistan. There was no change in the close relationship between the United States and Pakistan, but Mr. Blood was transferred to Washington and relegated to a sinecure in the office of human resources.[6] Even worse, a decade later, Ambassador Robert White was dismissed from the foreign service for ignoring Secretary of State Alexander Haig's order to cover up the killings of four American churchwomen in El Salvador. White exposed the cooperation of U.S. military advisors and CIA operatives in aiding El Salvador's brutal death-squad military.

The history of whistleblowing in the United States is as old as the Republic itself. Several years before the outbreak of the Revolutionary War, the colonies had to deal with the leak of confidential documents by Benjamin Franklin, the colonial representative to England. In an effort to quell the nascent rebellion in the colonies, which he feared, Franklin sent confidential letters from the colonists to the *Boston Gazette* to show that Massachusetts governor Thomas Hutchinson—not the British parliament—was responsible for the enhanced military presence in Boston. As a result, Franklin was sent home from London.

For too many, a whistleblower is a stool pigeon, an informer, a backstabber. But in 2002, *Time* magazine gave its "person of the year" award to "The Whistleblowers," three American women: Cynthia Cooper of World.com, Coleen Rowley of the FBI, and Sherron Watkins of Enron. These women were not quislings; all three identified serious malfeasance at their organizations, and all three were ignored. They didn't start out to be whistleblowers, but their warnings were leaked to the press. As a result, Cooper and Watkins could never get hired again, and eventually started their own consulting firms; Rowley was forced to retire.

The experiences of Thomas Drake, Chelsea Manning, William Binney, and Edward Snowden further reveal the risks of whistleblowing. Drake exhausted his life's savings to defend himself against charges under the Espionage Act, which was never intended to be used against whistleblowing, and is now working in an Apple store in my Bethesda, Maryland, neighborhood. Manning was arrested, abused while in detention, and given an outrageously long jail sentence, even though she exposed U.S. war crimes in Iraq. Edward Snowden was forced to take refuge in Russia because the United States confiscated his passport, making him a man without a country. The U.S. violations of law he exposed were far more serious than the ones he admits to committing. The heavy-handed actions of the government against these U.S. citizens were designed to deter future Americans of conscience from exposing the degree to which the national security state often acts beyond the rule of law.

My whistleblowing included confronting the CIA's deputy director of intelligence; reporting to the Office of Inspector General; meeting with the deputy director of the CIA when the director refused to see me; testifying to the U.S. Congress and media; publishing a widely cited book on the decline and fall of the CIA; writing a series of articles; and giving lectures. The commandant of the National War College pressured me not to testify, a form of harassment that I ignored. Some former CIA colleagues treated me like a turncoat. Like most whistleblowers, I was unprepared to testify before a congressional committee and was naïve about the consequences of going public. A study on whistleblowing confirmed that most whistleblowers admitted that they were naïve and had learned a painful lesson—never to do it again.[7] I'm proud of my efforts; I *would* do it again.

The Founding Fathers certainly believed in protecting whistleblowers. Hamilton, Jefferson, and Madison had different ideas about the formation of our government, but they agreed on the need for a carefully constructed nation based on checks and balances, a division of powers, and constitutional protection against unreasonable seizures and searches. They feared illegal government surveillance of citizens and, like Franklin, believed that "those who would give up essential liberty, to purchase a little temporary safety, deserve neither liberty nor safety." Now we have a government that has crafted a massive system of "safety," highlighted by a surveillance program to intimidate citizens and the use of state-secrets privilege to dismiss lawsuits or to disqualify plaintiffs for "lack of standing."

Whenever the United States has been at war, a major casualty has been the loss of personal and civil liberty for U.S. citizens, particularly dissenters. The war with France in 1798 led to the Alien and Sedition Acts, which permitted the United States to expel any non-citizen without a hearing. The Sedition Act made "peacetime treason" a crime entailing punishment for anyone who uttered "false, scandalous, or malicious" observations about the U.S. government or the Congress. The Espionage Act of 1917 repeated this language.

One of our nation's greatest presidents, Abraham Lincoln, had a dubious constitutional record during the Civil War. Lincoln suspended the writ of habeas corpus without congressional authorization, and created military tribunals for opponents of his administration. Private property was seized without compensation, and the North entered the Civil War without congressional approval or consultation.

Long before President George W. Bush circumvented the Fourth Amendment in the name of national security, President Lincoln—fearful that the telegraph was being used to organize Confederate sympathizers—ordered U.S. Marshals to enter telegraph offices in the North and seize all telegrams sent and received during the previous 12 months. It was the first time that national security was invoked to justify government surveillance of electronic communications.[8]

In 1862, Lincoln's secretary of war, Edwin M. Stanton, received permission to reroute telegraph lines through his office in order to monitor all communications, journalistic and personal. On the back of Stanton's request, Lincoln scribbled his approval: "The Secretary of War has my authority to exercise his discretion in the matter within mentioned."[9] Stanton ordered the arrest of dozens of journalists on dubious charges.

World War I led to additional prosecution of critics and dissenters. State sedition laws were passed, and the Montana law became the model for the Espionage Act passed in 1917. Following the war, there was a "red scare" that found a young FBI officer, J. Edgar Hoover, conducting raids and arrests against suspected communists. The Palmer Raids in 1919 led to more than 10,000 arrests, which was a part of the FBI campaign against the Industrial Workers of the World.

World War II was marked by the internment of tens of thousands of Japanese Americans, an executive decision upheld by the Supreme Court in 1944 in the infamous decision *Korematsu v. the United States*. Just as the Red Scare followed WWI, the years after WWII were marked by the fear-mongering antics and ramblings of Senator Joseph McCarthy, including the blacklisting of American writers, directors, and artists.

The surprise attack on Pearl Harbor and the start of the Cold War led directly to President Truman's creation of the CIA in 1947. But Truman was appalled at the misuse of the CIA by the Eisenhower and Kennedy administrations and in December 1963 wrote a memorandum that emphasized that the CIA "was not intended as a 'Cloak & Dagger Outfit'!"[10] Truman emphasized that the Agency was "intended merely as a center for keeping the president informed on what was going on in the world" and that the CIA "worked when I had control."[11] Too late. Truman's successors ignored these caveats.

The current constitutional battle over the massive surveillance of the NSA is not unprecedented. The investigations of the Church Committee 40 years ago revealed that the NSA obtained "millions of private telegrams sent from or through the United States from 1956 to 1975 under a secret arrangement with three U.S. telegraph companies."[12] The CIA and the FBI opened and photographed hundreds of thousands of first-class letters from the 1940s to as late as 1973, which produced a CIA computerized index of nearly 1.5 million names. The U.S. Postal Service has a program that photographs the outside of every piece of paper mailed in the United States, a powerful investigative tool.

I learned about postal surveillance in 1959, when one of my professors at Johns Hopkins University, Owen Lattimore, told his students about having to go to the post office to collect his mail from China. The government made no attempt to hide the fact that his mail had been opened, which should have required a warrant. Senator McCarthy falsely accused Lattimore of having communist affiliations; he was innocent, but never got the U.S. government off his back. In 1973, a high school student in New Jersey finally brought a suit against the FBI, which was tracking all mail sent to the Socialist Workers Party as part of an investigation. In that case, a federal judge issued a strong rebuke of the FBI.

The U.S. Army kept intelligence files on at least 100,000 Americans between the mid-1960s and 1971 because of their anti-war activities, and the CIA kept separate files on Americans and more than 100 domestic groups during this same period as a part of Operation CHAOS. One of my colleagues at the CIA, the late Mark Sullivan, secretly scoured such publications as the *New York Review of Books* to find names of domestic groups to pass to the White House so that the Johnson administration could conduct investigations. The CIA's deputy director for operations, Thomas Karamessines, warned counterintelligence chief James Angleton that such surveillance had "definite domestic counterintelligence aspects." The Internal Revenue Service played this game as well, maintaining files on more than 11,000 individuals and groups between 1969 and 1973 on the basis of "political rather than tax criteria."

More recently, the Bush administration simply coordinated surveillance activities with the major telecommunications companies, such as Verizon and AT&T. The only company that wouldn't cooperate, Qwest, was soon out of business. Qwest lost its government contracts, and its president, who testified that he refused to participate in the government's wiretapping before 9/11, is serving a prison sentence for insider trading.

Recent whistleblowers, Drake and Binney at the NSA or Kiriakou at the CIA, should be honored instead of being treated as traitors. I didn't expect any recognition from the CIA for pointing out the cancer of corruption, although I did receive letters of praise from the Democratic and Republican leaders of the Senate Intelligence Committee. Several years after I testified, the CIA established the position of ombudsman as a confidential counselor for those with complaints regarding manipulation of intelligence. Ironically, the position was given in 1998 to my closest friend at the CIA, the late Barry L. Stevenson, who 10 years earlier had advised me to stop my campaign for maintaining higher standards in the intelligence process.

But I never thought of myself as a public dissident, let alone a whistleblower. I didn't think I was committing an act of betrayal in protesting the CIA's manipulation of intelligence, nor did I think of myself as heroic in testifying to the Senate Intelligence Committee. Like any whistleblower, I simply reached a point where it was ethically intolerable to ignore a situation, in this case the CIA's methods for subverting the truth. But whistleblowers are naïve in assuming they can throw themselves in front of the moving train of government without consequences.

The psychology and pathology of whistleblowing remain elusive. No one sets out to become a whistleblower, and there are very few people who would consider such a move, let alone act on it. People resort to whistleblowing because they believe something is terribly wrong, and because they feel compelled to act on their conscience. I gave no thought to whether there would be consequences for trying to block the nomination of the CIA chief by the president of the United States. I had no qualms about meeting with the staff of the Senate Intelligence Committee or about testifying to the committee in a closed session. I didn't bother to request a subpoena to give myself some protection in case the Department of Defense decided to make my life difficult at the National War College. The Intelligence Committee initiated the subpoena as a form of protection.

There would have been a greater moral price to pay if I had decided not to give testimony. On one level, I was confronting leadership practices that were degrading the capacity for fairness and integrity in producing intelligence. The manipulation of intelligence for political ends is an unconscionable act. Matters of life and death on a mass scale hang in the balance. As a public servant who believed in the importance of government to serve and protect democracy, it would have been unethical *not* to testify.

If we were to fully investigate the massive terror, destruction, and misery that our unprovoked attack of Iraq has brought to millions of families, and the illegalities of the NSA's massive surveillance of our own population, the country might become more fair-minded in its assessments of Manning and Snowden. Several months before Snowden revealed the program to store phone records of U.S. citizens, NSA critics of the program gave a secret memorandum to NSA director General Keith Alexander that argued the program was not central to stopping terrorism and recommended that it be abolished. They were worried that there would be public outrage if the program were revealed. More recently, a federal appeals court termed the collection effort "illegal."

I continue to criticize the CIA because recent administrations have not exercised control over the intelligence community, and, as a result, the CIA has committed even greater crimes. Thanks to the Senate Intelligence Committee, we know these crimes included torture, in violation of constitutional and international law. There is no indication, however, that the revelations of the CIA's barbaric torture of people has led to any changes in public attitudes about these acts, let alone accountability for those who conducted them.

It is not only whistleblowers who draw the ire of the national security state. In 2004, Major General Antonio M. Taguba was directed to investigate the torture and abuse at Abu Ghraib prison in Iraq. The general's report documented "numerous incidents of sadistic, blatant, and wanton criminal abuses," which prompted a Senate Armed Forces Committee hearing.[13] The report described America's walk on the "dark side," directed by Vice President Dick Cheney.

A few months after General Taguba completed the investigation, however, he was reassigned to the Office of the Secretary of Defense, where he was closely monitored. In early 2006, he received an abrupt phone call from the Army's chief of staff, General Richard A. Cody, who stated: "I need you to retire by January of 2007."[14] The U.S. Army gave no reason why they were forcing the retirement of a general who was ordered to restore the moral compass of America's military.

Just as the military covered up torture, the CIA seven years later tried to block a congressional report on torture at its secret prisons. Senator Dianne Feinstein, a staunch defender of the CIA, conducted the most exhaustive probe of a CIA program in history. Her committee's report documented the sadistic measures that CIA employed, which went far beyond what the so-called "torture memoranda" of the Department of Justice endorsed, and revealed that senior CIA officials had lied to the Congress and the White House about the nature and results of the interrogations.

The CIA refused to cooperate with the committee, dumping 6.2 million pages of documents without any index, organization, or structure. CIA lawyers conducted a well-known game of "discovery warfare" that is common in high-stakes commercial litigation. CIA director Brennan's hostility to the committee's investigation and its report was palpable from the outset. He authorized CIA lawyers to break into the Senate computers to monitor the committee's work. When confronted with these charges, Brennan responded, "Nothing could be further from the truth. We wouldn't do that. That's just beyond the scope of reason in terms of what we would do."[15] Director Brennan was lying.

The klaxon that I sounded at the confirmation hearings for Gates in 1991 and in my book *The Failure of Intelligence* in 2008 seemed relevant. I had described the damage to the CIA's moral compass in the 1980s and its willingness to conjure intelligence to assist a White House hell-bent on launching a misguided war in 2002–2003. The crisis dealing with torture may be the worst of all. The CIA not only lied to the White House and Congress about torture, but it destroyed the tapes that documented its barbarity. The CIA used its lawyers to block congressional oversight that had been mandated in the 1970s. Nevertheless, the Department of Justice failed to declare obstruction of justice, and the CIA's Accountability Board—surprise, surprise—found no violations.

The media seemed to yawn, and much of the public remained asleep to the implications. "We did a whole lot of things that were right," President Obama blithely conceded at a press conference on August 1, 2014, "but we tortured some folks."[16] Well, if we "tortured some folks," then we need to know the "folks" who did the torturing and from whom they took orders, right up the chain of command. But the CIA made sure that even the pseudonyms of the operations officers who conducted the torture were redacted from the report. Meanwhile, senior intelligence officials publish books that deny torture occurred. It is "beyond the scope of reason" that the United States could bury the issue of torture so easily and effectively.

Since the Vietnam War, we have had a system of judicial tolerance, with the Supreme Court intervening in foreign policy only to endorse the powers of the president. This deferential attitude toward the White House has resulted in an absence of judicial scrutiny of illegalities including warrantless eavesdropping and the destruction of criminal evidence such as the torture tapes.

In addition to the failure of Congress and the courts to provide oversight of national security, the media have ignored their watchdog role. The job of the press is to expose those with power and the pretenders to power, particularly in regard to secret government. If we are to live in a democracy, we need whistleblowers to penetrate the secrecy of the intelligence community, and we need to support them when reprisals are taken against them. We also need a free and independent press that prioritizes truth and justice instead of today's lap-dog media that prefer to protect senior officials who dish them news.

Meanwhile, there is a false assumption that all government whistleblowers have protection from retaliation because President Obama signed the Whistleblower Protection Enhancement Act in November 2012. The bill was designed to provide millions of federal workers with the right to report government corruption and wrongdoing. The bill, however, does not cover national security whistleblowers who seek to make disclosures within agency channels, let alone those who go outside bureaucratic lanes. Federal workers do not even enjoy the right of a jury trial to enforce the new protections.

In fact, the Obama administration prosecuted more whistleblowers than all other presidencies in U.S. history. According to the legislative counsel of the American Civil Liberties Union, Gabe Rottman, the Obama administration issued 526 months of prison time for national security leakers as opposed to 24 months total jail time for all administrations since the American Revolution.[17] Obama's Justice Department sought lengthy prison terms for NSA whistleblowers Drake and Binney, and treated reporters who received leaks from whistleblowers as criminals. The Drake case demonstrates that whistleblowers in the field of national security lack a lawful path to document evidence of government corruption and crime.

Similarly, the Obama administration overreached on national security leaks to intimidate the legitimate pursuits of journalists. James Rosen, a Washington correspondent for Fox News, was called a "criminal co-conspirator" in a leak case, and Pulitzer Prize–winning journalist James Risen was threatened with prosecution. Pentagon officials have smeared journalists investigating dubious practices at the Pentagon, and the NSA has spied on journalists who receive leaks from whistleblowers.

President Obama, a Harvard-trained lawyer and former professor of constitutional law, not only tipped the scales of justice toward protecting rather than challenging authority, but exceeded most presidents in compromising liberties, particularly First Amendment issues involving freedom of the press. At his first inauguration, in January 2009, he echoed Benjamin Franklin's warning that those who were willing to trade liberty for security, deserved neither one. The president stated that he would never consider such a trade.

Nevertheless, President Obama resorted to the Espionage Act of 1917 more than twice as often as all previous presidents since Woodrow Wilson. Former attorney general Eric Holder admitted that the administration went too far in pursuing eight leak cases with criminal charges, compared to three cases for all other administrations since the law was passed during World War I. Eric Holder's Justice Department, moreover, conducted the most aggressive federal seizure of media records since the Nixon administration. The dean of Columbia University's Graduate School of Journalism, Steve Coll, called the administration's position on Risen a "low point" in First Amendment litigation.[18]

The pursuit of Risen was particularly troubling because the Department of Justice flatly rejected any notion of a reporter's constitutional privilege to protect sources in criminal proceedings. The judge who dissented in the Risen case, Roger Gregory, wrote that if a journalist cannot protect the confidentiality of sources, then there will be "damage to the way American democracy is supposed to work."[19] Such an outcome, according to Gregory, would not just hurt journalists, it would be "contrary to the will and wisdom of the founders."

When heads roll because of improprieties in U.S. national security policy, it is the heads of whistleblowers and not those who exceeded their authorities or violated the law. The clandestine operative who exposed the torture program went to jail for ostensibly outing a colleague; those who tortured, and the senior CIA official who destroyed the archive of evidence documenting torture, faced no punishment, and the latter wrote a CIA-approved book exonerating the agency of any wrongdoing. The NSA's Thomas Drake, William Binney, and Kirk Wiebe exposed fraud and mismanagement and lost their security clearances in the process. High-ranking NSA and CIA officials who conducted improprieties prospered in the bureaucracy, and the NSA's director, General Hayden, became the CIA's director.

Those who testified against Robert Gates and exposed corruption were marginalized by the press. Meanwhile, Gates and the analysts who tampered with intelligence were rewarded. To recap: Two analysts who submitted sworn affidavits against Gates were blocked from returning to their jobs and severely harassed by the Office of Security with intrusive polygraph tests. When Ambassador Robert White exposed the involvement of U.S.-supported death squads in the heinous rape and killing of four American nuns in El Salvador, as well as the CIA's association with Operation Condor in South America in the 1980s, he was fired from the Foreign Service by Secretary of State Alexander Haig.[20]

In addition to the use of the intelligence community to implement domestic security policy, there has been unimpeded surveillance at the local level. Since 2003, the New York City Police Department has conducted covert surveillance of people who exercise their First Amendment rights to protest. Police surveillance of public events was initiated by New York's deputy policy commissioner for intelligence, David Cohen, a former deputy director for operations at the CIA. In September 2002, Cohen wrote in an affidavit that the police department should not be required to have a "specific indication" of a crime before conducting an investigation.[21] In granting the city's surveillance requests, a federal judge in Manhattan ruled that the dangers of terrorism were "perils sufficient to outweigh any First Amendment cost."[22]

Cohen decimated internal oversight in the police department and invited the CIA to take part in the investigatory work of the New York Police Department, a violation of the CIA's charter stipulations against domestic intelligence collection. In the decade after 9/11, several CIA officers were embedded with the New York police, including one official who helped conduct surveillance operations in the United States. According to the CIA's inspector general report, the counterintelligence officer believed there were "no limitations" on his activities because he was on an unpaid leave of absence, and thus exempt from the prohibition against domestic spying.[23] Another embedded CIA analyst, who was on the CIA's payroll, said he was given "unfiltered" police reports that included information unrelated to foreign intelligence.

The CIA's inspector general concluded that the collaboration with the New York Police Department was fraught with "irregular personnel practices," lacked "formal documentation in some important instances," and received "inadequate direction and control" by agency supervisors, but that no illegal activity had occurred.[24] The problem, according to the inspector general, was the danger of "negative public perception," which was reminiscent of an agency investigation of politicization in the 1990s that found no evidence that intelligence was manipulated and merely concluded that there was evidence only of a perception problem.

Cohen's intelligence division created files on members of social movements such as Occupy Wall Street, as well as street theater companies, church groups, antiwar organizations, environmentalists, and even opponents of the death penalty. He monitored Muslim students far beyond the city limits, including at Ivy League colleges. The reports for the police commissioner included names, despite no evidence of wrongdoing. Informants and undercover officers were placed in Muslim student associations at colleges and universities. Liberals and progressives were seen as security risks, reminiscent of the dark days of Senator McCarthy and J. Edgar Hoover. I called attention to this activity in my writings as early as 2008, but the New York Police Department's illegal surveillance wasn't acknowledged by the mainstream media until an Associated Press article in 2011.

THE ESSENTIAL ROLE OF THE WHISTLEBLOWER

I will leave the debate to others whether Edward Snowden is a patriotic citizen or a subversive. For me, he is a whistleblower who provided essential information to Americans to protect our constitutional democracy. We learned from his revelations that U.S. officials lied to Congress about the monitoring of phone and Internet traffic of U.S. citizens; that the legitimate collection against al Qaeda morphed into massive surveillance of U.S. citizens; that intelligence agencies formed a Special Operations Division that provided access to information not related to terrorism; that intelligence collection was shared with foreign intelligence agencies with no regard to privacy protection; that the Foreign Intelligence Surveillance Court served as a "rubber stamp" for authorizing warrants and not as part of government oversight; and that all Internet traffic is stored at a huge NSA data center in Utah.[25] The impact of these trends is the emergence of an increasingly militaristic and authoritarian state in which rights of citizenship, basic accountability, and democracy itself are continually undermined by the powerful machinations of government surveillance and secrecy.

If it weren't for Edward Snowden, we would have an incomplete picture of the massive surveillance by the NSA; no awareness of the laws that have been broken regarding surveillance or the limited utility of much of the surveillance or and no debate on

362 | WHISTLEBLOWER AT THE CIA

the legality and effectiveness of the NSA's collection of unlimited records of telephone calls made to, from, and within the United States. Snowden's revelations gave legal "standing" to those taking surveillance issues to the judicial system; prior to Snowden, the Supreme Court ruled that plaintiffs had no "standing." As a result of his disclosures, a bloated surveillance apparatus that secretly invaded the privacy of hundreds of millions of Americans and recklessly compromised the security of the Internet has been subject to some oversight.

In 2015, a federal appeals court held that the NSA's collection of information about virtually every phone call made in the United States—a program revealed in 2013 by journalists working with Snowden—was illegal. The NSA surveillance case is headed for the U.S. Supreme Court due to a ruling, on December 16, 2014, by a federal judge in Washington, Richard J. Leon, that the indiscriminate hoarding of metadata violated the Fourth Amendment right to privacy and its prohibition of unreasonable searches.

Snowden's critics in the White House, the Congress, and the media refuse to acknowledge the legal, constitutional, and moral issues that surround his revelations. The NSA's massive surveillance of American citizens has not made Americans safer, and no one can guarantee that the U.S. government can be trusted with the data it has stored. The government's case against Snowden was severely compromised in January 2014, when a bipartisan, independent agency within the executive branch, the Privacy and Civil Liberties Oversight Board, declared the NSA program illegal and not useful. In its 238-page report, the Board called on the president to end the program for both constitutional and practical reasons. The Board concluded that it couldn't identify a "single instance involving a threat to the United States in which the program made a concrete difference in the outcome of a counterterrorism investigation."[26]

Snowden was further vindicated on May 7, 2015, when a

federal appeals court ruled that the NSA's program to collect information on billions of telephone calls was illegal. A three-judge panel from the New York–based Second Circuit Court of Appeals unanimously declared that a Congressional law allowing collection of information relevant to terrorism did not authorize the "bulk collection" of phone records on a massive scale. The Second Circuit is the first appeals court to rule on the legality of the "telephone metadata" program, which has been repeatedly authorized by the Foreign Intelligence Surveillance Court. Two other federal appeals courts are mulling similar challenges. The question of constitutionality was not raised, leaving the issue for the Supreme Court. Even former attorney general Eric Holder conceded that Snowden's revelations amounted to an important public service.

The complacency of the media was matched by the acquiescence of the U.S. Congress. On June 6, 2013, Senator Feinstein, then chair of the Senate Select Committee on Intelligence, assured the American public that the government's snooping into the phone records of Americans was fine, because the information it obtained was only "meta," meaning it excluded the actual content of the phone conversations.[27] Feinstein claimed the collection was "carefully done" and noted that the Foreign Intelligence Surveillance Court, made up of 11 special federal judges, had authorized the vast intelligence collection. She omitted the fact that the court meets in secret, and that one chief justice, John Roberts, named all 11 Foreign Intelligence Surveillance Court judges.

The White House issued similar statements, defending what was termed a "robust legal regime." President Obama emphasized that the government did not "listen in on anyone's telephone calls." However, if one president—George W. Bush—could illegally authorize warrantless eavesdropping, and another president—Obama—could elicit legislative cover for such action, then what is to stop a successor president from taking the next step in surveillance—wholesale monitoring of substantive conversation?

WHAT IS TO BE DONE?

In my 1991 testimony to Congress I reported that in the normal course of the NSA's electronic surveillance, there was the risk of violating the privacy and rights of U.S. citizens. Such surveillance may be authorized, but U.S. citizens should be protected by an anonymization process, which the NSA honored until its director, General Hayden, changed the rules in 2001. Privacy protections that existed prior to 9/11 must be restored, and targeting must be focused. The digital haystack is now too large to find the appropriate intelligence needles. The government must conduct a comprehensive review of all surveillance operations, and there needs to be independent and unobstructed surprise inspections and audits of these operations.

The United States has wasted huge amounts of money in attempting to protect itself from acts of terrorism. Billions of dollars have been devoted to airline security, with underwhelming results. The two terrorists who boarded international flights for the United States in 2002 and 2009 were stopped by passengers and stewards, not the Transportation Security Agency. Even though the would-be terrorists who targeted the United States were identified in intelligence collection, there was no effort to block their actions. The USA PATRIOT Act's electronic surveillance has made no contributions to security. The CIA's use of torture had no beneficial results. NSA officials knew that excessive surveillance was unnecessary, and CIA operatives at the secret prisons reported a lack of success.

Once again, campaign financing is a factor. A vote in the House of Representatives to curtail NSA surveillance missed by seven votes, and there was a huge difference in campaign funds given to representatives who wanted to continue NSA surveillance vs. those who wanted to end the program. On average, the supporters of surveillance received 122 percent more money ($41,635) from defense contractors than those hoping to end the program ($18,765). The Republican co-sponsor of the legislation, Rep. Justin Amash (R-MI), received only $1,400 from defense industry sponsors.[28]

Congressional intelligence committees have failed to conduct effective oversight over the past 25 years. With the exception of the Senate Intelligence Committee's report on torture, which no Republican member of the committee endorsed, there has been no genuine oversight of the secret surveillance system, let alone the abuses that have taken place at the CIA and NSA. Oversight and accountability must be part of the legislative branch in order to check executive power, particularly with regard to secret agencies that are antithetical to democratic governance. Congress has been on the sidelines while great harm was done to the United States and its reputation because of overzealous actions in the post-9/11 era. As a result, the Terror Wars have become a permanent fixture in our national security architecture as well as an economic cornucopia for private contractors.

What the CIA should be—and what it should do—are less clear than at any time since the beginning of the Cold War. The CIA has been out of control since 9/11. Its budget has more than doubled. U.S. citizens have little idea of what is done with this money, but those who live on the wrong end of CIA operations in Southwest Asia, North Africa, and the Horn of Africa have a good idea. The appointment of a former marine, an expert in paramilitary activity, to head the Directorate of Operations in 2015 points to more, and not fewer, covert operations that further bloat the budget of what has become a paramilitary organization.

The perils of corruption could be ended if CIA leaders simply observed the biblical inscription at the entrance to CIA headquarters, "the truth shall make you free." Too many CIA directors (e.g., Gates, Tenet, Goss, Brennan) suffered from the natural instinct to please and were unable or unwilling to present those in power with facts and analysis that didn't accommodate their agendas. In doing so, these directors have contributed to an authoritarian culture in which questioning leadership is equated with helping the enemy. An intelligence community that serves a democracy must be committed to telling the truth to all levels of decision makers. To do anything less would be to drift toward becoming the kind of militaristic society that we have historically dreaded and protected ourselves against.

THE IMPORTANCE OF SCRUTINY

The Founding Fathers understood that independent investigative reporting and the free press were central to government accountability and democracy, and that skepticism was essential on the part of the citizenry and the press. No event in recent history demonstrated the need for skepticism more than the suite of lies, manipulations, and strategies deployed by the Bush administration in order to conjure an excuse to send thousands of U.S. troops to war. Amidst the coercive barrage, the report that Secretary of State Powell delivered to the United Nations in February 2003 stands out. Powell ignored advisors who warned him not to travel to Langley to draft a speech based on the flawed intelligence estimate of October 2002. Most of Powell's assertions were unattributed in a speech that referred vaguely to "human sources" and "detainees." Powell eventually learned that CIA deputy director McLaughlin had lied to him about the so-called evidence, but by then men and women who enlisted to serve their country were already coming back in body bags.

Most of what appears in the media reflects what the government wants you to see, particularly in matters of foreign policy. The lies preceding the U.S. invasion of Iraq are a perfect example of accommodating presidential preferences, even if they are clearly *not* in the national interest. Tenet and McLaughlin added intelligence corroboration from the CIA, making no attempt to stop a rogue intelligence operation at the Pentagon that circulated intelligence even the CIA termed bogus.

Tenet should have been fired for manipulating intelligence. Instead, he left government in 2004 with the highest medal that can be given to a civilian, the Presidential Medal of Freedom. Congress fails to realize the cynicism created in government agencies when George Tenet receives a presidential award or Robert Gates is confirmed as director of the CIA. Meanwhile, the mainstream media, including public television, use McLaughlin as a credible source on the CIA, creating more conditions for cynicism.

George Tenet paved the way to his success with Bush Junior several years earlier when he named CIA headquarters after Bush Senior. If there were genuine oversight of the CIA, then someone on the intelligence committees would have questioned naming the key civilian intelligence facility after a figure who made no contributions to the Intelligence Community while serving as director of central intelligence. It is embarrassing to drive the George Washington Parkway in suburban Virginia and see signs for the George Bush Intelligence Center.

Meanwhile, the path to dissent has gotten more tortuous. In 2013, after the leaks of classified information by Snowden and Manning, the Obama administration introduced the Insider Threat Program to monitor the national security bureaucracy. The use of informant networks dates back as far as the Roman Empire, when Delatores (informants) were recruited from all classes of society. Prior to the death of Joseph Stalin, the Soviet Union used pervasive informant networks to eradicate "crimes." Chancellor Angela Merkel is particularly sensitive to the massive surveillance of the NSA because she grew up in East Germany and was exposed to the pervasive surveillance of the Ministry of State Security, the infamous Stasi. But the Stasi never had the kind of technology that the NSA has today.

The informant network of the Obama administration is insidious, with federal employees required to keep close tabs on co-workers, and managers facing criminal charges for failing to report their suspicions. There are government documents that equate leaks with espionage.[29] In February 2014, General James Clapper, the director of national intelligence, told the Senate

Armed Forces Committee that a system was being developed to monitor the behavior of employees with security clearances "on the job as well as off the job." Clapper's admonitions will ensure that much time and effort will be wasted in trying to pursue "suspicious" employees. Meanwhile, genuine spies, such as the convicted Aldrich Ames, pass their polygraph examinations.

In November 2010, the National Counterintelligence Office issued a memorandum to senior officials in an effort to identify insider threats, suggesting the use of psychiatrists and sociologists to assess changes in employees' behavior. This is a dangerous step in an intelligence community already using excessive polygraph examinations to intimidate employees and to pursue information with no relevance to a security. Shortly after submitting signed affidavits to the Senate intelligence community to oppose confirming Gates, Lyn Ekedahl and John Hibbitts were summoned by the CIA's Office of Security for intrusive polygraph examinations. A similar round of polygraph examinations followed for Ekedahl and others in the wake of leaks regarding CIA secret prisons that led to the forced resignation of an investigator in the Office of Inspector General, Mary O'Neil McCarthy, who had no knowledge of the prisons.

Witch-hunt fever is spreading beyond the intelligence community as the Insider Threat Program is taking root throughout the federal bureaucracy. A Department of Defense paper issued in 2012 exhorts employees to "hammer this fact home: leaking is tantamount to aiding the enemies of the United States."[30] The Department of Agriculture and the National Oceanic and Atmospheric Administration produced online tutorials titled "Treason 101" to teach employees to recognize the psychological profile of spies. Even the Peace Corps is implementing a program! General Clapper has opened another area for indictment by making declassified information off-limits to government personnel on their personal computers.

In April 2014, one of the few friends that whistleblowers

have on Capitol Hill, Senator Charles E. Grassley (R-IA), summoned the chief of the FBI's Internal Threat Program to his office to express concerns that the program would prevent whistleblowers from reporting wrongdoing in the FBI. According to the *Washington Post*, the FBI officials said that the program would protect whistleblowers by "registering" them. When Grassley's staff members asked them to elaborate, the FBI officials refused to answer any additional questions and headed for the door.[31] Any effort to "register" whistleblowers would surely put a target on their backs.

As long as the intelligence community treats whistleblowers as security threats, there will be reduced opportunities for accountability. Michael German, a former undercover FBI agent and whistleblower, called the Insider Threat Program a "dangerous" initiative for just this reason.[32] Once upon a time, intelligence officials could take serious transgressions to the inspector general with the assurance they could do so anonymously and without reprisal. Analysts today believe that the inspector general maintains an open-door policy in order to identify the brave few who are willing to enter. The Obama administration has turned the national security system against its own people, particularly whistleblowers who are trying to improve the system.

The intelligence community's hostile attitude toward whistleblowers reflects the militarization and authoritarianism that has taken hold over the past 20 years. Since the appointment of an undersecretary of defense for intelligence in 2004, the Pentagon has become the chief operating officer of the $70 billion intelligence industry. If President Eisenhower were giving his farewell address in current times, he would have cited the homeland security–intelligence complex in addition to the military-industrial complex. The Pentagon controls more than 85 percent of the intelligence budget and personnel, and deference within the intelligence community for the "warfighter" has meant that tactical military demands have outpaced strategic requirements.

The Pentagon's domination of satellite imagery marked a serious policy setback in view of the importance of such imagery to calibrating military budgets, deciding on military conflict, and monitoring arms control agreements. This capability should not be in the hands of the military.

General Powell's memoir, *An American Journey*, provided an example of the military's suppression of sensitive intelligence that didn't suit the administration's agenda. During Operation Desert Storm in 1991, General H. Norman Schwarzkopf reported that a smart bomb had destroyed four Iraqi Scud missile launchers. Satellite imagery demonstrated that the bomb had actually destroyed four Jordanian fuel tanks, not Scud missiles. General Schwarzkopf's intelligence officers lacked the courage to tell the general he was wrong. Not even General Powell, the chairman of the Joint Chiefs of Staff, would do so; he concluded that preserving General Schwarzkopf's "equanimity" was far more important than the truth.

The path of the whistleblower will remain difficult in our country. There will be tensions for family members who will not fully understand their motives or accept their veracity. There will be colleagues who will agree with whistleblowing in principle but will not appreciate criticism of their institutions. The mainstream media will be beholden to established sources. And there will be insiders who will fight to defend themselves regardless of the revelations. I experienced these challenges and criticisms. As long as congressional committees serve as advocates for the CIA and the Pentagon, we will need whistleblowers and institutions to support them.

Whistleblowers are an unusual and unpredictable lot, which explains why most organizations and even progressive politicians keep their distance from them. I volunteered to be a surrogate speaker for the John Kerry campaign in 2004, but the director for surrogate speakers, Ambassador Joe Wilson, told me that his colleagues were concerned with my background as a whistleblower.

Too many individuals and organizations are unnecessarily critical when a whistleblower puts loyalty to principle above loyalty to party or person.

Even Senator Feinstein encountered the media's marginalization of whistleblowers. In the wake of the release of the Senate Select Committee's torture report's executive summary, CNN's Wolf Blitzer audaciously suggested that Feinstein would have "blood on your hands" if the report led to fatal attacks on U.S. citizens.[33]

Former directors (Tenet, Hayden, and Goss) and deputy directors (McLaughlin, Morell, and Steve Kappes) continue to lie about the torture program. In the *Wall Street Journal*, they credited the CIA with reporting allegations of abuse to the inspector general and the Justice Department. They contend that "nothing was held back" in briefings to Congress. They deny that the CIA went beyond interrogation techniques authorized by the Justice Department. McLaughlin, who at Tenet's behest gave President Bush the specious "slam dunk" briefing to abet the case for invading Iraq, stated that the CIA went to "extraordinary lengths to assure" the program was "legal and approved." The record demonstrates the opposite. Yet Morell described McLaughlin as the "dean for his mastery of our profession."[34] The mastery of deception and manipulation?

CIA counsel Scott Muller lied to Vice President Cheney and Attorney General Ashcroft regarding U.S. acts of torture, and warned members of the National Security Council that "termination of this program will result in extensive loss of life."[35] The CIA provided inaccurate and incomplete information to the White House, and nearly 40 people were tortured before President Bush received an official briefing. The CIA stonewalled the Senate Select Intelligence Committee when it requested additional information on the barbaric activity. Hayden misrepresented the NSA's surveillance program and the CIA's torture program on numerous occasions.

President Obama stated eloquently that torture doesn't represent "our values," but did nothing to make sure our values were not compromised again. He indicated upon taking office that he would not seek accountability, that he would "look forward and not backward." He made poor choices in selecting CIA directors, particularly John O. Brennan, who lied to the Senate Intelligence Committee in order to block oversight. An editorial in the *Washington Post* credited President Obama with "fully" reining in the CIA, but the ugly reality is that the president has been unwilling to seek sufficient public accountability from the many layers of the U.S. intelligence infrastructure.

Manipulation of intelligence should never go unreported; the integrity of our secret intelligence services should count for something. Freedom from unreasonable searches should not be important only to Edward Snowden. Freedom of speech and association should not be important only to the "burglars" who stole classified documents from an FBI office in Media, Pennsylvania. The killing of innocent civilians in a war zone should have been reported at a higher level than Corporal Chelsea Manning. The CIA's use of torture in its secret prisons should not have led to the sentencing of the only CIA officer who blew the whistle.

There has been no accountability in the government for the deplorable acts of war, invasion, occupation, torture, indefinite detention, and abuse that the U.S. perpetrates against people in foreign countries. It was particularly shocking to learn that psychologists with the American Psychological Association fully participated in and supported inhumane interrogations, and even helped operatives to identify and manipulate the vulnerabilities of the people being detained and tortured. The involvement of health professionals is inconsistent with their professional obligations. Unlike the CIA, the American Psychological Association has banned further involvement in national security interrogations and has elected new leadership. Facing an existential crisis, the Association moved to restore its moral compass; the CIA needs to do the same.

There were CIA physicians and psychologists who opposed the torture program, but not a single one of them reported the torture and abuse to the CIA's inspector general or to members of Congress. Meanwhile, former CIA leaders responsible for allowing torture to become part of the agency's legacy are trying to rehabilitate their tarnished reputations in a book that denigrates the Senate's official and authoritative report.[36] The work itself is a classic example of the CIA's double standard, which scrutinizes and censors critics but allows high-level insiders to misuse classified information.

A CIA without stable and ethical leadership will continue to flounder and mis-serve the nation. There is no perfect résumé to indicate suitability for the role of a CIA director, but if presidents were to seek individuals with exceptional integrity and experience in the policy community, then perhaps the agency could move in a direction that supports, rather than subverts, our rights as citizens in an open and accountable constitutional democracy. President Truman believed that he had found such an individual in George F. Kennan, but Kennan rejected the position. If President Clinton had followed his instincts to appoint Ambassador Thomas Pickering to be the director in the early 1990s, the CIA could have had the strategic leader that it required.

With a stroke of a pen, President Obama could have removed CIA director John O. Brennan, appointed better leaders throughout the intelligence community, and released the Intelligence Committee's report that documented the brutality of CIA abuses and exposed lies to the White House. If the president wanted to roll back the misdeeds of the Bush administration, restore the rule of law at the CIA, and create necessary change, he needed to stop relying on senior officials who endorsed the shameful acts of the past. Former assistant secretary of state William Burns would have made an excellent CIA director.

Finally, there needs to be a recognition that the national security state created at the end of the Cold War has tilted too far in the direction of the military, which dominates the intelligence cycle. Strategic intelligence has suffered from the Pentagon's domination as priority is given to support the warfighter in an era of permanent war. There has been too much intelligence failure in the recent past, including strategic surprises that have taken place in Ukraine and Crimea; North Africa and the Middle East; and the Persian Gulf and Southwest Asia. The sudden emergence and virulent spread of the Islamic State, which "altered the political and military chessboard of the Middle East," was a strategic intelligence failure directly related to terror, misery, and chaos created by the unprovoked U.S. invasion and occupation of a Middle Eastern country.[37]

As long as the Pentagon is permitted to dominate the intelligence cycle, as well as the collection and analytic priorities of the community, there will be continued vulnerability to blowback and surprise. The Department of Defense dominates technical collection of intelligence and the political interpretation of satellite imagery. The secretary of defense and the Joint Chiefs of Staff have become dominant players in decision-making. The CIA has been relegated to a secondary role in intelligence assessment and reconfigured itself as a paramilitary institution. The intelligence tsar defers to the Pentagon's control over budget and personnel.

In July 2015 President Obama appointed a new chairman of the Joint Chiefs, General Joseph F. Dunford Jr., who immediately began to brandish Cold War rhetoric that pointed to greater pressure on the intelligence community. Dunford got out in front of the president when he supported weapons for Ukraine, which the administration didn't favor. Secretary of Defense Ashton Carter was a severe critic of Secretary of State John Kerry's efforts to gain a ceasefire in Syria.

Our government prides itself on openness, but it conducts national security policy on the basis of secrecy. In such a duality, the role of oversight is essential; without an aggressive press and the courageous whistleblower, there are reduced opportunities for oversight. The informed public cannot debate foreign policy as long as national security and intelligence are shrouded in secrecy. The congressional intelligence committees were created for this reason in the 1970s to correct the improprieties of the Vietnam War era; a statutory inspector general was created at the CIA in 1989 due to the crimes of the Iran-Contra operations. During the Terror Wars, however, the intelligence committees have not pursued oversight, and the CIA's interference with the Senate's investigation of torture has threatened the checks and balances central to democracy in America.

President Obama and his successors must be reminded that President Truman, who created the CIA in 1947 and the NSA in 1952, opposed the emergence of the CIA as a "Cloak & Dagger Outfit." Truman emphasized that he never intended for the CIA to "initiate policy or to act as a spy organization," but wanted an intelligence community that would keep the "President informed on what was going on in the world at large." He was particularly opposed to the use of covert actions in the Eisenhower and Kennedy administrations. President Truman would have considered the use of torture a catastrophic moral, legal, and political failure.

Obama's statements pointed to some understanding of Truman's demurrals, but his actions belied his rhetoric. In May 2013, the president told a high-ranking military audience at the National Defense University that our torture policies "ran counter to the rule of law;" that our use of drones will "define the type of nation that we leave to our children"; that "leak investigations may chill investigative journalism that holds government accountable"; and, in reference to Guantánamo, that holding "people who have been charged with no crime on a piece of land that is not part of our country" is also not "who we are."

President Obama at least appeared embarrassed when, in April 2015, he had to tell the American people that a U.S. counterterrorism operation had killed a U.S. aid worker in the Afghan-Pakistan border region in January 2015 in a "signature" strike, which meant that the United States lacked identities for its targets. Signature strikes and the bombing of a Doctors Without Borders hospital in Afghanistan should not be "who we are," and massive surveillance programs and informant networks should not be "who we are." The Obama administration also sold record amounts of lethal military weaponry to Saudi Arabia, which has conducted a campaign of brutality against civilians in Yemen over the past several years.

President Obama told his military audience that he was "troubled by the possibility that leak investigations may chill the investigative journalism that holds government accountable."[38] This statement is typical of the president's rhetoric that finds no change in policy. Former attorney general Eric Holder was tasked with providing a review of Department of Justice guidelines for investigations that involve reporters, but there has been no indication of a change and no sign of sponsorship of a media shield law to guard against government overreach.

There have been too many occasions in recent decades when the American people had to get essential information about intelligence agencies from whistleblowers and "burglars of conscience," and not Congressional oversight committees or the courts. In judging whether the actions of a whistleblower represent treason or civic duty, it is essential that interests of fairness trump interests of loyalty. Our democracy is embattled when a CIA director believes he can lie to his oversight masters to stop a legitimate intelligence committee investigation of illegal activities.

President Obama's efforts to weaken the role of the inspector general in the national security arena has complicated the job of reform of the intelligence community, particularly the CIA. One of the most significant reforms of the Watergate era was the passage in 1978 of the Inspector General Act; after the Iran-Contra scandal, the Congress finally created a statutory inspector general for the CIA. Obama consciously weakened the role of these internal watchdogs, which means that it has become even more difficult to ensure the integrity and efficiency of governmental operations. Hillary Clinton made sure there was no inspector general in place during her stewardship of the Department of State from 2009 to 2012; President Obama made sure there was no inspector general in place at the CIA during much of his two terms in office.

There is a fundamental problem in dealing with any intelligence agency in a democracy. The National Security Act of 1947 that established the CIA was simply too vague in outlining the goals and missions of the Agency. The National Security Agency and the National Reconnaissance Office were founded in secrecy, which was wrong, and the CIA was given too much power and influence, with very few standards and restraints regarding either operations or collection. The Congress was not given oversight responsibilities until 30 years after the creation of the Agency, and the CIA has fought against oversight every step of the way. CIA directors have authorization to protect their sources and methods, but this has led to actions that compromise the prohibition on "internal security functions."

A contributing problem is the mindset dominating counterintelligence thinking in the White House that views any sign of domestic protest as a national security threat. This led to the abuses during the Vietnam era in the 1960s and 1970s and to the militarization of U.S. society since 9/11. The CIA and the National Security Agency have dodged certain domestic prohibitions on collection by conducting illegal liaison with such foreign intelligence services as England's Government Communications Headquarters. The White House and the CIA have cooperated in the past decade to weaken internal oversight by ignoring the Office of the Inspector General.

As a result, it is difficult to control or even scrutinize secret agencies, and for the past 60 years our presidents have misused them. The absence of oversight makes it difficult to impose restraints on the misuse of government power, particularly those powers that threaten our own citizens, without the information that whistleblowers provide. The CIA's ability to brandish secrecy against the very committee responsible for its oversight stamps the Agency as an enemy of democracy.

Whistleblowers challenge the secrecy and lies that foster ignorance in the United States. The overuse of secrecy limits debate on foreign policy and deprives citizens of information needed to participate in genuine life-or-death issues. A culture of openness and a respect for the balance of power is needed to reverse the damage caused since the Bush administration's disastrous response to 9/11. As long as Congress defers to the president in the conduct of foreign policy; the courts intervene to prevent any challenge to the president's power in making foreign policy; and the media defer to authorized sources, we must rely upon and support whistleblowers.

It is possible that even President Obama regrets that he didn't do more in support of whistleblowing. During his last months in office, he released official documents to acknowledge that the CIA knew that former Chilean dictator Augusto Pinochet personally ordered the 1976 murder of a top dissident on Washington's Embassy Row, and that the U.S. had played a role in Argentina's "dirty war" against its own citizens in the 1970s and 1980s. President Obama was praised for trying to win friends in South America by revealing past misdeeds.[39] I prefer to think that the president understood the importance of whistleblowing.

I regret that I didn't do more in 1991 to defend and explain my protests. I turned down too many opportunities to give media interviews, particularly with network television such as NBC and ABC's *Nightline* with Ted Koppel. A former colleague, the late Barry Stevenson, had gotten some documents for me that described Bob Gates's efforts to tailor intelligence on arms control in order to portray the Soviets as opposed to disarmament, a depiction that was blatantly false. I took these documents to the home of Senator Sam Nunn, who lived close by, but at the last moment I drove away from his house in Bethesda, because I wrongly believed that I was overstepping my bounds. Whistleblowing is an important act of political resistance, and there should not be such bounds. Senator Nunn was the most important critic of Gates's confirmation, but he ultimately caved in to political pressure from the committee chairman to support him.

I wish that I had gone further as a whistleblower. I admire Edward Snowden for risking everything to reveal massive and unconstitutional spying on American citizens. I admire Thomas Drake for blowing the whistle on unlawful surveillance. As long as secret government manages to operate beyond the law and allows former officials such as Michael Morell, Jose Rodriguez, and John McLaughlin to lie about illegalities such as torture and abuse, the Agency will remain an enemy of democracy and I will champion a path of dissent. The uncertainty and disarray of the Trump administration and its ill-prepared national security team has made the importance of "telling truth to power" more essential than ever. Donald Trump would probably prefer to "replace and repeal" the First Amendment's defense of free speech and free press. It will be up to whistleblowers in the intelligence and policy communities to ensure that any misuse of power does not go unreported.

ACKNOWLEDGMENTS

In addition to wonderful mentors to whom this book is dedicated, I benefited from courageous friends and colleagues who did their best to stop and reverse efforts to corrupt intelligence at the Central Intelligence Agency in the 1980s. My wife, Lyn Ekedahl, was an exemplary intelligence analyst for three decades and then, while serving in the Office of the Inspector General, made every effort to bring to light the transgressions of the Bush administration in the realm of international security. Before they left the CIA to join the State Department's Bureau of Intelligence and Research, Jennifer Glaudemans and Wayne Limberg fought for objective and balanced intelligence analysis, and then cooperated with the Senate Select Committee on Intelligence in the investigation of Robert Gates's nomination as director of central intelligence. At the CIA, the late John Hibbits was an outstanding example of integrity and courage in his efforts to stop corruption. Brian MacCauley and Thomas Barksdale went to great lengths to prevent illicit efforts to sell military weaponry to a U.S. enemy, the Islamist government in Tehran. All of these colleagues compromised their careers at the CIA by taking on this struggle and all of them cooperated with the Senate Intelligence Committee. Finally, this book was shepherded into existence by my editor Greg Ruggiero, who provided invaluable support in clarifying my language. Any errors are, of course, my own.

GLOSSARY

Arms Control and Disarmament Agency—The agency devoted to conducting arms control and disarmament negotiations that was unfortunately disbanded by President Bill Clinton in 1997.

Board of National Estimates—The former senior panel for conducting the preparation of National Intelligence Estimates.

Center for the Study of Intelligence—Publishes historical studies on intelligence topics, including a series, the *Study of Intelligence*.

Central Intelligence Agency, CIA—The Defense Reorganization Act of 1947 created the CIA as a repository and consolidation place for intelligence. Its work is broken into two main areas: field operations and analysis.

CIA's Arms Control Intelligence Staff—The CIA staff for preparing intelligence support for arms control and disarmament talks and agreements.

Central Intelligence Agency Deputy Director—The deputy director assists the director in his duties as head of the CIA and exercises the powers of the director when the director's position is vacant or in the director's absence or disability. The current director of the Central Intelligence Agency is John O. Brennan.

Central Intelligence Agency Director—The director serves as the head of the Central Intelligence Agency and reports to the director of national intelligence. The director is nominated by the President of the United States and is confirmed by the United States Senate. The director manages the operations, personnel, and budget of the CIA and acts as the national human source intelligence manager. The current director of the Central Intelligence Agency is John O. Brennan.

CIA's Directorate of Operations—A key part of the CIA that is devoted to clandestine collection of intelligence and execution of covert missions.

CIA's Foreign Broadcast Information Service—This worldwide service once translated foreign news commentaries in the press and on radio. This work is now done by the Open Source Enterprise, which was established in 2005 to coordinate the exploitation of open-source materials.

CIA's Office of Current Intelligence—The former office for the preparation of current intelligence to U.S. policymakers in national security strategy. Current intelligence now plays a much smaller role in an expanded and renamed directorate of analysis.

CIA's Office of Inspector General—The office responsible for inspecting and investigating all areas of the CIA for possible malfeasance and improprieties.

CIA's Office of National Estimates—The former office responsible for the preparation of estimative and premonitory intelligence for the international security bureaucracy.

CIA's Office of Strategic Research—The former office for the preparation of economic intelligence to the policymakers in national security strategy in the U.S. government.

Central Intelligence Group—A short-lived intelligence group that served as a bridge between the OSS and the creation of the CIA.

communications intelligence, COMINT—Technical and intelligence information derived from the intercept of foreign communications.

counterintelligence—The thwarting of secret activities directed against the United States by foreign intelligence services, although this capability has also been used domestically (e.g., COINTELPRO).

covert action—U.S. term for influence operations in foreign countries, including regime change and assassination, that are not attributable to the sponsoring power.

DefCon, Defense Condition—A priority system for alerting the nuclear forces of the United States.

Defense Intelligence Agency—The intelligence component of the Department of Defense, which often duplicates the work of the CIA. It provides strategic military intelligence to the secretary of defense.

Department of Defense—Created after the end of World War II with the Defense Reorganization Act of 1947 to replace the War Department and to manage the military affairs and programs of the United States.

Department of Justice—The executive agency responsible for law enforcement and the administration of justice, given an expanded role in national security due to increased attention to tracking illegal immigration and pursuing terrorists.

Department of State—The first executive department created in 1789 for conducting the international relations of the United States. It is equivalent to the foreign ministries in most countries, but it has become the smallest of the cabinet-level national security offices, with a smaller budget and workforce than any other cabinet department.

Department of State's Bureau of Intelligence and Research—The bureau for providing intelligence information to the secretary of state and the senior officials of the Department of State.

détente—A diplomatic effort to improve relations with a former adversary such as the Soviet Union.

Director of National Intelligence (the "intelligence tsar")—A position created in 2004 to supplant the authorities of the director of central intelligence in coordinating the intelligence community.

Federal Bureau of Investigation, FBI—The FBI is the domestic intelligence and security service of the United States. In the 1990s and particularly after 9/11, the FBI's focus has moved steadily to national security rather than merely law enforcement. The bureau has had to adjust to a rapidly changing international system, and must now also try to track various groups around the world threatening the United States.

Foreign Intelligence Surveillance Act—The U.S. federal law that prescribes procedures for physical and electronic surveillance of communications between "foreign powers" and "agents of foreign powers," which may include American citizens.

Foreign Intelligence Surveillance Court—The federal court established in 1978 to issue surveillance warrants for the clandestine surveillance of communications.

foreign service officers—The elite corps that handles the complex diplomatic issues that confront the United States overseas.

GRU—Soviet Military Intelligence Service.

House Permanent Select Committee for Intelligence—The House committee for monitoring the intelligence community and conducting oversight.

human intelligence, HUMINT—Intelligence derived from human (not technical) sources through clandestine collection techniques.

Inspector General—The internal mechanism for monitoring and conducting oversight of U.S. intelligence agencies.

Intelligence Oversight Board—A committee of the National Foreign Intelligence Board that oversees the legality and propriety of U.S. intelligence activities.

Joint Chiefs of Staff—The senior military service chiefs who advise the Secretary of Defense, the Homeland Security Council, the National Security Council, and the President of the United States on military matters.

KGB—Soviet counterpart to the CIA.

Mutual and Balanced Force Reductions—The negotiations on the reduction of conventional arms in West and East Europe.

Multiple Independently Targetable Reentry Vehicle, MIRV—a ballistic missile designed to separate into multiple weapons of mass destruction and strike multiple targets.

National Foreign Assessment Center—Formerly the CIA's Directorate of Intelligence. Currently the Directorate of Analysis.

National Foreign Intelligence Board—An advisory board led by the director of national intelligence and consisting of leading figures in the U.S. intelligence community. It is tasked with the examination and acceptance of National Intelligence Estimates. The board advises the CIA director on production, review, and coordination of national intelligence, including liaison arrangements with foreign governments on intelligence matters.

National Geospatial-Intelligence Agency (formerly National Imagery and Mapping Agency)—The agency for analyzing satellite information and for enabling intelligence analysts and military commanders to "see" target areas remotely.

National Intelligence Council—Composed of national intelligence officers, their staffs, and an analytic group, the council advises the Director of National Intelligence in his/her role as head of the U.S. intelligence Community and serves as a bridge between the intelligence and policy communities.

National Intelligence Daily—The CIA's daily summary of political, military, and economic intelligence that reaches a large policy audience at home and abroad.

National Intelligence Estimate—The strategic intelligence synthesis of the entire intelligence community that estimates the capabilities, vulnerabilities, and probable courses of action of foreign nations and forces.

National Intelligence Officer—The senior staff officer of the director of national intelligence for an assigned area of functional or geographic responsibility. The national intelligence officer manages the estimative process and interagency intelligence production on behalf of the director of national intelligence.

National Photographic Interpretation Center—The former joint CIA-military center for the analysis of satellite photography.

National Reconnaissance Office—The office responsible for the construction and launch of satellites.

National Security Agency, NSA—The agency responsible for intercepting and monitoring signals and communications.

National Security Council—A coordination mechanism for national security policy that contains membership from the Departments of State, Treasury, and Defense as well as the intelligence community.

National War College—Created at the end of World War II from the vision of Generals Eisenhower and Marshall to ensure an interagency understanding of national security.

North Atlantic Treaty Organization, NATO—Self-defense organization of the United States, Canada, Western Europe, and Eastern Europe, created in 1949 and expanded in the 1990s.

Office of Soviet Affairs, SOVA—The office in the CIA responsible for monitoring and analyzing Soviet political, military, and economic policy.

Office of Strategic Services, OSS—The World War II intelligence organization that preceded the Central Intelligence Agency. Many CIA directors served in the OSS, including Allen Dulles, Richard Helms, William Colby, and William Casey.

President's Daily Brief—The sensitive all-source intelligence product for the president, the national security advisor, and key cabinet officers in the field of international security.

President's Foreign Intelligence Advisory Board —The presidential board designed to keep an eye on the intelligence community.

Senate Select Committee on Intelligence, SSCI—The Senate committee responsible for monitoring the agencies and departments of the intelligence community.

senior intelligence staff—The senior officers of the U.S. intelligence community.

senior research staff—The former CIA staff tasked with the preparation of historical studies with the use of intelligence information.

signals intelligence, SIGINT—Intelligence information from signals intercepts as well as electronic intelligence including radio or TV, the Internet, and telephone.

Strategic Arms Limitation Talks, SALT—The arms control and disarmament talks between the United States and the Soviet Union in the late 1960s and 1970s.

Special National Intelligence Estimate—An intelligence estimate that is typically prepared on an emergency basis with a short time frame on a sensitive issue.

U.S. intelligence community—A network of intelligence professionals that includes the CIA, the eight intelligence organizations of the Department of Defense as well as the intelligence bureaus of the Departments of Energy, State, and the Treasury.

walk-in—An person who becomes an intelligence source, usually a defector, who volunteers, as distinguished from a person who is recruited.

NOTES

INTRODUCTION

1. See *The Failure of Intelligence: The Decline and Fall of the CIA* (Lanham, MD: Rowman & Littlefield Publishers, 2008).

2. Andrew J. Bacevich, "How Manning and Snowden made secrecy impossible," *Washington Post*, August 18, 2013, p. B3.

3. Jose A. Rodriguez Jr., *Hard Measures: How Aggressive CIA Actions After 9/11 Saved American Lives*, New York: Simon and Schuster, 2013, p. 213.

4. *Meet the Press*, NBC, July 7, 2013.

5. CNN, July 27, 2013 and August 20, 2013.

6. David Carr, "Against One Another," *New York Times*, August 26, 2013, p. D1.

7. Burton Hersh, *Bookforum*, "What's Wrong with CIA," September 25, 2008.

8. Ben Zimmer, "The Role of the Whistleblower," *Wall Street Journal*, July 13, 2013, p. 4.

9. op. cit.

10. *Washington Post*, "The true VA scandal," editorial, January 17, 2014, p. 14.

11. Gary Ruskin, *Spooky Business: A New Report on Corporate Espionage Against Nonprofit Organizations*, Center for Corporate Policy, November 2013. http://www.corporatepolicy.org/2013/11/20/spooky-business/

12. Paul Farhi, "Washington Post wins Pulitzer Prize for NSA Spying revelations," *Washington Post*, April 15, 2014, p. S14.

CHAPTER ONE

1. Richard Helms, *A Look Over My Shoulder*, New York: Ballantine Books, 2003, pp. 292–293, 309.

2. A relatively junior CIA analyst in the field, Bob Layton, predicted the Tet Offensive in 1968, but he was similarly ignored by his senior managers. It is particularly frustrating when senior experts block the work of relative newcomers and thereby cause costly intelligence failures.

3. *The October War: A Retrospective*, Richard B. Parker (editor), (Gainesville: University Press of Florida, 2001), p. 213.

4. See Harold P. Ford, "CIA and the Vietnam Policymakers," Washington, DC: Center for the Study of Intelligence, CIA, 1998.

5. Louis G. Sarris, "McNamara's War, and Mine," *New York Times*, September 5, 1995, p. 23.

6. Dean Rusk, *As I Saw It* (New York: Norton, 1990), p. 392.

7. Robert S. McNamara, *In Retrospect: The Tragedy and Lessons of Vietnam* (New York: Random House, 1995), p. 95.

8. See Sam Adams, *War of Numbers: An Intelligence Memoir* (South Royalton, VT, 1994), half-finished memoir that was published posthumously.

9. Samuel Adams, "Memorandum for the Record: Comments on the Draft of the National Intelligence Estimate," CIA Records, 14.3–67, November 7, 1967.

10. Richard Helms, Memorandum for the President, November 14, 1967, CIA Files.

11. David Halberstam, *The Best and the Brightest*, New York: Fawcett Publishers, 1993, p. 644.

12. General Bruce Palmer, "U.S. Intelligence and Vietnam," *Studies in Intelligence* (Washington, DC: Center for the Study of Intelligence), 1997, p. 55.

13. CIA Files, Job No. 80R01580R, DCI/ER Subject Files, Box 15, Folder 5.

14. Lyndon B. Johnson, *The Vantage Point: Perspectives of the Presidency, 1963–1969* (New York: Random House, 1972), pp. 371–372. Walt Rostow wrote much of the former president's autobiography.

15. Walt Rostow, *The Diffusion of Power: An Essay in Recent History* (New York: MacMillan, 1972), pp. 464–465.

16. Carolyn McGiffert Ekedahl and Melvin A. Goodman, *The Wars of Eduard Shevardnadze* (State College, PA: 1997).

17. Henry A. Kissinger, *Crisis: The Anatomy of Two Major Foreign Policy Crises* (New York: Simon & Schuster, 2003), p. 13.

18. Ibid., p. 112.

19. Henry A. Kissinger, *The White House Years* (Boston: Little, Brown and Company, 1979), p. 1,295.

20. Richard B. Parker, *The October War: A Retrospective* (Gainesville: University Press of Florida, 2001), p. 168.

21. See CIA briefing paper entitled "USSR: Economics, Trends, and Policy Developments" in *Allocation of Resources in the Soviet Union and China—1983* (Washington, DC: GPO, Joint Economic Committee, 96th Congress, 1984); p. 306. It was easier for CIA intelligence analysts to get accurate information to the Congress because Deputy Director for Intelligence Gates paid little attention to congressional briefings. In my many briefings to the Senate Energy Committee and the Foreign Relations Committee in the 1980s, I could offer assessments that Gates would never permit in printed CIA assessments to policymakers.

22. Michael Morell, *The Great War of Our Time: The CIA's Fight Against Terrorism From Al Qa'ida to ISIS*, (New York: Twelve, 2015), p. 86.

CHAPTER TWO

1. Lyndon B. Johnson, *The Vantage Point: Perspectives of the Presidency, 1963–1969* (New York: Random House, 1971), p. 389.

2. Harry McPherson, *A Political Education* (Boston: Little, Brown, 1972), p. 217.

3. Zbigniew Brzezinski, *Power and Principle: Memoirs of the National Security Adviser 1977–1981* (New York: Farrar Straus Giroux, 1983), p. 461.

CHAPTER THREE

1. Harry S. Truman, "The Need for CIA Reform," *Washington Post*, December 22, 1963, p. 17.

2. Rick Perlstein, *The Invisible Bridge: The Fall of Nixon and the Rise of Reagan* (New York: Simon and Schuster, 2014), p. 332.

3. See the records of the Church Committee: "Operations with Respect to Intelligence Activities," U.S. Senate, 1976.

4. George Lardner, "The Streets of Washington," *The Washington Post*, March 11, 1976, p. 7.

5. Joseph E. Persico, *Casey: The Lives and Secrets of William J. Casey: From the OSS to the CIA* (New York: Viking, 1990), p. 201.

6. Robert White, "An Ambassador's Diary," *Fletcher Journal*, Winter 1982–1983, p. 94.

7. Joseph E. Persico, *Casey: The Lives and Secrets of William J. Casey: From the OSS to the CIA* (New York: Viking Penguin, 1990), p. 271.

8. Shultz, *Turmoil and Triumph*, p. 651.

9. Persico, *Casey*, p. 496.

10. Ibid., p. 439.

11. Gates, *From the Shadows*; U.S. Senate Select Committee on Intelligence, Testimony, Confirmation Hearings, October, 1991.

12. Claire Sterling, *The Terror Network* (New York: Reader's Digest Press, 1981).

13. John Ranelagh, *The Agency: The Rise and Decline of the CIA* (New York: Simon & Schuster, 1986), pp. 697–698.

14. Ranelagh, p. 698; interview with Phillip Stoddard.

15. Robert M. Gates, "The CIA and American Foreign Policy," *Foreign Affairs*, Issue #66, Winter 1987–1988, p. 227.

16. One of the few areas of disagreement Haig and Casey concerned the use of covert action. Casey ordered his clandestine operatives to stage covert interventions all over the world, but Haig believed that Casey's approach was wrongheaded and shortsighted, and that covert action should be ancillary to foreign policy, not get out in front of foreign policy.

17. Joseph E. Persico, *Casey: From the OSS to the CIA* (New York: Viking Press, 1990), p. 118; Bob Woodward, *Veil* (New York: Simon & Schuster, 1987), p. 329.

18. Peter Eisner and Knut Royce, *The Italian Letter: How the Bush Administration Used a Fake Letter to Build the Case for War in Iraq* (New York: Rodale, Inc., 2007), p. 149.

19. Gates, *From the Shadows*, p. 206.

20. Just as Director George Tenet told President George W. Bush that providing intelligence to support the war in Iraq would be a "slam dunk," Casey and Gates assured President Ronald Reagan that there would be sufficient intelligence to support the branding of the Soviet Union as an "evil empire."

21. Several decades after the National Intelligence Estimate was released and the secret archives of the Soviet Union and its East European allies were open, there was still no evidence that the Soviets had directly encouraged international terrorism. Nevertheless, Gates argued in his memoir that the East German archives pointed to East German sanctuary for West European terrorists as proof of Soviet activity and Bill Casey being "more right than the others." (Gates, *From the Shadows*, p. 206.)

22. Joseph E. Persico, *Casey: The Lives and Secrets of William J. Casey: From the OSS to the CIA* (New York: Viking, 1990), p. 287.

23. See U.S. Senate Select Committee on Intelligence, "Hearings: Nomination of Robert M. Gates," Senate Hearing 102–799, Volume II, September-October 1991.

24. See Bob Woodward, *Veil*.

25. Ibid, p. 554.

26. Ibid, p. 555.

27. Ibid, p. 557.

28. Gates, *From the Shadows*, p. 415.

29. Gates, *From the Shadows*; Gates, *Duty*.

30. Gates, *From the Shadows*, pp. 416–417.

31. See Craig Eisendrath, Melvin Goodman, and Gerald Marsh, *The Phantom Defense: The Illusion of the Star Wars Defense* (New York: Prometheus Press, 2000).

32. In addition to the fact the national missile defense would not work because of its inability to distinguish between genuine missiles and decoys, it is more likely that more conventional systems of attack would represent the threat to the United States, such as the terrorist attacks against the USS *Cole* in October 2000 and those against the World Trade Center and the Pentagon in 2001.

33. James Risen, "Iraqi Aims Were Shelved, Suit Says," *New York Times*, August 1, 2005, p. 8.

34. Peter Eisner and Knut Royce, *The Italian Letter: How the Bush Administration Used a Fake Letter to Build a Case for War in Iraq*, (New York: Rodale, Inc.), p. 56.

CHAPTER FOUR

1. See Janet Breslin-Smith and Clifford R. Krieger, *The National War College: A History of Strategic Thinking in Peace and War* (Washington, DC: Na-

tional War College Alumni Association, 2014). This excellent history was written by two of my faculty colleagues and reflects the strong attachment that so many faculty members have for the college, one of Washington's best-kept secrets.

2. Greg Miller, "A View from the Pentagon," *Washington Post*, February 9, 2011, p. 6.

3. See H.R. McMaster, *Dereliction of Duty: Johnson, McNamara, the Joint Chiefs of Staff, and the Lies That Led to Vietnam*, (New York: HarperCollins, 1997).

4. Duff Cooper, *Talleyrand*, (New York: Harper, 1926), p. 189.

5. President Harry S. Truman, December 1, 1963, The Truman Library.

6. President Harry S. Truman, oral history interview with Merle Miller, December 11, 1967, The Truman Library.

7. Phyllis I. McClellan, *Silent Sentinel on the Potomac: Fort McNair*, 1791–1991 (Bowie, MD: Heritage Press, 1993), p. 1.

8. Charlie Savage, "Pentagon Revamps Law of War Manual to Protect Journalists," *New York Times*, July 22, 2016, p. 17.

9. Stansfield Turner, "Intelligence for a New World Order," *Foreign Affairs*, Fall 1991, p. 162.

10. Ann Devroy, "Political Skirmish in Washington," *Washington Post*, January 30, 1993, p. 5.

11. Martin E. Dempsey, "Military leaders should be apolitical," Letter-to-the-Editor, *Washington Post*, July 31, 2016, p. 22.

CHAPTER FIVE

1. Gates, *From the Shadows*, p. 549.

2. Ibid, p. 548.

3. Robert M. Gates, *From the Shadows: The Ultimate Insider's Story About Five Presidents and How They Won the Cold War* (New York: Simon & Schuster, 1996), p. 418. The subtitle of the book tells a great deal about Gates's view of his own role and his efforts to insinuate himself into the White House, any White House.

4. Gates, *From the Shadows*, p. 550.

5. Ibid, p. 419.

6. Melvin A. Goodman, *National Insecurity: The Cost of American Militarism* (San Francisco: City Lights Books, 2013), p. 315.

7. Zbigniew Brzezinski, *Power and Principle*, p. 3.

8. In *Smiley's People*, Bill Haydon was a mole, and Control was working with Smiley to track him down. In 1991, Bill Casey was the protagonist demanding intelligence to support the policies of the Reagan administration, and Bob Gates provided the threatening reports on the Soviet Union to help Casey make his case.

9. Ann Devroy and Tom Kenworthy, "Gates Nominated to Head the CIA," *Washington Post*, May 15, 1991, p. A1.

10. Congressional Record, S 15833, November 4, 1991.

11. Congressional Record, S 151833, November 4, 1991.

12. While Chairman Boren was the leading cheerleader for Gates's confirmation, his Oklahoma colleague, Representative David McCurdy, who chaired the House Permanent Select Committee called on Gates to withdraw his nomination if he could not disprove charges of politicization "convincingly." (Bob Woodward, "McCurdy: Gates Should Withdraw," *Washington Post*, October 3, 1991, p. 1.

13. *CIA Employee Bulletin Number 2146*, November 18, 1991, p. 3.

14. I have known Marvin Ott for 25 years, including our 12 years spent as colleagues at the National War College. Much of the information on the politics of the nomination comes from my formal and informal chats with Mr. Ott, including a long session that took place on September 13, 2013.

15. There are some analysts who feel that this relationship was too close and that President Bush was committed to Bob Gates as CIA director because Gates knew the degree to which Bush was complicit in Iran-Contra and that his disavowals of any knowledge or activity were not to be believed. In any event, the Bush family took good care of Gates over the years: appointing him CIA director, dean of the Bush Library at Texas A&M (where he eventually became president of the university); and finally secretary of defense in 2007 to replace Donald Rumsfeld.

16. Robert M. Gates, "Trial by Fire," *New York Times*, March 19, 1997, p. 19.

17. Gates, *From the Shadows*, pp. 546–552.

18. Ibid., p. 548.

19. Testimony to the Senate Intelligence Committee, October 3, 1991.

20. Ibid.

21. Conversation with Harold Ford, November 22, 1991.

22. Conversation with Ron Marks, February 22, 1992.

23. Walter Pincus and George Lardner Jr., "Senate Confirms Gates as CIA Chief," *Washington Post*, November 6, 1991, p. 4. Pincus told me that he and Lardner were thoroughly opposed to confirmation because they were convinced that Gates was a liar; they wrote an opinion piece to that effect for the paper's "Outlook Section," but the editor of the opinion section, Meg Greenfield, personally blocked publication of the article with the support of the paper's publisher, Katherine Graham.

24. Stansfield Turner, *Foreign Affairs*, 1990. Revisionism is much in play about whether the CIA anticipated the collapse of the Soviet Union, but it is abundantly clear that social media provided better clues to the collapse of the Soviet Union (or, more recently, the Arab Spring) than any of the writings of the intelligence community, particularly the CIA.

25. Conversation with Ron Marks, February 22, 1992.

26. Hearings Before the Senate Select Committee on Intelligence, S. Hrg. 102-799, Volume 2, Washington, DC: Government Printing Office, 1992, p. 315.

27. Conversation with Art Grant, November 17, 1991.

28. My son Michael was a student at Wesleyan University in Middletown, Connecticut at the time of the hearings and, along with a group of friends, watched replays of the hearings on public television at a favorite campus drinking spot. He later recounted that he was extremely nervous during these scenes even though he was gratified by the fact that the mostly student clientele cheered my remarks and hissed and booed at every intervention by Rudman.

29. Johnny Carson remarked on the *Tonight Show* that every time Gates uttered "I don't recall," former president Ronald Reagan collected royalties. I foolishly believed that if Gates could make it to the Carson monologue in this fashion, then there would have been a good chance that he would not be confirmed.

30. During the period of Soviet decline, Gates was director of the Strategic Evaluation Center in 1980; executive assistant to Director Casey and national intelligence officer for the Soviet Union in 1981–1982; deputy director for intelligence from 1982 to 1986, chairman of the National Intelligence Council from 1986 to 1987; acting director of central intelligence from 1986 to 1989; and deputy director of CIA from 1989 to [provide info] Throughout the period, Gates was publicly issuing clarion calls about the Soviet threat and privately pushing CIA intelligence to the right, creating the image of a Russian Bear that was ten feet tall.

31. Conversation with Richard Combs, March 19, 1992.

32. Tom Polgar, Letter to Senators Nunn, Mitchell, Graham, and Leahy, October 22, 1991.

33. Conversation with Marvin Ott, staffer on the Senate Select Committee on Intelligence on Intelligence, September 18, 2013. Jack Nelson and Michael Ross, "Boren's Role in Efforts for Gates Questioned," *Los Angeles Times*, October 9, 1991, p. 12.

34. Matt Schudel, "Central Figure in Savings and Loan Scandal," *Washington Post*, April 2, 2014 p. B6.

35. Robert D. McFadden, "Charles Keating, Key Figure in Savings and Loan Crisis," *New York Times*, April 2, 2014, p. 23.

36. Several years later, a Democratic president, Bill Clinton, made Tenet the director of the CIA, the only congressional staffer ever serving in the post, and one of Tenet's first personnel moves was to bring Moseman to the Agency as a senior staff advisor to the director.

37. Conversation with Ron Marks.

38. Testimony to Senate Intelligence Committee, October 4, 1991.

39. Gates, *From the Shadows*, p. 511.

40. Walter Pincus and George Lardner Jr., "Gates Strikes Back at Critics in CIA," *Washington Post*, October 4, 1991, p. 8.
41. George Lardner Jr., "Committee Approves Gates at CIA," *Washington Post*, October 19, 1991, p. 1.
42. Charles R. Babcock, "Gates Passed Panel's Test on Lessons Learned from Casey's Controversies," *Washington Post*, October 19, 1991, p. 11.
43. Charles R. Babcock and Walter Pincus, "Gates's Intelligence Management at the CIA Becomes an Issue," *Washington Post*, September 27, 1991, p. 10.
44. John Gentry, *Lost Promise: How CIA Analysis Misserves the Nation* (New York: University Press of America, 1993), p. 135.
45. Walter Pincus and George Lardner Jr., "Panel May Place Gates in Confirmation Limbo," *Washington Post*, July 12, 1991, p. A16.
46. Lawrence E. Walsh, *Firewall: The Iran-Contra Conspiracy and Cover-Up*, New York: W.W. Norton & Company, 1997, pp. 290–292.
47. Lawrence Walsh was not the only prominent figure in Washington who may have been thinking there was jail time for Bob Gates in the Iran-Contra conspiracy. In my on background discussions with investigative reporter Seymour Hersh about the hearings, Hersh said that the "difference between me and you on Gates is that you are trying to deny Gates the position of DCI [CIA director], while I'm trying to put Gates in jail."
48. Haynes Johnson, "For CIA, Hearings' Legacy Could Be A New Beginning or Deeper Schism," *Washington Post*, October 4, 1991, p. 8.
49. Robert Gates, "The Role of Confirmation," *New York Times*, October 18, 1998, p. 21.
50. Conversation with James McCullough, January 18, 1992.
51. Gates, "Confirmation," *New York Times*, October 189, 1998, p. 21.

CHAPTER SIX

1. Jose A. Rodriguez Jr., *Hard Measures: How Aggressive CIA Actions After 9/11 Saved American Lives* (New York: Simon and Schuster, 2013), p. 169
2. Jose A. Rodriguez Jr., *Hard Measures: How Aggressive CIA Actions After 9/11 Saved Lives*, (New York: Threshold Editions, 2013), p. 216.
3. Ibid, p. 169.
4. Ibid, p. 169.
5. Ibid, pp. 170–171.
6. Tim Weiner, *Legacy of Ashes: The History of the CIA* (New York: Doubleday, 2007), p. 65.
7. "Report from the Chairman of the President's Board of Intelligence Consultants," January 5, 1961.
8. The late Arlen Specter was a Democrat from 1951 to 1965, a Republican from 1965 to 2009, and a Democrat from 2009 to 2012.

9. L. Britt Snider, "Creating a Statutory Inspector General at the CIA," *Studies in Intelligence* (Washington, DC: Central Intelligence Agency), p. 17.

10. Ibid., p 18.

11. Agencies and departments that have lacked an inspector general for more than a year include the Department of State, the Agency for International Development, the Department of the Interior, the Department of Veterans Affairs, and the General Services Administration. These agencies have a total estimated budget of nearly $250 billion.

12. Michael S. Schmidt and Matt Apuzzo, "FBI and Justice Dept. Said To Seek Charges for Petraeus," *New York Times*, January 10, 2015, p. 1.

13. See Michael Morell, *The Great War of Our Time*, New York: Twelve/Hachette Book Group, 2015.

14. Rick Perlstein, The Invisible Bridge: The Fall of Nixon and the Rise of Reagan (New York: Simon and Schuster, 2014), pp. 577–578.

15. See Philip Agee, *Inside the Company: CIA Diary*, New York: Dell, 1975.

16. David Brown, "Watching the Watchers," *American Civil Liberties Union Magazine*, Winter 2014, p. 20.

17. Eric Lichtblau, "CIA Chief Denies Charges," *The New York Times*, February 25, 2014, p. 17.

18. Truman Memorandum, Truman Library, Independence, Missouri, December 1, 1963.

19. Joby Warrick, "Intelligence Brief to Congress," *Washington Post*, January 21, 2014, p. 11.

20. Michael Cohen, "James Clapper Might As Well Be Called Director of US Fear Mongering," *The Guardian*, February 8, 2014, p. 5.

21. Greg Miller, "Warning from Intelligence Tsar," *Washington Post*, February 3, 2012, p. 7.

CHAPTER SEVEN

1. Greg Herken, *The Georgetown Set*, New York: W.W. Norton & Company, 2014, p. 138.

2. Clark Clifford with Richard Holbrooke, *Counsel to the President: A Memoir* (New York: Simon & Schuster, 1991), p. 165.

3. I left the CIA in the summer of 1986 to join the faculty of the National War College in Washington, DC, and therefore never worked for CIA director William Webster, who served from 1987 to 1991. I resigned from the CIA in 1990, and accepted a position on the War College faculty. I tried to see Webster to explain my reasons for resigning, but he had no interest in such a meeting, even with a member of his senior intelligence staff.

4. "Foreign Relations of the United States, 1969–1976," Volume II, document 230, December 7, 1970, Alexander Haig to Henry Kissinger, Washington, DC: Government Printing Office, 1979, p. 376.

5. Bob Woodward, *Veil: The Secret Wars of the CIA, 1981–1987* (New York: Simon & Schuster, 1987), p. 56.
6. Richard Helms with William Hood, *A Look Over My Shoulder: A Life in the Central Intelligence Agency* (New York: Ballantine Books, 2003), p. 410.
7. Transcript of Richard Nixon interview with Frank Gannon, Walter J. Brown Media Archives, University of Georgia; see http://www.libs.uga.edu/media/collections/nixon. Gannon interviewed Nixon for nine days in 1983. Full transcripts were published in 2002.
8. Helms and Hood, *Look Over My Shoulder*, p. 299.
9. Helms and Hood, *Look Over My Shoulder*, p. 423.
10. Richard Reeves, *President Nixon* (New York: Simon & Schuster, 2001), p. 483.
11. Harold P. Ford, *CIA and the Vietnam Policymakers: Three Episodes 1962–1968* (Washington, DC: Center for the Study of Intelligence, Central Intelligence Agency, 1998), p. 11.
12. Daniel Ellsberg, a former Pentagon defense analyst, had leaked the Pentagon's secret history of events leading to the Vietnam War to the *New York Times.*
13. Americans are in Schlesinger's debt for an even more important reason. In the days leading up to Nixon's resignation in August 1974, Schlesinger became so worried that Nixon was unstable that he instructed the Joint Chiefs of Staff not to react to White House orders, particularly on nuclear arms, unless cleared by him or Secretary of State Kissinger. Schlesinger even drew up plans to deploy troops in Washington in the event of any problems with a peaceful presidential succession.
14. Timothy R. Smith, "Acerbic economist held top defense and energy jobs," *Washington Post*, March 27, 2014, p. B-6.
15. Ibid.
16. Nearly all of my bosses from 1966 to the mid-1970s were graduates of Ivy League schools that made up the dominant educational background for the first generation of CIA leaders. I was probably part of the second generation of CIA officials who got their degrees from Big Ten schools and came from modest economic backgrounds with no social connections. Ironically, the school that sends more graduates to the CIA than any other institutions is Texas A&M University, where Gates was president from 2002–2006.
17. George H.W. Bush, *All the Best, George Bush: My Life in Letters and Other Writing* (New York: Scribner, 1991), p. 240.
18. Robert Parry, *Secrecy & Privilege: Rise of the Bush Dynasty from Watergate to Iraq* (Arlington, VA: The Media Consortium Inc., 2004), p. 50.
19. The mainstream media was extremely critical of Admiral Turner's stewardship of the CIA, while CIA director Helms, who was sentenced in

federal court in November 1977 for lying to the Church Committee was regularly praised for his efforts.

20. An excellent example of an intelligence failure caused by the military's control of satellite photography took place in 1998, when the CIA missed a series of India's missile tests because satellite collection was focused on developments in Iraq where the United States was enforcing no-fly zones.

21. *Washington Post* writer Bob Woodward, who is well known for his controversial revelations about major political figures, overreached in fingering Wilson as a possible suspect in the assassination of Orlando Letelier, a former Chilean ambassador to the United States, in September 1976. See the *Washington Post*, April 12, 1977, p. 1.

22. Casey had made a huge fortune in the stock market, and in his meetings with analysts took the position that if they were so smart they should also be rich. He had gained influence with Reagan in the 1970s by campaigning for his successful race for governor in California, and was a major fundraiser for Reagan's presidential campaign in 1980. Casey stuck by Reagan which his candidacy ran into rough spots on the campaign trail, and was rewarded with the position of director of central intelligence. Casey was disappointed, however; he wanted to be secretary of state. Richard Allen told Casey "You don't look like a secretary of state. You don't talk like a secretary of state. You only think like one." Well, not exactly!

23. John Rizzo, *Company Man: Thirty Years of Controversy and Crisis in the CIA* (New York: Scribners, 2014), p. 77.

24. Admiral Stansfield Turner, *Burn Before Reading: Presidents, CIA Directors, and Secret Intelligence* (New York: Hyperion, 2005), p. 206.

25. It is not widely known but Gates tried every possible stratagem he could devise to get President Clinton to extend his tour of duty at the CIA, including a request for a one-year appointment to bridge the outgoing Bush administration and the incoming Clinton administration. Clinton was inclined to go along with this, until Senator Bill Bradley, Gates's harshest and most effective critic in the confirmation process, convinced the president that Gates had serious issues of credibility and integrity.

26. Maggie Haberman, "CIA Director at the White House," *New York Times*, April, 17, 1993, p. 17.

27. Douglas Garthoff, *Directors of Central Intelligence as Leaders of the U.S. Intelligence Community, 1946–2005* (Washington, DC: Center for the Study of Intelligence, Central Intelligence Agency), p. 225.

28. Admiral Stansfield Turner, *Burn Before Reading: Presidents, CIA Directors, and Secret Intelligence* (New York: Hyperion, 2005), p. 227.

29. Michael R. Beschloss and Strobe Talbott, *At the Highest Levels: The Inside Story of the End of the Cold War* (Boston: Little, Brown and Co., 1993), p. 48.

30. Tim Weiner, David Johnston, and Neil A. Lewis, *Betrayal: The Story of Aldrich Ames, an American Spy* (New York: Random House, 1995), p. 283.

31. Ibid., p. 285.

32. Weiner, *Betrayal*, p. 284.

33. Helms and Hood, *Look Over My Shoulder*, p. 275.

34. In addition to the Presidential Medal of Freedom, the highest award that can be given to a civilian, Tenet published a profitable memoir, received a prestigious job on Wall Street, and like all other political celebrities who fail, millions of dollars in speaking fees over a ten-year period.

35. Tim Weiner, *Legacy of Ashes*, p. 499.

36. Ackerman, *American Way of Spying*, p. 42.

CHAPTER EIGHT

1. See Bob Woodward, *Veil: The Secret Wars of the CIA, 1981–1987* (New York: Simon & Schuster, 1991), 278.

2. Speech by Robert Gates in the CIA auditorium, February, 1989.

3. Conversation with Robert Gates, March 27, 1981.

4. Persico, *Casey*, p. 293.

5. Gates, *From the Shadows*, pp. 223–234.

6. Persico, *Casey*, p. 294.

7. Op. cit. Persico was totally clueless in his discussion of Casey's role in the formulating of intelligence, arguing that the director "reveled in dissent;" encouraging "his analysts to take conflicting, unpopular stands." Nothing could be further from the truth, and under Casey and Gates "footnotes" dissents gradually disappeared from all National Intelligence Estimates.

8. Memorandum from Robert Gates to CIA director William Casey, February, 1983.

9. Joseph E. Persico, *Casey: The Lives and Secrets of William J. Casey: From the OSS to the CIA* (New York: Viking, 1990), p. 3.

10. Gates's testimony to Senate Select Committee on Intelligence, October, 1991.

11. Congressional testimony, Senate Select Committee on Intelligence, May 1985.

12. Patrick E. Tyler, "CIA Analysts Said Iran Data Were Warped," *New York Times*, October 2, 1991, p. A19.

13. Memorandum from Brian McCauley to the Senate Select Committee on Intelligence, September, 1991.

14. Robert M. Gates, *From the Shadows: The Ultimate Insider's Story of Five Presidents and How They Won the Cold War* (New York: Simon & Schuster, 1996), pp. 547–548.

15. Gates, *From the Shadows*, p. 549.

16. John Hibbits joined CIA in 1974 and retired in 2000. He spent more than 30 years in government service as an intelligence officer, including more

than ten years in the U.S. Navy where he served as an operational intelligence officer in Japan during the Pueblo crisis with North Korea and the shoot down of a naval patrol aircraft off the coast of Korea in 1969. He was stalwart in dealing with the tough bureaucratic and political pressures involved in producing national and departmental intelligence.

17. MacEachin told a colleague of mine at the time that "if Goodman kept sticking his finger up his bosses's asses, pretty soon someone was going to bite it off."

18. John Hibbits, Statement to the Senate Select Committee on Intelligence, October 2, 1991.

19. For an excellent example of such reportage, see Thomas E. Rick's review of *Duty* in the *New York Times Book Review*, January 19, 2014, p 1. Ricks calls *Duty* "one of the best Washington memoirs ever," but merely cites a series of the author's anecdotes without mentioning Gates's inability to control his own Department of Defense.

20. Speech by Robert Gates to the American Enterprise Institute, October 2011.

21. Mac Thornberry and Andrew F. Krepinevich, "Preserving Primacy: A Defense Strategy for the New Administration," *Foreign Affairs*, September/October 2016,Volume 95, Number 5, p. 28

22. *PBS Newshour*, December, 2012.

23. See Robert Parry, *Secrecy and Privilege: Rise of the Bush Dynasty from Watergate to Iraq* (Arlington, VA: The Media Consortium Inc.), 2004.

24. Gates, *Duty*, p. 431.

25. Gates, *Duty*, p. 593.

26. Tim Weiner, *Legacy of Ashes: The History of the CIA*, New York: Doubleday, 2007, p. 379. Unfortunately, Weiner concluded that Bill Casey was as "smart, as capable, and as inspirational a leader an any man who ever ran the CIA."

27. Jennifer Glaudemans, "Has Gates learned his lesson," *Los Angeles Times*, November 21, 2006, p. 17.

28. George Shultz, *Turmoil and Triumph: My Years as Secretary of State* (New York: Charles Scribner's Sons, 1993), p. 864.

29. George P. Shultz, *Turmoil and Triumph: My Years as Secretary of State* (New York: Charles Scribner's Sons, 1993), p. 485. Shultz's memoirs would have been useful at the confirmation hearings two years before the publication of the memoir, but several of us could not even persuade Shultz to write a letter to the committee describing his dealings with the former CIA chief.

30. Ibid, op. cit, p. 864.

31. Shultz, *Triumph and Turmoil*, p. 864.

32. Ibid.

33. Ibid., p. 865.

34. Ibid., p. 866.

35. James Baker, *The Politics of Diplomacy: Revolution, War & Peace, 1989–1992* (New York: G.P. Putnam's Sons, 1995), p. 417.

CHAPTER NINE

1. Sean Willentz, *The Rise of American Democracy: Jefferson to Lincoln*, New York: W.W. Norton & Company, 2005, p. 66.

2. Robert M. Gates, Congressional testimony to Senate Select Committee on Intelligence, October, 1991.

3. Author's conversation with Robert Gates, February 1985.

4. Draft Assessment of the papal plot, March, 1985.

5. Conversation with Ross Cowey (co-writer of the internal review), November 17, 2006.

6. CIA Working Group Memorandum on Possible Delivery of MiGs to Nicaragua, October 4, 1984, Top Secret (Declassified by the Senate Select Committee on Intelligence).

7. Robert M. Gates, "Nicaragua," December 14, 1984, Top Secret (Declassified by the Senate Select Committee on Intelligence).

8. Gates Memorandum, *"Nicaragua,"* December 1984.

9. Graham E. Fuller, "The US-Soviet Struggle for Influence in Tehran," National Intelligence Council, May 7, 1985, Top Secret (Declassified by the Senate Select Committee on Intelligence). This memorandum was one of the more colorful examples of CIA sophistry, probably because Mr. Fuller was one of the more colorful examples of CIA operations officers.

10. McCauley Memorandum to Senate Select Committee on Intelligence, October 1991.

11. Author's Luncheon conversation with Elaine Sciolino, November 1991.

12. Unfortunately, Pincus has done a complete about-face and has become an apologist for the CIA. As recently as January 2015, he penned a long article to argue that there were parallels between President Eisenhower's support for the U-2 program and President Bush's support for torture and abuse.

13. Walter Pincus, "Recent CIA history and the Cold War parallels," *Washington Post*, January 6, 2015, p. 11.

14. Carl Bernstein, "CIA and the Media," *Rolling Stone*, April, 2012.

15. Gregg Herken, *The Georgetown Set: Friends and Rivals in Cold War Washington* (New York: Alfred A. Knopf, 2014), p. 376.

16. Jose Rodriguez, *Hard Measures: How Aggressive CIA Actions After 9/11 Saved American Lives*, (New York: Simon & Schuster, 2012), p. 117.

17. Melvin A. Goodman, "Ending the CIA's Cold War Legacy," *Foreign Policy*, Spring 1997, Volume 106, pp. 128–143. In their letter to *Foreign Policy*, Zelikow and May falsely state that the author of the case study, a former wire-service reporter, interviewed me for the study (not so), that Zelikow also talked to me (not so), and I had been given the draft of the case study

for my own comments (certainly not so). I was given a bootlegged copy of the case study from a senior CIA official who was shocked by the conclusions of the monograph. After all, if the CIA "got it right," then why did Secretary of State George Shultz, Chairman of the Joint Chiefs of Staff General Powell, CIA director Turner, and former senior members of the Senate Intelligence Committee (including Senators Bill Bradley and Daniel Patrick Moynihan) insist that the CIA got it wrong?

18. Spencer Ackerman, "The American Way of Spying," *The Nation*, July 14, 2008, p. 41. Ackerman was reviewing my *Failure of Intelligence: The Decline and Fall of the CIA*, in addition to Tim Weiner's *Legacy of Ashes: The History of the CIA*; Richard K. Betts' *Enemies of Intelligence: Knowledge and Power in American National Security*; and Amy Zegart's *Spying Blind: The FBI, the CIA, and the Origins of 9/11*.

19. Hank Steuver, "Colbert and the White House Dinner," *Washington Post*, April 19, 2006, p. 15.

20. David Gregory, *Meet the Press*, July 7, 2013. NBC's *Meet the Press*, is probably the most widely-quoted news program on television, but Gregory is one of the least substantive hosts the show has ever featured.

21. David Ignatius, "The Dangers of Whistleblowing," *Washington Post*, March 17, 2014, p. 21.

22. One of my colleagues at the CIA was a high school classmate of Cohen's and did his best to inform the op-ed writer about the specious intelligence that was used to justify the unnecessary and unwinnable war against Iraq, but he was treated to arrogant rebuttals from the pundit, who has at least spent the last several years apologizing for his support of the war.

23. Ruth Marcus, "The insufferable Snowden," *Washington Post*, January 1, 2014, p. 17.

24. Mary McGrory, "I'm Convinced," *Washington Post*, February 6, 2003, p. 21.

25. Roy Greenslade, "Self-Criticism in the U.S. Media," *The Guardian* (UK), January 31, 2015, p. 5.

26. Ibid.

27. Ibid.

28. James Risen, *Pay Any Price, Greed, Power, and Endless War* (New York: Houghton Mifflin Harcourt, 2014), p. 211.

29. Risen, *State of War*, p 174.

30. *Washington Post*, February 22, 2012, p. 12.

31. Forty years later, we only know the names of five of the eight "burglars of Media": Bonnie and John Raines, Keith Forsyth, Bob Williamson, and the late William C. Davidon. In the wake of the burglary, it still took two years for an aggressive journalist, Carl Stern of NBC, to use the Freedom of Information Act and a lawsuit against the Department of Justice and the FBI in order to learn the full extent of the program.

CHAPTER TEN

1. John Raines is one of the eight ordinary Americans, patriots, who burgled the district offices of the FBI in Media, Pennsylvania, and learned of the illegal and unconscionable spying on American citizens, particularly its civil rights leaders and anti-war protesters.

2. Megan McDonough, "CIA officer during Watergate era," *Washington Post*, November 28, 2014, p. 6.

3. Theodore Draper, *A Very Thin Line: The Iran-Contra Affairs* (New York, Doubleday, 1991), p. 73.

4. Ibid., p. 75.

5. Ibid., p. 76.

6. See Gary J. Bass, *The Blood Telegram: Nixon, Kissinger, and a Forgotten Genocide*, (New York: Vintage Books), 2013.

7. C. Fred. Alford, *Whistleblowers, Broken Lives and Organizational Power* (Ithaca, NY: Cornell University Press), 2011, p. 15.

8. After the first demonstration of the telegraph in the 1830s, the poet and writer Christopher Pearse Cranch wrote a story, "An Evening with the Telegraph-Wires," for the *Atlantic Monthly*, which appeared in September 1858, discussing the invention's potential for electronic surveillance. He even described telegraph wires in Paris built for the express purpose of spying on French citizens, and presciently warned that the technology could be turned against the government that deployed, which foreshadowed the exploits of Edward Snowden and WikiLeaks.

9. David T.Z. Mindich, "Lincoln's Surveillance State," *New York Times*, July 6, 2013, p. 17.

10. Special thanks to the Chief Archivist at the Truman Library, Ray Geselbracht, for locating this little known item dated December 1, 1963 in the Truman Library and forwarding it to me in July 2014, several weeks after I spoke at the Library on "The Presidency and CIA: From Truman to Obama." Shortly after penning this memorandum, President Truman published an op-ed in the *Washington Post*, which emphasized the danger of a secret Agency that initiated policy or acting as an espionage organization. Truman's warning about the CIA should have equal standing with President Dwight D. Eisenhower's warning regarding the military-industrial complex for its prescience.

11. Memorandum of the President, Harry S. Truman Library, Independence, Missouri, December 1, 1963.

12. See Senate Select Committee to Study Government Operations with Respect to Intelligence Activities, 1976.

13. Antonio M. Taguba, "Stop the CIA Spin on Torture," *New York Times*, August 6, 2014, p. 19.

14. Ibid., p. 19.

15. John Brennan, Lecture to the Council on Foreign Relations, March 18, 2014.

16. Charlie Savage, "Political Turmoil in the Intelligence Community," *The New York Times*, August 2, 2014, p. 11.

17. WashingtonsBlog.com, May 11, 2015.

18. Steve Coll, "A Test of Confidence," *The New Yorker*, September 2, 2003, p. 21.

19. Eric Lichtblau, "Judge Rules in Favor of *Times*' Reporter," *New York Times*, March 27, 2014, p. 17.

20. Ambassador White's cables in 1976 were the first solid evidence of CIA and DIA cooperation with Operation Condor, which was a campaign of political repression and terror involving intelligence officials. It has been axiomatic that clandestine operations and covert actions are most practiced where they are least needed, such as in South America. As Ambassador White's unpublished memoirs argue, covert operations are not only corrupt but self-defeating, contradicting official policy and common sense.

21. Jim Dwyer, "New York Police Covertly Join In at Protest Rallies," *New York Times*, December 22, 2005, p. 1.

22. Scott Shane, "CIA Involvement with New York Police," *New York Times*, June 17, 2008, p. 15.

23. Charlie Savage, C.I.A. Sees Concerns on Ties to New York Police, *New York Times*, June 27, 2013, p. 1.

24. James Risen, "Leaks in the Pentagon," *New York Times*, June 17, 2008. p. 15.

25. The collection of Internet and phone traffic is performed under the BOUNDLESS INFORMANT program; Internet traffic from Gmail, Facebook, Skype, and Yahoo is under the PRISM program; and additional Internet monitoring is under the X-KEYSCORE program. There are also special relationships such as the NSA-Israeli exchange that is covered under a secret "Memorandum of Understanding." See Glenn Greenwald's *No Place to Hide* that was published in 2014.

26. Serge Schmemann, "Distrust in America," *New York Times Sunday Review*, January 26, 2014, p. 2.

27. Jane Mayer, "The Problem with Metadata," *newyorker.com*, June 6, 2013.

28. Lee Fang, "Lawmakers Protecting NSA Surveillance Are Awash in Defense Contractor Case," www.thenation.com/blog/175464

29. Taylor and Landay, "Informants in the Obama Administration," McClatchey News Service, June 20, 2012.

30. *New York Times*, October 20, 2013, p. 18.

31. Scott Higham, "For whistleblowers, a threat," *Washington Post*, July 24, 2014, p. 17.

32. Ibid, p. 17.

33. CNN, December 9, 2014.
34. Michael Morell, *The Great War of Our Time: The CIA's Fight Against Terrorism from Al Qa'ida to ISIS* (New York: Twelve/Hachette Book Group, 2015), p. 92.
35. Greg Miller, "CIA Misled White House on Torture Policy," *Washington Post*, April 20, 2014, p. 7.
36. See *Rebuttal: The CIA Responds to the Senate Intelligence Committee's Study of Its Detention and Interrogation Program*, Edited by Bill Harlow (Annapolis, MD: Naval Institute Press), 2015.
37. Alex Stubin, nationalinterest.com, April 2014.
38. President Obama, National Defense University, May 23, 2013.
39. "Sunlight Diplomacy," *The Economist*, September 24, 2016, p. 35.

INDEX

Abizaid, John, 135
Able Archer military exercise, 95
Abramowitz, Morton, 290
Ackerman, Spencer, 332
Acton, Lord, 239
Adams, Samuel, 50, 51, 52
Afghan civil war, 85
Afghanistan, 5, 6, 17, 70, 84, 86, 87, 89, 90, 126, 133, 150, 151, 163, 283, 303, 304, 305, 308, 324, 376
Afghan War, 304
Agar, Herbert, 69
Agee, Philip, 226
The Agents of Influence, 326
Agni missile program, 132
Air Force, 44
Albright, Madeleine, 167
Alexander, Keith, 354
Allen, Charlie, 171
Allende, Salvador, 246, 293
Allen, John, 167
Allison, Royal, 76
Al Qaeda, 6, 8, 14, 21, 68, 136
Alsop, Joseph, 111, 314, 326
Alsop, Stewart, 326
Amash, Justin (R-MI), 365
American Civil Liberties Union, 357
American Enterprise Institute, 302
American protest movement, 6
American Psychological Association, 372
American Revolution, 357
Ames, Aldrich, 228, 240, 265, 368
Ames, Robert, 325
Amin, Hafizullah, 87, 90
An American Journey, 370
Andropov, Yuri, 92
Angleton, James, 157, 352
Angola, 92, 106

Anti-Ballistic Missile (ABM) Treaty, 4, 57, 65, 74, 75, 79, 132
Anti-Iraq War, 147
Anti-Vietnam War, 101, 147
Arab-Israeli confrontations, 62
Arab Spring, 303
Arab success, 60
Argentina, 320
Armed Forces Committee, 368
Armies of the Night, 46
Arms Control, 66
Arms Control and Disarmament Agency, 74, 75, 76, 79, 254
Arnold Auditorium, 165
Arnold, Henry, 153
Ashcroft, Attorney General, 371
Aslund, Anders, 159
Aspin, Les, 165, 262
Assange, Julian, 8, 9
Association of Computing Machinery, 13
Association of Retired Intelligence Officers, 226
Athens, 143, 226
Atomic Energy Commission, 249
9/11 attacks, 166
Azerbaijan, 36
Azrael, Jeremy, 114

Baader-Meinhof Gang, 122
Bacevich, Andrew, 6
Baker, Howard, 171
Baltimore Orioles, 43
Baltimore Sun, 17
Baluchistan, 89
Banani, Amin, 30
Baquet, Dean, 340
Bay of Pigs, 83, 239
Bearden, Milton, 89

Beijing, 57
Beirut, 97, 104
Belarus, 161
Berger, Samuel, 222
Berkeley, 6
Berlin, 57
Berlin agreement, 79
Berlin blockade in 1948, 92
Berlin Wall, 2, 79, 200
Bernstein, Carl, 326
Bernstein, Leonard, 278
Bethesda, 349, 379
Biden, Joe, 111, 166, 303, 306
bin Laden, Osama, 136, 303
Binney, William, 52, 349, 353, 357, 359
Blackwell, Robert, 159
Blitzer, Wolf, 227, 371
Blix, Hans, 121
Blood, Archer, 348
Board of National Estimates, 52, 55
Boatner, Hayden, 120
Bohlen, Charles E. (Chip), 55
Boren, David L., 171, 182, 347
Boston, 348
Boston Gazette, 348
Boston Marathon bombings, 126
Bourne, Randolph, 345
Bradley, Bill, 146, 172, 182
Brennan, John O., 2, 14, 214, 245, 373
Brezhnev, Leonid, 61, 66
British-French-Israeli invasion of Egypt, 3
Broder, David, 324
Brodie, Bernard, 148
Brokaw, Tom, 331
Brown, Harold, 76
Brussels, 85
Brzezinski, Zbigniew, 58, 86, 158, 314
Buckley, William, 106
Bulgaria, 80, 123, 161

Bulgarian airfield, 318
Bundy, McGeorge, 314
Bureau of Intelligence and Research, 4, 35, 113, 114, 141
Burns, William, 373
Burr, Richard, 15, 227
Burt, Richard, 314
Bush administration, 22, 334, 345
Bush, George H. W., 2, 4, 9, 24, 37, 44, 48, 64, 75, 103, 109, 114, 118, 126, 127, 131, 135, 165, 241, 254, 363
Bush, George W., 350
Bybee, Jay, 6, 324

Cairo, 96
California, 6, 271
Cambodia, 106
Camp David, 247
Capitol Hill, 160, 270, 369
Carlucci, Frank, 171, 310
Carns, Michael, 266
Carr, David, 9
Carter, Jimmy, 84, 258, 314
Carver, George, 54
Casey-Gates stewardship, 174
Casey, William J., 2, 9, 18, 100, 103, 144, 146, 172, 240, 243, 246, 306
Castro, Fidel, 32, 81, 84, 102
Center for Army Lessons Learned, 231
Center for International Policy, 154, 164
Central America, 105, 115, 129, 288, 308, 320
Central Europe, 163
Central Intelligence Agency (CIA), 1, 2, 3, 4, 5, 6, 7, 10, 11, 21, 29, 77, 80, 83, 84, 88, 100, 101, 108, 109, 113, 119, 122, 124, 128, 131, 134, 138, 141, 170, 226, 301, 307, 311, 313
    at American University, 53

Directorate of Intelligence, 10, 202

Directorate of Operations, 34, 47, 88, 132, 217, 225

Foreign Bureau of Information, 47

Office of Current Intelligence, 31, 43

Office of Inspector General, 22

Office of National Estimates, 40

Office of Training, 207

Publications Review Board, 335

Publications Review Board censors, 327

Central Intelligence Group, 152

Charm City, 43

Cheney, Dick, 2, 7, 54, 64, 67, 75, 165, 323, 340, 355

Cherne, Leo, 106

Chicago, 338

Chicago Sun Times, 333

Chile, 7, 320

China, 6, 45, 57, 78, 79, 131, 352

Chinese invasion of Vietnam, 48

Christopher, Warren, 262

Church and Pike Committees, 226

Church Committee, 101, 177, 215, 253

Church, Frank, 82, 101

CIA Family Inn, 43

Citizenfour, 22

Civil War, 114, 350

Clapper, James R., 134, 229, 236, 367

Clark, Dick, 227

Clarke, Bruce, 74

Clarridge, Dewey, 202

Cleave, William Van, 64

Clifford, Clark, 71

Clinton, Bill, 80, 165

Clinton, Hillary, 5, 45, 167, 220, 331, 377

CNN, 9

Coats, Dan, 135, 232

Cody, Richard A., 355

Cohen, Bill, 321

Cohen, David, 45, 176, 359–360

Cohen, Richard, 324, 337

Cohen, William, 165

COINTELPRO, 226

Colbert Nation, 333

The Colbert Report, 332

Colbert, Steven, 332

Colby, William J., 2, 14, 101, 114, 156, 240, 243, 298

Cold War, 1, 2, 4, 12, 31, 79, 92, 100, 141, 152, 155, 161, 163, 172, 250, 265, 302

Cold War McCarthyism, 55

Collins, James, 36

Coll, Steve, 358

Combat brigade, 81

Combs, Richard, 143

Comey, James, 222, 275

Congo, 32

Congress, 11, 14, 16, 19, 22, 23, 24, 50, 52, 64, 152, 159, 301

Congressional Intelligence Committees, 41

Contras in Nicaragua, 7

Cordesman, Anthony, 302

Corinto, 319

Costa Rica, 39

Council on Foreign Relations, 11

Counterintelligence Center, 265

Counterterrorism Center, 15

Cranston, Alan, 182

Crewsdon, John, 333

Crimea, 46, 90, 374

Croatia, 161

Crocker, Chester, 158

Crowe, William, 263

Cuba, 11, 32, 58, 80, 81, 83, 106
 military, 318
 missile crisis, 59, 79, 80, 91, 92

Cushman Jr., Robert E., 346

Cynthia Cooper of World.com, 348

Czech-built L-39 jet trainer, 318
Czechoslovakia, 48, 77
Czech Republic, 301

Dalglish, Lucy, 342
D'Amato, Alphonse, 123
Danforth, John, 192
Dardanelles, 61
Dark Alliance, 20
David Gregory, 9
Davis, Lynn, 94
Dayan, Moshe, 71
DeConcini, Dennis, 182
Defense Condition III (DefCon-III),
   61
Defense Intelligence Agency, 51, 116,
   119, 231, 257, 284
Democratic Party, 325
Democrats, 173, 177, 182, 286
Dempsey, Martin, 149, 167, 237
Denton, 30
Department of Agriculture, 108
Department of Defense, 4, 19, 65, 66,
   75, 76, 153, 249, 264, 306
Department of Energy, 249
Department of Health and Human
   Services, 16
Department of History, 35
Department of Justice, 12, 324
Department of State, 4, 5, 46, 66,
   70, 76
Department of Veteran's Affairs, 16
Der Spiegel, 340
Deutch, John, 242
Diem, Ngo Dinh, 102
Dillard, Hardy, 148
Directorate of Intelligence, 38, 40,
   42, 68, 172, 233, 277, 283
Directorate of Operations, 31, 33, 38,
   40, 42, 255, 281
Directorates of Intelligence and
   Operations, 39, 41
Disarmament Agency, 66

Dobrynin, Anatoly, 78
Doctors Without Borders, 17
Dole, Robert, 82
Dominican Republic, 233
Donaldson, Sam, 158
Donovan, Wild Bill, 246
Dracula, 64
Drake, Thomas, 17, 52, 338, 341,
   349, 359, 379
Dulles, Allen, 39, 239, 314, 326, 331
Dunford Jr., Joseph F., 374
Dunn, Michael, 152

Eagleburger, Lawrence, 155, 194
Eastern Europe, 159
East Europe, 32, 163
East Germany, 367
East Pakistan, 348
Eatinger, Robert, 230
Egypt, 48
Egyptian military operation, 59
Egyptian-Syrian attack, 58, 60
Ehrlichman, John, 347
Eisenhower, Dwight D., 11, 42, 63,
   151, 166, 214, 303, 314
Ekedahl, Carolyn McGiffert, 36, 109,
   116, 120, 122, 170, 179, 211, 288,
   331, 368
Ellsberg, Daniel, 9, 13, 18, 19, 23, 52,
   342, 346
El Salvador, 320
Enders, Rudy, 319
Erdogan, Recep, 126
Ermarth, Fritz, 288
Eshkol, Levi, 72
Espionage Act, 16, 24, 218, 336, 349,
   350, 358
Essential Information, 21
Estonia, 56
Europe, 325
European Security and Cooperation,
   79
Evil Empire, 297

Fadlallah, Muhammad Hussein, 126

The Failure of Intelligence: The Decline and Fall of the CIA, 10, 11, 12, 356

Falkland Islands, 103

FBI agents, 17, 18

Federal Emergency Management Agency, 16

Feinstein, Dianne, 11, 14, 15, 230, 272, 355, 363, 371

Feith, Douglas, 113, 135

Fells Point, 43

Ferrell, Robert, 30, 140

Feshbach, Murray, 159

Fielding, Lewis, 346

Fiers, Alan, 177

Florida, 104

Flynn, Mike, 167

Foggy Bottom, 110, 113

Ford administration, 101, 114

Ford, Dan, 219

Ford, Sewell, 12

Foreign Intelligence Surveillance Act (FISA), 17, 238

Foreign Intelligence Surveillance Court, 17, 363

Foreign Policy, 329

Foreign Relations and Armed Services, 74

Foreign Service, 31, 164, 302

Forrestal, James, 154

Forward Operating Base Chapman, 234, 324

Franklin, Benjamin, 313, 348, 350

From the Shadows, 173

Fryer, John, 165

Fulbright, William, 227

Fuller, Graham, 125, 195, 289, 309

Gannon, John, 217, 335

Garthoff, Douglas, 109, 145, 298

Garthoff, Raymond L., 76, 91

The Gatekeepers, 7

Gates, Robert M., 2, 3, 8, 9, 18, 36, 41, 44, 45, 50, 63, 89, 91, 100, 107, 116, 125, 144, 152, 156, 169, 170, 208, 240, 277, 278, 282, 285, 304, 312, 316, 347, 359

Gelb, Les, 314

Gellman, Barton, 23

Gelman, Harry, 327

General Services Administration, 346

Geneva, 309

George, Clair, 108, 130, 202, 265

George H.W. Bush Intelligence Center, 269, 367

George H.W. Bush School of Government, 303

Georgetown, 326

George Washington Parkway, 367

George Washington University, 205

Georgia, 29, 56

Gerber, Burton, 265

German invasion, 93

German, Michael, 369

Germany, 49, 319

Gershwin, Larry, 95, 197, 309, 310

Gerson, Louis, 140

Ghraib, Abu, 5, 355

Gibney, Alex, 22

Gingrich, Newt, 80

Glaudemans, Jennifer, 179, 293, 307

Glenn, John, 182

Glickman, Dan, 228, 266

Goble, Paul, 159

Golan Heights, 48

Goldwater, Barry, 228

Gonzales, Alberto R., 222

Gorbachev, Mikhail, 38, 70, 124, 149, 172, 260, 286, 287, 304, 309

Gordievsky, Oleg, 90

Gordon, Michael, 342

Goss, Porter, 2, 10, 14, 269

Graham, Bob, 241

Graham, Danny, 64

Graham, Katherine, 322

Graham, Philip, 331
Grassley, Charles E., 369
Gray, Boyden C., 174
Greece, 167
Greenfield, Meg, 322
Greenwald, Glenn, 8, 23, 337
Greenwald, Robert, 22
Gregory, Roger, 358
Grunwald, Michael, 9
Guardian US, 23
The Guardian US, 23
Guatemala, 32, 320
Guinness, Alec, 173
Gulbiddin Hekmatyar, forces of, 89
Gulen, Fethullah, 126
Gulf of Suez, 48

Haig, Alexander, 103, 110, 164, 246, 284, 359
Halberstam, David, 150
Hale, Nathan, 37
Hamilton, 349
Hanoi, 49, 54
Haqqani network, 89
Harold Saunders, 48
Harper's magazine, 52
Harry Truman's CIA, 10
Harvard Intelligence and Policy Project, 329
Harvard's Kennedy School, 329, 330
Harvard University, 41, 176
Hastings, Michael, 306
Hayden, Michael, 2, 219, 241
Helgerson, John, 20, 22
Helms, Jesse, 80, 104
Helms, Richard McGarrah, 2, 49, 71, 157, 220, 240, 268, 314, 330, 331
Hersh, Seymour, 12, 157, 313, 323, 333
Herzstein, Robert E., 346
Hiatt, Fred, 324
Hibbits, John, 297, 368
Hillenkoetter, Roscoe, 239

Hill, Anita, 192
Hill, Harry, 154
Hodnett, Grey, 310
Hoekstra, Peter, 229
Holder, Eric, 324, 358, 363
Hollings, Ernest, 182
Holmes, Oliver Wendell, 313
Honduras, 318, 320
Hoover, J. Edgar, 243
Horton, John, 286
House Homeland Security Committee, 23
House Intelligence Committee, 252, 266, 270
Hungarian Revolution, 3
Hunter, Robert, 170
Hunt, Howard, 140, 346
Hussein, King of Jordan, 62
Hussein, Saddam, 68, 118, 123, 125, 202, 307, 320
Hutchinson, Thomas, 348
Hyland, William, 140

ICBMs, 74
Ignatius, David, 314, 324, 325–326, 337
India, 39, 89
Indiana University, 1, 26, 30, 34, 36
Indian Ocean, 85, 95
Inman, Bobby Ray, 173, 201
Institute of Defense Analysis, 53
Intelligence and Operations Directorates, 34
Intelligence Community, 367
Intelligence Directorate, 54, 117, 258, 290
Intelligence Reform Act of 2004, 134
Intermediate Nuclear Forces agreement, 268
Internal Revenue Service, 16, 352
International Red Cross, 161
Iran, 2, 32, 33, 88, 89, 125, 126, 129, 131, 146, 309, 319, 324

Iran-Contra, 24, 116, 124, 300, 301, 310
    Committee, 171
    investigation, 323
    operations, 262, 292, 315
    scandal, 127, 128, 157, 171, 176, 186, 204, 221, 319, 376
Iranian ballistic missiles, 301
Iranian hostage crisis, 48
Iranian Revolution, 59
Iran's nuclear program, 6
Iraq, 6, 7, 17, 25, 26, 39, 43, 68, 70, 75, 100, 111, 118, 119, 131, 132, 134, 136, 151, 163, 241, 303, 307, 315, 320, 366
Iraq War, 19, 54, 68, 340, 345
Islamic State (ISIS), 8, 21, 43, 101, 136, 303, 374
Israel, 7, 48, 58, 59, 62, 96, 126
Israelian, Victor, 157
Israeli Defense Minister Moshe Dayan, 60
Israeli intelligence, 58
Israelis, 48, 59, 61, 62
Italian Communist Party, 252
Italian Military Intelligence and Security Service, 118
Italian Red Brigades, 113

Jackson, Henry, 64, 79, 81
Jackson, Moynihan, 64
Japan, 108, 122
Jefferson, Thomas, 342
Jehl, Doug, 323, 333
John Paul II, Pope, 110
Johns Hopkins University, 18, 26, 30, 352
Johnson, Haynes, 321
Johnson, Lyndon B., 49, 54, 150, 237
Joint United States Military Mission in Greece, 3, 29
Jones, James, 160

Justice Department, 229
    memoranda, 6, 328

Kabul, 87, 90, 305
Kaiser, Robert, 158
KAL 007, 323
Kalugin, Oleg, 157
Kansi, Aimal Khan, 37
Karzai, Hamid, 304
Kennan, George F., 33, 55, 148, 154, 156, 263, 373
Kennedy, John F., 11, 42, 47, 50, 60, 63, 69, 150, 277
Kent, Sherman, 40, 52, 148, 278
Kerrey, Bob, 191
Kerr, Richard, 171, 177, 262, 300
Kerry, John, 370
Kessler, Ronald, 331
KGB, 76, 92, 143
Khan, Genghis, 283
Khomeini, Ayatollah, 289
Khost, Afghanistan, 234
King, Ernest, 154
King, Martin Luther, 101
King, Peter T., 23
Kirkland, Lane, 64
Kissinger, Henry, 34, 48, 58, 59, 60, 61, 62, 66, 75, 140, 158, 244, 246, 314
Kleindienst, Richard, 249
Knoche, E. Henry, 65
Kolt, George, 310
Korea, 59, 336
Kraft, Joseph, 314, 326
Kremlin, 46, 77, 87, 93, 94, 110, 112, 120, 124, 126, 161, 317
Kunduz, 17

Lake, Anthony, 256, 266
Landay, Jonathan, 339
Lardner, George, 322
Latin America, 288

Lattimore, Owen, 35, 352
Lautenberg, Frank, 194
Law of War, 158
Laxalt, Paul, 208
Layton, Bobby, 54, 55
Lazar, Emily, 332
Lebanese civil war, 126
Lebanon, 62, 97, 103, 126, 326
Ledeen, Michael, 113
Lehman, Richard, 119
Leon, Richard J., 362
Lewis, Anthony, 321, 323
Library of Congress, 31
Libya, 6, 129
Lichtblau, Eric, 18, 313, 323, 341
LIFE magazine, 43
Limberg, Wayne, 179
Lincoln, Abraham, 350
Lithuania, 56
Little Red Riding Hood, 337
London Observer, 340
Long Island Newsday, 333
Lumumba, Patrice, 32, 102

MacEachin, Doug, 85, 145, 146, 176,
    285, 292, 310
Machiavelli, Niccolò, 29
Madison, James, 239, 303, 313, 349
Malinovsky Tank Academy, 162
Maloof, Michael, 135
Manning, Chelsea, 5, 7, 6, 8, 9, 13,
    19, 25, 64, 65, 316, 337, 338, 349,
    372
Mansbach, Richard, 122
Marcus, Ruth, 337
Marine Colonel Oliver North, 300
Marks, Ron, 181
Marshall, George, 153, 154
Massachusetts Institute of Technol-
    ogy, 267
Matlock, Jack, 162
McCain, John, 150
McCarthyism, 35, 55

McCarthyite inquisition, 194
McCarthy, Joseph, 351, 352
McCarthy, Mary O'Neil, 325, 368
McCartney, Paul, 194
McCauley, Brian, 179
McChrystal, Stanley, 166, 300, 304,
    306
McCone, John, 240, 298
McConnell, Mike, 271
McCullough, James, 129, 208
McDonough, Denis, 160, 274
McFarlane, Robert, 95, 97, 290
McGovern, Raymond, 44, 45, 309
McGrory, Mary, 321
McKim, Charles, 155
McLaughlin, John E., 41, 67, 203,
    245, 331, 338, 340
McMahon, Bernie, 107
McMahon, John, 108, 121, 129, 281
McMaster, H.R., 150
McNair, Leslie, 147
McNamara, Robert, 49, 50, 72, 73
McPherson, Harry, 72
Meany, George, 64
Meet the Press, 9, 337
Meigs, Montgomery, 149
Merkel, Angela, 367
Metzenbaum, Howard, 182
Mexican-American War, 345
Middle East, 48, 60, 61, 62, 70, 96,
    119, 151, 303, 374
Middleton, Drew, 314
MiG-21 fighter aircraft, 317
Military institutions, 303
Miller, Greg, 323
Miller, Judith, 342
Mirage, 73
Miranda, David, 9
MIRVs, 74
Miscik, Jami, 68
Mitchell, George, 177
Mitchell, John, 46
Mitrokhin, Vasili, 137

Modus operandi, 329
Montana law, 351
Moorer, Thomas, 61
Morell, Michael, 199, 223, 331, 335, 379
Morris, Bernard, 35
Moscow, 56, 60, 62, 63, 66, 77, 78, 89, 122, 143, 146, 154, 159, 309, 317, 338
    disarmament policy, 309
    Institute for International Affairs, 154
Moseman, John, 176, 198
Moskowitz, Stanley, 129, 179, 194
Movimento Popular de Libertação de Angola (MPLA), 58
Moynihan, Daniel Patrick, 11
Mozambique, 107
Mudd, Roger, 321
Mullen, Mike, 304
Muller, Scott, 371
Mundy, Carl, 165
My Lai, 323

Nader, Ralph, 12, 13, 21
Nasser, Gamel Abdel, 59, 71
National Archives, 31, 222
National Cathedral, 45
National Counterintelligence Office, 368
National Daily Bulletin, 48
National Defense University, 152, 375
National Geospatial Intelligence Agency, 235
National Imagery and Mapping Agency, 267, 268
National Intelligence, 234, 315, 319
National Intelligence Council, 170, 176, 279, 282
National Intelligence Estimate, 21, 42, 47, 48, 49, 65, 229, 231, 241, 279

National Military Command Center, 71
National missile defense system, 132
National Photographic Interpretation Center, 268
National Reconnaissance Office, 4, 235, 257, 377
National Security Act of 1947, 26, 42, 153, 243, 308
National Security Agency (NSA), 4, 8, 13, 17, 19, 21, 30, 47, 70, 80, 83, 97, 102, 105, 153, 235, 238, 241, 271, 313, 361
National Security Council, 57, 61, 64, 71, 72, 77, 120, 124, 129, 153, 232, 259, 284, 289, 305, 308, 310, 325, 371
National War College, 3, 4, 19, 20, 39, 45, 87, 130, 137, 147, 152, 156, 165, 193, 237, 255, 271, 298, 319, 321, 322, 354
NATO force, 94, 148
Navajo language, 180
Naval War College, 157
Navy League convention, 301
NBC, 9, 337
Nedzi, Lucien, 102
Negroponte, John, 134, 232
Neo-Stalinists, 304
New Jersey, 352
Newsweek, 37
New York City, 12, 31, 37, 44, 45, 102, 161, 336
New York City Police Department, 176, 359
New Yorker, 333
New York Review of Books, 56, 352
New York Times, 9, 18, 23, 60, 157, 309, 314, 320, 331
Nicaragua, 92, 107, 146, 206, 287, 289, 317, 319
Nicaraguan counter-revolutionaries, 309

Nicaraguan leftists, 317
Niger intelligence, 118
Nitze, Paul, 76
Nixon, Richard, 38, 46, 58, 63, 66, 69, 90, 103, 133, 346
Nixon White House, 49, 79
Nolo contendere, 225
Noren, James, 109, 145, 298
North Africa, 365, 374
North Atlantic Treaty Organization (NATO), 79, 85, 88, 149
North Korea, 131
North Vietnam, 57
North Vietnamese, 49
No Such Agency, 241
Nuclear Freeze Movement, 253
Nuclear war, 78, 136
Nuclear weapons program, 134
Nunn, Sam, 143, 182, 379
Nye, Joseph, 176

Obama administration, 22, 302, 303, 334
Obama, Barack, 14, 15, 16, 17, 22, 24, 44, 47, 102, 151, 166, 217, 304, 305, 325, 338, 358
Oberdorfer, Don, 158
Occupy Wall Street, 360
October War, 59, 60, 61, 83
Odom, William, 80
Office of Current Intelligence, 44, 46
Office of Inspector General, 22, 23, 235
Office of National Intelligence, 235
Office of Strategic Services (OSS), 39, 40, 152, 281
Oliver, Kay, 310
Olson, Frank, 102
Operation Ajax, 33
Operational and Intelligence Directorates, 243, 280
Operation Barbarossa, 93
Operation Gladio, 109

Operation RYAN, 94
Orwell, George, 22
Ott, Marvin, 178
Oval Office, 254

Pakistan, 17, 39, 89, 133, 348
Palestine Liberation Organization, 112, 120
Palmer, Raids, 351
Panetta, Leon, 14, 245, 264, 335
Panetta Review, 15, 273
Papal Plot, 118, 124, 191, 295, 316
Parker, Richard, 62
Parry, Robert, 302
Pazienza, Francesco, 118
Pearl Harbor, 93, 153, 351
Penkovsky, Oleg, 60, 137
Pennsylvania Railroad, 3
Pentagon, 17, 18, 19, 46, 49, 57, 65, 66, 69, 77, 85, 94, 95, 136, 152, 153, 158, 167, 232, 257, 304, 358
    Defense Mapping Agency, 267
    Joint Chiefs of Staff, 243
    Selected Acquisition Reports, 301
Pentagon National Photographic Interpretation Center, 268
Pentagon Papers, 346
Perle, Richard, 162
Perry, William, 267
Persian Gulf, 151, 374
Persico, Joseph, 115, 282
Peru, 226, 334
Petraeus, David Howell, 44, 134, 245, 221, 304
Philadelphia Inquirer, 339
Philippines, 167
Phillips, David Atlee, 226
Phoenix Program, 32, 251
Pike Committee, 101, 215
Pike's Pique, 194
Pillar, Paul, 125, 228
Pincus, Walter, 314, 322, 324, 337
Pinochet, Augusto, 378

Pipes, Richard, 63, 254
Poindexter, John, 295
Poitras, Laura, 23
Poland, 59, 124, 301
Polgar, Thomas, 177, 255
Polish Pope, 123, 124
Powell, Colin, 160, 338, 366
Prague, 160
Priest, Dana, 325
Privacy and Civil Liberties Oversight Board, 362
Public Service, 303
Pulitzer Prize, 9, 23
Putin, Vladimir, 92, 109

Qaddafi, Muammar, 157
Quakers, 69
Queeg, Philip, 284

Raborn, William, 240
Raines, John, 345
Reagan, Ronald, 2, 9, 10, 12, 47, 58, 83, 90, 93, 97, 101, 206, 226, 240, 283, 294, 308, 315, 330
Regan, Donald, 127
Reagan, Nancy, 127
Republicans, 15, 174, 182
Republican White House, 314
Reuters journalists, 8
Reykjavik, 309
Richardson, Elliot, 249, 254
Risen, James, 18, 313, 323, 336, 341, 358
Rizzo, John, 223, 327
Roberts, John, 363
Rockefeller Commission, 101
Rodman, Peter, 62
Rodriguez, Jose, 23, 327, 379
Rogers, Kenny, 46
Rolling Stone magazine, 166, 306, 326
Roman Empire, 367
Rome, 123

Roosevelt Library in Hyde Park, 31
Roosevelt, Theodore, 148, 155
Root, Elihu, 155
Rosen, James, 336, 357
Rostow, Eugene, 54, 55, 71, 97, 314
Rostow, Walter, 49, 52, 54, 55, 71, 244
Rottman, Gabe, 357
Rouge, Khmer, 51
Rowe, Eugene, 47
Rowley, Coleen, 348
Royce, Knut, 333
Rudman, Warren, 19, 177, 319
Rumsfeld, Donald, 45, 64, 65, 75, 131, 316
Rusk, Dean, 49, 73, 50
Russia, 93, 109, 131, 151, 338
Russian aggression, 46
Russian military, 59
Russian studies, 30
Rutgers University, 316
Rutherford, Ben, 145

Sadat, Anwar, 60, 95
Sadat's "bombshell," 61
Safire, William, 115, 173
Saigon, 54
SALT agreement, 79
SALT II agreement, 80
SALT team in Vienna, 64
Salvadoran insurgency, 318
Salvetti, Lloyd, 330
Sandinista government, 317, 320
Sandinistas, 294, 317
Santovito, Giuseppe, 118
Sarris, Louis, 49, 53
Saudi Arabia, 376
Saunders, Harold, 48
Savage, Charlie, 323
Sayre Stevens, 60, 66
Schlesinger, James, 59, 61, 62, 243, 267
Sciolino, Elaine, 320, 321, 333

Scowcroft, Brent, 64
Secret Service, 16
Sedition Act, 350
Semenov, Vladimir, 78
Senate and House Intelligence Committees, 18
Senate Armed Forces Committee, 191, 355
Senate Congressional Committee, 157
Senate Ethics Committee, 197
Senate Foreign Relations Committee, 82, 225
Senate Select Committee on Intelligence, 2, 3, 9, 10, 11, 12, 14, 15, 18, 19, 24, 39, 107, 116, 128, 130, 152, 169, 170, 174, 178, 182, 203, 218, 219, 229, 235, 241, 245, 267, 271, 272, 274, 305, 307, 317, 320, 324, 330, 353
Senate Select Committee on Intelligence, Richard Burr (R-NC), 15
Senate Select Intelligence Committee, 347, 371
Shackley, Ted, 157
Shane, Scott, 334
Shaw, George Bernard, 1
Shevardnadze, Eduard, 56
Shevtsova, Lilia, 159
Shinseki, Eric, 160
Shipler, David, 158
Shorty McCabe, 12
Shulman, Marshall, 87
Shultz, George P., 67, 107, 284
Sino-American relations, 78
Sino-Soviet dispute, 256
Six-Day War, 244
SLBMs, 74
Slovenia, 161
Smiley, George, 173
Smith, Gerald, 75
Smith, John, 155
Smith, Walter Bedell, 40, 239

Snepp, Frank, 224
Snowden, Edward, 5, 6, 8, 9, 13, 19, 24, 25, 337, 343, 349, 361, 372
Socialist Workers Party, 352
Sofia, 123
Somalia, 6
South Africa, 58
South Asia, 133
Southeast Asia, 49, 51, 57
Southern Africa, 308
South Korea, 239
South Vietnam, 57, 233
Southwest Asia, 365, 374
South Yemen, 107
Soviet-American relations, 38, 304
Soviet-American weaponry, 63
Soviet combat brigade, 90
Soviet Evil Empire, 306
Soviet force, 87
Soviet intelligence, 76
Soviet invasion, 3
    of Czechoslovakia, 46
    of Hungary, 29
Soviet-Iranian rapprochement, 204
Soviet military, 63, 318
Soviet threat, 7, 12
Soviet Tudeh Party, 293
Soviet Union, 3, 4, 7, 26, 36, 47, 56, 57, 58, 65, 66, 80, 81, 87, 93, 105, 112, 116, 123, 126, 141, 151, 153, 156, 160, 234, 240, 254, 265, 284, 298, 304, 306, 308, 310, 314, 316, 328, 367
    U.S. government, 32
Spain, 167
Spanish-American War, 345
Specter, Arlen, 215
Sputnik, 3
SSBN, 74
Stadler, Gerald, 152, 321
Stadler, Walter, 19
Stafford, Roy, 156
Stalin, Joseph, 153, 339, 367

Stanton, Edwin M., 350
Star Wars, 285
Starzak, Alissa, 15, 219
State Department Bureau for Intelligence and Research, 35, 49, 56, 112, 231, 261, 290
Stavridis, James, 149
Sterling, Jeffrey, 225
Stevens, John Paul, 65, 66, 233
Stevenson, Barry L., 45, 46, 353, 378
Stevens Point, 30
Stoddard, Phillip, 112
Stoertz, Howard, 65
Stone, Richard, 82
Strategic Arms Limitation Talks (SALT), 3, 73
Strobel, Warren, 339
Studies in Intelligence, 330
Sudan, 325
Suez crisis, 29, 72
Sullivan, Mark, 352
Summers, Larry, 335
Sunday Outlook, 322
Sund, Gordon, 60
Supreme Court, 22
Syria, 6, 17, 43, 48, 63, 70
Syrian, 71

Taguba, Antonio M., 355
Taiwan, 167
Talbott, Strobe, 268
Tamm, Thomas, 18
Taraki, Nur Mohammad, 90
Teicher, Howard, 125, 289
Tenet, George, 2, 10, 14, 41, 67, 176, 178, 335, 340, 367
Terror Wars, 2, 6, 13, 15, 16, 24, 238, 242, 271
Texas, 30, 48
Texas A&M, 303
20th Century Fund, 11
The New Yorker, 9
Third World, 88, 122, 146, 299, 315

Thomas, Clarence, 192, 208
Thompson, Paul, 261
Thompson, Tommy, 55
Thunder, Rolling, 49
Tiananmen Square, 59
Tighe, Eugene, 121
Toobin, Jeffrey, 9
Toon, Malcolm, 118, 142
Transportation Security Agency, 364
Treaty of Berlin, 77
Treverton, Gregory, 170, 176
Trident submarine program, 79
Trujillo, Rafael, 102
Truman, Harry S., 10, 11, 41, 42, 57, 68, 69, 100, 121, 152, 308, 351, 375
Truman Library, 11
Trump, Donald, 27, 167, 379
Tsarnaev, Ruslan, 126
Tudeh Party, 289
Turmoil and Triumph: My Years as Secretary of State, 308
Turner, Stansfield, 156, 240
Twain, Mark, 169
Twitter, 9

Ukraine, 46, 56, 85, 88, 90, 109, 163, 374
Uncle Leon, 271
The Uncounted Enemy: A Vietnam Deception, 53
Uncovered, 22
United Nations, 37, 229
United States, 1, 4, 5, 6, 7, 8, 13, 21, 24, 25, 32, 33, 37, 40, 47, 50, 60, 61, 62, 65, 78, 80, 91, 92, 93, 109, 131, 151, 301, 302, 303, 316, 318, 350, 362, 364
  Air Force, 94, 153
  Army, 3, 8, 143, 231
  bombing of Vietnam, 49
  borders, 237
  Congress, 26, 118, 125

Congressional Intelligence
    Committees, 18
Congress members, 74
Constitution, 13, 27
    Fourth Amendment of, 242
Department of Commerce, 159
Department of State, 155
drone attacks, 102
embassy, 39, 326
foreign policy process, 3
intelligence, 5, 67, 303
intelligence community, 77, 91
invasion, 100
invasion of Lebanon, 3, 29
laws, 8, 9
military-surveillance grid, 305
national security, 24
national security system, 3
Navy, 94, 157
Office of Inspector General, 213,
    219
personnel in Iraq, 8
Supreme Court, 242
war in Iraq, 7
war in Vietnam, 35
wars, 6
United States Army, 15
United States Foreign Service, 30
USA PATRIOT Act, 17, 272
USSR, 39, 90
USS Theodore Roosevelt, 165
Uzbekistan, 56

Verizon, 353
Vienna, 55, 78, 86, 161, 309
Viet Cong, 50, 54, 251
Viet Cong-North Vietnamese, 54
Vietnam, 1, 6, 31, 45, 48, 49, 50, 51,
    54, 57, 70, 96, 98, 106, 139, 150,
    163, 244, 314, 318, 319
Vietnamese people, 32
Vietnam War, 14, 22, 24, 38, 41, 53,
    69, 98, 100, 101, 226, 238, 245,

    251, 255, 304, 326, 342, 345, 356,
    375
Virginia, 3, 45, 367
Virginia police, 37

Wagner, Karl, 346, 347
Walpole, Robert, 125
Walsh, Even, 323
Walsh, Lawrence, 300
The War on Whistleblowers, 22
Warren, Elizabeth, 335
Warsaw Pact, 2, 79, 200
Washington, 36, 40, 43, 45, 46, 47,
    49, 54, 61, 70, 302, 322
Washington, George, 155
Washington National Cathedral, 251
Washington Post, 11, 20, 23, 158,
    306, 309, 314, 323, 331
Washington press corps, 322
Washington Times, 67, 304
Watergate, 24
Watkins, Sherron, 348
Webb, Gary, 20
Webster, William, 215
Weiner, Tim, 333
Weiser, Benjamin, 320, 321
Weiss, Seymour, 64
Welsh, Richard, 226
We Steal Secrets: The Story of
    WikiLeaks, 22
Western Europe, 119, 159
Western Hemisphere, 319
West German Baader-Meinhof
    Gang, 113
West Germany, 122
Westmoreland, William C., 53
White House, 6, 7, 10, 12, 14, 15, 19,
    20, 22, 31, 33, 36, 42, 44, 52, 54,
    55, 57, 66, 71, 72, 73, 84, 98, 101,
    115, 127, 152, 157, 229, 236, 305,
    314, 323, 363
White, Robert E., 104, 133, 348, 359
White, Stanford, 155

Wicklund, Eugene, 45, 54
Wiebe, Kirk, 359
WikiLeaks, 8, 9
Wilkerson, Larry, 229
Wilson, Edwin, 157, 258
Wilson, Joe, 370
Wilson, Woodrow, 24, 358
Wisconsin, 30
Wisner, Frank, 111
Wolfowitz, Paul, 64, 111
Woodward, Bob, 127, 306, 331
Woolsey, James, 240, 245, 246
World Health Organization, 161
World Trade Centers, 242
World Trade Towers, 66
World War I, 351, 358
World War II, 39, 49, 92, 93, 108, 147, 151, 153, 212, 252, 319, 351
    resistance, 251
Worthen, James, 330
Worthen, Ruth, 103
Wurmser, David, 113, 135
Wyden, Ron, 169, 230

Yariv, Aharon, 72
Yeltsin, Boris, 151, 263, 304
Yemen, 6, 17, 71, 376
Yoo, John, 6, 324

Zinni, Tony, 160
Zubaydah, Abu, 327

ABOUT THE AUTHOR

Melvin A. Goodman was a Soviet analyst at the CIA and the Department of
State for 24 years, and a professor of
international relations at the National
War College for 18 years. He served
in the U.S. Army in Athens for three
years, and was intelligence advisor to
the SALT delegation in 1971–1972.
Currently, Goodman is the Director of the National Security Project
at the Center for International Policy in Washington, DC, and
adjunct professor of government at Johns Hopkins University.
He has authored, co-authored, and edited seven books, including
National Insecurity: The Cost of American Militarism; *Gorbachev's
Retreat: The Third World*; *The Wars of Eduard Shevardnadze*; *The
Phantom Defense: America's Pursuit of the Star Wars Illusion*; *Bush
League Diplomacy: How the Neoconservatives Are Putting the World
at Risk*, and *Failure of Intelligence: The Decline and Fall of the CIA*.
His articles and op-eds have appeared in numerous publications,
including the *New York Times, Harper's, Foreign Policy, Foreign Ser-
vice Journal*, the *Baltimore Sun*, and the *Washington Post*. He lives
in Bethesda, Maryland.